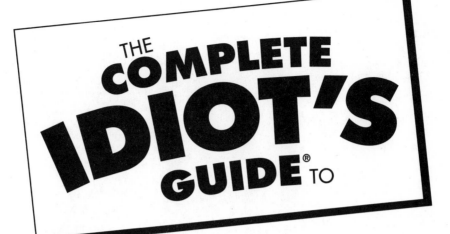

# THE COMPLETE IDIOT'S GUIDE® TO

# The ASVAB

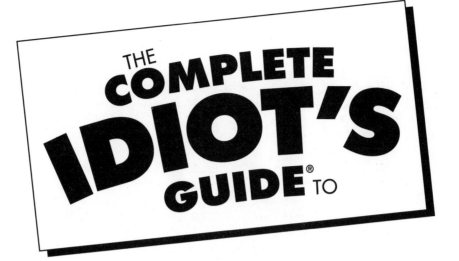

THE COMPLETE IDIOT'S GUIDE® TO

# The ASVAB

*by Laura Stradley and Robin Kavanagh*
*Illustrated by Kara LaFrance*

ALPHA

A member of Penguin Group (USA) Inc.

## ALPHA BOOKS

Published by the Penguin Group

Penguin Group (USA) Inc., 375 Hudson Street, New York, New York 10014, USA

Penguin Group (Canada), 90 Eglinton Avenue East, Suite 700, Toronto, Ontario M4P 2Y3, Canada (a division of Pearson Penguin Canada Inc.)

Penguin Books Ltd., 80 Strand, London WC2R 0RL, England

Penguin Ireland, 25 St. Stephen's Green, Dublin 2, Ireland (a division of Penguin Books Ltd.)

Penguin Group (Australia), 250 Camberwell Road, Camberwell, Victoria 3124, Australia (a division of Pearson Australia Group Pty. Ltd.)

Penguin Books India Pvt. Ltd., 11 Community Centre, Panchsheel Park, New Delhi—110 017, India

Penguin Group (NZ), 67 Apollo Drive, Rosedale, North Shore, Auckland 1311, New Zealand (a division of Pearson New Zealand Ltd.)

Penguin Books (South Africa) (Pty.) Ltd., 24 Sturdee Avenue, Rosebank, Johannesburg 2196, South Africa

Penguin Books Ltd., Registered Offices: 80 Strand, London WC2R 0RL, England

## Copyright © 2010 by Laura Stradley and Robin Kavanagh

International Standard Book Number: 978-1-59257-983-9
Library of Congress Catalog Card Number: 2009938581

12   11   10      8   7   6   5   4   3   2   1

Interpretation of the printing code: The rightmost number of the first series of numbers is the year of the book's printing; the rightmost number of the second series of numbers is the number of the book's printing. For example, a printing code of 10-1 shows that the first printing occurred in 2010.

*Printed in the United States of America*

**Note:** This publication contains the opinions and ideas of its authors. It is intended to provide helpful and informative material on the subject matter covered. It is sold with the understanding that the authors and publisher are not engaged in rendering professional services in the book. If the reader requires personal assistance or advice, a competent professional should be consulted.

The authors and publisher specifically disclaim any responsibility for any liability, loss, or risk, personal or otherwise, which is incurred as a consequence, directly or indirectly, of the use and application of any of the contents of this book.

Most Alpha books are available at special quantity discounts for bulk purchases for sales promotions, premiums, fund-raising, or educational use. Special books, or book excerpts, can also be created to fit specific needs.

For details, write: Special Markets, Alpha Books, 375 Hudson Street, New York, NY 10014.

**Publisher:** *Marie Butler-Knight*
**Editorial Director:** *Mike Sanders*
**Senior Managing Editor:** *Billy Fields*
**Executive Editor:** *Randy Ladenheim-Gil*
**Development Editor:** *Lynn Northrup*
**Senior Production Editor:** *Janette Lynn*
**Copy Editor:** *Krista Hansing Editorial Services, Inc.*

**Cover Designer:** *Kurt Owens*
**Book Designer:** *Trina Wurst*
**Indexer:** *Angie Bess Martin*
**Layout:** *Rebecca Batchelor, Brian Massey*
**Proofreader:** *Laura Caddell*

*This book is dedicated to my husband, for his unwavering love, support, and encouragement; to my children, who have brought immeasurable joy to my life; and to my sister, my best friend.*
—Laura Stradley

*To the Matthews and Kavanagh families, who have been an enormous support throughout this project. Also to my friends and acquaintances who are serving or have served in the military.*
—Robin Kavanagh

# Contents at a Glance

# Contents

# Introduction

Thinking about a career in the military? Congratulations! You're considering one of the most honorable professions in the world. Unlike most other types of jobs you could be exploring right now, you have to go through a long process for the military to determine whether you've got the right stuff to succeed in a specific branch.

You'll be tested on all types of things, such as your physical appearance and health, your psychological health, your character, and even your financial responsibility. But before you get to these assessments, you have to jump one big hurdle: you must pass the Armed Services Vocational Aptitude Battery (ASVAB from here on out).

If you don't know by now, this is a battery of up to 10 tests designed to predict how you will perform once you're in the Army, Navy, Marine Corps, Air Force, or Coast Guard. It will also determine which jobs you're qualified to train for. What you should know right now is that you need to get a minimum score on certain sections of this test to be eligible to enlist.

We offer this book as a general guide to help you prepare for the ASVAB and get your scores to where you want them to be. You may not agree with all of our advice, and some parts may not work for you as an individual—and that's okay. No piece of advice is right for every person. We encourage you to make your test-prep experience your own and pursue whatever works best for you.

When you're using this book, we ask that you keep in mind that we are giving advice based on our extensive research and personal experience with this subject. The information we provide is the most up-to-date that we can offer as of the date this book was written, and we have made every effort to ensure the accuracy of the information we provide.

Please be aware that regulations and conditions in the military can change very quickly, which may render some of the information in this book incorrect by the time you read it. It's always best to contact a recruiter for the most up-to-date information about enlistment, the ASVAB, scores, and anything else related to your pursuit of a military career.

## How to Use This Book

Studying for a large exam like the ASVAB is a huge undertaking, especially when you consider the amount of math and science you'll be tested on. To help, we've tried to make reading and using this book as easy as possible for you by breaking down all the information you need into five main sections; you can pick and choose what you want to read, and when.

**Part 1, "A Little Intel Goes a Long Way,"** gives you lots of information about the different branches of the military, career options, and recruitment. You'll also find out how the test is broken down, what to expect, and the best ways to approach both taking the test and studying for it.

**Part 2, "Word Up! All About Communication Skills,"** explains how the ASVAB is divided into two main parts: the Armed Forces Qualifying Tests (AFQT) and the Technical Tests. The AFQT tests you on verbal communication and math abilities. This part takes you through what you'll see on the verbal subtests and gives you plenty of room to practice.

**Part 3, "Math as Easy as Hup-2-3,"** breaks down the two math subtests for you and gives you a comprehensive review of the type of math you'll likely encounter on the ASVAB. You'll see a lot of practice questions in the chapters, as well as a separate chapter filled with more chances to practice.

**Part 4, "Get It Together: Technical Sections,"** describes all the other subtests, which are considered "technical sections." This is not only because they count toward your job eligibility, but also because they test you on general science, physics, electronics, automotive and shop information, and visual logic. Each of the chapters in this part of the book provides review on the subject at hand, plus questions that will help you get some good practice.

**Part 5, "After Action Review: Practice Tests,"** contains three complete practice tests that include both AFQT and job specialty sections. You'll also find an additional test that has only math and verbal sections, so you can get some more practice taking the crucial AFQT (in case you didn't know, this is the part of the test you need to pass to join the military).

We also include three appendixes that give you score breakdowns for each branch of service, locations of testing sites throughout the United States and Puerto Rico, and a listing of resources you can check out to help make the most of your test-prep experience.

## Extras

Along the way, be sure to look for these power-packed extras:

## def•i•ni•tion
These mini lessons give you a better understanding of terms you'll hear a lot during the recruiting process, and give you a better understanding of the ASVAB in general.

### Heads-Up
These little facts and hints help you steer clear of trouble on the exam and give you the info you need to make smart decisions about your future.

### Test Tip
These are quick and effective ways to increase your ASVAB scores and plan for your career ahead.

### Classified Intel
These are interesting facts about the test, those who've taken it, how it's used, and other tidbits, to help you keep things in perspective.

## Acknowledgments

Laura Stradley:

Special thanks to Rick May for his automotive expertise; to all the recruiters at the Army and Navy recruiting stations in Greece, New York, who offered their suggestions and advice; to the managers at Bryant & Stratton College in Rochester, New York, who truly value the military and support local recruiting and veterans initiatives; and to everyone who has helped with the completion of this book.

Robin Kavanagh:

Special thanks to Keri Cerami, math professor extraordinaire, who was invaluable to this project. Also to Tom Kavanagh for his awesome automotive knowledge; Wendy Mamilovich, who helped an old friend; Marilyn Allen, best agent in the world; and all those who have contributed their experiences and tips to this book. And of course, thank you to our team of fabulous editors: Randy Ladenheim-Gil, Lynn Northrup, Janette Lynn, Krista Hansing, and David Jordan.

## Special Thanks to the Technical Reviewer

*The Complete Idiot's Guide to the ASVAB* was reviewed by an expert who double-checked the accuracy of what you'll learn here, to help us ensure that this book gives you everything you need to know about preparing for and taking the ASVAB. Special thanks are extended to David Jordan.

David Jordan grew up all around the world in an Army family. He is currently a graduate student and teaching assistant at Massachusetts Institute of Technology, where he studies mathematics. His hobbies include biking, making stained-glass windows, engaging in political activism, and doing technical editing for Alpha Books.

## Trademarks

All terms mentioned in this book that are known to be or are suspected of being trademarks or service marks have been appropriately capitalized. Alpha Books and Penguin Group (USA) Inc. cannot attest to the accuracy of this information. Use of a term in this book should not be regarded as affecting the validity of any trademark or service mark.

# Part 1

# A Little Intel Goes a Long Way

There's an old saying, "Work smart, not hard." It may sound cliché, but there's quite a bit of wisdom in these tried and true words. Doing your homework (literally, in the case of test prep) can help make you better informed and ready to strike when the chance arises—which is why gathering intelligence is so important in the military. It's also essential when scoping out your current enemy: the ASVAB.

In this part, we get you up to speed on the different sectors of the military you may be interested in, what to expect from the recruitment process, military careers, and how the ASVAB fits in. Then we get down and dirty about how to take the test and how best to prepare for it, no matter where you are in life.

# Chapter 1

# So You Want to Be in the Military ...

## In This Chapter

- ◆ Choosing the right military branch
- ◆ What to expect in the recruitment process
- ◆ What recruiters wish for
- ◆ Questions to bring to the recruitment office
- ◆ Military career counseling

College just isn't for you or isn't affordable right now. A relative you admire served. You feel called to duty as a patriotic American. You're looking to take your life in a new direction. It's a family tradition.

Young people consider joining the military for a lot of reasons, and each is deeply personal and unique. Regardless of your motivation for choosing to serve, it's important to learn as much as you can about this life-altering decision and the world you are preparing to step into.

This chapter gives you an overview of the five main branches of the military, what you can expect during recruitment, what recruiters wish candidates knew before signing up, and essential questions to ask along the way.

## The Decision of a Lifetime

Enlistment is a decision that will impact your career choices throughout your life. You may find that once you're in the military, it's the place you want to spend the rest of your working years. You could also view your time in the military as a stepping stone toward larger educational and career goals.

Joining the military is a great way to train for different professions while getting paid for gaining hands-on experience in a private-sector industry that you're interested in. It can also be a place to grow and explore yourself (and the world) while you consider college or your long-term career options.

All of these scenarios make researching the different branches of the military extremely important before you decide which one is right for you. Because the Army, Navy, Air Force, Marines, and Coast Guard offer different opportunities and have different requirements of recruits, now is the time to determine which is the best for helping you reach both short-term and long-term goals.

### Heads-Up

The United States Military Entrance Processing Command (USMEPCOM) website (www. mepcom.army.mil) is a great resource for learning more about what you can expect when you go through enlistment. You can also find a full listing of Military Entrance Processing Station (MEPS) locations in Appendix B.

## Air Force

In 1947, the Air Force became an official entity of the U.S. Armed Forces. For the 40 years earlier, it had been a part of the Army. After the heavy use of aircraft during World Wars I and II, it was clear that airpower would be a key factor in national defense, especially since the Korean War was well underway only a few years after the end of World War II. President Harry Truman created the Department of the Air Force with the National Security Act of 1947, and the U.S. Air Force has been responsible for guarding the skies ever since.

The Air Force's official mission is to "fly, fight, and win." Today that mission applies to the air, space, and cyberspace. Protecting the United States against missile and airborne attacks, guarding against cyber-attacks, and overseeing the national space program are just a few of the branch's charges.

The Air Force is made up of nine major commands in Virginia, Texas, Ohio, Georgia, Colorado, Florida, Illinois, Hawaii, and Germany. Additionally, there are 35 field operating agencies and 4 direct reporting units. The Air Force also offers two reserve units: the Air Force Reserve and the Air National Guard.

In the Air Force, you can explore four main types of occupational specialties that encompass a variety of different jobs. These include the following:

◆ **Mechanical.** These are generally technical specialties, such as Aerospace Maintenance, Air Traffic Controller Operations, Biomedical Equipment, Electrical Power Production, Aircraft Fuel Systems, HVAC, Munitions Systems, Missile and Space Systems Electronics Maintenance, Nuclear Weapons, Tactical Aircraft Maintenance, and Vehicle Operations.

◆ **Administrative.** These positions center on the behind-the-scenes work that make everything run smoothly. A sampling of jobs includes Air Transportation, Aviation Resource Management, Information Management, Logistics Plans, Personnel, Materiel Management, Regional Band, and Vehicle Maintenance Control and Analysis.

◆ **General.** Jobs in this category are anything but general. They encompass a wide variety of abilities, interests, and industries—many of which you might not expect. Just a few of the opportunities here include Aerospace Control and Warning Systems, Aerospace Physiology,

Airborne Battle Management Systems, Airfield Management, Bioenvironmental Engineering, Cardiopulmonary Laboratory, Communications Signals Intelligence, Contracting, Dental Assistant, Diagnostic Imaging, Graphic Arts, Diet Therapy, Paralegal, Pest Management, Still Photography, and Pararescue.

◆ **Electronics.** These technical specialties deal primarily with electronics systems. Possible jobs include Aerial Gunner, Airborne Mission Systems, Avionics Test Station and Components, Computer Systems Control, Electrical Systems, Ground Radar Systems, Integrated Avionics Systems, Missile and Space Facilities, Wideband and Telemetry Satellite Systems, and Visual Imagery and Intrusion Detection Systems.

If you're interested in learning more about the Air Force, you can get a lot of good information from its official website, www.af.mil/. The recruitment site is www.airforce.com/.

---

### Classified Intel

Each branch of the military has two websites. One is the official organization site and has a .mil extension on the address. The other is a recruiting site, which has a .com extension. An official site will say "official site" on the home page, and you can assume that the information on the site is accurate and up-to-date. Any other site is produced and maintained by a private company, which means the information may or may not be up-to-date.

---

## Army

When many people talk about the military, they use "Army" as their go-to reference—and with good reason. It's the oldest and largest branch of America's Armed Forces. As of September 2008, nearly 1.1 million soldiers were serving in the Army, about half of them currently active (as opposed to reserve). The National Guard and the Army Reserves make up the remainder of these troops.

The Army's mission is to "fight and win our Nation's wars by providing prompt, sustained land dominance across the full range of military operations and spectrum of conflict in support of combatant commanders." To achieve this, the Army is broken up into operational and institutional organizations. The operational Army is the units stationed worldwide that are on the ground conducting operations. The institutional Army is the infrastructure that keeps the operational Army ready for action by providing training, administration, and resource-management and logistic functions.

Within each of these subdivisions are more than 217 different jobs that you can pursue, depending on your interests and qualifications. General areas of occupation include these:

◆ **Administrative Support.** If you're interested in a career in human resources, general administration, law, finance, information services, or even religion, this category is for you. Some of these jobs include Chaplain, Human Resource Specialist, Financial Management Technician, Shower/Laundry and Clothing Repair Specialist, Unit Supply Specialist, and Personnel Systems Manager Officer.

◆ **Intelligence and Combat Support.** In these jobs, you'll work behind the scenes to help collect intelligence and get it to units engaged in combat. Some of these jobs include Interpreter/Translator; Cryptologic Linguist; Chemical, Biological, Radiological, and Nuclear (CBRN) Specialist; Civil Affairs Specialist; and Small Arms/Artillery Repairer.

◆ **Arts and Media.** Those who work in this category straddle the lines of civilian and military communication. If graphic design, media, music, or journalism is your passion, this is one area you should explore. Some jobs include Public Affairs Specialist, Multimedia Illustrator, Army Bandsperson, and Visual Information Equipment Operator–Maintainer.

◆ **Legal and Law Enforcement.** These jobs are all about keeping the peace and making sure military personnel and property stay safe. Some include Military Police, Firefighter, Attorney, Paralegal, and Criminal Investigations Special Agent.

◆ **Combat.** These soldiers are on the front lines gathering reconnaissance and employing defensive and offensive tactics wherever action is needed. Some jobs include Special Forces Candidate, Cannon Crewmember, Air and Missile Defense Crewmember, Infantryman, and Cavalry Scout.

**Heads-Up** _____

Women are ineligible for all combat jobs.

◆ **Mechanics.** These jobs help make sure all of the Army's basic and highly advanced equipment stays in good working order. Some jobs include Avionic Communications Equipment Repairer, Artillery Mechanic, Machinist, Biomedical Equipment Specialist, and Multiple Launch Rocket System (MLRS) Repairer.

◆ **Computers and Technology.** All sorts of different jobs fall into this category, including ones dealing with communications, intelligence gathering, graphic arts, mechanics, and explosives. Some include Computer/Detection Systems Repairer, Imagery Analyst, Counterintelligence Agent, Information

Technology Specialist, and Avionic and Survivability Equipment Repairer.

◆ **Medical and Emergency.** This is a great way to gain free training and experience in the general, veterinary, and dental medical fields. Some jobs include Animal Care Specialist, Medical Laboratory Specialist, Mental Health Specialist, Optical Lab Specialist, Mortuary Affairs Specialist, and Dental Corps Officer.

◆ **Construction and Engineering.** Interested in carpentry, engineering, plumbing, electrical, or masonry? These are the jobs you should check out. Some include Combat Engineer, Bridge Crewmember, Interior Electrician, Petroleum Supply Specialist, Quarrying Specialist, and Water Treatment Specialist.

◆ **Transportation and Aviation.** These jobs are responsible for the management, coordination, use, and anything else involved in the transport of Army equipment and personnel. Some jobs include Avionic Mechanic, Air Traffic Control (ATC) Operator, Parachute Rigger, Unmanned Aerial Vehicle Operator, and Cargo Specialist.

If you're interested in learning more about the Army, go to the official website, www.army.mil/, or the recruiting site, www.goarmy.com.

## Coast Guard

The U.S. Coast Guard's domain is the sea and shores that surround the United States and its territories. It is responsible for protecting "the public, the environment, and the United States economic and security interests in any maritime region in which those interests may be at risk, including international waters and America's coasts, ports, and inland waterways." This includes enforcing maritime law, providing search-and-rescue operations, and supplying assistance to mariners in U.S. waters. During peacetime, the Coast Guard acts under the direction of the Department of Homeland Security. However, during wartime or under the direction of the President, the Coast Guard falls under the Navy.

It takes a certain type of personality to be a "Coastie," says Petty Officer Albert Scales, a recruiter in West Orange, New Jersey. He says most members of the service are looking to give of themselves more and that they're more interested in protecting and saving lives. For example, Scales says that when faced with a huge wave (a "big surf," in Coastie-speak), "the average person would say, 'That's a 40-foot wall of water. Why would I want to go into that?' We don't think that way. We just go because someone on the other side needs our help."

The Coast Guard has five main missions: national defense, maritime security, protection of natural resources, maritime mobility, and maritime safety. Compared to the other branches of the service, the Coast Guard has relatively few positions to offer recruits.

---

**Classified Intel**

The life of a Coastie is never boring. Every day, on average, the Coast Guard saves 14 lives; conducts 74 search-and-rescue operations; seizes or removes more than 1,000 pounds of illegal drugs at an estimated $12.9 million in value; boards 193 ships and boats; and ensures the safe, secure, and efficient navigation of ships carrying $5.5 billion worth of commerce.

---

However, if the job you're interested in is unavailable at the time you enlist, you can enter this service as a nonrated officer, which means that no one job is assigned to you. You will work and be paid as a member of the Coast Guard while you wait for your name to come up for the particular training

school. You can also train for many different types of jobs throughout your time in the service.

Generally, enlisted Coast Guard jobs are divided into four main categories:

- **Aviation.** As the name suggests, these jobs involve technical positions that include maintenance of fixed-wing and rotary aircraft. Responsibilities can include inspecting, servicing, and repairing avionics systems; working with airframe systems; repairing aircraft engines, fuselages, wings, rotor blades, and more; filling aircrew positions; and performing search-and-rescue operations.

- **Deck and Ordnance.** These jobs deal with the running and operation of Coast Guard vessels, including law enforcement; small arms and weapons systems; pyrotechnics; tactical command, control, and communications; intelligence gathering; and cryptology.

- **Hull and Engineering.** These jobs deal with the maintenance, running, and operation of Coast Guard vessels. Duties include general and emergency repairs; installation, maintenance, repair, and management of electronics systems and components; maintenance of navigation and communication systems; information management; and mechanical support.

- **Administrative and Scientific.** All the other jobs in the Coast Guard fall under this broad category. Duties can include environmental protection, health-care services, restaurant and catering, writing and photography, human resources management and administration, and accounting.

For more information about the Coast Guard or recruitment, or to see the Coast Guard in action, go to www.uscg.mil/, www.gocoastguard.com/, or www.thecoastguardchannel.com.

## Marines

The United States Marine Corps recruitment website says: "Marines are made, not born. Twelve weeks of the toughest training in the world transforms civilians into members of the United States' most noble brotherhood." If this sounds like fun, you just may have what it takes to become a Devil Dog, gyrene, jarhead, or leatherneck—whichever nickname you prefer.

### Heads-Up

The Marines is a very conservative branch of the military, which means standards of appearance are high. If you have tattoos, body art, or piercings, you may not be able to join. Prohibited items include tattoos on the head or neck; sleeve tattoos; and markings that depict gang colors, have sexist or racist messaging, or are related to drugs or illegal activity.

The Marines is an infantry-based command, which means its primary mission is combat and combat support for other branches of the military. At just about 200,000 active-duty personnel as of May 2009, the Marine Corps has the smallest workforce, after the Coast Guard. This is partly because of the level of skill and dedication needed to succeed in the Marines, but also because of the need for units to be able to deploy task forces anywhere worldwide within 24 hours of receiving orders.

The Marine Corps is a kind of amalgamation of all the other services wrapped into one ultra-efficient unit. Marines can execute operations by land, by sea, and by air with efficiency and stealth.

Career opportunities with the Marine Corps are vast. As one recruiter put it, "There's something for everyone" if you qualify physically, academically, and psychologically for the rigors of the more than 300 jobs under 80 categories that make this branch

function. Because of this, we just list a sampling of the job categories so you can get an idea of whether there's a job that may fit with your interests:

- Air Control/Air Support/Anti-Air Warfare/Air Traffic Control
- Aircraft Maintenance
- Airfield Services
- Ammunition and Explosive Ordnance Disposal
- Aviation Logistics
- Aviation Ordnance
- Avionics
- Chemical, Biological, Radiological, and Nuclear Defense
- Combat Camera
- Communications
- Electronics Maintenance
- Field Artillery
- Financial Management
- Food Service
- Ground Ordnance Maintenance
- Infantry
- Intelligence
- Legal Services
- Linguist
- Logistics
- Marine Corps Community Services
- Meteorology and Oceanography
- Military Police and Corrections
- Music
- Navigation Officer/Enlisted Flight Crews
- Personnel and Administration
- Public Affairs
- Supply Administration and Operations
- Traffic Management
- Training
- Utilities

For more information about the Marine Corps or Marine Corps recruitment, go to www.marines.mil or www.marines.com/.

## Navy

The Navy is the branch of the U.S. Armed Forces responsible for defending the country and its interests by sea. The Navy's official mission is to "maintain, train, and equip combat-ready Naval forces capable of winning wars, deterring aggression, and maintaining freedom of the seas."

To carry out this mission, the Navy maintains bases, ships, and other assets worldwide to support offensive and defensive military operations. This means a huge variety of opportunities for those looking for careers that include travel, adventure, and personal challenge—not to mention a ton of variety! Navy jobs are not all about sailing. Navy recruits train in just about any type of job you can think of, from aviation and mechanics, to law enforcement and information technology.

Although you don't need to be an expert swimmer to join the Navy, you should be prepared to spend a good deal of time at sea. As a new Navy recruit, you will most likely be assigned to a ship after boot camp, but not always. You could explore some land-based jobs. If you have an aversion to water, talk with your recruiter about these options.

---

**Classified Intel**

You can join the Navy even if you don't know how to swim. They will train you until you're a pro. Take it from one recent recruit who had never had a swim lesson in his life before he enlisted. By the time he completed his training, he was certified as a rescue diver.

---

Because enlisted and officer personnel in the Navy have more than 1,000 different career options, we list only some of the job categories so you can get an idea of whether there's a job that may fit your interests:

- Arts and Photography
- Aviation
- Business Management
- Computers
- Construction and Building
- Education
- Electronics
- Emergency, Fire, and Rescue
- Energy and Power
- Engineering
- Finance and Accounting
- Food, Restaurant, and Lodging
- Information Technology
- Intelligence and Communications
- Law Enforcement and Security
- Law
- Medical and Dental
- Music
- News and Media
- Office and Administrative Support
- Religion
- Science
- Telecommunications
- Transportation and Logistics
- World Languages

For more information about the Navy or Navy recruitment, go to www.navy.mil or www.navy.com/.

# The Recruitment Experience

Now that you have a general overview of what each branch of the military has to offer, let's talk about recruitment. If you're interested in joining a particular branch, or even just want more information, contacting a recruiter is your best bet.

It's important to understand a recruiter's role before going any further. You may have heard horror stories from friends or on the Internet about people having bad experiences with recruiters. Complaints often arise about promises being made and then not fulfilled, high-pressure tactics, and even misleading information.

The truth is that it's a recruiter's job to maintain and increase the numbers of active and reserve personnel in our voluntary Armed Forces. They have their own goals to meet and are trained in how to counsel and lead potential recruits through the decision-making process.

However, they also must abide by stringent ethical standards. They are knowledgeable career counselors who are responsible for guiding you through the whole enlistment experience.

> **Classified Intel**
>
> A recruiter or guidance counselor can't promise a specific assignment, location, or job. He also can't promise that you will not deploy or force you into signing anything.

The smartest thing for you to do is learn as much as you can about the branch you're interested in, independent of your recruiter. The Internet, friends, and family who have had experience with the branch you're thinking about joining are great resources and will help you make the most informed choice. We also give you a taste of what to expect.

## From the Door to Contract

When you connect with a recruiter, you'll do a lot of talking. During this time, he or she will discreetly look to see if you and the branch of service you're considering joining are a good fit. Through conversation, the recruiter will try to see if you meet minimum qualifications based on age, physical appearance, prior service record, law violations, education history, marital status, dependants, and testing. You may even take some sample ASVAB

tests to indicate how you would score on the real exam.

From there, your recruiter will decide whether you will likely make it through the enlistment process and fulfill the military's needs. Even if he's not 100 percent sure that you're military material, he'll probably send you to take the ASVAB, as an additional assessment tool.

> **Heads-Up**
>
> We get into exactly what the ASVAB is in Chapter 2. For now, you just need to know that taking the test doesn't obligate you to enlist—if a recruiter sends you to take it, you've got nothing to lose.

You'll be sent to either a Military Entrance Processing Station (MEPS) or a Military Entrance Test (MET) site to take the real ASVAB. Larger MEPS sites can provide one-stop shopping for military recruits, so if your recruiter feels you'll do well on the ASVAB, you may complete some of the other entrance requirements:

- **Physical and psychological examinations.** Basics like blood pressure, height/weight, vision, and hearing are tested and recorded. Expect blood and drug screenings, and possible strength or stamina tests.

- **Moral character assessment.** This test also takes place at a MEPS location. These may include extended interviews, credit and criminal background checks, and even a financial history. Requirements for this vary.

Where you go from the ASVAB depends on your scores. If you don't make the grade, you'll have to retake the ASVAB in 30 days. If you do make the grade (see Chapter 2), your next step is to meet with a guidance counselor (if available) or your recruiter to discuss your career options. Now it's up to you to figure out what those options are. Remember that you still have control over where you go from here. After you've gone through all these steps, you'll get an offer from the military stating what your job will be, how much you'll be compensated, and the time of service you'll be responsible for fulfilling (among other things).

Keep in mind that deciding whether to take the deal might involve more than your career goals. According to S. Douglas Smith, Public Affairs Officer with the U.S. Army Recruiting Command, recruits sign on because of incentives that are offered, the location they're offered, and the length of enlistment, in addition to the type of job that's available. Incentives can include signing bonuses of up to $40,000, money for college or help paying back student loans, start-up funds for a business or to buy a house, or even bonuses for prior education and work experience. If you're interested in these incentives, ask about them when discussing your contract.

When you've reviewed the contract, if you're not happy with the deal they're offering, you're free to walk away without signing. If you decide to sign, make sure that you read the contract carefully and that you understand and agree to all of what's stated before signing.

Also keep in mind the importance of your short-term and long-term goals. A $40,000 signing bonus may seem like a great deal when you're 18, but it could come with an obligation to stay in the military for at least four years. Ask yourself how this affects your career and education goals before you accept.

## After You Sign

Once you sign on the dotted line, you may be raring to pack up and head off to basic training. In reality,

most new recruits wait a minimum of three to four months before they have to show up for active duty. If you don't get orders to report for training within a month of enlistment, you'll likely be enrolled in the Delayed Entry Program (DEP). The DEP is designed to control the number of new enlistees who are assigned to training schools by assigning them specific dates when they will begin active duty. Those in the DEP can wait up to a year, although the average wait time is four months.

**Heads-Up**

Even after you sign a contract with the military, provisions can help you get out of it if you get a case of buyer's (or, in this case, signer's) remorse.

If exceptional circumstances arise, you can ask for your active duty date to be pushed back up to an additional year, even if you've been delayed for a full year already. Some high school students can also apply for DEP status so that they can graduate before beginning their service.

## Recruiters' Wish List

The fact that you're reading this book means you've probably given some serious thought to joining the service. Probably one of your main concerns is whether military life will be a good fit for you. Believe it or not, your recruiters have wondered the same thing! As ambassadors of the military, they know firsthand the benefits that await you upon enlistment. At the same time, they also know that not everyone is cut out for life in the service.

That's why it's important to look at this equation from their perspective as well. Your recruiter can provide you with the tools and the means to successfully enlist in the military, but they need you to hold up your end of the bargain, too.

Most recruiters wish for a few things, to ensure a smooth process for you and for them:

- **A clean record.** In recent decades, very few people have been able to join any branch of service with more than a misdemeanor in their past.

- **A reasonable body fat composition.** Each branch of the military differs in what it will allow in terms of height and weight standards. However, each branch has certain minimum qualifications in this department; ask your recruiter for more information if this concerns you.

- **Honesty.** When your recruiter asks you questions about your past or your health, or requests information of a personal nature, the best policy is full disclosure. They will most likely find out the truth eventually, and it will save everyone a lot of time if you are honest from day one. Often there are circumstances where disqualifications can be waived.

- **The ability to pass the ASVAB.** We saved the best for last! The ASVAB can be challenging for the ill-prepared test-taker. Many recruiters recommend websites like March 2 Success, military.com, and others (see Appendix C) so that you will be familiar with the types of questions on the exam. Other recruiters may require you to take a practice test in their office before they go to the trouble and expense of sending you to a test site. Some recruiting stations even have a portion of their operating budget set aside for ASVAB tutoring.

The point is, the ASVAB is not the type of test that people should just assume they can pass without preparation. The more time you spend reviewing the subject matter and answering sample questions, the more likely you will be able to pass the ASVAB on your first try.

Of course, recruiters wish for many other things in addition to this list: punctuality at appointments, returned phone calls, happy moms and dads, cooperative high school officials and guidance counselors, and so forth. That being said, the most important items on their list are the four qualifying areas just mentioned. As you continue to navigate this book, you will most definitely improve your ability to qualify for military service—and check off a box on your recruiter's wish list!

# Essential Questions to Ask Your Recruiter

Joining the military is a major decision. Much like the other major decisions you've made in life, you'll want to be sure you have all the facts before you sign on the dotted line. The question is, what facts should you have? When something is new to us, sometimes it's hard to know what questions to even ask. You'll want to know answers to these questions, based on veteran experience:

1. What rank will I be when I enter basic training?

2. If I have college credits already, will I be able to enter at an advanced rank? (Most branches of service value college credits and will allow you to enter at an advanced rank—the rate of advancement varies by branch, as does the number of college credits required for this program.)

3. How quickly can I get promoted after basic training?

4. How long is basic training?

5. What will be required of me when I arrive at basic training? (Some branches require you to do a certain number of push-ups upon arrival; failure to do so could result in spending extra time at basic training, something no one wants to do!)

6. What happens if I get injured or sick during basic training?

7. What kind of education benefits will I have when I enter the service? Are any of these benefits available to me before I leave for basic training? (Some branches provide tuition assistance up to $250 per credit hour before you even leave for basic!)

8. Am I eligible for any enlistment bonuses, such as the Army College Fund, college loan repayment, signing bonuses, and station of choice?

9. After I choose the career field I want in the military, is this guaranteed? (Some branches can guarantee better than others.)

10. What is the maximum commitment I will have to the service? (Even if you enlist for four years of service, you are generally obligated to eight years of combined active and inactive service. Inactive simply means that if the military wants you back when your four years are up, they can recall you.)

11. If I don't like the job I enlist for, can I reclass to a different job?

12. If I'm married, will the service pay to have my spouse moved to my assignment?

13. How soon can my spouse join me? After basic training, after Advanced Individual Training (also known in some branches as on-the-job training), or when I arrive at my first assignment?

14. What kinds of benefits will my spouse be eligible for as a dependent?

15. What is the likelihood that I will get deployed, and what are the average lengths of deployments? (Length of deployment varies by branch.)

16. How much traveling and/or time away from home is required with the job I have selected?

17. Does my career field have a crossover to the Commissioned Officer Ranks?

18. What type of pay will I receive besides my base pay? (Generally, you will be eligible for a housing allowance, a food allowance, travel expenses as needed, and a plethora of additional stipends.)

19. What civilian jobs are similar to the military job I have chosen?

20. What type of transition assistance will be provided for me when I'm ready to transfer back to civilian life? (Different branches vary on this—the Army actually contracts this assistance out to the largest outplacement agency in the country, providing a full-service program to soldiers, including resumé writing, job fairs, job preparation workshops, counseling, interviewing skills, and the like, all for free!)

You may want to ask your recruiter dozens of other questions, but hopefully this list has given you a starting point. One last tip: if your recruiter doesn't know the answer, he knows someone who does. Be sure your questions are answered to the extent that you are comfortable with, even if it means a few extra phone calls are made or e-mails are sent. You won't regret having too much information in the days and months ahead.

 **Test Tip**

If the information your recruiter or counselor is giving you doesn't match up with your goals, make sure you say so. This is your future and you have to make the decisions that are right for you.

## The Least You Need to Know

- It's best to learn about the different branches of the military to see if they can offer you the type of training you're interested in.

- There are many requirements and steps in the recruitment process that you have to pass in order to enlist.

- Recruiters can be a great resource for career counseling, but remember they have quotas to meet when considering the information they give you.

- Think about where you'd like your career to take you and what your long-term goals are before heading to a recruiter.

- You're under no obligation to enlist until you sign a contract, and even then you may still be able to change your mind.

- Preparing a list of questions about the issues you're most concerned with in regard to serving in the military can be a big help.

# Chapter 2

# Know Thy Enemy: ASVAB Essentials

## In This Chapter

◆ How the ASVAB is divided up

◆ Taking the computer adaptive version

◆ Taking the paper version

◆ How the tests are scored

◆ Retaking the test

By now, you know that being in the Army, Navy, Air Force, Marines, or Coast Guard isn't all about jumping out of airplanes and heading off to combat. For most members of the service, it's a career choice or a training ground to gain the skills they need to work in private-sector industries. Any way you slice it, the military is a world unto itself, and it needs skilled labor just like any other society.

That's where the ASVAB comes in. Just about anyone can walk into a recruiter's office and say they want to enlist. But it's the recruiter's job to figure out whether those who come to them have the right stuff to make it in the military. To do this, recruiters adhere to their branch's code of ethics and entrance standards that every new recruit must meet.

The ASVAB is a standardized way to assess the skills of the thousands of strangers who come knocking on recruiters doors coast to coast. This chapter gives you an overview of what the ASVAB is, how it's divided up, and what you can expect when you take the exam.

# ASVAB Breakdown

The ASVAB is a series of short tests aimed at giving the military an idea of your abilities before they hire you. It might be weird to think of the military as an organization that hires people, but that's really all enlistment is about. Each branch of the military wants to fill its ranks with the best and brightest candidates for the myriad jobs that make the organization run.

The ASVAB subtests are designed to reveal a person's natural strengths and abilities so that they can be placed in a job where they will succeed. This is done not only for the benefit of the recruit—after all, a happy serviceperson is one who sticks around—but for the benefit and safety of the organization as a whole. Placing someone who has a low aptitude for mechanical science in the cockpit of an F-15 fighter plane can end up costing lives and millions of dollars in expenses.

---

**Classified Intel**

Each of the ASVAB subtests is based on general knowledge that anyone with a high school diploma or GED would know. The majority of the questions contain information that should at least be somewhat familiar to you, even if only vaguely.

---

With this in mind, the ASVAB is divided into two main parts: the Armed Forces Qualifying Test (AFQT) and the technical tests. One allows you entrance into the military; the other qualifies you for specific jobs within each of the branches.

## Armed Forces Qualifying Test

The AFQT is nothing more than a big math and English exam, very similar to what you'd find on the SAT or ACT. It consists of two math subtests and two verbal subtests, each with specific skill sets being tested.

What can math and English skills tell the military about you? A lot more than you might think.

Take a look at the four subtests that make up the AFQT:

- **Word Knowledge (WK).** On the surface, this section tests your vocabulary knowledge. Underneath, it's really measuring your communication skills and ability to use context clues to draw logical conclusions.

- **Paragraph Comprehension (PC).** Here you're asked to read short passages and answer questions based on what you read. This is kind of a wolf-in-sheep's-clothing test, since what's really being tested are your analytical skills.

- **Arithmetic Reasoning (AR).** This whole test is all about word problems. You're asked to think through these problems, develop the best (and fastest) approach to solving it, and then choose the correct answer out of the four you're given. You're really being tested on your ability to follow directions, think logically, and develop an analytical approach to problem solving.

- **Mathematics Knowledge (MK).** On this test, you're asked to demonstrate your elementary math skills, as well as your knowledge of algebra and geometry. This test is straight-up, in that it is designed to measure how good you are at math.

**Heads-Up**

When you take the ASVAB, you sit down and take one long test divided into sections. You will not see any section labeled "AFQT" or "Technical Tests." It's up to you to prepare for the sections that matter most to you. Since everyone has to pass the AFQT to enlist, math and verbal prep is a must.

## Technical Tests

Unlike with the AFQT, how you perform on the technical tests (or technical subtests) does not affect your entrance eligibility. These are a series of subject-specific tests that determine what career path options are open to you:

- **General Science (GS).** This tests you on the basics of physical, earth, and life sciences. Don't worry if you slept through bio; brushing up should be enough to get you through this part of the test.

- **Electronics Information (EI).** If you like tinkering with your DVD player, this test is right up your alley. Here you'll find all sorts of questions about electrical systems, components, circuitry, terminology, and other technical basics.

- **Automotive and Shop Information (AS).** Strut your stuff (ha, ha!) about all things related to cars, tools, and hardware. Here's where your industrial arts and weekends working on your car pay off.

- **Mechanical Comprehension (MC).** No, you won't find automotive questions in this section. Mechanical comprehension is mostly about physical science, how machines work, and applications of mechanical principles in real life.

- **Assembling Objects (AO).** This section focuses on perception of spatial relationships. Basically, you're given multiple parts of an object, and then you need to answer questions about how they would fit together.

## Why You Need to Do Well

We know the prospect of being tested on math, English, science, logic, automotive and shop

information, and visual acuity is not the happiest thought in the world. The good news is that you don't have to be an ace in everything to achieve your goals in the military.

What you do need to ace is the AFQT. This is the part of the test that determines whether you can enlist. Each branch of the military has a minimum AFQT score that recruits must achieve to be eligible for enlistment. These scores vary and can change from month to month. Check with your recruiter for the current minimum score for the branch you're looking to join.

> ### Classified Intel
> The Coast Guard has the highest AFQT score requirement of all of the Armed Forces. Why? Most Coast Guard jobs are heavily based in academics. If you're interested in being a Coastie, be prepared to study hard and take lots of tests during your service.

Technical subtest scores have a much different function in the recruitment process. For some jobs, you need to have only the right math and verbal scores. However, most jobs require recruits to have a certain amount of knowledge and skill (as determined by the ASVAB technical scores) to be able to perform safely and successfully.

For example, it makes sense to have a high aptitude in science, math, and electronics for jobs that concentrate on electrical engineering or weapons programming. These are highly scientific, analytical, and technical specialties that may not suit the strengths of someone who is more naturally inclined toward the arts or humanities. The technical subtests give the military an educated guess about your strengths so that you and your recruiter can make the best decision for your future.

# The Two Faces of the ASVAB

The ASVAB actually comes in three versions: the paper and pencil test (PAP), the computer adaptive test (CAT), and the student test. If you were given an aptitude test in high school, you may well have already taken a version of the ASVAB already. The student version is used as a career-counseling tool for high school students.

If your goal is not necessarily to figure out your career path, but to gain entrance into the military, you need to be familiar with both the PAP and CAT tests. Although the information you're tested on is the same, how these tests are administered makes a difference in how well you do. It's not because of the difficulty of the questions or because one test is easier or harder than the other. It's simply a matter of strategy.

Think of it like washing your car. You prepare differently to go to a full-service car wash than you do when washing your car yourself in your driveway. The result—a clean car—is the same, but the method of preparation and execution is different.

Knowing how to approach both tests puts you at an advantage. As mentioned in Chapter 1, you may not have a choice of where you take the ASVAB. Although the CAT is becoming increasingly available, many MET sites can offer only PAP testing. Conversely, at sites where CAT is available, you may not have the option to take a paper version of the ASVAB. Being prepared no matter what the situation will help you perform better.

**Heads-Up**

Don't be surprised if your technical scores indicate that you'd be great in a variety of occupations. At the end of the day, the ASVAB is a career-planning tool designed to give insight into a person's strengths.

## Computer Adaptive Test (CAT)

The CAT offers test-takers an alternative to the traditional fill-in-the-bubble paper test. Major standardized tests such as the GMAT, GRE, MAT, and other academic evaluations are administered through a CAT system.

Questions on the CAT ASVAB adapt to how you perform on the test. For example, the first question in every section is at a medium level of difficulty. If you get that one correct, the next question will be a little harder. If you get that first question wrong, the second will be a little easier.

One thing that's important to understand about the ASVAB is that not all questions are counted equally. Two people can take the ASVAB, get the same number of questions correct, and come back with different scores. All ASVAB questions, regardless of which version you take, are scored as either a 0 or a 1. However, this doesn't mean that each question is worth the same. Scaled ASVAB scores are based on Item Response Theory, which takes into consideration several factors:

◆ Assigned difficulty of questions

◆ How a question discriminates among those at different levels of ability

◆ The likelihood that a guess from a test-taker with a low level of ability will result in a correct answer

So why is this important to know about the CAT ASVAB? Knowing that the difficulty of questions has an impact on your scaled score can help you strategize. Try to get as many questions correct as you can in the beginning of the test. This will ensure that you have harder questions at the beginning, which will increase your scaled score right off the bat. If you start out with a high score, maintaining it is a lot easier than trying to build it up from a lower one.

## What to Expect

Like any standardized test, the CAT ASVAB is timed. You'll have a certain amount of time to complete the questions within the section you're working on. The following table shows how the CAT ASVAB is broken up.

### Computer Adaptive Test ASVAB Sections and Times

| Subject | Number of Questions | Minutes |
|---|---|---|
| General Science (GS) | 16 | 8 |
| Arithmetic Reasoning (AR) | 16 | 39 |
| Word Knowledge (WK) | 16 | 8 |
| Paragraph Comprehension (PC) | 11 | 22 |
| Mathematics Knowledge (MK) | 16 | 20 |
| Electronics Information (EI) | 16 | 8 |
| Auto Information (AS)* | 11 | 7 |
| Shop Information (AS)* | 11 | 6 |
| Mechanical Comprehension (MC) | 16 | 20 |
| Assembling Objects (AO) | 16 | 16 |
| **Total** | **145** | **154** |

*The Auto Information and Shop Information scores are presented under one label: AS.*

The questions will come up one at a time. After you choose your answer, you make your selection electronically. You're then prompted to verify that the selection you made is your final answer.

### Test Tip

Don't just blindly click through the answer verification after you make your selection. Double-check to make sure you didn't make a mistake between the answer you were thinking of and the one you marked. It just might save you from submitting a wrong answer.

Once you verify your answer, you're presented with the next question. This goes on until either the time runs out or you've completed the section. When you're done with one section, you simply move on to the next. At the end of the test, you get a computer-generated score report that instantly lets you know how you did. Decoding it may take a degree in cryptology, but we walk you through score reports a little later in the chapter.

The CAT ASVAB is also designed so that even the least computer-savvy person can complete the exam. As long as you can move a mouse and click a button, the CAT will be no problem for you. Every testing site gives very detailed and easy-to-follow directions and training on how to take the computerized test. There's also a tutorial that you take before starting the test so that you can try out answering questions without any risk. This gives you good practice and helps familiarize you with what you'll be doing over the coming hours.

## Paper and Pencil Test (PAP)

This is the more traditional standardized test most people are used to taking. The PAP ASVAB comes complete with test booklets, answer sheets with rows and rows of tiny bubbles, no. 2 pencils, and a *proctor* to make sure everyone is completing the exam according to the rules.

## def•i•ni•tion

A **proctor** is someone who is charged with administering an exam. It's this person's responsibility to make sure that all the administrative duties are carried out, all the paperwork is in order, the test is properly timed, and everyone adheres to the rules.

You're most likely to find this test given at MET sites, since they are smaller and often are a part of designated space in a building dedicated to other purposes. The computer and communications equipment needed to administer the CAT requires specific facilities to maintain the integrity of the test. With the PAP, all you need is the test materials, a room, a clock, chairs, and a proctor.

## What to Expect

When you get to the site, you'll be checked in and given instructions on where to go, what to do, and when (good practice for life in basic training). Make sure you bring a picture ID and a few sharpened pencils. Leave the calculator, food, and beverages at home.

When all the administrative stuff is out of the way, the proctor will begin reading instructions and test booklets, and handing out answer sheets. You will be expected to follow these instructions to the letter.

When administrative duties are taken care of, the test begins. The following table shows how the PAP ASVAB is broken up.

### Paper and Pencil ASVAB Sections and Times

| Subject | Number of Questions | Minutes |
|---|---|---|
| General Science (GS) | 25 | 11 |
| Arithmetic Reasoning (AR) | 30 | 36 |
| Word Knowledge (WK) | 35 | 11 |
| Paragraph Comprehension (PC) | 15 | 13 |
| Mathematics Knowledge (MK) | 25 | 24 |
| Electronics Information (EI) | 20 | 9 |
| Auto and Shop Information (AS) | 25 | 11 |
| Mechanical Comprehension (MC) | 25 | 19 |
| Assembling Objects (AO) | 25 | 15 |
| **Total** | **225** | **149** |

You must wait for the time in each section to run out before you can move on to the next. If you have time left in the section you're working on, you can go back and check answers in that section only. You can't move ahead to the next subtest or leave when the section is over.

When all is said and done, expect the PAP to take three to four hours. Your scores will be sent to your recruiter within a few days.

## CAT and PAP Head-to-Head

As you can see, the CAT and paper ASVAB have major differences, aside from how you record your answers. One of the most important is the difference in time and number of questions. You have slightly more time to complete the CAT than you do the PAP; you also have fewer questions to answer with the CAT, and you don't have to wait for time to run out on a section before moving on to the next. As a result, the average test-taker completes the CAT ASVAB in about 90 minutes.

You may have also noticed that the CAT contains 10 subtests, while the PAP has only 9. The Automotive and Shop Information section of the CAT ASVAB is broken up into two sections. However, the score is reported as a combined scaled total under the AS label.

Because of how the PAP is structured and administered, you can choose to leave questions blank on your answer sheet. You don't have that luxury on the CAT. What's more, you're not penalized for leaving answers blank on the PAP. You do incur a penalty for not completing a section of the CAT. The penalty is in direct proportion to the number of questions left unanswered. This means that not finishing one or two questions will have less of an effect on your score than not finishing 10 questions.

**Test Tip**

No matter which version of the test you take, always answer every question. Try to narrow your answer choices and make an educated guess—one based on logic instead of chance.

Scheduling is also a major difference. Test times for the CAT ASVAB are much more flexible than those for the PAP because a proctor is not needed to administer the test. With the PAP, a proctor must be present to handle all the paperwork and maintain a controlled environment. PAP ASVABs are also frequently given at MET sites, where personnel may be sparse. A whole group of recruits may be assembled before a test date is assigned, which makes availability unpredictable.

When considering which test you would prefer, consider the pros and cons of each. Be aware, though, that you may not have a choice in where you're sent to take the ASVAB. Still, knowing which fits better with your skill set and personality can help open a dialogue between you and your recruiter about your options for taking the test.

**Computer Adaptive Test**

*Pros:*

- The test takes less time and has fewer questions.

- The test adjusts to your skill level.

- You get your results immediately after you finish the test.

- You have more flexible scheduling options.

- You can leave when you're done.

- Headphones are available to help you tune out the world around you and concentrate on taking the test.

*Cons:*

- The test may not be available at every testing center.

- You have to answer every question you're given, in the order it's given. You can't jump around.

- You can't change an answer once you finalize it.

- If you don't answer a question, you'll receive a score penalty.

**Paper and Pencil Test**

*Pros:*

- You can jump around within a single section of the test and play to your strengths more easily.

- You can go back over questions in a section or change your answers if you have time at the end of a subtest.

- The paper test may be more comfortable for those more familiar with this type of format.

- You can skip questions and not receive a score penalty.

*Cons:*

- There's room for error in marking your answers on a form that has bubbles to fill in.

- You have to wait for days to get your results.

- Scheduling options are not as flexible.

- No facilities near you may offer the PAP ASVAB.

- You have to wait for the allotted time for each section to run out before you can move on to the next.

# Interpreting Your Score Report

The most important part of the ASVAB actually comes after the test. After all, it's the scores you're really interested in, not the test itself.

Seeing a score report for the first time can be intimidating. You'll see all sorts of numbers and abbreviations. Even with a recruiter's help, figuring out what it all means can be tough, so we break it down for you here.

You'll get three main types of scores on your score report:

◆ Standard scores

◆ Composite scores

◆ AFQT Percentile score

## Standard Scores

Standard scores (also known as line scores) are given for each of the AFQT and technical subtests. They can be anywhere between 0 and 100, based on the number of questions you answered correctly. On the ASVAB, you're not penalized for a wrong answer; you just don't get any points for it. Standard scores look like this:

| GS | AR | WK | PC | MK | EI | AS | MC | AO | VE |
|----|----|----|----|----|----|----|----|----|----|
| 75 | 69 | 58 | 77 | 52 | 46 | 82 | 62 | 55 | 69 |

Each of the two-letter designations represents a subtest (see the listing of subtests earlier in the chapter), with the exception of the VE, which indicates your total verbal score.

**Heads-Up**

According to the Official ASVAB Enlistment Testing Program, the VE score is a "weighted composite of WK and PC scores and is not computed by simply adding the PC and WK scores."

## Composite Scores

Next, you'll see your composite scores. These determine your occupational eligibility. They're divided into four branches of the military: Army, Air Force, Navy/Coast Guard, and Marines. The scores are broken down into subcategories specific to the types of jobs offered in each branch. See Appendix A for more detailed information on how these scores are used.

They are also calculated differently, depending on the area of service. For example, the Marines, Army, and Air Force use different scaled formulas to arrive at their composite scores. The Navy and Coast Guard simply add the line scores you got in the required subtests for each of their job categories. You'll see something like this in this section of your score report (explanations of the categories are discussed later in Appendix A):

| Army: | GT | CL | CO | EL | FA | GM | MM | OF | SC | ST |
|---|---|---|---|---|---|---|---|---|---|---|
| | 123 | 124 | 125 | 126 | 127 | 128 | 129 | 130 | 131 | 132 |

| Air Force: | M | A | G | E |
|---|---|---|---|---|
| | 80 | 81 | 82 | 83 |

| Navy/CG: | GT | EL | BEE | ENG | MEC | MEC2 | NUC | OPS | HM | ADM |
|---|---|---|---|---|---|---|---|---|---|---|
| | 120 | 216 | 217 | 121 | 122 | 123 | 218 | 219 | 124 | 125 |

| Marines: | MM | GT | EL | CL |
|---|---|---|---|---|
| | 122 | 123 | 124 | 125 |

## AFQT Percentile Score

The final score on your report is the AFQT Percentile. This is the most important score because it determines your overall eligibility. It's determined based on the following formula: 2(VE) + AR + MK. This means that your VE line score is multiplied by 2 and then added to your AR and MK scores. Then the score is converted into a percentile that shows how your performance places in relation to others who took the test during a sample period (in 1997, no less!). For example, if your score report places you in the 90th percentile, only about 10 percent of test-takers in a fixed sample scored higher on the overall AFQT than you did.

To see how all this looks when put together, you can see a good sample score report at en.wikipedia.org/wiki/ASVAB#Composite_scores.

# What If I Don't Make the Grade?

Don't freak out if your scores are not where you need them to be the first time you take the ASVAB. It happens all the time, especially if it's been a long time since you've actively engaged in the subject matter or taken a standardized test.

You can retake the ASVAB 30 days after your first test. If your scores are still not where you'd like them to be, you can take it again 30 days later. If by the third time you take the exam you're not making the grade, you have to wait six months before you can take the ASVAB again.

This is a lot of time to get ready to do your best. The fact that you're reading this test guide in the first place shows that you're already on the path toward success. Also work with your recruiter to prepare. They have resources at their disposal to help you study on your own or get tutoring.

However, keep in mind that even if you scored well on all of the necessary tests to qualify for your dream job, there is no guarantee that you will be placed in that position. You may be wait-listed until a spot becomes available in that training school.

# ASVAB Scores and Your Military Career

After you enter the service, your ASVAB scores will affect your career only if you want them to. They're not used for general promotions, awards, or other favorable actions. If you want to reclass into another career field or, in some branches of service, be promoted to a more advanced version of the same job, then your scores may come into play. In most cases, though, non-entry-level positions (in all branches) have "NA" for ASVAB score requirements.

## The Least You Need to Know

- ◆ The ASVAB is divided up into ten subject-specific subtests, depending on which version you take.

- ◆ The computer adaptive and paper and pencil versions of the ASVAB are not the same and each have their share of pros and cons.

- ◆ It's important to find out which version of the test you'll take and practice strategies specific for each.

- ◆ You will get a variety of different scores, but it's only your math and verbal scores that determine whether or not you can enlist.

- ◆ All of your other scores determine job eligibility.

- ◆ If you don't score high enough to meet the minimum requirements for your branch, you can retest in 30 days.

# Plan of Attack: General Test-Taking Strategies

## In This Chapter

- ◆ How to approach taking a standardized test
- ◆ Strategies for choosing the best answer
- ◆ Tips for taking the CAT
- ◆ Tips for taking the PAP

At some point, somebody must have told you that you can't study for a standardized test. If that were true, test-preparation companies wouldn't be making millions teaching high school and college students how to pass their college/grad school entrance exams—and there wouldn't be books like this one on the library shelf.

The truth is, test prep works! But knowing the material you're being tested on is only one piece of the puzzle. Taking the test correctly is as much a part of your score as finding the right answers, and this is what most test-preparation courses focus on. And believe it or not, your scores do go up when you understand how the questions are structured, what to look for, and what to expect at every turn.

This chapter reintroduces you to how to take a standardized test and gives you strategies that help you use the test structure to your advantage.

# Rethink Your General Approach

The phrase "standardized test" often evokes sweat and panic among potential test-takers. For some reason, people have been taught to fear these types of exams, a fact that just doesn't make sense to us.

In school you're given a variety of different types of tests with lots of types of questions. What were the ones you liked best? If you answered multiple choice, you're with just about everyone else. Now think about why you like this type of question instead of, say, fill-in-the-blank or definition. Maybe it's because you can more easily figure out the correct answer because you're given several possibilities.

So why should a whole test full of multiple-choice questions be so daunting? All the answers are already there! The ASVAB is a test based on general knowledge, which someone who has completed high school (or its equivalent) should be familiar with. So with a little brushing up on the subject matter, you should be in good shape for handling the questions.

But that's not the end of the story. It's your job to choose the answer that will get you the points, which can be more complicated than it sounds. Multiple-choice exams are essentially guessing games. How you would phrase the answer isn't necessarily how the answers you have to choose from are presented.

If you adjust the way you approach taking the exam in the first place, you'll be able to get to the correct answers more easily and quickly. These general tips are a good guideline to start with.

## Read Carefully

First, always start by making sure that you read the directions and your question very carefully before deciding what a likely answer is. One of the biggest mistakes test-takers make is to assume they know what they're supposed to do on every question. And since you're under tight time constraints, it's very tempting to do this.

However, this is a surefire way to end up missing crucial information in the question itself that leads to the correct answer. Always take your time and make sure you fully understand what the question is asking.

**Test Tip**

Pay close attention to questions that have the word *not* in them. They ask you to do the reverse of what you normally would on a question. For example, instead of searching for the one answer choice that the question content supports, you'd be looking at three answer choices that the question backs up and one that doesn't fit. That one is your answer.

## Speak for Yourself

After reading the question, your first instinct may be to go right to the answer choices. But doing this may sway your opinion on the correct answer, which you want to avoid.

Instead, take a minute to jot down your own answer to the question. You can use your test booklet if you're taking the PAP or scratch paper if you're taking the CAT. This will help ensure that your answer makes sense to you and that you remember it once you look at the answer choices. Believe it or not, it's very easy to forget your original answer when you start evaluating the answers on the test.

## Make the Most of Multiple Choice

Now that you have the answer you think is right, it's time to look at the answer choices you have to work with. Most standardized questions don't ask you to choose the right answer; they ask you to find the best answer out of the four choices you're given.

This is all part of the test design strategy. Those who write these exams want to see that you can not only come up with the correct answer, but also recognize it in varying forms.

Process of elimination is your best friend with the ASVAB—and for multiple-choice exams in general. If you think about it, it makes more sense to look for answers that are wrong simply because there are more of them. Some will be so obviously wrong that you can cross them off quickly. However, others will give you pause. This is where having an answer in mind will help you the most.

Use the answer you came up with on your own to help you narrow down possible "best" answers when there is more than one possibility. Consider each choice and eliminate anything that doesn't fit your original answer. If you can get your odds down from one correct answer out of four to something like one correct answer out of two, your chances of selecting the correct answer go way up.

**Heads-Up**

Always choose an answer choice that makes a logical connection to the information—don't just take an instinctual guess.

Always go through all the answer choices before making your selection—even if you're 100 percent sure that your answer is right. Often answer choices are arranged to make you think one is correct at first glance. Using process of elimination will slow you down a little, but you'll be able to think your answer through a little more before marking your answer. Remember that wrong answers are not penalized on the ASVAB; you simply don't get any points. The number of questions you complete is not as important as the number you get correct.

It's also important to be flexible when it comes to your answers, because the choices you're given may not match what you were thinking. When this happens, try thinking about the question and your answer from a different direction, or go over the way you came up with your answer to make sure you didn't miss something.

## Putting It Together

Now that you have a new general approach to your test questions, let's try out the steps on an Electronics Information question.

> Which of the following is an example of a conductor?

*Read carefully:* What is this question asking? Essentially, it's asking you to figure out what a conductor is and be able to identify one.

*Speak for yourself:* Since this is the Electronics Information section, it's pretty safe to assume that when they say "conductor," they're not talking about a railroad employee. The question has something to do with electricity.

If you know anything about being safe during a lightning storm, you know something about conductors. Conductors transmit electricity and help it move from place to place. Lightning rods are made of metal to attract the electricity away from other objects. It's not safe to swim when there's a thunderstorm. Why? Metal and water are both conductors. They attract electricity and help it travel from one place to another. While this is far from a definite answer, it's a good place to start. You have a general idea of what you're looking for.

*Make the most of multiple choice:* Now that we know what a conductor is, let's take a look at the answers and ask, "Is this made of metal or wood?" If the answer is "yes," then you have a possible answer:

(A) garbage bag

(B) plastic storage box

(C) TV antenna

(D) rubber boots

**Test Tip**

If one of the answers fits with what you're looking for, don't stop checking the rest of the choices. One of the other answers may be a better fit.

Garbage bags are usually made of plastic or, in some cases, paper, neither of which is metal or water. The same is true of the plastic storage box and the rubber boots. A TV antenna, on the other hand, is usually made of metal. This is the best choice out of the ones you're presented with.

Let's try this question again, this time with a little twist:

Which of the following is NOT an example of a conductor?

*Read carefully:* By adding one little word to the question, we've changed your whole purpose in finding an answer. Essentially, the question is asking you to look at a list. Three of the items on the list will be conductors. One will not. You have to choose which one doesn't belong.

*Speak for yourself:* We said before that metal and water are both conductors. Use this as your starting place again.

*Make the most of multiple choice:* Now that we know what a conductor is, let's take a look at the answers and ask, "Is this made of metal or water?" Instead of looking for a "yes," this time look for the one for which the answer is "no":

(A) wire fence

(B) pond

(C) TV antenna

(D) rubber boots

Wire fences are made of metal, so answer A is not a possibility. Ponds are full of water, one of our conductors, and as we said before, TV antennae are usually made of metal. This leaves rubber boots as the best answer.

# The Guessing Game

One question most test-takers have is whether they should guess on the test. For some exams, this is a viable strategy because of the way the test is scored. For others, no advantage is gained by guessing.

With the ASVAB, you're not penalized for wrong answers—you simply don't get credit for them. This makes guessing a good idea throughout the test. You have nothing to lose and everything to gain.

Does that mean you should just randomly select answers on questions you're having trouble with? No way. This is a wasted opportunity. If you don't know what the answer to the question is, you can still eliminate answer choices that you know are not correct and then make an educated guess based on what's left. When we say "educated guess," we mean that you choose an answer based on some kind of logic or using information that you have. It's always best to make an educated guess instead of a random one, because it increases your chances of getting the question correct.

Eliminating answers that you know are not right is a great way to start making your educated guess. It automatically increases your chances of getting the question right. Think about it: on any given question …

- You have a 25 percent chance of choosing the answer that will get you points.

- If you can eliminate one of those answers, you increase your chance to 33 percent.

- Eliminate one more, and you have a 50 percent chance of choosing the right answer.

Even if you have no idea what the question is asking, you tip the odds in your favor by eliminating at least one of the answers. Here are some specific things to look for in answer choices, usually telltale signs that those choices are not the best answer:

- **Extremes or absolutes.** ASVAB test writers like to keep things neutral. If an answer choice has words that indicate some type of condition that is too far to one side, this is not likely what you're looking for. Watch out for words like *never, always, furious, enraged,* or *overjoyed,* or anything else that hints at an extreme situation.

- **Contradictory information.** Many times, particularly in the verbal sections, answer choices directly contradict the information given in the question, information you're asked to read, and even another answer choice. If it goes against what's in the question or passage, that's a dead giveaway that the choice is most likely wrong. If it goes against another answer choice, this is a signal that at least one of these answers is wrong—and that one is right. Spend some time here to figure out which one is your best bet.

- **Similarities.** When you see two answers that are very close in meaning, it's easy to get stuck trying to figure out whether there's a trap there. Generally when this happens, neither answer is correct, and the only thing you gain is more time passed on the clock. If your instincts are telling you that there is some-

thing there, see what other answer choices you can eliminate; then come back to these and look for specific reasons you think one might be correct.

## Test-Specific Strategies

As we discussed in Chapter 2, the CAT and PAP versions of the ASVAB have some pretty big differences. This means that there are some specific strategies for each type, in addition to the general tips we give you throughout this book.

Here are some tips for taking the CAT:

- **Start off strong.** Since the first question of any CAT section is at a medium level of difficulty, if you get it right, the next question will be harder. Remember that, on the CAT ASVAB, harder questions mean more points. Because it's harder to build up to a high score when you start with a low one, try to get your first five questions correct. This will get your score up at the beginning of the test and make it easier to maintain throughout.

- **Watch where you click.** Choosing a different letter than the choice you mean to mark is a common mistake on the CAT. To avoid this, use your scrap paper to write down the answer choices and cross off the ones you want to eliminate. Circle the one that you believe is correct, then check and double-check that that's the answer you're selecting onscreen. Once you make your selection, you'll be prompted to confirm that this is your choice. Take this opportunity to check again. Better safe than sorry.

- **Know before you go.** Get as familiar with the CAT ASVAB as possible before test day. Visit the official ASVAB website for more detailed information: www.official-asvab.com/catasvab_app.htm. When you sit down for the test, spend as much time going through the tutorial as you need so that you're comfortable moving forward.

---

**Classified Intel**

The time spent on the tutorial is free time. Think of it like free air time when you check your wireless account information on your cell phone.

---

◆ **When in doubt, click through.** You have only so much time to complete each section, so don't spend too much on any one question. If you're not sure of the answer, choose an answer and move on. If time is running short, finish the section by randomly choosing answers. You may not get any right, but at least you'll avoid a score penalty by not finishing the section.

Here are some tips for taking the PAP:

◆ **Take notes.** Make use of the test booklet (which you can write on) or scratch paper you're given during the test. Writing down your thoughts, taking notes, and even making lists of A-B-C-D so that you can check off which answer choices you don't need can be invaluable ways to work through questions, especially if you learn best by both seeing and doing.

◆ **Watch where you mark.** Filling in the right bubble on the wrong line is common. Use your test booklet or scratch paper to block out all the answer bubbles for the questions following the one you're answering, to prevent this mistake. Also, always check and double-check that you are filling in the right bubble in the right space. If you make a mistake, make sure you completely erase your mark.

◆ **Skip carefully.** You can move back and forth among questions in a single section. Use this to your advantage by skipping questions that you're having difficulty answering and move on to something else. When you do this, make sure that you continue to mark your answer in the correct spaces on the answer sheet.

◆ **Keep an eye on the clock.** If you know how many questions you have in a section, you can pace yourself accordingly. Be aware of the time as you work on the test. As with the CAT, if it looks like you're running out of time, finish the section you're working on by filling in random answers. You won't be penalized for not completing the section, but you could pick up a few stray points by doing this.

---

**Test Tip**

One of the best study strategies that is most overlooked is taking timed practice tests. Make sure that, in addition to studying the subject matter for each section, you practice completing those sections in the time frame you'll face when taking the real thing.

---

## The Least You Need to Know

◆ Rethinking your general approach to taking a standardized test can help you score better.

◆ You can use the multiple-choice format of the test to your advantage by eliminating incorrect answers.

◆ When in doubt, taking an educated guess on a question you're not sure about can increase the chances of you getting a correct answer.

◆ You can use different strategies to approach the CAT and PAP versions of the ASVAB, so know which one you're taking and study accordingly.

# Chapter 4

# Prepare, Prepare, Prepare

## In This Chapter

◆ General ASVAB study strategies

◆ How to make the most of studying

◆ What to do before the test

◆ Where to turn for help

Let's face it, studying for what amounts to 10 tests that you have to take in one sitting is a daunting task. You've got to brush up on your algebra and learn a whole bunch of new vocabulary words. Since there are essentially three science sections on the ASVAB, you've got to break out your old textbooks and bone up on biology, chemistry, and physics. On top of all that, you need to get your knowledge of tools, hardware, and automotive systems up to snuff, in addition to having to figure out how to visually put puzzles together!

If you feel like there's just too much to learn and not enough time before you have to take the ASVAB, you're going to psych yourself out before you get anywhere near the test. The best way to get over the anxiety of preparing for what might seem like an insurmountable task is to break it down into smaller, more manageable pieces.

This chapter walks you through some general preparation strategies that will help make your studying more effective, not to mention take some of the pressure off.

## Practice Tests and Planning Strategies

It's time to put everything that you've learned about the ASVAB into perspective. Although studying the subject areas you'll find on the test and learning about new strategies for taking this type of exam are extremely helpful tools, practicing is the best way to prepare.

But blindly taking practice test after practice test just to get experience doesn't make much sense. It also takes a lot of time that you could be using more wisely. Your best bet is to think strategically about what you need to accomplish when you take the actual ASVAB and then plan your study approach accordingly.

## Using Scores as a Guide

Because the ASVAB gives you scores for general entrance eligibility and job qualification, doing well on every section of the test is not absolutely necessary. One way to strategically prepare for the ASVAB is to determine your specific goals and concentrate on getting the scores you need to make them happen.

### Heads-Up

Remember, even if you score well on all the necessary tests to qualify for your dream job, there's no guarantee that you will get the job. Placement depends on the availability of spots in the designated training school and the needs of that branch of the military.

- Talk with your recruiter about your interests and aspirations to determine career paths that may interest you.

- Find out what technical scores you need to qualify for those jobs.

- Assess your skill and comfort level with the subject matter of each subtest required for that job. The best way to do this is to take practice tests (like those in this book) at home or at your recruiter's office.

- When you know what you need the most help with, concentrate most of your study efforts on those subjects.

## Your Recruiter, Your Coach

Recruiters are a great resource for what you can realistically expect to encounter as you move forward through recruitment and the ASVAB, in particular. But believe it or not, many people who are preparing for the ASVAB overlook their recruiter as a tool to help them get where they need to be.

At the end of the day, your recruiter is there to help you get through the ASVAB. Your recruiter wants you to succeed, if only to increase his or her enlistment numbers. In many ways, recruiters are like salespeople, and enlistment is a numbers game—but instead of meeting sales goals, they're trying to meet enlistment goals.

That's not to say that they don't genuinely care about your future. They do. People choose recruiting as their profession because they like working with people and want to help them succeed. For all these reasons, many recruiters will do anything they can to help you prepare and get the scores you need. This can include the following help:

- Recommend a personal tutor, and in some cases, pay for the tutoring via the branch's recruiting budget

- In-office timed practice testing

- Guidance on what to concentrate on, based on your goals

If you're feeling anxious about taking the test, have questions, or just need a quiet place to study, your recruiter should be your first point-of-contact. Recruiters don't mind putting in extra time or effort, so don't feel bad about asking for help.

# Maximize Your ASVAB Workouts

Chances are, if you're reading this book, you're serious about preparing for the ASVAB. Nothing will stop you from getting the scores you want, and you will dedicate yourself to hours upon hours of studying for however many weeks you have between now and the date of your test.

Okay, so that's a little bit extreme, but that's how many people feel when they get ready to study for any type of test in earnest. The point is that, over the coming weeks, you plan to invest quite a bit of time and effort into preparing for this exam—in addition to school, work, family, friends, sports, or whatever else you have going on in your life.

That's why it's important that you get the most out of your study time. Let's look at some often overlooked, yet highly effective, ways to make sure your efforts will make the most impact on test day.

## Timing Is Everything

Sure, study and practice will help you increase your ASVAB score. However, all the correct answers in the world won't mean much if you don't have the time to record the answers.

One Marine Corps recruiter in New Jersey said that one of the biggest mistakes potential recruits make when preparing for the ASVAB is not timing themselves on practice tests. If you remember our discussion in Chapter 2 about how the test is broken down, you'll note that, for many of the ASVAB subtests, you have many more questions than you have minutes to answer.

A certain amount of anxiety accompanies any timed test, let alone one in which you have to answer 20 questions about the science of electrical components in 9 minutes. If you're a slow reader or have marked test-taking anxiety issues, these can become even more pronounced when taking the ASVAB. The best remedy for this is to practice under the same time constraints you'll face on test day. The more you practice at home, the better idea you'll have about what pace to set, how much time to spend on your questions, and how to keep yourself on target with the clock.

### Heads-Up

Unlike many other standardized exams, the ASVAB does not have provisions for test-takers with learning disabilities or those who may need extra time or a special environment to complete the test.

Timing yourself also goes a long way toward making you more comfortable with working against the clock. The calmer you are when you take the test, the better the experience will go. If you think you might have trouble with this on your own, talk to your recruiter to see if you can come into the office and be timed there.

## Study Strategically

It doesn't matter whether you're studying for every section of the ASVAB or only one or two subtests—break down the material you're studying into smaller parts. This will keep you from feeling too overwhelmed with information in one sitting. Keeping your mind concentrated in one area will also increase your chances of retention.

Additionally, always make sure no matter what you're studying, you work on a handful of practice questions. Reading and memorizing is great, but you'll benefit from it more if you can apply it right away. For example, if you're studying roots to prepare for the Word Knowledge subtest, answer a few practice questions in the book or online, to apply what you learned to actual questions.

### Test Tip

Completing practice questions is a good way to study. You'll learn new information from the ones you got wrong. And because you missed the right answer the first time, you're more likely not to miss it if you see a similar question later.

## Slow and Steady Is the Way

When you sit down to take the ASVAB for real, you'll want to be as comfortable with it as possible. So it's not very realistic to expect to be ready for the test in a week, or even two. To effectively study for the ASVAB, you need time.

But nowadays, time is hard to come by, especially when you're trying to learn the structure of a new test, refresh yourself on the subjects and topics you'll be tested on, and test your knowledge by answering practice questions.

Our advice is to schedule a little time every day over a few weeks to work on your ASVAB skills, so it doesn't seem like such a huge task. An hour a day is all you need. This will spread out the work and keep your stress level down. Some tips for doing this include the following:

- Give yourself enough time to realistically prepare for the test. There's no rush to enlist. Take the time you need to study now so you can do your best the first time around.

- Look at your schedule for the next six to eight weeks and pencil in some study time every day. Then stick to it.

- Choose a place where you're comfortable and where you'll be undisturbed, preferably someplace without a phone or computer.

- Leave the rest of your hectic life behind. Your study time is yours. Don't let any other worries or concerns about other aspects of your life take precedence.

- Have everything you need close at hand. Having to go from one room to another wastes a lot of time.

- Don't beat yourself up for missing a study session or two. Life can be unpredictable. Try to adjust your routine if you need to, or sneak in some extra study time later.

### Heads-Up

You're not allowed to use a calculator on the ASVAB, so don't get into the habit of relying on it when you're studying. Breaking out the scrap paper and getting back to basics will better prepare you for the actual test.

## Relax, It's Only a Test

After weeks of preparing and thinking about the worlds of possibilities riding on your results, your blood pressure may be sky-high the week you're scheduled to take the test. Putting everything in perspective now is more important than ever.

Taking the ASVAB is not rocket science, nor is it your one-and-only shot at a prosperous future. It's a test, plain and simple. It's made of paper and ink (or, in the case of the CAT ASVAB, software coding). Spill your water on it, and it goes back to being so much man-made material that just sits on a desk.

Now that you've got your head in the game, here are some other things you can do the week leading up to the test, to make sure you're in the best shape possible for taking the ASVAB—and they have nothing to do with studying.

- **Take some time off.** A day or so before the test, ease back on the preparation. Better yet, stop altogether. This will give your brain a chance to rest so that it's in top shape on test day. Instead, schedule in some leisure time with friends, family, or your favorite Xbox game.

- **Get some sleep.** Try to get as much sleep as you can the week of the test. One night's rest is not enough if you want to be as rested and relaxed as possible for the test.

- **Eat something.** Have a little something packed with protein the morning of the test. This will help keep your blood sugar up and hunger at bay. The last thing you want is a grumbling stomach while you're trying to concentrate. You also don't want to be overly full, so keep it light. Protein bars are a good idea.

- **Pack what you need the night before.** Make sure you have everything you need for the exam with you and ready to go. A photo ID is a must. If you have to borrow or sharpen pencils in the middle of the test, you'll lose precious time. Bring at least five sharp #2 pencils for the PAP. Find out from your recruiter other specifics you'll need and what you can't bring to the site.

- **Arrive early.** Arrive at least 15 minutes before the test begins, to take care of any administrative business and ensure you get the seat you want. Traffic and unforeseen events are no excuses for being late to the test, so allow yourself ample time.

- **Come up with a plan B.** If you're not feeling well, have a fever, or have recently gone through a stressful or emotional event (good

or bad), your test scores may not accurately reflect your abilities. Don't be afraid to reschedule the test. Talk to your recruiter about options if your personal circumstances are not optimal on test day or the days leading up to it.

## The Least You Need to Know

- You can maximize your study time by developing a strategy based on your goals.

- Recruiters are excellent resources if you're looking for help preparing for the ASVAB.

- There are a lot of sections to the ASVAB, so concentrate on preparing for only one section at a time and doing a little studying every day.

- Getting your answers down in time is crucial on test day, so make sure when you take your practice tests you time yourself.

- Don't spend the week before the test cramming; you'll want to be as relaxed as possible on test day.

# Part 2

# Word Up! All About Communication Skills

Words, words, and more words. No matter where you go, you're surrounded by them. And for good reason! We live in the age of information, and effective communication makes the world go round. When you enter the military, however, communication takes on a whole new significance. Your ability to accurately transmit and decode messages in various ways—written and verbally— is crucial when lives are on the line. That's why the ASVAB devotes two whole sections of the Armed Forces Qualifying Test (AFQT) to communication skills.

In this part, you'll learn about the Word Knowledge and Paragraph Comprehension subtests and get some good practice for the types of questions you'll likely face on test day. Plus, you'll get lots of tips for improving your vocabulary, breaking down questions, and translating those pesky paragraphs into real English.

# Chapter 5

# Word Knowledge

## In This Chapter

◆ Why you're tested on this

◆ Types of questions you'll see

◆ Essential strategies

◆ Vocabulary-building tips

Just about every teacher you've had in school probably stressed the importance of building your vocabulary skills. Back then, you needed it to pass your tests and write papers that made you sound like the greatest living expert on whatever your topic was. Today you need it to pass the Word Knowledge (WK) section of the ASVAB.

This section of the ASVAB is really nothing more than a big vocabulary test, only better. If you remember back to high school, your vocab tests were probably nothing more than a list of words you had to define. On the ASVAB, you get four answers to choose from and context clues to help you make the right choice.

This chapter gives you the tools you need to ace this subtest. You'll see what types of questions the Word Knowledge subtest has, essential strategies for approaching them, and ways to build up your vocabulary skills so that you can figure out the correct answer, even when you don't know what the words mean.

## Why Do I Have to Take This?

"A picture is worth a thousand words." The truth of this adage has certainly been proven throughout history. But when you're giving orders for executing a mission or putting together a weapon, expressing what you want and need in words is often more effective—not to mention safer.

That's why the ASVAB tests you on your knowledge of vocabulary. This subtest is a way for the military to gauge your communication abilities. When a failure to accurately communicate can result in lives lost, ensuring that new recruits have a minimum-level ability in this area is essential.

New recruits are often shocked at the amount of writing they have to do throughout training and eventually for the job they're placed in. To make it through whatever school you're placed in, perform an administrative task, and even command entire units, you'll be writing in some form pretty much on a daily basis. Your success depends on being able to clearly and efficiently communicate.

# What to Expect

The ASVAB tests your understanding of the words, how they're used in context, and their general meaning. You'll encounter two types of questions on the Word Knowledge section of the ASVAB— and they both test you on synonyms. This simply means that the correct answer choice means pretty much the same thing as the underlined word in the question.

On the CAT version of the test, you'll have 8 minutes to answer 16 questions, giving you about 30 seconds per question. On the PAP, you'll have to answer 35 questions in 11 minutes. That's less than 20 seconds per question! So both speed and preparation are essential for getting the best score you can on this section.

When faced with a Word Knowledge question, following the multiple-choice general strategies outlined in Chapter 3 should be your first line of defense. But for this to work, you have to know or figure out what all the words in the question mean. We walk you through some ways to do this for both types of questions you'll see on the test.

## Simple Definition

The first type of question we look at is the most straightforward: simple definition. You're given a word, and your job is to choose the answer choice that is closest to the meaning of that word:

> Joyous most nearly means
> > (A) happy.
> > (B) drab.
> > (C) original.
> > (D) different.

Seems simple enough, right? Sure, if you know what everything means. If you don't, you still have lots of ways to narrow your answer choices and get some clue to a word's meaning.

### Get to the Root of the Problem

Just about every word in the English language is made up of smaller parts. If you've ever wondered why the word *contradict* is used to describe saying something that goes against something else, just look at the word roots:

♦ The prefix *contra* means "against" or "opposite."

♦ The root *dict* means "speak."

Now put these meanings together, and you can see a clear definition: to speak against or oppose. Many of the words commonly used on standardized tests like the ASVAB use words that have Greek and Latin word roots, prefixes, and suffixes. Don't forget that you're looking for the answer that most nearly matches the word you're given, not the definition that is exactly the same. That's why roots can be a powerful tool for eliminating answer choices.

You can make this work for you by memorizing a handful of these roots (more on this in "Learn Your

Roots," later in this chapter). Then when you see them in a word, you can get a good idea of what the word generally means. Based on this intel, you can then eliminate answer choices that do not match up with this idea.

**Test Tip**

When you have a larger, more complex word, look for smaller words within. They can give you a hint at the definition.

Try it with the following example:

Enamored most nearly means
(A) angry.
(B) melodious.
(C) infatuated.
(D) angelic.

Look at the root word in the middle, *amor*. Pretty much everyone knows that *amor* means "love," thanks to American pop culture. So the correct answer choice will have something to do with love.

Now look at your answer choices. *Angry* just isn't going to do it. If you don't know what *melodius* means, see if you can pick out a familiar word within the main roots. Look closely, and you'll pick out "melody," which doesn't mean love. Try the same strategy with *angelic*, and you have "angel." Although angels often are associated with love, angels are defined as heavenly beings. Love is not used to define what an angel is. That means this answer choice is likely wrong.

Even if you didn't know that *infatuated* means "possessed of an unreasoning passion or love," you've eliminated all of the other answer choices as being unsuitable for "most nearly" meaning the same as the word in the question.

## What's the Connotation?

If you're not sure what the definition of a word is, ask yourself if it has a positive or negative *connotation*.

## def•i•ni•tion

**Connotation** is the implied meaning or the feeling associated with a word. You may choose to say "car accident" instead of "wreck" or "crash" because "accident" doesn't imply as much violence as the other words. Don't confuse connotation with its opposite, denotation, which is the literal or dictionary definition.

A correct answer choice will have the same connotation as the word in the question, so depending on what word you're struggling with, you can use this technique to help you eliminate answer choices:

1. If you know that the word in the question is positive, you can eliminate any negative answer choices right away.

2. If you're not sure what one of the answer choices means, see if you can determine whether it is positive or negative. Then compare it to the question word's connotation.

3. If the word you're given in the question is neither positive nor negative, the correct answer must also be neutral. Eliminate any obviously positive or negative answer choices.

To determine the connotation of a word, think about how you've heard it used before and in what context. Say you don't know what the word *malicious* means, but there it is in a practice question. Ask yourself where you've heard that word before and in what situations. What can you connect to it?

Chances are the context in which you've heard this word used have been negative, since *malicious* describes something as being intentionally harmful.

This means you can be pretty confident that its connotation is negative, too.

Prefixes and suffixes can also give you a good idea of whether the word you're looking at is positive or negative. Again, memorizing word roots will be a big help here. Here are some to get you started:

◆ Prefixes that connote positive meanings: *am/ ami/amor, ben/bene, gen, grat, pac*

◆ Prefixes that connote negative meanings: *ant/ anti, bel, dys, mal, mis, mor/mort, neg, pug*

## Determine Part of Speech

The correct answer choice will be the same part of speech as the word in the question. If you know the word you're given is a noun, you can eliminate any answer choice that is not a noun.

In case you've forgotten your parts of speech, here's a quick review:

◆ Noun: Word that names a person, place, thing, or idea. "Cat," "home," and "mother" are all nouns.

◆ Verb: Word that signifies action. "Run," "speak," and "smile" are all verbs.

◆ Adjective: Word that describes or modifies a noun. "Willing," "beautiful," and "old" are all adjectives.

◆ Adverb: Word that describes or modifies a verb, adjective, or another adverb; often ending in *ly*. "Happily," "nearly," and "expertly" are all adverbs.

Looking at parts of speech can work both for and against you. It can work against you because some words have multiple definitions and have multiple parts of speech; it can work for you because looking at the part of speech of other words in the question

can help you determine which definition of the word is being used in this instance. Look at the following example:

> Cow most nearly means
>
> (A) energize.
> (B) levitate.
> (C) aggravate.
> (D) intimidate.

Your first instinct is likely to define *cow* as a noun, an adult female bovine, whale, elephant, manatee, or other animal. But if you look at the answer choices, you'll see that they're all verbs: to energize, to levitate, to aggravate, to intimidate. This means that the definition of *cow* you need to concentrate on is the verb form, which means "to frighten or threaten."

## Words in Context

The second type of question you'll see on the Word Knowledge subtest of the ASVAB gives you sentences with a single underlined word. Your job is to choose the answer choice that gives the meaning of how the word is used in the sentence:

> Thanks to her <u>acute</u> sense of hearing, the woman picked up the kitten's faint cries for help from the sewer below.
>
> (A) dirty
> (B) sharp
> (C) transparent
> (D) luxurious

The sentence isn't there just to make the test question longer. It actually gives you more information that will help lead you to the correct answer. The strategies we discussed earlier for simple definition questions can still be used with these. However, two additional techniques work specifically for these types of questions.

## Look for Clues

The sentences in these questions are like gifts from the ASVAB fairy, and you either use them or lose them. Look for context clues within the sentence that hint at the meaning of the word. Some are very obvious, like specific words that modify or apply to the underlined word. Others require a little logic on your part to draw conclusions about what's going on in the sentence and how it relates to the underlined word.

In the example, the word you need to define is *acute*. You know that the word is being used to describe hearing (a noun), which means it's an adjective. What else does the sentence tell you? Acute hearing helped the woman hear faint cries.

What do you know about faint cries? They're quiet and hard to hear. You would need to have sensitive hearing to pick them up. So if acute hearing enabled the woman to hear something that wasn't loud, you can infer that the meaning of the word has something to do with being able to be very precise or sensitive.

Now look at the answer choices:

(A) dirty
(B) sharp
(C) transparent
(D) luxurious

You know that *dirty* has nothing to do with being precise or sensitive. *Sharp* is a possibility, since it has multiple definitions, one of which is sensitive. But you still need to eliminate the other answer choices to be sure. *Transparent* means something is see-through, and *luxurious* is the adjective form of "luxury." Neither of these have meanings close to what you're looking for, which makes B your best answer.

### Heads-Up

Remember that many words you'll find on the ASVAB have multiple definitions. Read the sentence carefully, to see which definition applies to the word and how it works in that specific sentence.

## Swap It Out

The second approach is to simply replace the underlined word with the answer choices. This works well when you know the definitions of the answer choices but are not sure about what the underlined word means. If the answer choice makes sense in the sentence without changing the meaning, chances are, that answer is a keeper.

Read the following example:

Mark was such an <u>affable</u> guy, it was no wonder that his many friends voted him the most popular boy in his class.
(A) lackluster
(B) unusual
(C) likable
(D) original

Now replace *affable* with the answer choices, and see what works best:

(A) Mark was such a <u>lackluster</u> guy, it was no wonder that his many friends voted him the most popular boy in his class.
(B) Mark was such an <u>unusual</u> guy, it was no wonder that his many friends voted him the most popular boy in his class.
(C) Mark was such a <u>likable</u> guy, it was no wonder that his many friends voted him the most popular boy in his class.

(D) Mark was such an <u>original</u> guy, it was no wonder that his many friends voted him the most popular boy in his class.

If you don't know what *lackluster* means, you can use one of our previous strategies to get a clue to its meaning: look for smaller words in this complex one that are familiar. The word *luster,* when it stands alone, means "shiny." *Lack* suggests that something is missing—in this case, shine, since that's part of the word. A good guess would be that *lackluster* means "dull" (which it does).

Now that you're familiar with all of the words, what fits? Would a dull or unusual guy have lots of friends and be voted Mr. Popularity? Probably not. How about an original guy? Original is a neutral word, suggesting neither positive nor negative connotations. The sentence, however, leans more to the positive than anything else, so "original" is likely not your answer. Would a likable guy have lots of friends and be popular? Of the answers you're given, this makes the most sense.

> **Heads-Up**
>
> You're not limited to using only one strategy at a time when attacking Word Knowledge questions. Combining those that make the most sense will get you to the correct answer fastest.

# Build Your Vocab

Probably the best thing that you can do to raise your score on the Word Knowledge section of the ASVAB is to simply increase your vocabulary. The more words you know or are familiar with going into the test, the faster and more efficient you'll be on this subtest.

The key to bulking up your vocab is to do it slowly and steadily. A little work on this each day can pay off big-time in terms of words you know walking into the exam. The following are easy and even entertaining ways to get started.

## Word-of-the-Day

You can subscribe to a word-of-the-day website that will e-mail you a new vocabulary word and definition every day. Just click open your message and use that word sometime during the day, for maximum retention. You can also have words-of-the-day sent to your phone via text message. A quick online search nets several services that you can subscribe to. We like Merriam-Webster's Word of the Day (see Appendix C).

## Hit the Books

Simply reading will help you increase your vocab. It doesn't matter much what you read, as just about anything you pick up will likely introduce at least one new word to you. Yes, that romance novel, mystery, issue of *Sports Illustrated*, or even daily newspaper can help you pick up new words. The increased interaction with language will seep into your mindset and familiarize you with more words than you could ever imagine—and it happens automatically.

You can also head to your local library in search of vocabulary guides. Use one of these books to make a list of words you want to learn, and work on learning them a few at a time over a couple weeks.

## Memorize in Clusters

So many of the words you'll likely encounter on the ASVAB have similar meanings. For example, *florid, embellish, bombastic, ornate, overblown, flowery,* and *elaborate* all have similar meanings: excessively decorated, spoken, or written. Use a good thesaurus and make a list of synonyms for any vocabulary word on your list. This is a great way to get the most out of your study time.

## Learn Your Roots

We talked earlier about being able to recognize prefixes, suffixes, and word roots. This is really an invaluable tool for improving your vocabulary because it gives you the tools for understanding how words are built—which, in turn, clues you into their meaning. The following table compares some common roots, prefixes, and suffixes.

### Common Roots, Prefixes, and Suffixes

| Root | Meaning | Example |
| --- | --- | --- |
| acer/acri | sour, sharp, bitter | acid |
| bene | good | benefit |
| beli/bel/pug | fight, war | pugnacious |
| circ | around | circuit |
| chron | time | chronological |
| dic/dict/dit | speak, talk | dictate |
| loqu/locut/log | speak, talk | dialogue |
| luc/lum/lun/lus | light | illuminate |
| mal | bad | malaise |
| phot/photo | light | photograph |
| omni | all, ever | omnipresent |
| path | feel | sympathy |
| pop | people | population |
| simil/simul | same | simultaneous |
| spec/spic | see | conspicuous |
| sym/syn | together | synchronize |
| terr/terra | earth | terrain |
| ver | true | verify |

| Root | Meaning | Example |
| --- | --- | --- |
| vid/vis | see | visual |
| viv/vita/vivi | life | vitality |

| Prefix | Meaning | Example |
| --- | --- | --- |
| a/ab/an | away from, without | abdicate |
| ante | before | antechamber |
| anti/de | against, opposite | antihero |
| com/con | with, fully, together | congregation |
| contra/counter | against, opposite | counteract |
| inter | between | interoffice |
| intra | within | intramural |
| post | after | posthumous |
| super/supra | above or over | supersede |

| Suffix | Meaning | Example |
| --- | --- | --- |
| able | worth or ability, suggests adjective | capable |
| acy/cy | state of, suggests noun | accuracy |
| ant/ent | noun that does something | defendant |
| ary | relating to, suggests adjective | reactionary |
| ed | past, suggests verb | walked |
| ism | belief, suggests noun | feudalism |
| ist | person, suggests noun | nudist |
| ful | having/giving, suggests noun/adjective | bountiful |
| ation/ness | action or condition, suggests noun | intimidation |

*continues*

## Common Roots, Prefixes, and Suffixes (continued)

| Prefix | Meaning | Example |
|--------|---------|---------|
| fy/ify | to cause or form, suggests verb/ adjective | justify |
| ly | in the manner of, suggests adverb | normally |
| ise/ize | cut off, suggests verb | excise |

Let's get in some practice figuring out the meanings of words based on looking at their roots. For each of the following, list as many roots as you can in the first column. Then write what you think the word means in the second column. Look them up in the dictionary to check.

| Word | Roots | Meaning |
|------|-------|---------|
| Interoffice | _____ | _____ |
| Acerbic | _____ | _____ |
| Luminous | _____ | _____ |
| Circumvent | _____ | _____ |
| Omnipotent | _____ | _____ |
| Antebellum | _____ | _____ |
| Pugilistic | _____ | _____ |
| Malodorous | _____ | _____ |
| Anachronistic | _____ | _____ |
| Sympathetic | _____ | _____ |

 **Test Tip**

Prefixsuffix.com (www.prefixsuffix.com) has an extensive list of word roots that you can access for free.

## Make Associations

One of the easiest and most lasting ways to learn new words is to associate their meanings with something that makes sense to you. You can do this in a few ways. The first is to come up with a little rhyme or word association that reminds you of the meaning. These are called mnemonic devices, and as long as it makes sense to you, they can consist of just about anything. Here are a few to get you started:

- Pretentious: Pretends to be all that
- Nullify: Make nada or nothing
- Miser: Scrooge was a miserable miser
- Levity: Levitates or lifts your mood
- Concrete: Hard evidence
- Intrepid: Bold, gutsy, like the famous aircraft carrier

You can also make associations with words based on where you heard them (a conversation, a book, a movie, a song, and so on), what you were doing when you heard it, the context of what was going on, how you were feeling, and more. A few that work for us include these:

- *Curious:* Mr. Olivander, the wandmaker in *Harry Potter and the Sorcerer's Stone*, used *curious* when Harry's wand ended up having the same core as his arch enemy's.
- *Indubitably:* Burt, in *Mary Poppins*, would say "Indubitably" when agreeing with her.
- *Vapid:* In the movie *10 Things I Hate About You*, a character used *vapid* to describe the boring and unoriginal student population.

Now it's your turn. Look up and write out the definitions of the following words. Then think of an association for each that means something to you.

**Uproar**

Definition: _____

Association: _____

**Trepidation**

Definition: _____

Association: _____

**Slovenly**

Definition: _____

Association: _____

**Acrid**

Definition: _____

Association: _____

**Jettison**

Definition: _____

Association: _____

**Vacuous**

Definition: _____

Association: _____

**Misanthrope**

Definition: _____

Association: _____

**Torpid**

Definition: _____

Association: _____

**Enigmatic**

Definition: _____

Association: _____

With a little time and practice, you will be in excellent shape to take the ASVAB's Word Knowledge subtest, no matter how much you may have shivered at the thought of studying English in school. And all your hard work will pay off—not only on the test, but for the rest of your life as well. A great vocabulary is an asset that can give you an advantage when applying for future jobs and help you make a good impression on new people you meet.

# Chapter 6

# Paragraph Comprehension

## In This Chapter

◆ Why you're tested on this

◆ How Paragraph Comprehension questions work

◆ Types of questions you'll see

◆ Techniques for choosing the best answer

You're most likely not going to have to take another test in the military that asks you to read a passage and then answer questions about what you read. You will, however, apply the same skills you would to pass such a test on a daily basis.

The military needs to know the strength of your communication and analytical skills before they will allow you to enlist. Believe it or not, that's where Paragraph Comprehension (PC) comes in. Answering questions based on complex passages about generalized topics actually shows how you think and understand the world around you.

This chapter introduces you to what you can expect to see on this section of the test, how to approach each type of question, and how to get through this subtest as painlessly as possible. If English has never been a strong subject for you, this chapter will definitely help you.

## Why Do I Have to Take This?

The ability to read and understand written materials is something that every branch of the military takes very seriously. Unlike in most civilian jobs, mistakes in communication can end up costing people their lives in the military.

So how does reading boring little paragraphs and answering questions tell anyone how you communicate? It's all about analysis. The ASVAB's Paragraph Comprehension subtest gauges your ability to effectively take in information, process it, and be able to make decisions based on what you've read. When you get the correct answer, you show that you can do this effectively.

You need to score well on this section for two reasons:

◆ It's part of the AFQT, and in calculating your percentile scores, your verbal raw score is counted *twice*. If you don't make the grade here, you won't be eligible to go further through the enlistment process.

◆ Many jobs require a good PC score to qualify for training. Make sure you know what line scores you need for the jobs you're interested in, so you can study accordingly.

# What to Expect

For this section, taking the CAT version of the ASVAB gives you an advantage, especially if you're a slow reader. The PC subtest on the CAT is 11 questions in 22 minutes. On the other hand, you have only 13 minutes to answer 15 questions on the PAP version. That's less than a minute per question!

You can expect to see a short passage (most are just one paragraph, but they can go up to three), with one or more questions that follow. Each question refers to that particular passage.

The good news is that you most likely won't have to read 11–15 paragraphs to complete this section in time. It just doesn't make sense when you've got less than a minute per question. Instead, some simple tweaks to your general approach will save you time and brainpower:

1. **Read the question first.** You'll find several different types of questions, which we detail later in the chapter. If you know what type of question you're dealing with, you'll know what to look for in the passage. For example, if you get a question that asks you what a word means in a particular sentence, you have to read only enough to figure out how it's used in that one instance. Also make sure you read through the answer choices and understand what they mean.

2. **Attack the passage.** Depending on what type of question you have, deploy the appropriate technique for best finding the information in the passage that will get you the answer you need. Analyze the information and answer the question in your own words.

3. **Eliminate what doesn't fit.** Look for answers that are backed up directly with information from the passage. Get rid of answer choices that are not supported by a specific phrase or sentence in the passage.

### Test Tip

Check reality at the door when you approach a PC question. The only information that matters is what's in the passage. Make your inferences based on your own logic and specific statements from the passage—not what you know to be true in real life.

Now let's take a look at the six main types of questions you'll see on the PC subtest.

## Main Idea

Often you'll be asked to identify the overall point of a passage. Most passages have a predictable format: some kind of topic sentence states or implies the point of the passage, and the rest of the sentences give details or support to that point. Your job is to find that sentence. To make this easier, look for sentences that explain what the passage is about instead of how or why something is what it is. These can appear anywhere in the passage. They often are the first or last sentence, but they can also come in toward the middle.

Plan of attack:

1. Read the passage carefully, making notes when you can.

2. Ask yourself what the passage is about.

3. Eliminate answer choices that don't match your idea.

### Heads-Up

Main idea questions may not come right out and ask you to identify the point. When you see questions that ask you to choose the best title or what the passage is primarily about, think main idea.

## Purpose

This is a variation on the main idea question. You're not looking for what the passage is about; you're looking for what the speaker hopes to accomplish. Some purposes of a passage can include these:

♦ Inform the reader about something

♦ Show or explain a process

♦ Educate or instruct

♦ Persuade

♦ State an opinion or position

♦ Reason something out

♦ Tell a story

Plan of attack:

1. Figure out what the main idea of the passage is.

2. Ask yourself why the speaker would try to communicate this message. What is he or she hoping to accomplish?

3. Eliminate answer choices that don't match your idea.

## Tone

As we discussed in Chapter 5, words can have more to their meaning than what's written in the dictionary. They can also evoke a feeling in the person communicating with them and the person receiving the message.

On the ASVAB, you'll be asked to figure out what feelings the *speaker* in a passage is trying to communicate through words. This is called tone. When you have a tone question, pay close attention to the language in the passage and the impression you get based on what's said.

## def•i•ni•tion

When we say **speaker**, we're talking about the narrator of a passage, not the author. Narrators give accounts of events and stories, and may or may not be involved in what's being told. Every piece of writing has a speaker. When you read the following example, ask yourself who the speaker is. If you think it's a runner, you're right!

Read the following passage:

The wind gently blows the hair away from my face. My muscles burn with the strain of the motion as my arms and legs work in synchronization with each other. Blood pumps through my veins in time with my steps. The faster I go, the more exhilarated I feel. I love to run.

What kind of vibe do you get from reading this paragraph? Affectionate, energized, and savoring are all good answers. The loving and elaborate description of the everyday action of running tells us that this person doesn't think of it as ordinary, but rather as something reverent.

Plan of attack:

1. Look at the language being used, punctuation, and context clues in the passage.

2. Determine whether the speaker in the passage is excited, somber, apprehensive, happy, and so on.

3. Eliminate answer choices that don't match.

Try it here:

The tone of this passage can best be described as
(A) reminiscent.
(B) argumentative.
(C) mysterious.
(D) relishing.

*Reminiscent* means that you're remembering something fondly, which doesn't really apply here, since the speaker is using present tense. *Argumentative* and *mysterious* just don't make sense for this passage. This leaves *relishing*, which means "to take pleasure in." Answer D fits best.

As with main idea questions, you'll have to read the whole passage for tone questions. Vocabulary also plays a key role in this type of question, since many of the answer choices may be more sophisticated than what you'd use every day. Be sure to check out our vocab-building tips in Chapter 5.

## Specific Details

Like the name suggests, this type of question asks you to find a specific piece of information in the passage. The beauty of this type of question is that the answers are right in the passage, and often the question will use language similar to what's written in the answer. Knowing this will save you time if you use the general approach outlined earlier in the chapter.

Plan of attack:

1. Read and determine what information the question is asking you to find.

2. Skim the passage to determine where the information you need is located. Read just enough to answer the question in your own words.

3. Eliminate answer choices that don't match your answer.

### Heads-Up

Beware of questions that ask you to determine what's *not* in a passage or can't be inferred from what's written. This runs counter to what you're used to (finding the correct answer), and it's easy to overlook that you're seeking something different.

Give it a try:

A component that can decrease the amount of power in a circuit is a
(A) bulb.
(B) socket.
(C) resistor.
(D) switch.

The question is asking you to look for a word that has something to do with decreasing power. Now skim the passage for those words and see what you find:

> Most electrical circuits require a precise balance of components in order to work properly. If too much power travels from the socket into which a lamp is plugged to the bulb, it will overheat and sustain damage. Introducing resistors into the circuit can help decrease the amount of power that reaches the bulb so that it matches exactly what is needed to make the bulb work properly.

The last sentence in the passage talks about resistors being able to decrease power in a circuit. Answer C is correct.

## Vocabulary-in-Context

These questions are probably the easiest on the test, especially since, by the time you get to them, you've already had lots of practice with them.

The Word Knowledge (WK) subtest, which comes just before Paragraph Comprehension, has lots of vocabulary-in-context questions—just without an accompanying paragraph. This means you can use Word Knowledge strategies here as well. The Swap It Out technique discussed in Chapter 5 also works for this type of question.

Your job is to figure out how the underlined word is being used in a specific sentence. The great thing about this type of question is that you usually have to read only one sentence!

Plan of attack:

1. Go back to the passage and read the sentence that contains the word in the question.

2. Use context clues to determine how the word is being used and what it's intended to mean.

3. Eliminate answer choices that don't match your definition.

**Test Tip** _____

Use your test booklet and/or scratch paper to write down notes about the passage as you read along. This will help keep you on your toes and increase your chances of getting the correct answer.

## Inference Questions

Many people consider inference questions to be difficult or tricky because the questions don't give you the answers, as they do in specific detail or vocabulary-in-context questions. It's up to you to draw conclusions (or infer) based on information in the passage.

As with every other question in this section, you'll be presented with a passage of information and a question. Common questions that follow include these:

◆ The author is most likely to agree with which of the following statements?

◆ Based on the passage, it can be inferred that ….

◆ According to the passage, it can be assumed that ….

Then you'll get four statements to consider. They might ask you about what happens next, thoughts the author might have, where the story takes place, and other conclusions that could be based on the passage.

Now, you may be asking how you're supposed to know what happens next or what the speaker is thinking. That's where the critical thinking comes in. It's your job to compare the answer choices to information in the passage. Correct answers will always be supported by specific details in the passage.

Plan of attack:

1. Read the question first.

2. Read the passage.

3. Go to each answer choice and ask yourself, "What in the passage tells me this would likely happen or be true?"

Now try this:

According to the passage, it can be assumed that ….

The setup of the question tells us it's a straightforward inference question. Next, read the passage:

> Owning a pet can result in several health benefits. Studies have shown that cat and dog owners tend to suffer fewer cardiovascular ailments, such as high blood pressure or cholesterol. Interacting with pets can also result in increased brain activity and have a calming effect on the body.

Now look at the answer choices, and go through them one by one to see what's supported by information in the passage and what's not.

(A) Pet owners live longer.

(B) Cats and dogs are inappropriate pets for children.

(C) The health benefits of owning a dog are greater than those of owning a cat.

(D) A cat would be a good gift for someone who has anxiety issues.

The passage doesn't mention anything about pets affecting length of life or children, so you can eliminate answers A and B. Although the passage does talk about different health benefits from owning dogs and cats, it does not provide a judgment on which is better. This eliminates answer C. Because the passage says that interacting with a pet can have a calming effect on the body, and a cat is a pet, it can be reasonably assumed that answer D is correct.

### Heads-Up

It's really tempting to choose an answer that sounds logical or possible. But remember, it must also be supported by specific information in the passage. If you can't point to a line in the passage as the reason you feel the answer is correct, chances are, it's wrong.

# The Paragraph Breakdown

Now that you know all about the types of questions you'll see on the test, you can practice on getting the information you need out of them. Write down the main idea, purpose, tone, and major details for each of the following passages.

> William Henry Harrison had the shortest presidency in American history. He took office on March 4, 1841, and died 32 days later. Harrison was the first president to die in office, and controversy about the title and term of his successor soon developed.

Main idea: _____

_____

Purpose: _____

_____

Tone: _____

Main details: _____

_____

Wine is the result of a fermentation process involving grapes or other fruits whose chemical compositions are conducive to creating alcohol. Wine grapes are first crushed and strained, the skins discarded. Yeast is added to the mixture. As the yeast consumes the natural sugars in the grape juice, alcohol is produced.

Main idea: _____

_____

Purpose: _____

_____

Tone: _____

Main details: _____

_____

When you fall asleep, your brain literally slows down. The brain waves you create when you're awake take a break and different, slower waves are produced. These theta and delta wave patterns become slower the deeper you sleep. Your body temperature and respiration also decrease, while your brain's need for oxygen increases.

Main idea: _____

_____

Purpose: _____

_____

Tone: _____

Main details: _____

_____

Laws regarding car seats vary from state to state. It is important for parents to know what their local regulations are, not only for the safety of their children, but also to comply with the law. Car dealerships, community groups, and health-care agencies often hold free clinics to check that your car seat is installed properly and give out informational material about car seat age, height, and weight requirements. Every parent can benefit from attending these clinics.

Main idea: _____

_____

Purpose: _____

_____

Tone: _____

Main details: _____

_____

# Chapter 7

# Communication Skills Workout

Practice really does make perfect—and it's the best way to increase your comfort with any section of the ASVAB. Use this section to test out what you learned in Chapters 5 and 6. And remember, you can learn just as much from incorrect answers as you can from those you get right.

## Word Knowledge Workout

The following questions test your knowledge of and ability to use vocabulary. Read each question and choose the answer choice that most nearly means the same as the underlined word.

1. Adhere most nearly means
    (A) vent.
    (B) attribute.
    (C) stick.
    (D) sense.

2. Mutation most nearly means
    (A) character.
    (B) lampoon.
    (C) ambassador.
    (D) change.

3. Profuse most nearly means

    (A) beautiful.

    (B) lavish.

    (C) horrid.

    (D) graceful.

4. Strict most nearly means

    (A) lax.

    (B) uncaring.

    (C) rigid.

    (D) parental.

5. He had a voracious appetite after having fasted for three days.

    (A) unquenchable

    (B) healthy

    (C) average

    (D) enviable

6. Respite most nearly means

    (A) surge.

    (B) bastion.

    (C) well.

    (D) break.

7. Zealot most nearly means

    (A) fanatic.

    (B) arbitrator.

    (C) expert.

    (D) leader.

8. Upbraid most nearly means

    (A) reprimand.

    (B) tie.

    (C) fashion.

    (D) lift.

9. The murder was so egregious that the person convicted was given four life sentences.

    (A) questionable

    (B) monstrous

    (C) slight

    (D) average

10. Disdain most nearly means

    (A) contempt.

    (B) comedy.

    (C) disappointment.

    (D) approval.

11. Boon most nearly means

    (A) insight.

    (B) tragedy.

    (C) impediment.

    (D) gain.

12. Because he didn't heed his mother's warning, the boy ran into the poison ivy and got a rash.

    (A) slow

    (B) observe

    (C) initiate

    (D) argue

13. Fervent most nearly means

    (A) excess.

    (B) original.

    (C) mocking.

    (D) heartfelt.

14. Caustic most nearly means

    (A) poisonous.

    (B) scathing.

    (C) believable.

    (D) excessive.

15. <u>Articulate</u> most nearly means

    (A) think.

    (B) arrange.

    (C) create.

    (D) enunciate.

16. The sun's warmth felt so good, all she could do was <u>bask</u> in it.

    (A) heat

    (B) forget

    (C) enjoy

    (D) seek

17. After our first date, Mike and I said good night and went to our <u>respective</u> houses.

    (A) relative

    (B) visual

    (C) individual

    (D) regretful

18. My <u>equivocal</u> response neither confirmed nor denied my involvement.

    (A) definite

    (B) instant

    (C) evasive

    (D) missing

19. <u>Cow</u> most nearly means

    (A) comfort.

    (B) brace.

    (C) repair.

    (D) bully.

20. Our orders are to <u>plaster</u> the downtown area with the 5,000 flyers that were delivered last night.

    (A) blend

    (B) bluster

    (C) cover

    (D) avert

# Answers and Explanations

1. **C.** To *adhere* means "to stick," which is why tape is called an adhesive—it sticks to things! To *vent* is to "talk out your frustrations." When you *attribute*, you "give credit," and when you *sense*, you "perceive."

2. **D.** If you're an *X-Men* fan, you know a thing or two about mutation. In the context of the comic or cartoon, mutants are people who have genes that have mutated (changed from the norm) and given them superpowers. So we're looking for a word that implies change. *Character* and *ambassador* refer to people, so those are not possible answers. A *lampoon* is a type of satire (think the *National Lampoon* movies), which doesn't make sense. That leaves *change*. Since a definition of *mutation* is "the process of changing," that makes this your best bet.

3. **B.** *Profuse* means "extensive," "abundant," "extravagant"—basically, a lot of something! The only answer that applies to quantity is *lavish*, which means "using or giving in great amounts."

4. **C.** Someone who is strict adheres to the rules with little or no deviation. *Lax* is the opposite of this, while *uncaring* implies apathy; people who are strict feel strongly about the importance of convention or rules. And while many parents may be strict, they are not, by definition. This leaves *rigid* as the best answer.

5. **A.** If you had nothing to eat for three days, chances are, you would be extremely hungry. The answer you're looking for reflects this type of urgency. *Healthy* and *average* are simply not strong enough to match a starved appetite. *Enviable* has to do with jealousy and nothing to do with hunger. Your answer is *unquenchable*, which means "unable to be satisfied." It's not

an exact match, but remember, you're looking for the best choice out of the four you're
given.

6. **D.** When you get a respite, you get a rest (this
is a good mnemonic). *Surge* is the opposite
of resting. A *bastion* is a protective structure,
and a *well* is a hole dug that provides water—
neither has anything to do with what you're
looking for. *Break* is the best choice.

7. **A.** A zealot is someone who is extremely
devoted to an ideology. While this person may
be an *expert*, *arbitrator*, or *leader*, they don't
have to be any of these things in order to be a
zealot.

8. **A.** When you see this word, *tie* or *fashion* may
look like a good answer choice because you see
*braid* in the underlined word. Don't be fooled
here. To upbraid is to scold or reprimand.

9. **B.** Context clues in the sentence indicate that
the answer we're looking for shows an unusu-
ally horrible crime. The only answer choice
that reflects this is B. If you're not familiar
with what *monstrous* means, you can easily
associate it with monster, which implies horror
that is out of the ordinary.

10. **A.** *Disdain* is a strong negative word. As a
noun, it means "a sense of contempt or scorn."
That eliminates *comedy* and *approval* as possible answers. *Disappointment* means "expecting
something and then not having that expec-
tation met." Although it's negative, it's not
strongly so. *Contempt* is a feeling that something is horrible or vile, both strong negatives.

11. **D.** When you get a boon, you gain something
that you want, or something that is useful.
This makes *boon* a positive. That eliminates
*tragedy* as a possible answer. Both *impediment*
(something that blocks your way) and *insight*
(knowledge) are neutral and have nothing to
do with gaining something.

12. **B.** The context clues in this sentence tell us
that if the boy had listened to his mother, he
would not have suffered the effects of poison
ivy. *Observe* is the only answer that makes sense
here.

13. **D.** When you do something with fervor, you
do it with great emotion and feeling. You put
your heart into it. *Fervent* is the adjective form
of this word. Although all the answer choices
can be done fervently, the only one that
defines the word is D, *heartfelt*.

14. **B.** Your first instinct with this question may be
to choose *poisonous*. After all, many household
cleaners are considered to be caustic. Making
the association between the word and "poison"
would be natural. However, not all poisons
are *caustic*, which refers to "something that
is corrosive" or "something that is extremely
critical or malicious." *Believable* and *excessive*
don't make sense as answers. However, *scathing*
refers to something that's bitingly critical or
hurtful.

15. **D.** This one is a little tricky. *Articulate* can be
either an adjective or a verb. When you are
articulate, you have a way with words and can
speak clearly and distinctly. When you articulate, you are actively giving a clear description
of something. The answer choices tell us that
we're dealing with the verb here, since they
are all verbs. *Think*, *arrange*, and *create* have
nothing to do with speaking. *Enunciate* means
to speak clearly, which makes this the correct
answer.

16. **C.** This sentence is talking about how the
warm sun makes you feel really good. *Enjoy* is
the only answer choice that matches this.

17. **C.** This is a good question to use the Swap It
Out method discussed in Chapter 5:

After our first date, Mike and I said good night
and went to our <u>relative</u> houses.

After our first date, Mike and I said good night and went to our <u>visual</u> houses.

After our first date, Mike and I said good night and went to our <u>individual</u> houses.

After our first date, Mike and I said good night and went to our <u>regretful</u> houses.

The answer that makes the most sense is C.

18. **C.** In this sentence, the response being discussed doesn't really give any firm information. Is it *definite?* No. *Instant*, maybe, but instant implies time, which has nothing to do with not giving exact information. The response can't be *missing*, since the speaker says that they gave it. So even if you don't know that *evasive* refers to trying to avoid or dodge, it's still the most logical answer.

19. **D.** The obvious answer here may be the big farm animal that makes milk. Unfortunately, that's not one of your answer choices. *Cow* is used here as a verb, which means "to threaten." *Comfort* and *brace* mean the opposite of this, and *repair* has nothing to do with threatening. *Bully* is your best choice.

20. **C.** When you apply plaster to something, you cover it in the substance. So it makes sense that when you distribute a lot of something, like flyers, throughout an area, it's also called plastering. In the sentence, the orders are to get as many flyers out in the downtown area as possible. *Cover* is obviously the best choice.

# Paragraph Comprehension Workout

Read each passage and answer the questions that follow. Choose the answer choice that best answers the question.

*Use the following passage to answer questions 1–2:*

While you may think it's the acid in fresh pineapple that causes your tongue to burn if you eat too much, it's actually the work of an enzyme found in the fruit. Bromelain, found in abundance in pineapples, is a natural enzyme that breaks down proteins found in muscles, such as your tongue. This enzyme is also the main substance in commercial meat tenderizer. However, the pain associated with a bromelain burn on the tongue lasts only as long as it takes for the damaged cells to regenerate.

1. Based on the information in the paragraph, it can be inferred that

 (A) adding pineapple juice to a marinade will help tenderize meat.

 (B) burns caused by bromelain cause permanent damage.

 (C) bromelain is what gives pineapple its sweet taste.

 (D) bromelain is a main nutritional component of pineapple.

2. The word <u>abundance</u> in this paragraph most nearly means

 (A) just enough.

 (B) inadequate.

 (C) in great quantities.

 (D) reserved.

*Use the following passage to answer question 3:*

Babies have 144 more bones than do adults. Throughout a person's physical development from birth to adulthood, the 350 bones they are born with grow and expand, causing many to fuse together. By the time a person stops growing, they have only 206 bones.

3. The purpose of this passage is to

   (A) entertain.

   (B) inform.

   (C) postulate a theory.

   (D) dismiss a claim.

*Use the following passage to answer questions 4–5:*

Increased interest in the ideals of The Enlightenment throughout eighteenth-century Europe was one of the main causes of the French Revolution. As talk of nationalism, individual rights, and democracy spread throughout the starving populace, the inequity between the nobility and the church, and the commoners became more apparent. This led to an extended period of civil unrest and violence as the country struggled to redefine its government.

4. Which of the following would be the best title for this passage?

   (A) The Rise of Napoleon

   (B) The French Revolution's Definitive Cause

   (C) Viva la Révolucion!

   (D) The Enlightenment's Role in the French Revolution

5. Which was NOT an effect of The Enlightenment ideals on the French populace?

   (A) The masses felt empowered to change their government.

   (B) More people emigrated to other countries in Europe.

   (C) Tolerance for the excesses of the nobility decreased.

   (D) France became increasingly unstable.

*Use the following passage to answer questions 6–7:*

Rock candy is a sweet treat that is easy to make. Simply create a solution of supersaturated sugar syrup and water. Place the liquid in a container that can sit undisturbed for a number of days. Then put a stick or string in the solution and keep it in a cool, dry place. Within a few days, sugar crystals will have formed on the stick or string.

6. Based on the information in the paragraph, it can be inferred that

   (A) food coloring is needed to make rock candy.

   (B) you have to have a good knowledge of chemistry to make rock candy.

   (C) making rock candy is the simplest task in the world.

   (D) you can't make rock candy in one day.

7. The word <u>solution</u> in this paragraph most nearly means

   (A) a mixture of sugar and water.

   (B) a way to solve a problem.

   (C) a chemical reaction.

   (D) a candy.

*Use the following passage to answer questions 8–9:*

My favorite band is finally coming to town! I have been a huge fan of their music since the group's first album came out five years ago. Since then, they have only gotten better. I live in such a small town that musicians hardly ever come here to perform. I am the luckiest person, and I can't wait for the concert!

8.  Based on the information in the paragraph, it can be inferred that

   (A) the speaker has never attended a concert before.
   (B) the speaker will attend the concert.
   (C) the speaker is a new fan of the band.
   (D) the speaker only casually listens to the band's music.

9.  The speaker in this passage is

   (A) angry.
   (B) confused.
   (C) excited.
   (D) ill.

*Use the following passage to answer questions 10–11:*

Simple, handmade soap is the product of a chemical reaction when fat and lye are combined in precise proportion. Handmade soap is becoming increasingly popular because soap makers often use vegetable oils, such as olive or coconut, as the base for their products. This produces a naturally moisturizing soap that is gentle on the skin, whereas the additives in commercial soap can irritate and dry out skin.

10. The author would most likely agree with which of the following statements?

   (A) Commercial soap is the best you can buy.
   (B) Selling commercial soap is more profitable than selling handmade soap.
   (C) Handmade soap smells better than commercial soap.
   (D) Handmade soap is better for sensitive skin than commercial soap.

11. According to the passage,

   (A) fat and lye must be combined in precise proportion to make soap.
   (B) animal fat cannot be used to make soap.
   (C) vegetable oils are unpopular ingredients among soap makers.
   (D) lavender is a main ingredient for making soap.

*Use the following passage to answer questions 12–13:*

Medieval castles served an important function throughout European history. They were tall, strong fortresses that housed military units and protected the surrounding areas. They also acted as homes to ruling nobility and royalty in feudal systems. However, today the roles of castles have been romanticized by their portrayal in children's fairy tales and popular media.

12. According to the passage

    (A) castles are still important in the defense of present-day Europe.

    (B) today general ideas about medieval castles have been romanticized.

    (C) commoners often lived in medieval castles.

    (D) castles had only one function in medieval history.

13. The main idea of this passage is best described as

    (A) the role of fairy-tale castles in today's world.

    (B) the architecture of medieval castles.

    (C) how the nobility of medieval England once lived.

    (D) the changing roles of castles in Europe.

*Use the following passage to answer questions 14–15:*

A vaccine helps protect people and animals from a specific disease by teaching the body how to recognize and destroy the pathogen that causes it. First, a portion of a virus or bacteria, called an antigen, is introduced into the body through the vaccine. Then the immune system fights off the antigens. The next time that pathogen makes its way into the body, the body recalls what needs to be done to destroy the invader, thus preventing illness.

14. The word <u>pathogen</u> nearly means

    (A) an immune system response.

    (B) an antidote.

    (C) an invading virus or bacteria.

    (D) a vaccine.

15. This passage illustrates

    (A) a process.

    (B) a decision.

    (C) a memory.

    (D) an incident.

*Use the following passage to answer questions 16–17:*

I don't understand how I could've lost my keys! They were in my hands when I walked into the room. I went straight to the table and put down my things. Then I went to the kitchen for a snack. When I checked the table for my keys, they weren't there.

16. The speaker of this passage most likely feels

    (A) relaxed.

    (B) confused.

    (C) tired.

    (D) energized.

17. Which of the following is NOT a reasonable inference based on the passage?

    (A) The keys could have fallen out of sight.

    (B) Other things on the table could be covering the keys.

    (C) She didn't have the keys in her hand when she put her things on the table.

    (D) The keys could have been taken by someone else in the house.

*Use the following passage to answer questions 18–20:*

Napoleon Bonaparte was forced into exile in 1814, after having tried to dominate Europe through more than a decade of military campaigns. The self-proclaimed emperor was sent to the Italian island of Elba to live out the remainder of his life.

However, he soon escaped to retake his throne, though unsuccessfully. Napoleon was finally defeated at the Battle of Waterloo in 1815 and was exiled again, this time to Saint Helena in the Southern Atlantic.

18. The word <u>exile</u> most nearly means

   (A) expulsion.
   (B) repentance.
   (C) subservience.
   (D) terror.

19. According to the passage

   (A) Napoleon won the Battle of Waterloo.
   (B) Napoleon died on Elba.
   (C) Napoleon was not an elected official.
   (D) Napoleon was a hero to the French people.

20. The author of this passage would most likely agree with which of the following statements?

   (A) Napoleon's exile was a just consequence for causing more than a decade of war throughout Europe.
   (B) France never recovered from Napoleon's fall.
   (C) Napoleon is considered a despot by historians.
   (D) Exiling Napoleon so close to Europe was not an effective way to prevent continued aggression from France.

# Answers and Explanations

1. **A.** The passage states that bromelain is a main component of commercial meat tenderizer. Since the enzyme is found in abundance in pineapple, it stands to reason that soaking meat in a marinade with pineapple juice would work to tenderize it. The passage does not talk about the nutritional value of bromelain or its effect on taste. The passage also says that cells regenerate from bromelain damage, which contradicts answer B.

2. **C.** Because you can suffer from bromelain burns if you eat pineapple, it's logical to think that there is a lot of it in the fruit. The other answer choices don't make sense.

3. **B.** Because of the factual nature of the content, this passage is clearly intended to inform.

4. **D.** This is a main idea question. Answers A and C are not supported by the information in the passage. Answer B is contradicted by the first sentence, which implies that the French Revolution has more than one cause.

5. **B.** Each of the answer choices except answer B can be proven by specific lines in the passage. The passage does not mention emigration.

6. **D.** Because the passage says that sugar crystals will form in a few days, it's logical to infer that you can't make rock candy in one day. Food coloring isn't mentioned anywhere in the passage, nor is any reference to chemistry made. Answer C is an opinion that the passage does not support. Even if you agree with it, answer D is directly supported by information in the passage, thus making it your best choice.

7. **A.** *Solution* in some contexts could mean a way to solve a problem. In this case, though, it's a sugar/water mixture.

8. **B.** Nothing in the passage suggests that the speaker has never been to a concert. The information in the passage indicates that the speaker is an avid fan and has been so for a long time. The final statement about not being able to wait for the concert suggests that the speaker will attend.

9. **C.** The context of the passage clearly shows that the speaker is excited.

10. **D.** The final sentence in the passage talks about the effects of soap on the skin and how handmade soap is gentler than commercial soap. None of the other answer choices is supported by the passage.

11. **A.** This is a specific detail question. If you look at the passage, the first sentence uses language similar to the first answer choice. Animal fat and lavender are not mentioned in the passage. The popularity of vegetable oil is mentioned, but this contradicts answer C.

12. **B.** This is another specific detail question. Again, the language in the correct answer is similar to where you find it in the passage. All of the answer choices presented except for B are contradicted by information in the passage.

13. **D.** This is an explicit main idea question, but no one sentence states the purpose of the passage. Because the passage starts talking about the role of castles in medieval Europe and their roles today, answer D is the best choice.

14. **C.** *Pathogen* isn't really defined in the sentence it's presented in; it's defined in the following sentence. Based on this information, you can conclude that a pathogen is an invading virus or bacteria.

15. **A.** This is a different take on the purpose question. The only choice that fits is "a process" because the passage takes you through the steps of how a vaccine works.

16. **B.** The speaker is clearly confused. The facts don't add up to her, and she can't come up with a reason for her keys to be missing.

17. **C.** Watch out for the NOT here. The passage specifically states that the speaker had the key in her hand when she walked in the room. Because no other information is introduced to suggest that she did anything other than put the keys down on the table, answer C is the best choice.

18. **A.** In this passage, *exile* is used to describe how Napoleon was forced to leave his native country after his fall from power—basically, his expulsion. *Repentance* is to make up for a wrong committed, *subservience* is to be like a servant, and *terror* is extreme fear. The passage doesn't support any of these definitions.

19. **C.** The passage contradicts choices A and B. How the French people viewed Napoleon is not mentioned. However, the passage says Napoleon was a self-appointed emperor, which means he, not the French people, named himself as leader.

20. **D.** The passage does not touch on the justice of Napoleon's exile. The passage also makes no reference to France after Napoleon, historians, or despots, which eliminates answers B and C as possibilities. It is logical to infer that because the passage says that Napoleon escaped from Elba and immediately launched another military campaign, exiling him off the coast of Italy was not effective.

# Part 3

# Math as Easy as Hup-2-3

The good news is that, to qualify for entrance into the military, you don't have to be a math genius. You just need general skills in arithmetic, algebra, geometry, and logic. The bad news is that you have to show off what you know on two math subtests: Arithmetic Reasoning is all word problems, and Math Knowledge has lots of equations, shapes, and figuring involved.

Never fear, though. This part will refresh your memory and skills in areas of math that you likely haven't thought about since grammar school, such as adding fractions with different denominators. We also take you through more complex types of math that you may not have understood all that well the first time you touched on them in high school—but you sure will this time, with a little practice.

# Chapter 8

# Arithmetic Reasoning

## In This Chapter

- ◆ Why the military tests you on this
- ◆ Types of questions to expect
- ◆ Strategies for success
- ◆ Essential review for each subject area

When most people hear the word *arithmetic*, they envision simple math: adding and subtracting, multiplying and dividing, maybe the occasional percent or fraction. No biggie, right? We all learned that in grade school.

Well, that's exactly what the Arithmetic Reasoning (AR) section of the ASVAB tests you on—but it takes everything a step further using word problems. On this section, your understanding and application of basic math skills is put to the test. However, since you're breaking down word problems to get to that basic math, your reading, analytical, and reasoning skills are also being assessed.

This chapter walks you through ways to make these reasoning problems more, well, reasonable. We show you how to break these questions into bite-size pieces (and give you some practice at it), in addition to giving you a review of basic concepts you'll likely encounter on the test.

## Why Do I Have to Take This?

Basic math is a skill that everyone in life must have. But as we've said, this section isn't just about the math; it's about how you think. All branches of the military want to make sure their recruits can follow instructions carefully and logically. This is more crucial in the military than in any other type of civilian job, since the security of the nation and the lives of our men and women in the service depend on how well military personnel make decisions. That's why this section is part of the AFQT and is required for military entrance.

# What to Expect

The majority of the Arithmetic Reasoning section is made up of word problems that ask you to apply logic and simple arithmetic skills. Your mission here is to pick the mathematical objectives out of a short description of circumstances. To do this, you analyze the word problem and decide what's important to your task and what's not.

Try it with the following word problem that breaks down the difference in the amount of time you have to answer each question on the CAT and PAP versions of this subtest. Then we'll tackle how to break down the question in the next section:

> On the CAT version of the Arithmetic Reasoning subtest, you'll have 39 minutes to answer 16 questions. On the PAP, you'll have 36 minutes to answer 30 questions. How much more time per question do you have on the CAT versus the PAP?

# Word Problems? No Problem!

Just mentioning the phrase "word problem" is enough to make a lot of people nervous. But with a little strategy and practice, you can build up your confidence to where you're doing better than ever on this section of the ASVAB.

# Basic Approach

Since you're taking a test to get into the military, we think you should approach these word problems like you were running a mission. Here are the steps you take:

1. **Gather intel.** In the field, you'd send someone on a reconnaissance mission to get information about a target. On the ASVAB, you simply read the question from beginning to end and try to figure out what it's asking you to do.

2. **Assess the situation.** After you've read the question, translate it into words that make sense to you. This will give you a better understanding of what the question is asking you to do, and give you a simpler version to work off of when moving forward.

3. **Devise a plan of attack.** Write out the steps and equations you'll need to solve the problem. Seeing them on your scratch paper will help you keep track of your work as you go along and make sure you're taking a logical approach to solving the problem.

4. **Execute the mission.** Complete all steps needed to formulate the answer. Check and double-check your math to make sure that it's accurate and makes sense.

5. **Debrief.** In real life, this is when you would report the results of your mission. On the ASVAB, this is when you eliminate answer choices that don't match the one you've come up with.

Let's try this approach on the word problem from the previous section:

1. **Gather intel.** On the CAT version of the Arithmetic Reasoning subtest, you'll have 39 minutes to answer 16 questions. On the

PAP, you'll have 36 minutes to answer 30 questions. How much more time per question do you have on the CAT versus the PAP?

2. **Assess the situation.** The question is asking us to find the difference (red flag for subtraction) between two times. But to get those times, we have to figure out how much time there is to answer each question (red flag for division) in each section.

3. **Devise a plan of attack.** We can set up three expressions to help us work through the problem: one to figure out how long you have to work on these questions on the CAT, one to do the same for the PAP, and one to calculate the difference. What you write on your scratch paper may look something like this:

$$\text{Minutes per CAT question} = \frac{39}{16}$$

$$\text{Minutes per PAP question} = \frac{36}{30}$$

Minutes per CAT question –
minutes per PAP question =
final answer

4. **Execute the mission.** Now let's solve the expressions we've written and find out what answer choice we need to look for:

$$\text{CAT} = \frac{39}{16} = 39 \div 16 = 2.4375$$

(minutes per CAT question)

$$\text{PAP} = \frac{36}{30} = 36 \div 30 = 1.2 \text{ (minutes}$$

per PAP question)

$$\text{CAT} - \text{PAP} = 2.4375 - 1.2 = 1.2375$$

5. **Debrief.** If this were a question on the ASVAB, you'd now eliminate answer choices that are not in the ballpark of 1.2375 minutes.

## Practice Makes Perfect

Not too bad, right? Now let's get some practice in breaking down some more word problems. The point is to get used to the word problem format and working through the question to get to the stage where you can start calculating.

For each of the following word problems, read carefully and write in your own words what you think the question is asking you to find out. Then write out the steps and/or equations you would use to solve the problem.

1. The owner of Arty's Furniture Emporium is planning a holiday sale. A five-piece dining room set is one of the main items he wants to feature. He bought the set wholesale for $1,000 and set the retail price at $2,000. If he wants to make at least a 25% profit when selling the set, what's the lowest amount that he can set the sale price?

   What it's asking: _____

   _____

   How you would solve: _____

   _____

   _____

2. A car salesman makes a 5% commission on every sale he closes. If the average car sells for $18,500, about how many cars in a month would the salesman have to sell in order to make enough to pay his $1,500 rent?

   What it's asking: _____

   _____

   How you would solve: _____

   _____

   _____

3. If a factory can produce 45 widgets in 15 minutes, how many widgets can it produce in an 8-hour work day?

   What it's asking: _____

   _____

   How you would solve: _____

   _____

   _____

   _____

4. A graduating class has 135 students. If $\frac{8}{20}$ of the class's population are women, what number of students are men?

   What it's asking: _____

   _____

   How you would solve: _____

   _____

   _____

   _____

# Arithmetic Review

Now that you're feeling more comfortable with word problems, it's time to review some of the math you'll be using on the AR subtest. To start, take a look at some basic terms and symbols. Some may be familiar, while others may be new.

## Arithmetic Vocab

| Term | Definition |
|---|---|
| Natural numbers | Counting numbers, like 1, 2, 3, and so on. Natural numbers are always positive, and 0 is not a natural number. When a set of natural numbers includes 0 (0, 1, 2, 3), you're dealing with whole numbers. |

| Term | Definition |
|---|---|
| Integer | Any whole number and its opposite (the opposite of 3 is –3; the opposite of 5 is –5). –2, –1, 0, 1, and 2 are all integers; –3.1 or 2.5 are not. |
| Prime number | An integer that can be divided by only 1 and itself. 2, 3, 5, 7, 11, 13, and 17 are prime numbers. 1 is not a prime number because 1 is its only factor. |
| Factor | A number that can be evenly divided into a number. Factors of 12 are 1, 2, 3, 4, 6, and 12. They all divide into 12 evenly. |
| Multiple | The product of two natural numbers: 36 is a multiple of 9 since $9 \times 4$ is 36. 14 is a multiple of 7 since $7 \times 2 = 14$. |
| Product | Answer to a multiplication problem. This and words like *times*, *double*, and *of* in a word problem can indicate the need for multiplication. |
| Quotient | Answer to a division problem. This and words like *per*, *out of*, and *into* in a word problem can indicate the need for division. |
| Sum | Answer to an addition problem. This and words like *total* and *combined* in a word problem can indicate the need for addition. |
| Difference | Answer to a subtraction problem. This and words like *minus*, *decrease*, and *fall* in a word problem can indicate the need for subtraction. |

## Order of Operations

You may remember the "Please Excuse My Dear Aunt Sally," or PE(MD)(AS), rule from grade school. This mnemonic applies to order of operations, or the order in which you perform mathematical processes in an expression with more than one type of the following symbol: +, ×, ÷, and −.

You need to follow a specific order to solve these problems correctly. First, look for any expressions that are separated into parentheses and solve these first, applying any exponents (discussed later in the chapter) that may be present.

Next, move on to multiplication and division, and solve these parts of the expression moving left to right. Finally, perform the addition and subtraction operations, moving left to right. Once the expression in the parenthesis has been reduced to a number, repeat the order of operations on the entire expression.

### Heads-Up

When you see a number or expression in parentheses, but no operation directly before or after, this is an indication that the operation that needs to be applied to that value is multiplication.

Try this with the following expression:
$(3)(4 − 1)^3 + 2 − 4$

1. **Parentheses.** Solve the expression in parentheses: $4 − 1 = 3$.

2. **Exponent.** Apply the exponent to the 3 in the parentheses. This is the same as saying $3 × 3 × 3$. The product is 27.

3. **Multiplication.** The new expression is $27(3) + 2 − 4$. Because the 3 is alone in parentheses, we know we have to multiply it by 27. This gives us 81.

4. **Addition and subtraction.** Now the expression is $81 + 2 − 4$. We solve left to right to finish: $81 + 2 = 83$ and $83 − 4 = 79$.

Always keep order of operations in mind when you have a mixed expression like this. Solving in a different order can lead you to a wrong answer.

## Positive and Negative Numbers

If you think of numbers in terms of a line, you'll be able to understand positives and negatives. At the center of the line is 0. All numbers to the right of 0 are positive, and all numbers to the left are negative (0 is a neutral number).

Easy enough, right? The tricky part with positives and negatives come when you start moving up and down that line through addition and subtraction. Remember:

- The number on the right of an expression tells you how many units to move and in which direction on the line.

- When you see an addition sign (+), you move to the right on the number line.

- When you see a subtraction sign (-), you move to the left.

Look at the following expression: $2 − 1$. Your first instinct might be to read this as 2 minus 1, but really, what you're seeing in terms of the number line is $+2 + (−1)$. This expression is telling you to start at the +2 position on the number line and move one step to the left, or −1. The result is that you end up at +1 on the number line. Try it on the previous number line.

This is the basic idea of how we deal with adding and subtracting positives and negatives in math. Use the previous number line to illustrate the following:

- **Positive + Positive =** Move up the number line; for example, 1 + 1 = 2.

- **Positive + Negative =** Move down the number line; for example, 3 + (–4) = –1.

- **Negative + Positive =** Move up the number line; for example, –2 + 4 = 2.

- **Negative + Negative =** Move down the number line; for example, –3 + (–1) = –4.

- **Negative – Negative =** When you have two negative symbols, they cancel each other out and make a positive. For example, –2 – (–2) is the same as –2 + 2, and you would move up the number line when you solve. The answer is 0.

- **Positive – Negative =** With this type of problem, you have two negatives as well: 1 – (–1). The negatives become a positive, so you need to move up the number line: 1 – (–1) = 1 + 1 = 2.

Multiplication and division problems are a little different:

1. Multiply or divide the numbers in the problem like you normally would.

2. Then figure out whether the result is positive or negative. Only the negatives affect the sign of the answer:

   - An odd number of negatives will result in a *negative* answer: –14 / 7 = –2 (one negative); (–2)(–4)(–5) = –40 (three negatives).

   - An even number of negatives will result in a *positive* answer: –27/–3 = 9 (two negatives); (–4)(–6)(–8)(–10) = 1,920 (four negatives).

# Exponents and Roots

What you see a term like $x^2$, you may automatically think "exponent." However, this is actually a "power." The main number or variable in the term is called the base, while the raised number is the exponent. For example, in $4^3$, 4 is the base, $^3$ is the exponent, and all together it's called 4 to the third power (or 4 cubed).

No matter how you say it, though, exponents tell you one thing: how many times to multiply the base times itself. All $4^3$ means is $4 \times 4 \times 4$.

Some rules to remember with exponents:

- A base to the first power ($x^1$) is just the base shown. A base to the zero power ($x^0$) equals 1.

- When you multiply like variables, you get an exponent: $y \times y = y^2$

- When multiplying two like variables with exponents, keep the variable the same and add the exponents: $x^2 \times x^4 = x^6$

- When you apply an exponent to terms in parentheses that have powers, you multiply exponents to simplify the expression: $(x^3)^3 = x^{3 \times 3} = x^9$

- When you multiply separate powers, you multiply the coefficients and then add the exponents: $3x^2 \times 2x^2 \times 2x^2 = 12x^6$

- When you divide powers, treat it like a fraction and reduce. Write out the base the number of times indicated in the exponent and cancel out like terms:

$$x^4 \div x^3 = \frac{x^4}{x^3} = \frac{x \times x \times x \times x}{x \times x \times x} = \frac{\cancel{x} \times \cancel{x} \times \cancel{x} \times x}{\cancel{x} \times \cancel{x} \times \cancel{x}} = \frac{x}{1} = x$$

♦ When you multiply unlike variables with exponents, combine them into one term: $x^2 \times y^2 = x^2 y^2$

♦ A negative exponent, such as $4^{-2}$, doesn't tell you the number of times to multiply the base by itself. Instead, it tells you how many times to divide the number itself from 1. Take a look at how this works with $4^{-2}$:

1. Calculate the value of $4^2$: $4 \times 4 = 16$.
2. Write the answer as a fraction: $\frac{16}{1}$.
3. Flip the fraction: $\frac{1}{16}$.

A number or variable that is raised to the second power is called a square. The opposite of a squared base is a square root, the number that, when multiplied by itself, equals that power. For example, $10^2 = 10 \times 10 = 100$. If you wanted to find the square root of 100, you would use a radical sign, which would make your expression look like this: $\sqrt{100} = 10$.

For the ASVAB, it's easier to learn some common square roots than to learn how to break them down. Exponents from 1 to 10 are easy: $\sqrt{4} = 2$, $\sqrt{9} = 3$, $\sqrt{16} = 4$. When you're asked to find a square root of a number you're unfamiliar with, knowing the squares of the first 20 natural numbers can help you quickly zero in on the correct square root answer.

## Multiples and Factors

When you need to factor a number, what you're doing is figuring out how many pairs of natural numbers can be multiplied to get the number you're factoring. For example, what numbers can you multiply to get 12? Just three: $1 \times 12$, $2 \times 6$, and $3 \times 4$. Guess what? You just calculated the factors of 12! 1, 2, 3, 4, and 6 are all factors of 12.

You need to know three things when calculating with multiples and factors.

## Prime Factorization

This action breaks down a number into the product of its prime factors.

1. Divide out a prime number again and again until you have 1 as an answer.
2. List all the primes you used and multiply.

Let's try this with the number 27:

```
3|27
3|9
3|3
  1
```

Now list the prime numbers you used on the outside (3, 3, and 3) and then multiply: $3 \times 3 \times 3 = 27$

A good place to start dividing with prime factorization is 2 if you have an even number, 3 if the sum of the digits is a multiple of 3 (for example, 3,654; $3 + 6 + 5 + 4 = 18$, which is a multiple of 3), and 5 for numbers ending in 0 and 5.

## Greatest Common Factor (GCF)

The general idea here is to multiply all the common prime factors of two numbers. The product is the highest factor they have in common.

To find the GCF of two numbers:

1. Use prime factorization.
2. Multiply the common factors.

Try it with 32 and 36:

```
2|32        2|36
2|16        2|18      32 = [2 × 2] × 2 × 2 × 2
2|8         3|9       36 = [2 × 2] × 3 × 3
2|4         3|3
2|2          1
  1
```

The only shared factor here is 2 × 2, or $2^2$, which, when multiplied, gives you a highest common factor of 4. If there had been more than one shared factor, you would have multiplied them all, and the product would be your greatest common factor.

## Least Common Multiple (LCM)

This is the smallest number that can be divided by two specific numbers.

To find the LCM of two numbers, follow these steps:

1. Use prime factorization.
2. Multiply each factor by the greatest number of times it appears in any one factorization.

Take a look at the following example, where you need to find the LCM of 15 and 25:

$$15 = 3 \times 5$$
$$25 = 5 \times 5$$
$$3 \times 5 \times 5 = 75$$

The factors are 3 and 5. The greatest number of times we see these factors is 5 = twice; 3 = once. Combine each of these occurrences in the expression 3 × 5 × 5, and find that 75 is the smallest number that 15 and 25 can both divide into evenly.

## Fractions

Fractions represent a part of a whole, which means that every whole number can be expressed as a fraction: $4 = {}^4\!/_1$. They follow a specific format: $\frac{3}{4}$. The bottom number (denominator) tells us how many pieces make up the whole. The top number (numerator) tells us how many parts of that whole we are dealing with.

**Test Tip**

The line between numerator and denominator can also indicate division, which is an essential operation when dealing with fractions. If the sight of a fraction in a problem freaks you out a little, think of it as a division problem instead and treat it that way.

Here are a few things to remember:

- When the numerator is less than the denominator, you have a proper fraction: $\frac{2}{3}$
- When the numerator and denominator are the same number, the fraction equals 1: $\frac{2}{2} = 1$
- When the numerator is either equal to or greater than the denominator, you have an improper fraction, which represents something that is either more than or equal to 1: $\frac{10}{4}$
- When you simplify an improper fraction, you break it down into a mixed fraction (a whole number and a fraction together in one term). To do this, divide the bottom number into the top (that result is your whole number) and use the remainder as the numerator of a new fraction, with the denominator remaining the same: $\frac{13}{6} = 2\frac{1}{6}$.

For the most part, you'll be working with proper fractions on the ASVAB. For proper fractions, you need to know how to do the following:

- **Simplify.** Reduce a fraction to its simplest form. Always reduce your fractions before attempting any other action with them. Break down both the numerator and denominator into prime factors, and get rid of any factors each side has in common. What's left is the simplified fraction:

$$\frac{9}{36} = \frac{3 \times 3}{2 \times 2 \times 3 \times 3} = \frac{\cancel{3} \times \cancel{3}}{2 \times 2 \times \cancel{3} \times \cancel{3}} = \frac{1}{4}$$

◆ **Add.** Add only the numerators when the denominators are the same. If your fractions have different denominators, you have to get them to match. Multiply each fraction by the opposite denominator as both numerator and denominator.

For example, if you wanted to add $\frac{1}{2} + \frac{1}{3}$, you would multiply the first fraction by $\frac{3}{3}$, since the denominator opposite the first fraction is 3. You would multiply the second fraction by $\frac{2}{2}$, since the denominator opposite the first fraction is 2. The result is $\frac{1}{2} \times \frac{3}{3} = \frac{3}{6}$ and $\frac{1}{3} \times \frac{2}{2} = \frac{2}{6}$. Now add the numerators on the resulting fractions and find that: $\frac{3}{6} + \frac{2}{6} = \frac{5}{6}$

So what do you do if you have to add mixed fractions? Add the fractions first and then add the whole numbers, including any that result from adding the fractions:

$2\frac{5}{8} + 3\frac{1}{2}$

Add fractions first: $\frac{5}{8} \times \frac{2}{2} = \frac{10}{16} \qquad \frac{1}{2} \times \frac{5}{8} = \frac{5}{16}$

$$\frac{10}{16} + \frac{5}{16} = \frac{15}{16}$$

Now add the wholes (since you have a proper fraction, add only the whole numbers in the problem): 2 + 3 = 5.

Your final answer is $5\frac{15}{16}$.

◆ **Subtract.** Apply the same rules you use for addition:

$$\frac{1}{2} - \frac{1}{3} = \frac{3}{6} - \frac{2}{6} = \frac{1}{6}$$

If you have to subtract mixed numbers, turn them into improper fractions before doing anything. To do this, multiply the whole number by the denominator. Then add the product

to the numerator. Your denominator stays the same. Try it with $2\frac{3}{8} - 1\frac{1}{2}$:

$$2\frac{3}{8} = 8 \times 2 + 3 = 16 + 3 = 19 = \frac{19}{8}$$
$$1\frac{1}{2} = 2 \times 1 + 1 = 2 + 1 = 3 = \frac{3}{2}$$
$$\frac{19}{8} - \frac{3}{2} =$$

Once all your fractions are converted, follow the same steps you would to subtract proper fractions, and simplify your answer back to a mixed fraction:

$$\frac{19}{8} \times \frac{2}{2} = \frac{38}{16} \qquad \frac{3}{2} \times \frac{8}{8} = \frac{24}{16}$$

$$\frac{38}{16} - \frac{24}{16} = \frac{14}{16} = \frac{7}{8}$$

◆ **Multiply.** Multiply the numerators and denominators straight across. Then simplify the resulting fraction:

$$\frac{1}{3} \times \frac{2}{4} = \frac{2}{12} = \frac{1}{6}$$

If you have to multiply mixed numbers, turn them into improper fractions and follow the same steps as above. When you simplify the answer, turn it back into a mixed number.

◆ **Divide.** Set up your problem as if you were multiplying. Then flip the numbers of the second fraction, which is called a reciprocal, and multiply across:

$$\frac{1}{3} \div \frac{2}{4} = \frac{1}{3} \times \frac{4}{2} = \frac{4}{6} = \frac{2}{3}$$

When dividing mixed fractions, turn them into improper fractions and proceed as you would with any other division problem.

# Decimals

Just as every whole number is a fraction, every whole number is a decimal. The decimal place is directly behind the whole number: 4 = 4.0. Everything after the decimal point is a portion of a whole.

Here are some important things to remember:

◆ **Add and subtract.** Perform these operations like you would with any other problem. Line up your decimal points before you attempt to solve these problems. This ensures that you keep your numbers in line and that your answer has the decimal in the right place:

$$
\begin{array}{r}
12.3 \\
+1.2 \\
\hline
13.5
\end{array}
$$

◆ **Multiply.** Multiply the problem as you normally would. Then count up the *total* number of decimal places in *each* factor of the original expression, and put the decimal point that many places to the left of the last number in your product. Try it with 5.4 × 2.3:

1. Multiply like normal:
$$
\begin{array}{r}
54 \\
\times 23 \\
\hline
1242
\end{array}
$$

2. Since there are two decimal places (one number after the decimal in each of the factors) in the original expression, place the decimal in the answer two places from the right:
$$
\begin{array}{r}
54 \\
\times 23 \\
\hline
12.42
\end{array}
$$

---

**Classified Intel**

You can drop any zeroes at the end whenever you deal with decimals.

---

◆ **Divide.** The trick to dividing decimals is working with a whole-number divisor. Turning decimals into whole numbers is as simple as moving the decimal point in the right direction. Here's how you'd approach 215.65 ÷ 1.729.

1. Write out the expression like this:
$$1.729 \overline{)215.65}$$

2. The outside number is the divisor. Move the decimal point three places to the right so that you have a whole number:
$$1729 \overline{)215.65}$$

3. Now move the decimal point of the dividend (the inside number) three places to the right. Since the decimal point is only two places in, add in as many 0s as needed to make up three places:
$$1729 \overline{)215650}$$

4. Divide like normal and get 124725. Since the decimal point in the dividend is after the 0, just move it straight up into the quotient:
$$1729 \overline{)215650}^{\,124.725}$$

◆ **Decimals to fractions.** To convert a decimal to a fraction, make the decimal the numerator and make 1 the denominator. Then move the decimal point to the right until you have a whole number. For each place you move the decimal to the right, add a zero to the denominator. Finally, simplify the fraction:

$$.25 = \frac{.25}{1} = \frac{25}{100} = \frac{1}{4}$$

To turn a fraction into a decimal, simply divide the numerator by the denominator:

$$\frac{1}{2} = 1 \div 2 = .50$$

# Percent

Percents represent a part of 100. Whenever you have a question that involves percent, you're dealing with either decimals or fractions (whichever works best for you).

In decimals, 100% is the same as 1. Anything less than 100% is shown to the right of the decimal place: 4% = .04; 50% = .50.

In fractions, 100% is $\frac{100}{100}$. When you want to turn a whole number into a percent expressed as a fraction, simply make the number the numerator and use 100 as the denominator: $4\% = \frac{4}{100}$. Then, if possible, reduce.

In the AR section of the ASVAB, you may be asked to find what percentage one value is of another. When asked to do this, divide the smaller number by the larger to find the percentage.

Try it here:

> You just got notification that you will receive a $2,160 increase in your salary of $36,000 per year. By what percent did your pay just go up?

This question is asking you to calculate what percent of $36,000 is $2,160. To do this, you divide: $36000\overline{)2160.00}^{.06}$. This means your salary increased by 6 percent.

# Ratios

Ratios compare two values and are expressed in three main ways: with fractions, with a colon (:), or using the word *to*. On the ASVAB, they usually express some sort of group relationship. The easiest way to work with ratios is to turn them into fractions and reduce.

A dance club has 25 men and 45 women. What's the ratio of men to women?

Here you're being asked to write a mathematical statement that shows the relationship of men to women. Write the fraction the way you read it. That means the value for men is the numerator and the value for women is the denominator: $\frac{25}{45} = \frac{5}{9}$.

# Proportions

When you compare ratios, you use proportions. Like with ratios, it's easiest to treat these as fractions. Two must-knows for the ASVAB:

♦ **Test for equality.** Cross-multiply the fractions. If the products are the same, your proportions are equal. Test to see if $\frac{7}{8}$ is proportional to $\frac{21}{24}$. If $7 \times 8 = 8 \times 21$, then it is. In this case, the values on either side of the equals sign are not the same ($7 \times 8 = 56$ and $8 \times 21 = 168$), so these two fractions are not proportional.

♦ **Solve for an unknown quantity.** Cross multiply the two proportions in fraction format and use a variable (see Chapter 9) for the unknown value. Try it with the following: $\frac{3}{5} = \frac{x}{10}$. Start by cross multiplying: $3 \times 10 = 30$    $5 \times x = 30$. To find the value of $x$, divide both sides of the second equation by 5:

$$\frac{\cancel{5}}{\cancel{5}} \times x = \frac{30}{5}$$
$$x = 6$$

This gives you a final answer of $x = 6$.

$$\frac{3}{5} = \frac{x}{10}$$
$$3 \times 10 = 30$$
$$5 \times x = 30$$
$$\frac{5}{5} \times x = \frac{30}{5}$$
$$x = 6$$

## Rates

Rates are special ratios that compare two different measurements. Examples include: unit price $\left( \dfrac{\text{Price}}{\text{Number of items}} \right)$, speed $\left( \dfrac{\text{Distance}}{\text{Time}} \right)$, distance (rate × time), interest (amount borrowed × interest rate × time of loan), and time $\left( \dfrac{\text{Distance}}{\text{Rate}} \right)$.

On the AR section of the ASVAB, figure out what the question is asking and plug your values into the appropriate equation. Solve for the missing value.

## Averages

Calculating averages is simple math. When asked for an average of something, add up all the terms that are given and then divide by the number of terms. For example, the average of 3, 4, 6, and 7 = $\dfrac{3+4+6+7}{4} = \dfrac{20}{4} = 5$.

## Scientific Notation

Scientific notation is a way of using exponents to shorten a long number and still have it represent the correct value. To do this:

1. Move the decimal point to the right of the leftmost digit. With 248,500,000, you'd move the decimal eight places to the left, to get 2.48500000.

2. Drop all the 0s at the end of the number: 2.485.

3. Multiply by the power of 10 the number of places you moved the decimal: $2.485 \times 10^8$.

## Factorials

These look strange but are really easy. Say you get a question that looks like this: 3! All you do is list all the numbers in order from 1 to 3 and multiply them together: 3! = 3 × 2 × 1 = 6. Use this same pattern whenever you see a number with an exclamation point after it.

# Chapter 9

# Mathematic Knowledge

## In This Chapter

◆ Why the military tests you on this

◆ Types of questions to expect

◆ Strategies for success

◆ Essential review for each subject area

If you're anything like we were in high school, the thought of having to sit through an algebra or geometry class was not the most pleasant of your day. With all the lines, letters (some even in Greek!), shapes, and rules, learning and applying these math skills can be confusing and overwhelming.

The military doesn't expect you to be a math genius, however. The Math Knowledge (MK) section of the ASVAB tests you on only basic math, algebra, and geometry skills that you likely acquired by the time you were a sophomore in high school. The problem is, you probably haven't used these skills since then, either.

This chapter goes over what types of questions you'll see on this section of the ASVAB, strategies for working them out, and a thorough review of the main subject areas you'll encounter on the test.

## Why Do I Have to Take This?

The purpose of taking algebra in high school isn't as much about learning skills that you'll apply in everyday life as it is to teach you how to think logically. Unless you pursue a technical career that involves math or science, you will likely never have to worry about solving inequalities or manipulating polynomials in real life.

Still, testing you on your ability to work with these types of math problems is a good way to measure your abilities to reason, follow a multistep process, and apply logic to solve a problem. All of these are skills you need to perform just about every job in the military, which could explain why Math Knowledge is part of the AFQT.

The bottom line is that you need to do well on this section to gain entrance to the military as a whole, in addition to qualify for many jobs.

## What to Expect

Mathematics Knowledge is a relatively short section. On the CAT, you need to answer 16 questions in 20 minutes (1.25 minutes per question). For the PAP, you've got 25 questions in 24 minutes (just under a minute each).

### Test Tip

If math isn't your strong suit, make sure that you time yourself when you practice for this section. This will help increase your confidence and give you a better idea of what types of questions you can answer quickly and what types require more time.

The questions in this subtest are much more straightforward than those on the Arithmetic Reasoning test. Here you're asked to solve equations, apply algebraic and geometric concepts, and tackle the occasional short word problem. Oh yeah, there are also some basic arithmetic questions.

Keep in mind that many questions will require you to take several steps to come up with the correct answer, so be prepared to look beyond the surface before attacking any of these questions. You'll also have to figure out the answers to all of the math questions on the ASVAB the old-fashioned way.

That's right, calculators are not allowed. The only tools you're allowed are pencils and scratch paper, so it's best to get into the habit now.

## Plan of Attack

People tend to get flustered on the math sections of standardized tests, for many reasons. While this is perfectly normal, we're here to tell you that there really is nothing to fear if you know what to expect to see and how to approach the questions. Here are a few tricks to take some of the guesswork out of working on this section of the ASVAB:

- **Translate the question.** Standardized math tests are notorious for asking you to complete complex questions with many steps. Take some time to really read and understand the question before diving in. Put it in your own words, if you can. You may find that it's asking you to do something other than what you thought at first glance.

- **Estimate the answer.** After reading the question, try to estimate the answer. For example, if you need to find a factor of 12, you know you're looking for either 1 or a number less than 12. Eliminate anything that doesn't fit these criteria. This is a quick way to narrow your choices and help you decide whether the answer you've calculated is reasonable. In some cases, it can even lead you to the right answer without having to do much math at all.

- **Substitute.** If the question you're dealing with asks you to solve for a variable, try to plug the answer choices into the equation you're working with. This means you don't have to deal with unknowns and you can do simple math with real numbers. The right answer is the one that works in the equation.

◆ **Eliminate.** Again, we can't stress enough how important it is to eliminate answer choices you know are wrong.

# Algebra Review

The language of mathematics is very complex. If you're not familiar with the words used to describe numbers, parts of equations, and actions you're supposed to take in a problem, you'll be confused throughout our discussion about the types of math you need to know. So before we dive into the basic concepts of algebra, familiarize yourself with the terms in the following table.

## Algebra Vocab

| Term | Definition |
|------|------------|
| Expression | Mathematical statement that combines terms and operations, such as $9 + 1$, $5x(9)$, or $4x^2 + 7x - 10$. |
| Operation | Action you need to take with a value: addition, subtraction, division, or multiplication. See Chapter 8 for more on this. |
| Equation | A mathematical statement that shows two equal expressions: $7 + 4 = 11$ or $8x = 16$. |
| Variable | Letter in an equation or expression that stands in place of an unknown quantity; in $4x = 12$, $x$ is the variable. |
| Coefficient | Number that multiplies a variable; in $4x = 12$, 4 is the coefficient and means $4 \times x$. |
| Term | A single number, variable, or combinations thereof. Examples: $8x$, $x$, $xy^2$, 15. |
| Constant | A number that stands by itself in an expression or equation; in $5x + 2$, 2 is the constant. |

| Distributive law | This just means that whenever you see a number, variable, or expression outside a set of parentheses, you multiply that to each term inside the parentheses. With the expression $x(x + 6)$, you multiply $x$ by every term in the parentheses, which gives you $x^2 + 6x$. |
|------------------|------------------------------------|

Now let's look at some initial concepts that will help you on a number of ASVAB questions.

## Equations

Working with equations is one of the most basic tasks in algebra. If you remember the definition of equation discussed earlier, you're dealing with two amounts that equal each other. It's your job to either solve the equation or solve for one term in the equation. To do this, you'll have to move terms around and make sure what you do to one side of the equation, you do to the other.

Let's say that you're asked to solve for a variable. You do this by isolating the variable to one side of the equation and the numbers to the other. How do you do that? Get rid of the numbers on one side of the equation by canceling it out with a reverse operation (subtraction is the reverse of addition, division is the reverse of multiplication, and so on). Then do the same to the other side.

Check out this example: $14 + x = -4$

You want to get rid of the 14 so that the $x$ is alone on the left side of the equation. Because the 14 is positive, you add a negative 14 to cancel it out, and then you do the same to the expression on the other side of the equals sign.

$$14 - 14 + x = -4 + (-14)$$

The rest is simple arithmetic. If you remember from Chapter 8, when you add a negative to a negative, you go down the number line, which means your sum is a negative. In this case, $-4 + (-14) = -18$, which leaves you with a final answer of $x = -18$.

Unfortunately, not every problem will have such a nice and neat answer. More often, you're going to have to solve for a variable equaling an expression. Your answers can look more like $x = y + 2$ instead of a simple $x = 2$. If the question you're working on asks you to solve for one variable "in terms of" another, this is what you're going to have to do.

Isolate the variable you're asked to solve for on one side of the equation, the same as you would with a number. The only difference is that you're moving around terms, not just numbers. For example, if you're asked to solve for $a$ in terms of $y$ if $12a - 8y = 9a + 4y + 6$, your goal is to solve until you have $a$ by itself on one side of the equals sign.

Start by adding $8y$ to both sides:

$$12a \cancel{-8y + 8y} = 9a + 4y + 6 + 8y$$

Now combine *like terms:*

$$12a = 9a + 12y + 6$$

Next, add $-9a$ to both sides:

$$12a + (-9a) = \cancel{9a + (-9a)}\ 12y + 6$$

Now combine like terms again:

$$3a = 12y + 6$$

Finally, divide every term on both sides of the equation by 3:

$$\frac{3a}{3} = \frac{12y + 6}{3}$$

$$a = 4y + 2$$

**def•i•ni•tion**

**Like terms** refers to terms that have the same variables and exponent. For example, with $8 \times 2 + 10x + x - x^2$, the only terms you can add are $10x$ and $x$ to make $11x$ because they share the exact same variable and exponent. (In this case, the exponent is 1, which is implied. See our explanation of exponents in Chapter 8.)

Some equation problems will give you the values of the variables. When you see this, just plug in the numbers and solve according to order of operations.

## Inequalities

When you see something that looks like an equation but has a $>$, $<$, $\leq$, $\geq$, or $\neq$ sign, you're dealing with an inequality. Here's what these symbols mean:

- **Greater than symbol ($>$).** The value to the left is greater than the value to the right.

- **Less than symbol ($<$).** The value to the left is less than the value to the right.

- **Less than or equal to symbol ($\leq$).** The value to the left is greater than or equal to the value to the right.

- **Greater than or equal to symbol ($\geq$).** The value to the left is less than or equal to the value to the right.

- **Not equal symbol ($\neq$).** The values are unequal.

Without getting too mathematical on you, your job with inequalities is not to find one answer, but to find a range of answers (which you don't have to write out). To do this, work an inequality through like you would any other equation:

$$14 + a < 25$$
$$\cancel{14 + (-14)} + a < 25 - 14$$
$$a < 11$$

Here, your answer is saying that the value of *a* is some number less than 11.

Simple, right? However, when you multiply or divide an inequality by a negative number, you have to flip the inequality symbol. Take a look:

$$20 > -10a$$

This says 20 is greater than –10. To solve for *a* in this inequality, you have to divide both sides by –10:

$$\frac{20}{-10} > \frac{-10a}{-10}$$

The 10s on the right cancel each other out, leaving only the *a*. Divide 20 by 10 and **flip the symbol,** and you're done: $-2 < a$.

# Polynomials

Okay, it's a big word, but all it really means is that you're looking at an expression involving one or more terms that may be separated by an operation. Any expression that has one or more terms is called a polynomial. A term with more than three terms is referred to only as a polynomial and does not have a special name. You should be aware of three basic types of polynomials:

- **Monomial.** This is a polynomial that has just one term: 5, 10*x*, and $4xy^2$ are all monomials.

- **Binomial.** This is an expression with two terms joined by operations: $8xy + 4$ and $6 - 2$ are binomials.

- **Trinomial.** These are expressions with three terms joined by operations, such as $x^2 + 6y + 4$.

On the ASVAB, you're asked to add, subtract, multiply, and divide much more complicated polynomial expressions and equations than the ones you've seen so far. Remember a few rules when you're dealing with polynomials:

- **Simplify before you solve.** Combine like terms. To do this, simply add the coefficients.

- **Multiply or divide.** Where you can, apply multiplication and/or division operations. To do this, multiply or divide coefficients like you normally would. Then do the same to the variables and exponents. For multiplication, you can multiply and combine unlike bases: $(8x)(2xy^3) = 8 \times 2$ and $x \times x \times y \times y \times y = 16x^2y^3$.

  With division, treat the operation like a fraction. For example, with $\frac{24a^2}{4a^6}$, you would reduce the coefficients like you would any fraction: $\frac{6a^2}{a^6}$. Next, reduce the exponents. An easy way to do that is to write out the base the number of times indicated in the exponent: $\frac{a \times a}{a \times a \times a \times a \times a \times a}$. In this example, the top two *a*'s cancel out two of the *a*'s on the bottom: $\frac{\cancel{a} \times \cancel{a}}{\cancel{a} \times \cancel{a} \times a \times a \times a \times a}$, leaving four behind in the denominator. Your final answer to this problem would be $\frac{6}{a^4}$.

- **Use FOIL when multiplying or dividing binomials.** FOIL stands for "first, outer, inner, and last," or the order in which you would multiply or divide terms (most often multiplication). Take a look:

  $(3x + 1)(2x - 4)$, you multiply *first* terms $3x \times 2x$, *outer* terms $3x \times -4$, *inner* terms $1 \times 2x$, and *last* terms $1 \times -4$. The resulting equation looks like this:

  $$(3x + 1)(2x - 4) = (3x \times 2x) + (3x \times -4) + (1 \times 2x) + (1 \times -4)$$

  Now solve what's in parentheses:

  $$(3x + 1)(2x - 4) = (6x^2) + (-12x) + (2x) + (-4)$$

Finally, simplify the expression by combining like terms:

$(3x + 1)(2x - 4) = 6x^2 + (-10x) + (-4)$

**Test Tip** _____

The final expression you have in this example is a quadratic expression. We explain more about this later in this chapter. For now, memorize this format so you can recognize it easily.

## Simple Polynomial Factoring

Factoring polynomials is a common algebraic task that challenges you to find out what smaller expressions make up a larger expression. Unfortunately, this means you have to work backward to figure out what was multiplied to get the expression or equation you're given. It's not as bad as it sounds. We break it down for you piece by piece.

Let's start with simple factoring. The first thing you need to do is figure out the GCF (see Chapter 8), or the largest factor that two or more terms share (variables included). If variables are also involved, you need to look for the variable term with the lowest common exponent. For example, if you're looking for the GCF for $27x^2 + 15x$, your GCF would actually be $3x$, because 3 is the greatest factor 27 and 15 have in common and $x^1$ is shared by both terms.

After you've determined the GCF, divide each term by the GCF. Place the simplified terms separated by their operations in parentheses and place the GCF outside.

Let's try it. Factor the previous expression: $27x^2 + 15x$. We know the GCF is $3x$, so we start by breaking down each term into prime factors:

$27x^2 = 3 \times 3 \times 3 \times x \times x$

$15x = 3 \times 5 \times x$

What do both of these have in common? One $3 \times x$. Simplify each of these by crossing out one $3 \times x$ in each expression:

$27x^2 = 3 \times 3 \times \cancel{3 \times x} \times x \times x$

$15x = \cancel{3 \times} 5 \times x$

Now combine like terms and place the new expression in parentheses with $3x$ outside: $27x^2 + 15x = 3x(9x + 5)$. To check to see if you're right, multiply each term in parentheses by $3x$: $3x \times 9x = 27x^2$ and $3x \times 5 = 15x$.

## Factoring Quadratic Expressions

Now that you have a good idea of how to work simple factoring, let's move on to something a little more complicated: factoring quadratic expressions.

If you're presented with an expression that has the following structure or if the expression you're left with after factoring out the GCF has this structure, think quadratic expression: $ax^2 + bx + c$. Here, the $x$'s can be any variable, $a$ and $b$ are coefficients, and $c$ is a constant. All of the following are quadratic expressions:

$y^2 + 13y + 30$; $x^2 + 10x + 25$; $a^2 + 7a + 12$

When you factor quadratic expressions, you're actually working FOIL backward to find the two binomials that, when multiplied, make up the quadratic. You do this in a few simple steps, which we show you using $x^2 + 9x + 14$.

First, create two sets of binomials, with the expression's variable as the first term: $(x \quad)(x \quad)$.

To figure out the second terms in each of the parentheses, list out the factors of the last term. Now find one that, when added together, equals the coefficient of the middle term. With the previous example, we would break down 14 into factors: 1 × 14 and 2 × 7. (It's a good idea to do this with negatives as well.)

When you add 2 and 7, you have 9, which is the coefficient of the middle term. Plug these numbers into the parentheses: (x + 2) (x + 7). Finally, figure out whether you need positive or negative signs and where. Because both 2 and 7 are positive, use an addition sign in both sets of parentheses (shown previously). If the 2, 7, or both had negatives, you would use a subtraction sign in the parentheses.

To check your work, FOIL the binomials you've made. The answer should be the original equation:

$(x + 2)(x + 7) = (x \times x) + (x \times 7) + (2 \times x) + (2 \times 7)$

$(x + 2)(x + 7) = (x^2) + (7x) + (2x) + 14$

$(x + 2)(x + 7) = x^2 + 9x + 14$

**Test Tip**

If you want to save a lot of time and brain power, when you're asked to factor a quadratic expression, FOIL the answer choices. The one that equals the expression in the question is your answer.

# Geometry Review

Many people find geometry to be much easier to handle than algebra. This could be because there are more steadfast rules in geometry and fewer exceptions. Like algebra, geometry is meant to teach you logic. Unlike algebra, geometry has many more practical applications, such as figuring out how much flooring you need for a room based on its dimensions.

The type of geometry that's on the ASVAB concentrates mostly on a handful of concepts that you need to brush up on to get you through. Familiarize yourself with the terminology in the following table.

## Geometry Vocab

| Term | Definition |
|------|-----------|
| Polygon | A closed two-dimensional shape made up of at least three sides. Examples are a triangle, a hexagon, and a quadrilateral. |
| Area | The space an object occupies. Usually measured in square units. |
| Perimeter | The distance around an object. |
| Vertex | The point where the two lines that make up an angle intersect. |
| Line | A 180° angle that stretches infinitely in two directions. |
| Ray | Part of a line that has one finite endpoint but goes on infinitely in one direction. |

## Lines

Lines form the basis of geometry, and you'll see them in many forms. The most important things to know about lines are that they're infinite (they stretch in either direction without end) and can be segmented, for the purposes of an ASVAB question. Some specific line types you should know include the following:

♦ **Line segment.** This is a part of a line with two endpoints. It's often broken up into several smaller segments that are labeled with letters. The midpoint is the marking directly in the center of the line.

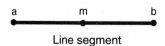

Line segment

You may be asked to identify certain parts of a line segment, such as its midpoint; calculate the length of a line segment based on information given; or apply properties of certain types of lines to figure out lengths or angle values.

◆ **Parallel lines.** These are special types of lines that run next to each other but never meet.

Parallel lines

◆ **Perpendicular lines.** Two lines are perpendicular if they intersect at a point and the resulting angles are all 90°. See the following diagram for an example.

Perpendicular lines

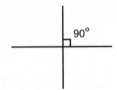

# Angles

Angles are simply formed when two lines, rays, or line segments intersect at a common point; they are measured in degrees. Angles you should know include these:

◆ **Right.** Angle that looks like an *L*. It measures 90°; the lines are perpendicular.

◆ **Acute.** Any angle that is less than 90°.

◆ **Obtuse.** Any angle that is more than 90°.

◆ **Straight.** A straight line is actually a 180°-angle. This is an important number to remember because it can help you calculate the degrees of other angles in a geometry question.

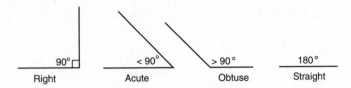

Now that you know the basics, memorize these special types of angles and their properties. Not only can you be asked to identify these types of angles on the test, but knowing the rules associated with them will enable you to figure out missing values of angles in ASVAB questions.

◆ **Adjacent.** Two angles that share a common side. Adjacent angles look like one large angle that's split at the vertex. The sum of the two angles is equal to the larger angle.

◆ **Supplementary.** Two angles that together make a straight line. The sum of the angles equals 180°.

◆ **Complementary.** Two angles that together make a right angle, so the sum of the angles equals 90°.

◆ **Corresponding.** You'll often see these as a set of parallel lines with another line, called a transversal, running through both. This creates a set of angles with specific properties and relationships. Memorize the relationships outlined on the following diagram.

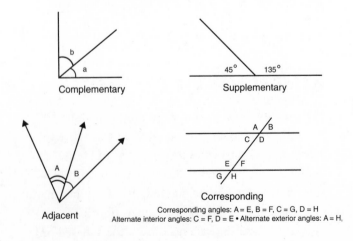

# Triangles

Triangles are an ASVAB favorite. Learning the types of triangles there are and the rules associated with them will help you through many types of questions. A lot of times, questions involving triangles ask you to determine missing values before you get to the main part of the problem, which may be calculating area or some other task.

Memorize these basic rules about angle relationships in triangles. They'll help you quickly calculate missing values:

♦ Triangles have three internal angles. They also have external angles. Each internal angle is adjacent to an exterior angle (see the following diagram).

♦ The three internal angles of a triangle always add up to 180°.

♦ The sum of an internal angle and its adjacent external angle always is 180°.

♦ You can calculate the value of an internal angle if you know the value of the adjacent external angle. Simply subtract the value of the external angle from 180. In the following diagram, the external angle is 45°. $180 - 45 = 135$, which means the adjacent internal angle is 135°.

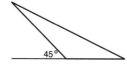

♦ You can figure out the value of an external angle by adding the two internal angles that do not touch the external angle. In the following diagram, you would add $88 + 42$ to find the value of angle $x$ (130°).

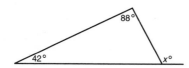

You should also be familiar with several special triangles:

♦ **Similar triangles.** These are two triangles that have internal angles that are equal to each other and, therefore, have proportional sides. In the following diagram, the degrees of angles $g$, $d$, and $f$ are the same in each triangle. This means that side $a$ is proportional to side $x$, side $c$ is proportional to side $y$, and side $b$ is proportional to side $z$ (with the same proportion).

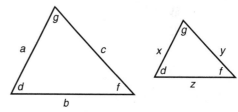

♦ **Congruent triangles.** Two triangles whose corresponding side lengths and angles are the same values.

Congruent

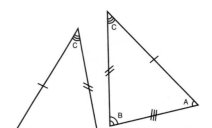

To test if two triangles are congruent, ask the following questions. If the answer to any of these is yes, you have congruent triangles:

♦ Are all three corresponding side values equal?

♦ Are two corresponding sides and the angle they make equal?

• Are two corresponding angles and the side they share equal?

• Are two corresponding angles and a side they don't share equal?

Common triangles include the following:

◆ **Isosceles.** A triangle with two sides of equal length and, therefore, two angles that are equal.

◆ **Equilateral.** A triangle with all side lengths and angles equal. Angles are always 60°.

◆ **Right.** A triangle with one angle equal to 90°.

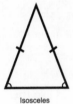 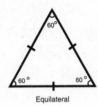 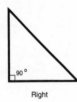

Isosceles                    Equilateral                    Right

Now that you're familiar with common triangles and their properties, let's talk about what you'll be asked to do with this information on the test. Most often you'll need to find the perimeter (value of the length around), area (value of the space within), or a missing value. Here's what you do:

◆ **Perimeter.** Add the lengths of all three sides.

◆ **Area.** Determine the length of the base of a triangle, divide by half, and then multiply by the height using the equation $A = \frac{1}{2}bh$. Take a look at the following diagram.

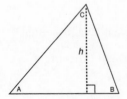 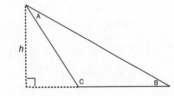

The base of a triangle is the length of the bottom line, and the height is the distance between the triangle's highest point and the base. Often you'll see this indicated as a dotted line running from the base to the top angle. A triangle's area is represented in square units ($cm^2$, $ft^2$) when units of measure are given in the problem.

◆ **Missing value of an angle(s).** Determine what type of triangle you're looking at, and label the diagram with the values you're given in the problem. Then use the rules discussed earlier in this section to calculate the values you need. For instance, if you're given a right triangle and told that one angle is 30°, you know the other is 60°.

◆ **Missing side of a right triangle.** When you know the value of any two sides of a right triangle, you use the Pythagorean Theorem to calculate the other: $a^2 + b^2 = c^2$. Memorize this formula and the following diagram. Substitute the two sides for the corresponding letters in the equation. Then solve for the missing side.

Pythagorean Theorem

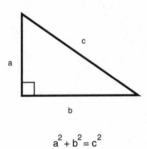

$$a^2 + b^2 = c^2$$

**Heads-Up**

When you solve for a missing side of a right triangle, you have to figure out the square root to get the actual length of the side, because in the equation, each of the sides are squared.

# Quadrilaterals

Quadrilaterals are polygons that have four sides and corners. You need to know these quadrilaterals:

♦ **Parallelograms.** These are quadrilaterals that have opposite sides that are parallel and equal in length. This makes the opposite angles also equal. Rectangles, rhombi, and squares are all parallelograms.

♦ **Rectangles.** These are parallelograms with four right angles. The sides that run parallel to each other are equal.

♦ **Squares.** All four sides are congruent and angles are right angles. A square is a special type of rectangle.

Square      Rectangle

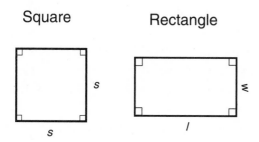

Like with triangles, you should know how to calculate area and perimeter for each of these. With perimeter, you add the values of all the sides. With area, you multiply the value of the length times the value of the width. In the previous rectangle, if length = 4 in and width = 2 in, you'd multiply 4 × 2 and find that the area is 8 in². For a parallelogram, you'd multiply the base times the height. The height is found in the same way as for a triangle.

You should know two special types of quadrilaterals:

♦ **Rhombus.** This is a paralellogram that has four sides of equal length and diagonals that intersect at right angles (a square is one type of rhombus). Take a look at the following diagram.

Rhombus

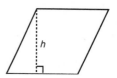

To calculate the area of a rhombus, you multiply the base by the height. For example, if the height line in the previous diagram is 10 in and the base (which can be any side) is 8 in, the area would be 80 in².

♦ **Trapezoid.** This is a quadrilateral with at least two sides that run parallel to each other. To calculate the area of a trapezoid, you use the following formula: $A = \frac{1}{2} \times h(b_1 + b_2)$. In this case, $b_1$ and $b_2$ are the values of the bases (top and bottom lines of the following figure).

Trapezoid

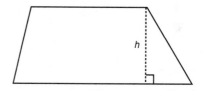

If in the previous diagram $b_1$ = 12 in, $b_2$= 18 in, and $h$ = 6 in, this is how you would work the equation:

$$A = \frac{1}{2} \times 6 \times (12 + 18)$$

$$A = \frac{1}{2} \times 6 \times 30$$

$$A = \frac{1}{2} \times \frac{6}{1} \times 30$$

$$A = \frac{6}{2} \times 30$$

$$A = 3 \times 30$$

$$A = 90 \text{ in}^2$$

## Circles

Circles are a lot easier to work with than you might think. Memorize a few essential bits of information, and you'll do fine:

- **Radius (*r*).** This is a segment that's drawn from the center of a circle to the edge. A circle can have an infinite number of radii.

- **Diameter (*d*).** This is a segment whose end-points are on the circle and that goes through the center of the circle. Double the value of any radius, and you get the diameter.

- **Circumference (*c*).** This is the distance around a circle.

- **Chord.** This is a segment in a circle that touches any two points of the edge. A diameter is a type of chord.

- **pi (π).** This is a mathematical constant that appears in many formulas involving circles. All you need to know is that it equals about 3.14 or $\frac{22}{7}$, which is enough to get you through your ASVAB calculations.

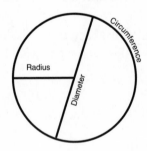

These gems of wisdom about circles and the following formulas should help you tackle just about any circle question on the ASVAB:

- Circumference: $C = 2\pi r$

- Area: $A = \pi r^2$

## Solid Figures and Volume

If you see a solid figure on the ASVAB, it will likely be either rectangular or cylindrical. You're most often asked to figure out volume or surface with rectangular solids (think cubes).

### Cube

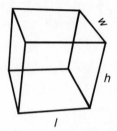

The two main tasks you'll be asked to complete with solids are volume and total surface area:

- **Rectangular solids.** Use the following formula to figure out volume: $V = l \times w \times h$. Plug in the values for length, width, and height, or solve for a missing value based on the information given in the question. These values will always be notated with *l*, *w*, and *h*. To calculate surface area, use the following formula: $2lw + 2wh + 2lh$.

- **Cylindrical solids.** For cylindrical solids, the formula is $V = \pi r^2 h$. Plug in the values of the radius, pi, and height to get your answer or solve for a missing value based on the information given in the question. To calculate total surface area, use the formula $TSA = 2\pi r(r + h)$.

# 10

# Math Skills Workout

## Arithmetic Reasoning

Carefully read the following word problems and choose the best answer for each.

1. A concert hall can hold 1,253 people. If tonight's show sold out only 82% of the hall, about how many tickets were sold?

    (A) 226

    (B) 568

    (C) 1,027

    (D) 1,171

2. Erin bought half as many bolts at the hardware store as Jason and double the number that Brooke bought. If Brooke bought 18 bolts, how many did Jason buy?

    (A) 28

    (B) 36

    (C) 56

    (D) 72

3. Which of the following is the same as 4,683,000,000?

    (A) $4.683 \times 10^9$

    (B) $4.6830 \times 10^{10}$

    (C) $4.6830 \times 10^{11}$

    (D) $4.683 \times 10^{12}$

4. A flight leaves New York City traveling at 520 miles per hour. After three hours in the air, how far will that plane have traveled?

    (A) 1,040 miles

    (B) 1,560 miles

    (C) 1,875 miles

    (D) 2,056 miles

5. Your test grades for the semester are 82, 73, 94, 87, and 78. What will your test average be?

    (A) 82.8

    (B) 85.3

    (C) 87.65

    (D) 96.4

6. The cost of tuition at the local college is increasing by $255 per credit. Last year, you paid $9,900 for 12 credits worth of classes. How much will you pay this year for the same number of credits?

    (A) $825
    (B) $1,081
    (C) $9,990
    (D) $12,960

7. A carnival grab bag game has 36 prizes. Of the prizes available, 14 are for boys, 14 are for girls, and 8 are unisex. If you closed your eyes and picked, what is the probability of drawing a girl or unisex prize?

    (A) $\frac{1}{2}$

    (B) $\frac{1}{3}$

    (C) $\frac{11}{18}$

    (D) $\frac{13}{18}$

8. It takes Bob $1\frac{1}{2}$ hours to mow one lawn. There are 15 lawns on his block, and $\frac{1}{3}$ of the homeowners want Bob to mow their lawn today. If Bob starts the first lawn at 10:00 A.M., when will he finish the last one?

    (A) 7:30 A.M.
    (B) 4:00 P.M.
    (C) 5:30 P.M.
    (D) 6:00 P.M.

9. Mrs. Menkin's class is going to the zoo. There are 24 students in the class, plus Mrs. Menkin and two class parents. If each car can seat four people, how many cars are needed to drive everyone to the zoo?

    (A) 6
    (B) 7
    (C) 8
    (D) 9

10. Marge can carry up to 22 pounds in her backpack. She needs to move 10 five-pound bags of sugar from her car to the store. What is the fewest number of trips she would have to make in order to move all of the sugar from the car to the house?

    (A) 1
    (B) 2
    (C) 3
    (D) 4

11. You buy a new car for $12,465. At the dealership, you write a check for $3,000 as your down payment, and then sign a five-year loan for the remainder of the purchase price at an interest rate of 6%. By the end of the loan, how much will you have paid for the car in total?

    (A) $2,839.50
    (B) $9,465.00
    (C) $13,032.90
    (D) $15,304.50

12. A class of 789 students declare their majors. About 14% will study biology, 23% will study English, 46% will study business, and the rest will study liberal arts. About how many students total will study business and liberal arts?

    (A) 363
    (B) 497
    (C) 542
    (D) 694

13. Tom begins walking to Journal Square at a rate of 4 miles per hour. At the same time, Adrienne begins walking toward the same destination at 2 miles per hour. If Tom lives 8 miles away and Adrienne lives 3 miles way, how long could Adrienne stop for coffee in order to get to Journal Square at the same time as Tom?

    (A) $\frac{1}{2}$ hour

    (B) $\frac{3}{4}$ hour

    (C) 1 hour

    (D) 2 hours

14. 5!

    (A) 15
    (B) 56
    (C) 120
    (D) 132

15. On the whale-watching trip, $\frac{3}{4}$ of the 216 participants registered online. What is the ratio of people who did not register online to those who did?

    (A) 1:2
    (B) 1:3
    (C) 2:3
    (D) 3:4

16. You need to buy bread, eggs, milk, and orange juice at the store. The bread is $2.33, the eggs are $3.69, the milk is $2.65, and the juice is $3.45. The cashier rings you up and adds 6% sales tax. If you give her $20 to pay for your groceries, what will your change be?

    (A) $4.45
    (B) $5.67
    (C) $6.28
    (D) $7.15

17. Your new office is 365 ft². The office manager estimates one cubicle will take up 12 ft² of space. If you wanted $\frac{1}{5}$ of the office to house cubicles, how many cubicles would you need to purchase to fill this space?

    (A) 5
    (B) 6
    (C) 7
    (D) 9

18. You just found a library book that is a year and a half overdue. If the library you took it from charges 10¢ per day in fines, how much money will you owe when you return it?

    (A) $5.42
    (B) $36.50
    (C) $54.75
    (D) $541.50

19. A gallon of gas is $2.68, and your car has a 15-gallon tank. You start a 650-mile road trip with an empty tank and fill up every 325 miles. Assuming you do not use any gas while at your destination and you fill up your tank once home, how much money will you spend on gas round-trip?

    (A) $80.40

    (B) $120.60

    (C) $160.80

    (D) $210

20. Music lessons for your child will cost $1,265 per year. If you get a part-time job that pays $6.05 per hour, how many hours will you have to work in a year to pay for the music lessons?

    (A) 209.09

    (B) 290.90

    (C) 2,090.90

    (D) 2,909.90

# Answers and Explanations

1. **C.** This question is all about percents. Calculate 82 percent of 1,253: .82 × 1,253 = 1,027.

2. **D.** The wording here is tricky, so ask yourself what the question is really looking for. You need to find out how many bolts Jason bought. You know that Brooke bought 18 bolts and that Erin bought twice as many as Brooke did. Multiply 18 × 2, and you'll find that she bought 36 bolts. You also know that Erin bought half as many bolts as Jason, which is another way of saying he bought twice as many as she did. Multiply 36 × 2, and you have your answer: 72.

3. **A.** Notice the answer choices. This involves scientific notation. Discard answers B and C, since they retain a 0 at the end of the number, which is not done with scientific notation. If you count the total number of places in the original number, you'll see that there are only 10 of them, so the correct answer can't be D. This leaves A, which follows the correct format for scientific notation.

4. **B.** This is a simple rate problem. Use the Distance = Rate × time formula to solve for the distance: D = 520 × 3.

5. **A.** You need to figure out the average here, so add all the numbers together and divide by the number of terms you added. Your equation will look like this: $\frac{(82+73+94+87+78)}{5} = 82.8$

6. **D.** You need to take several steps to solve this problem. First, you have to figure out how much each credit cost last year. To do this, divide $9,900 by 12, which results in $825 per credit. Next, calculate how much the tuition increase raised the price per credit: $825 + $255 = $1,080. Finally, multiply the new price per credit by the number of credits from last year: $1,080 × 12 = $12,960.

7. **C.** This is a probability problem. There are 36 total possible outcomes. Because you're being asked the chances of drawing two types of prizes, you need to add the number of possible positive outcomes, which would be 14 girl's prizes and 8 unisex prizes. Use these numbers to make your fraction and reduce:

$$P = \frac{\text{Number of positive outcomes}}{\text{Number of total possible outcomes}}$$

$$P = \frac{14+8}{36}$$

$$P = \frac{22}{36} = \frac{11}{18}$$

8. **C.** Start by calculating the number of lawns Bob has to mow: $\frac{15}{1} \times \frac{1}{3} = \frac{15}{3} = 5$. Then multiply the answer by how long it takes Bob to mow one lawn:

$$\begin{array}{r} 1.5 \\ \times\ \ 5 \\ \hline 7.5 \end{array}$$

. Finally, count 7.5 hours past 10:00 A.M., and you'll see Bob will be done by 5:30 P.M.

9. **B.** There are 27 people who need to get to the zoo. Divide this number by 4 (the number of people who can fit in one car) and you'll get 6.75. Since there's no such thing as .75 of a car, round up to the next whole number. They will need seven cars total.

10. **C.** Since each bag of sugar weighs 5 pounds, the backpack can hold only 4 at a time ($5 \times 4 = 20$). Two trips will take eight bags to the store, leaving two bags left. This means it will take three trips to transport all the bags into the store.

11. **D.** You need to do many things to find the answer to this problem. First, subtract the down payment from the price of the car: $12{,}465 - 3{,}000 = \$9{,}465$. This is the amount that will be financed through the loan. Next, use the rate formula for calculating interest discussed in Chapter 8: amount borrowed × interest rate × time of loan. Plug in the values you have: $9{,}465 \times .06 \times 5 = 2{,}839.50$. Because the question asks how much you've paid for the car in total, add this value to the total price of the car, which gives you $\$15{,}304.50$.

12. **B.** Add the total percentages you're given in the problem and subtract that from 100. This gives you 17, which is the percent of students who declared liberal arts as their major. Add this value to 46, the percent of business majors, to find that the total percent you're working with is 63. Turn 63 into a decimal and multiply by the total number of students: $.63 \times 789 = 497$.

13. **A.** You need to figure out how long it will take Tom and Adrienne to reach Journal Square based on their individual paces. Apply the formula Distance = Rate × time for each of them:

Adrienne: $3 = 2t$

$$\frac{3}{2} = t$$

$$1\frac{1}{2} = t$$

Tom: $8 = 4t$

$$\frac{8}{4} = t$$

$$2 = t$$

Now subtract Adrienne's time from Tom's to find that she will arrive at Journal Square a half hour before Tom.

14. **C.** This is a factorial: $5 \times 4 \times 3 \times 2 \times 1 = 120$.

15. **B.** If $\frac{3}{4}$ of the participants registered online, then $\frac{1}{4}$ did not. Figure out how many people this is by multiplying $\frac{1}{4}$ (or .25) by 216 (the total number of participants): $.25 \times 216 = 54$. Subtract this value from 216 to find the number of people who did register online: $216 - 54 = 162$. Now set up a ratio (54:162) and reduce it to lowest terms using 54 as the greatest common factor. The final ratio is 1:3. More simply, we can note that the total number 216 is irrelevant, as $(\frac{1}{4}):(\frac{3}{4}) = 1:3$.

16. **D.** Add all the prices together: $\$12.12$. Next, multiply the total by .06 (the sales tax): .73. Then add those two amounts together and subtract from the total amount of money you give to the cashier: ($20):

$$\begin{array}{r} 20.00 \\ -12.85 \\ \hline 7.15 \end{array}$$

17. **B.** To figure out how many feet can be dedicated to cubicles, you need to calculate how much $\frac{1}{5}$ of 365 is. In mathematical terms, this translates to $\frac{1}{5} \times \frac{365}{1} = 73$. Now that you know that only 73 ft² can be used, divide that amount by 12, the area one cubicle will take up. You'll get 6.08, which, rounded to the nearest whole number, is 6.

18. **C.** One year is 365 days. Divide that by 2 to find that half a year is 182.5 days. Add the two numbers together (365 + 182.5 = 547.5) and multiply by 10¢ (which is the same as saying .10):

$$
\begin{array}{r}
547.50 \\
\times \quad .10 \\
\hline
00000 \\
+\,547500 \\
\hline
54.7500
\end{array}
$$

The amount of the fine is $54.75.

19. **D.** Start by figuring out how much a full tank of gas would cost at the price indicated: $2.68 × 15 = $40.20. Now figure out how many times you'll gas up based on the information in the question. Since 325 is half of 650, you'll fill up five times: once before leaving, once at the 325-mile mark, once when you get to or leave your destination, once 325 miles into your return trip, and once when you get home. Multiply the price per tank by 5, and your answer is $210.

20. **A.** Divide the amount of money needed by the hourly rate to get the number of hours that you will have to work:

$$
6.05\overline{)1265.00}
$$

$$
605\overline{)126500.00} \quad 209.09
$$

$$
\begin{array}{r}
-1210 \\
\hline
550 \\
-000 \\
\hline
5500 \\
-5445 \\
\hline
550 \\
-000 \\
\hline
5500 \\
-5445 \\
\hline
55
\end{array}
$$

# Mathematics Knowledge

For each question, choose the best answer.

1. Reduce the following expression into lowest terms: $\frac{4x+2}{6x+4}$

    (A) $x + 1$

    (B) $2x + 1$

    (C) $\frac{x}{2x+1}$

    (D) $\frac{2x+1}{3x+2}$

2. Solve for $x$: $x^2 + 12 = 48$.

    (A) 2

    (B) 4

    (C) 5

    (D) 6

3. A letter in an equation or expression that stands in place of an unknown quantity is a

    (A) ray

    (B) variable

    (C) constant

    (D) coefficient

4. Solve for $y$: $4y = 128$.

    (A) 32

    (B) 36

    (C) 38

    (D) 42

5. $\dfrac{6a}{3a^4} \times \dfrac{4b^3}{a^3} =$

    (A) $\dfrac{8ab^3}{a^7}$

    (B) $\dfrac{8ab^3}{3a^7}$

    (C) $\dfrac{8b^3}{a^6}$

    (D) $\dfrac{24ab^3}{a^6}$

6. Factor $y^2 + 8y + 15$.

    (A) $(y + 4)(y + 3)$

    (B) $(y + 2)(y + 6)$

    (C) $(y + 5)(y + 2)$

    (D) $(y + 5)(y + 3)$

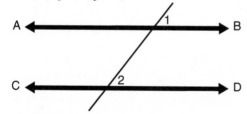

7. In the figure, $\overline{AB}$ and $\overline{CD}$ are parallel. If angle 1 is 53°, then angle 2 is

    (A) 43°

    (B) 53°

    (C) 68°

    (D) 127°

8. If two triangles have three corresponding sides of equal value, they are

    (A) congruent

    (B) similar

    (C) right

    (D) acute

9. A circle's radius is 8 in. What is its circumference?

    (A) 22.58 in

    (B) 25.32 in

    (C) 50.24 in

    (D) 201.06 in

10. $\sqrt{81}$

    (A) 8

    (B) 9

    (C) 10

    (D) 11

11. Solve for $b$: $ab + c = d^2$.

    (A) $b = d^2 + c - a$

    (B) $b = d^2 - c - a$

    (C) $b = \dfrac{d^2 + c}{a}$

    (D) $b = \dfrac{d^2 - c}{a}$

12. $\dfrac{14a}{10b} \div \dfrac{7b^2}{5a}$

    (A) $\dfrac{a^2}{b^3}$

    (B) $\dfrac{a^{-2}}{b^{-3}}$

    (C) $\dfrac{98ab^2}{50ab}$

    (D) $\dfrac{50ab^2}{98ab}$

13. $\dfrac{9}{11} \times 2\dfrac{4}{6}$

    (A) $1\dfrac{9}{10}$

    (B) $1\dfrac{4}{5}$

    (C) $2\dfrac{2}{11}$

    (D) $2\dfrac{1}{12}$

14. 24.45$\overline{)794.3}$

    (A) 25.854

    (B) 28.936

    (C) 32.487

    (D) 46.289

15. A trapezoid has a base of 9 in, a second base of 7 in, and a height of 5 in. What's the area?

    (A) 16 in²

    (B) 28 in²

    (C) 35 in²

    (D) 40 in²

16. $(3y \times 4z)(7y \times 3z)$

    (A) $252yz$

    (B) $322yz$

    (C) $252y^2z^2$

    (D) $322y^2z^2$

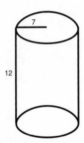

17. The volume of the cylinder above is about

    (A) 1,846 in³

    (B) 1,923 in³

    (C) 2,421 in³

    (D) 3,556 in³

18. If one angle in a right triangle is 42°, the remaining angle will be

    (A) 20°

    (B) 36°

    (C) 48°

    (D) 90°

19. If $14a + 2 > 100$, $a >$

    (A) 2

    (B) 4

    (C) 5

    (D) 7

20. If the $a$ side of a right triangle is 4 ft and the $b$ side is 6 ft, the area of the triangle is

    (A) 10 ft²

    (B) 12 ft²

    (C) 16 ft²

    (D) 36 ft²

# Answers and Explanations

1. **D.** Factor each of the expressions on either side of the fraction bar. You can factor 2 out of both: $\dfrac{4x+2}{6x+4} = \dfrac{2(2x+1)}{2(3x+2)}$.

2. **D.** Isolate the $x$ by adding –12 to each side of the equation. This leaves you with $x^2 = 36$. Now figure out the square root of 36, which is 6.

3. **B.** A ray is a part of a line with one endpoint and another side that stretches to infinity. A constant is a number that stands by itself in an expression or equation. A coefficient is a number that multiplies a variable. A variable is a letter that stands in place of an unknown quantity.

4. **A.** This is a simple equation. Isolate the $y$ by dividing each side by 4. This gives you 32 as your answer.

5. **C.** Treat this like any other problem multiplying fractions. Multiply the terms straight across: $\dfrac{6a}{3a^4} \times \dfrac{4b^3}{a^3} = \dfrac{24ab^3}{3a^7}$. Then reduce. 3a can go into $24ab^3$ once, which leaves you with $\dfrac{8b^3}{a^6}$.

6. **D.** This is a quadratic equation. Sure, you could do the math to break everything down, but this problem can actually be solved very easily. Take a quick look at the answers to see which numbers, when added, equal 8. That leaves you with B and D. Next ask if the numbers, when multiplied, equal 15. The only one you're left with is D, which is correct.

7. **B.** These two angles are corresponding, which makes their value the same.

8. **A.** This is one of the tests you can apply to see if two triangles are congruent. Right and acute triangles have specific types of angles, and *similar* refers to two triangles that have internal angles that are equal to each other and have proportional sides.

9. **C.** Apply the C = 2πr formula here: 2 × 3.14 × 8 = 50.24.

10. **B.** The square root of 81 is 9, since 9 × 9 = 81.

11. **D.** The only difference between this type of equation and one with numbers is that you're not solving for a specific quantity. You approach it the exact same way. Since we're solving for $b$, we need to isolate it to one side. Start with $c$ and subtract that quantity from both sides. Then divide both sides by $a$. This gives you your final answer:

$$ab + c = d^2$$
$$ab + \cancel{c} - \cancel{c} = d^2 - c$$
$$\frac{\cancel{a}b}{\cancel{a}} = \frac{d^2 - c}{a}$$
$$b = \frac{d^2 - c}{a}$$

12. **A.** Approach this like you would any other division of fractions problem. Turn it into a multiplication expression and flip the second fraction. Multiply straight across and reduce:

$$\frac{14a}{10b} \times \frac{5a}{7b^2} = \frac{70a^2}{70b^3} = \frac{a^2}{b^3}$$

13. **C.** The easiest way to approach this is to turn the mixed fraction into an improper fraction and multiply straight across:

$$\frac{9}{11} \times 2\frac{4}{6} = \frac{9}{11} \times \frac{16}{6} = \frac{144}{66}$$ . Then divide the denominator into the numerator and write out the remainder as a fraction. Reduce where you can:

$$\frac{144}{66} = 2\frac{12}{66} = 2\frac{2}{11}$$

14. **C.** This is simple division of decimals. Move the decimal point in the divisor two places to the right. Then do the same with the dividend and add a 0 after the 3. Divide down and move the decimal point straight up into the quotient:

$$24.45\overline{)794.3}$$

$$
\begin{array}{r}
32.4867 \\
2445\overline{)79430.0000} \\
-7335\phantom{00000} \\
\hline
6080\phantom{0000} \\
-4890\phantom{0000} \\
\hline
11900\phantom{000} \\
-9780\phantom{000} \\
\hline
21200\phantom{00} \\
-19560\phantom{00} \\
\hline
16400\phantom{0} \\
-14670\phantom{0} \\
\hline
17300 \\
-17115 \\
\hline
185 \\
\end{array}
$$

15. **D.** Apply the $A = \frac{1}{2} \times h \times (b_1 + b_2)$ equation here:

$$A = \frac{1}{2} \times h \times (b_1 + b_2)$$
$$A = \frac{1}{2} \times 5 \times (9 + 7)$$
$$A = \frac{1}{2} \times 5 \times 16$$
$$A = \frac{1}{2} \times 80$$
$$A = \frac{1}{2} \times \frac{80}{1} = \frac{80}{2} = 40$$

16. **C.** Order of operations applies here. Solve what's in parentheses first. Start with the coefficients and then move on to the variables:

   $(3y \times 4z)(7y \times 3z)$
   $3 \times 4 = 12$
   $y \times z = yz$
   $7 \times 3 = 21$
   $y \times z = yz$
   Combine each to get $12yz \times 21yz$.
   Repeat with the remaining expression:
   $12 \times 21 = 252$
   $y \times y \times z \times z = y^2z^2$
   Your final answer is $252y^2z^2$.

17. **A.** Use the formula for finding the volume of a cylinder for this question: $V = \pi r^2 h$
   When you plug in the numbers from the question, you find:

   $V = 3.14 \times 7^2 \times 12$
   $V = 3.14 \times 49 \times 12$
   $V = 153.86 \times 12$
   $V = 1,846.32$

18. **C.** We know that right triangles are named so because they have one 90° angle. If another angle is 42°, all you have to do is subtract the measure of these two angles from 180 to figure out the value of the third angle: $180 - (90 + 42) = 48$.

19. **D.** Approach this like you would a regular equation and solve for the value of $a$. Start to isolate $a$ by adding −2 to each side of the inequality: $14a + 2 + (-2) > 100 + (-2)$. The new inequality is $14a > 98$. Next, divide both sides by 14: $\dfrac{14a}{14} > \dfrac{98}{14}$. The final inequality is $a = 7$.

20. **B.** In a right triangle, the $b$ side is the base and the $a$ side is the height. Plug in the values given into the formula for calculating the area of a triangle:

   $$A = \frac{1}{2}bh$$
   $$A = \frac{1}{2}6 \times 4$$
   $$A = \frac{1}{2} \times \frac{24}{1}$$
   $$A = \frac{24}{2} = 12$$

# Part 4

# Get It Together: Technical Sections

So far, we've helped you bone up on the skills you need to pass the math and verbal sections of the ASVAB, on which you need to get minimum scores to even qualify for entrance. Now it's time to start thinking about what job you might want to pursue and what tests you'll need to pass to get you there.

In this part, we go over each of the Military Occupational Specialty qualifying subtests and their accompanying subject areas: General Science, Electronics Skills, Auto Information, Shop Skills, Mechanical Comprehension, and Assembling Objects.

# Chapter 11

# General Science

## In This Chapter

♦ Why you're tested on this

♦ What to expect on this section

♦ Essential life, earth, and physical science review

*"The whole of science is nothing more than a refinement of everyday thinking."*
*—Albert Einstein*

Often referred to as the father of modern physics, Albert Einstein is arguably one of the most famous scientists in the history of the world. He published over 450 works during his lifetime, developed legendary scientific theories, and possessed extreme intelligence. For that reason, this quote seemed like the perfect introduction to this chapter. After all, if *Einstein* thinks science is based on everyday thoughts, it must be so!

Throughout this chapter, we discuss terms and concepts commonly found on the General Science (GS) section of the ASVAB, as well as in everyday life. Your ability to apply textbook theories to the world around you will greatly enhance your understanding of science, as well as your ability to score well on the science subtest of the ASVAB.

## Why Do I Have to Take This?

For many people, the word *military* brings to mind images of combat, war, and people dressed in camouflage who defend our nation's liberty. This is certainly true, but it's only a piece of the military puzzle, not the complete picture.

Hundreds of jobs in the military support the combat professions. And like any employer, the military wants to be sure that the right people are hired for the right jobs. So far, the best tool they have for this is the ASVAB.

The technical subtests on the ASVAB are a good indicator of skill and aptitude. In the chapters that follow, we tell you about each of these tests and what types of jobs require you to do well on them. That's right, all the technical subtests count toward your MOS score requirements, and how well you do on them directly influences your career options.

> ### Classified Intel
>
> Although training costs vary by branch and job, most estimates suggest that the cost of training for *each* service member is between $50,000 and $100,000. Clearly, the military wants to get selection right on the first try!

Here's where knowing what you want to do with your career can help you on the ASVAB. Look up the job you're interested in pursuing in your area of service and see what line scores you need for them. You'll likely find General Science (GS) listed in those dealing with general maintenance, technical applications, electronics, and medicine. If your future career lies along these lines, acing the GS subtest is critical.

## What to Expect

The General Science section of the ASVAB covers a wide variety of concepts, primarily from the life, physical, and earth sciences. As we begin to "dissect" these disciplines, you may start having flashbacks to your junior high and high school science class. The good news is that you don't have to sit through years of those classes again!

Even better, you've probably already learned most of the information on the ASVAB tests. And despite the fact that the GS section covers a wide range of topics, there are actually only 25 questions on the PAP and 16 questions on the CAT that you'll have to answer.

Most of the strategies outlined in earlier chapters of this book lend themselves nicely to the science subtest as well. The other advantage you have is that science is all around us. Although you may not remember all the terminology from your teenage school years, you now have the ability to apply these terms to actual life experiences. For example, you can envision how much a liter measures if you've ever bought a 2-liter bottle of soda. You can also envision how much a milliliter measures if you've ever had to give a young child medicine in one of the prepackaged droppers. That being said, you know that liters and milliliters are a form of liquid measurement, with the latter of these being much smaller than the former.

Using your experiences in life to help understand and remember scientific terms is one of the biggest advantages you have on this section of the test. Now let's turn our attention to some of the main subjects you may see on the test.

## Life Science Review

Life science is a broad field of study that deals with living organisms, their life processes, and their relationship with the environment. It actually encompasses several other branches of science, including the many derivatives of biology, such as cellular biology (which includes genetics), health, and nutrition. Let's examine each of these in greater detail.

# Biology Basics

Biology is the study of life and living organisms. Due to the magnitude of this subject, scientists have broken biology down into smaller, more manageable subcategories, including zoology (the study of animals), botany (the study of plants), ecology (the study of the environment), and so forth.

**Heads-Up**

The Greek root *ology* means "study of." If you see a word with this suffix and are not sure what the word means, you already know that it means the study of something. Look to the other parts of the word to see if you can figure out the meaning. For example, the root *bio* means "life," so *biology* translates into "the study of life."

We get into some of these subcategories momentarily. First, however, let's discuss five basic principles that cover everything under the biology umbrella:

◆ **Cell theory.** All living organisms are made of cells, which are the basic units of life. From bacteria, to fungi, to plants and animals, cells make up the structure of every life form on Earth.

◆ **Gene theory.** Traits such as intelligence, physical characteristics, and the like get passed on from generation to generation through genes. Genes are located on chromosomes, which are threadlike strands of DNA found in cells.

◆ **Evolution theory.** Genetic changes in a population are inherited over several generations, no matter how large or small. For example, after being introduced into a foreign environment in Australia, toxic toads grew longer legs that helped them escape to other sections of the country in order to survive. Their modern descendants actually have legs that are 6 centimeters longer than their ancestors and can hop 24 miles farther per year!

◆ **Homeostasis theory.** This principle addresses an organism's ability to maintain a constant internal environment, regardless of external changes. Think of the human body. It has to be at the right temperature at all times for the internal environment to be able to sustain all vital functions. This is why you sweat when you exercise or sit too long in the sun; it's also the reason you shiver in the cold. The body is trying to balance the internal and external environments.

◆ **Thermodynamics theory.** Energy never disappears; it's simply converted into other forms. This principle also talks about how energy transformation is not completely efficient. One of our favorite activities involves energy transformation: eating! When our bodies consume food, we convert the chemical energy from the food to a new mechanical energy known as thermal energy.

These five principles demonstrate how easily we can relate to the science of biology. Let's look now at some sample concepts from the specific biological subcategories just listed.

## Zoology

As you can guess from the name, zoology is the study of animals. One of the most important things for you to know about zoology for the ASVAB is a concept called taxonomy, also known as biological classification. This is a method by which scientists classify living things. Living organisms can be divided into the following classifications (listed from largest to smallest).

- ◆ Kingdom
- ◆ Phylum
- ◆ Class
- ◆ Order
- ◆ Family
- ◆ Genus
- ◆ Species

A good way to remember the order of classifications is to use a mnemonic device. In this case, you take the first letter of each word and turn it into a silly sentence, such as "Keen People Can Often Find Good Sales."

Any living organism on the planet can be classified using the previous ranks, as well as their specific subclassifications. Take a look at the following table to understand how a human being is classified:

| Rank | Classification | Explanation |
| --- | --- | --- |
| Kingdom | Animalia | Animals: Multicellular, heterotrophic, eukaryotic organisms. |
| Phylum | Chordata | Chordates: Animals with skulls. |
| Class | Mammalia | Mammals: Animals that have hair and give milk to their young. |
| Order | Primata | Primates: Includes monkeys and apes; adapted for climbing trees, rely on vision, and have large brains. |
| Family | Hominidae | Fist-walking and knuckle-walking hominids, or great apes. |
| Genus | Homo | Humans possessing specific and specialized development of memory, learning, and teaching. |

| Rank | Classification | Explanation |
| --- | --- | --- |
| Species | Homo Sapien | Literal translation: "Wise man." Highly developed, with specialized ability to learn; able to actively transform environment; can acclimatize, control, and farm; can create urban establishments, infrastructures, and advanced technology. |

Scientists are in constant debate about what should be included in each rank. For example, the kingdom classification traditionally includes five subcategories: animalia (animals, vertebrates, invertebrates), plantae (plants, mosses), fungi (mushrooms, molds), protista (slime molds, some algae), and monera (bacteria, some pathogens).

Some biologists also want to include a new kingdom called archaea, but no official addition has been made. Some scientists would also like to add a category above kingdom, called domain, but no official change has been made here, either.

## Botany

Botany is the study of plants. An important concept to know in this branch of biology is photosynthesis. This is a process that green plants use to turn sunlight, water, and carbon dioxide into energy, in the form of oxygen and sugar.

The process of photosynthesis takes place in the chloroplasts, which are located in the leaves of the plants. The chloroplasts, which are so tiny they must be viewed through a microscope, use an element called chlorophyll to facilitate the photosynthetic process. Chlorophyll absorbs red and blue light, making it impossible to see these colors with our eyes. Green light, on the other hand, is not absorbed and, therefore, causes plants to appear green.

The energy from the absorbed red and blue light interacts with the water within the plant. This action results in the creation of molecules that the plant uses to turn its water and carbon dioxide into sugars. When photosynthesis occurs, a chemical reaction takes place:

$$6CO_2 + 6H_2O \ (+ \text{ light energy}) \rightarrow C_6H_{12}O_6 + 6O_2$$

In plain English, this equation says that carbon dioxide (the air we exhale) plus water and sunlight gets converted into sugar and oxygen (which we inhale). This is one reason environmentalists are concerned with deforestation. Believe it or not, we actually have plants to thank (in part) for our ability to breathe!

## Ecology

Ecology is the study of the environment and how organisms live and interact within different habitats. Habitats are an important aspect of biology because they need to have a balance of elements for organisms to survive.

If you've ever been to the zoo, you may have heard someone say that a particular animal, such as the polar bear, is not in its natural habitat. That means that the environmental conditions are different than those where the organism would typically call home. However, conditions have been artificially re-created to ensure the survival of whatever species lives there.

The following is a list of the major habitats located throughout the world:

- **Polar regions.** These are the coldest places on Earth, with the lowest temperature recorded at −129° Fahrenheit in Antarctica. Most of the region is covered in snow and ice, reflecting sunlight rather than absorbing it. The air is dry, elevation is high, and foliage consists of low-lying bushes and grasses. The land is covered with a permanent layer of frozen soil, called permafrost.

- **Coniferous forests.** These are found primarily in the Northern Hemisphere, thriving in short summers and long winters. The forests are comprised mainly of cone-bearing trees, such as what we buy every year for Christmas. The soil tends to be poor quality, and there are few flowering plants.

- **Temperate forests.** There are many types of temperate forests, including Mediterranean forests, deciduous forests, and rainforests. Long, hot summers in the Mediterranean forest result in the growth of small oaks and pines. Deciduous forests are characterized by trees with big, thin-skinned leaves that are delicate and tend to shed their leaves in the fall. Finally, temperate rainforests are known as such because of excessive rainfall. They may include *coniferous* or *deciduous* trees.

## def•i•ni•tion

Coniferous trees have cones or yews; they also usually have needles. These trees do not lose their needles or cones during any particular season, which is why they're best known as evergreens. An easy way to remember this is with the mnemonic "Conifers have cones." **Deciduous** trees have leaves that change color and fall off in autumn.

◆ **Grasslands.** These areas are basically a cross between forests and deserts. They don't have enough rain or trees to be a forest, but they aren't dry enough to be a desert. They have few trees, because of the dry climate or animal grazing, and are usually found in flat areas. In the United States, these areas are called prairies.

◆ **Deserts.** Covering more than 20 percent of Earth's surface, these areas are dry, with few animals, sparse plants, and barren landscapes. Deserts are so dry, in fact, that it might take years for a rainstorm to occur in the same place. Deserts might be covered in sand, stony plains, or rocky hills.

◆ **Mountains.** These cover another 20 percent of Earth's surface (some of which are under the ocean) and can be found on every continent. Mountains offer a wide variety of plants and temperatures, depending on elevation and location within the mountain. Mountains are formed by movements in the Earth's crust.

◆ **Tropical forests.** These are known as some of the most beautiful places on Earth, largely because of their diversity. They are comprised of enormous trees, lush plants, gorgeous colors, and a variety of mammals. They are primarily located in Central and South America, West and Central Africa, and Southeast Asia.

◆ **Oceanic islands.** These isolated little land masses tend to be wet, cloudy, and windswept, with constant temperatures year-round. They rise from the ocean floor, often as a result of volcanic activity. Tahiti is an example of an oceanic island.

◆ **Freshwater wetlands.** These regions are covered by shallow waters, such as marshes and ponds. They are plagued by floods, but they are full of life. Fish, birds, mammals, amphibians, and multiple plants call freshwater wetlands home.

◆ **Oceans.** Oceans cover nearly 75 percent of Earth's surface. Because all the oceans join one another, this is the world's largest habitat. Ocean waters and ocean floors have layers, each one supporting a variety of life forms. There are five oceans: the Pacific, Atlantic, Indian, Arctic, and Southern oceans.

## Cellular Biology

Cellular biology examines what cells do, what they're made of, and what their purpose is. There are billions (if not trillions) of cells in the adult human body. These cells break down into groupings, as follows:

◆ **Tissue.** A family of cells that live close together is called tissue. One example of tissue is muscle tissue. Muscle tissue in the heart, for instance, is called cardiac muscle.

◆ **Organ.** A group of tissues that work together forms an organ. Cardiac muscle tissue, for example, works together to create the heart.

◆ **System.** Organs work together to form a system. Using the same example as above the heart, blood vessels, and blood form the cardiovascular system.

◆ **Body.** Multiple systems that work together form a body of life, such as a human.

Although cells are microscopically small, they are actually comprised of several important components called organelles. Check out these simple illustrations of the two main types of cells.

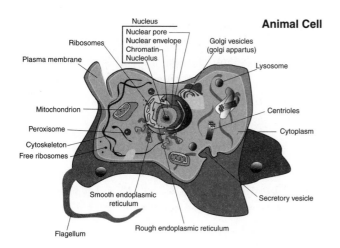

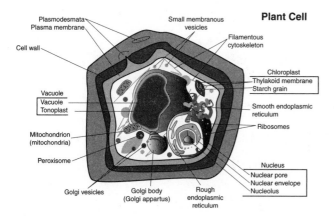

As you prepare for the ASVAB, you should become familiar with some of the terms noted in each illustration:

♦ **Nucleus.** This is the central part of the cell, which contains the DNA and RNA for growth and reproduction.

♦ **Plasma cell membrane.** This is a semiporous enclosure that surrounds the cell. It acts as a boundary, holding all the contents inside the cell and preventing foreign substances from entering the cell.

♦ **Endoplasmic reticulum.** This transports cellular materials. It's also involved with synthesis and modification of those materials.

♦ **Ribosome.** These units use RNA (a molecule similar to DNA, discussed later in this section) to build proteins.

♦ **Golgi.** This is the location in the cell where newly made proteins can mature and become functional.

♦ **Mitochondria.** This is the unit in which nutrients are converted into energy. Mitochondria have a membrane enclosure around them.

♦ **Lysosome.** This organelle contains the necessary digestive enzymes for the cell.

Cells have a variety of processes that they undergo on a regular basis, one of the most important being cell division. There are two main types of cell division:

♦ **Mitosis.** This is the process of dividing one cell into two cells, each with its own complete nucleus. All cells (except those involved with sexual reproduction) undergo mitosis. Your body undergoes mitosis every time you get a cut and new skin grows back. Or when your children pull each other's hair, it grows back because of mitosis. Weightlifters also experience mitosis when they grow bigger muscles from working out.

♦ **Meiosis.** This method of cell division is used in sexual reproduction. In animals, the number of chromosomes per cell is halved, which results in a gamete cell. When two gamete cells combine, the outcome is a new cell with a combination of information from each gamete. In other organisms, meiosis may result in a spore. A spore is a reproductive structure often found in bacteria, plants, algae, fungi, and some protozoans.

# Genetics

Within discussions of cell reproduction, you often hear about genetics, which is a branch of science that examines heredity and variation in living organisms. As you can see, when cells divide, they either create an exact copy of themselves or create a cell with half its genetic material that waits to join with another similar cell.

Some key terms to understand in this subject area include:

- **Gene.** This is the basic unit of heredity and contains the information needed to build, maintain, and reproduce cells.

- **DNA.** Thanks to popular television shows like *CSI: Miami* and *Bones*, most people are familiar with the term *DNA*, which is short for *deoxyribonucleic acid*. DNA contains the genetic instructions used in the development and functioning of all known living organisms and some viruses.

- **Chromosome.** This is a specific type of DNA that is joined with protein and contains information about genes, as well as nucleotide sequences and regulatory elements specific to the organism.

- **RNA.** Short for *ribonucleic acid*, RNA is similar to DNA. The two differ slightly structurally; RNA is single-stranded, compared to the double-stranded composition of DNA. RNA is needed to synthesize proteins.

- **Nucleotides.** These are molecules that, when joined, comprise the structural units of RNA and DNA. They play an important role in metabolism.

- **Metabolism.** This is the set of chemical reactions that allows organisms to grow, reproduce, maintain structure, and respond to the environment. Metabolism also breaks down organic matter to harvest energy, and it influences how much food an organism requires. It is in this capacity that we typically hear of metabolism, especially in connection with weight gain or weight loss issues.

- **Amino acids.** These molecules are critical to life. They also play a key role in metabolism. Amino acids form linear chains of proteins, which catalyze the chemical reactions of metabolism. Amino acids are used in the food industry as flavor enhancers, as well as in biodegradable plastics and drugs.

- **Proteins.** These linear chains of amino acids are also known as polypeptides. Proteins are organic compounds that are essential to cellular processes. They are a necessary component of animals' diets as well. Through the process of digestion, proteins are broken down into free amino acids, which are then used in metabolism.

# Health

Our bodies are incredibly complex machines. They truly "embody" the concept of teamwork, from the organs working together within each system to the microscopic units working together in each cell. In this section, we examine some of the major systems that operate within the human body.

## Circulatory System

- **The team.** This system controls the flow of blood in the body using vessels, muscles, arteries, veins, capillaries, and the heart to accomplish the mission.

- **The process.** Blood leaves the heart through the left ventricle, picking up oxygen in the aorta on its way out. (The aorta is the largest artery in the body.) The oxygen-rich blood enables cells in the rest of the body to do their work. After circulating throughout the body, the blood heads back to the heart through veins. As it filters through the lungs, the blood deposits the carbon dioxide (which we exhale) and replaces it with oxygen (which we inhale).

## Respiratory System

- **The team.** The respiratory system works hand-in-hand with the circulatory system. This is the team that actually supplies the blood with oxygen. The "team" is comprised of the mouth, nose, trachea, lungs, and diaphragm.

- **The process.** Oxygen enters the body through the mouth and nose, passing through the trachea into the chest cavity. To get to the lungs, the oxygen then travels through a little maze of pipes known as the bronchi and bronchial tubes. Upon arrival in the lungs, it settles in small sacs called alveoli to await the diaphragm pumping out carbon dioxide. Finally, the diaphragm pulls the oxygen all the way through the lungs and completes the process.

## Digestive System

- **The team.** Main players in this system that convert food to energy are the mouth, throat, esophagus (food tube), stomach, liver, gall bladder, intestines, rectum, and anus.

- **The process.** Food enters the mouth and begins to be broken down when you chew, mixing the food with saliva. When you swallow, you move the food into the esophagus, which brings it down into the stomach. Here, acid and other chemicals your body makes break down the food even more. Juices from the pancreas and liver (by way of the gall bladder) combine with the contents of the stomach in the small intestine to perform most of the

digestive work. Nutrients are broken down and routed to the right systems, while solid wastes are passed on to the large intestine through the rectum and out the anus.

## Excretory System

- **The team.** This system regulates the chemical composition of the body by removing waste, retaining the right amount of water, and balancing all of this with salt and nutrients. The kidneys, liver, lungs, and skin are all involved with the excretory system.

- **The process.** The kidney's job is to filter waste from the blood and excrete it with water through urine. The liver also serves as a filter, removing unnecessary amino acids. The skin, often referred to as the largest organ in the body, is another excretory agent that generally filters out salt and water in the form of perspiration.

---

### Classified Intel

You've probably heard of people who've died of dehydration, meaning they did not have enough water in their body. But people have also died of overhydration because the salt amounts weren't balanced with water levels, something controlled by the excretory system.

---

## Reproductive System

- **The team.** This system was designed to ensure survival of the species. Female reproductive organs are located within the pelvis and are designed to produce eggs, transport and sustain these cells, nurture and develop offspring, and produce hormones. The male reproductive organs have essentially the same function (using sperm instead of eggs), with their location being both inside and outside the pelvis.

♦ **The process.** Remember back to your sex ed classes for this one. A woman's ovaries hold eggs, each of which can be fertilized by a single sperm to create a baby. Every month, an egg is released from an ovary and travels into the fallopian tube, where it stays until fertilized. If it is fertilized, it embeds in the lining of the uterus and begins to grow and form a placenta. If it isn't fertilized, it is shed along with the lining of the uterus through menstruation.

# Nutrition

As you prepare for the military, you are most likely training intellectually for the ASVAB (using this book) and physically for the fitness demands of the service. In fact, nutrition and fitness will actually be intertwined with one another, your career, and your success in the military.

Most branches of the Armed Forces have rigorous standards for cardiovascular and muscular fitness, as well as height, weight, and body fat composition. Your ability to excel in these areas will have a direct impact on your level of success in the military. Your knowledge of this information will also positively affect your score on the General Science section of the ASVAB, so learning about nutrition is a win-win situation! Let's take a few minutes to cover some of the basics.

Every physical activity requires energy, which we gain through our body stores and the food we eat. This energy is measured in calories. Caloric intake is not the only important factor in the creation of energy, though. Nutrient balance is critical for both energy and health. Many of us probably remember the old food pyramid that taught us about balanced nutrition when we were kids.

The U.S. Department of Agriculture has revamped the former horizontal model in favor of a vertical pyramid; the purpose is to give each food group more balanced representation. You can check it out at www.mypyramid.gov/pyramid/index.html.

Some of the specific nutrients that you should be familiar with include the following:

♦ **Proteins.** We discussed these earlier; in terms of nutrition, they are essential to growth and repair of muscle and other body tissues. They can be found most commonly in meats, eggs, dairy, seeds, and nuts.

♦ **Fats.** This is one source of energy that we need, but we should try to consume it in moderation. Good fats are found in olive oil, salmon, almonds, and avocados.

♦ **Carbohydrates.** Our main source of energy, these are found in foods like whole grains, fruits, chocolate, and honey.

♦ **Minerals.** These are inorganic elements that are critical to its normal functions and are found in many foods. Some examples of minerals include iron, zinc, copper, calcium, and magnesium.

♦ **Vitamins.** These are essential to many chemical processes in the body and are also found in a variety of foods. Some examples include vitamin A, found in fish oil, eggs, milk, and dark leafy vegetables; vitamin D, found in cheese, eggs, and breakfast cereals; vitamin K, found in spinach, parsley, and broccoli; and vitamin C, found in citrus fruits, melons, peppers, and tomatoes.

♦ **Water.** This is essential to normal body function. It serves as a vehicle for carrying other nutrients; furthermore, more than 60 percent of the human body consists of water.

♦ **Roughage.** This is the fibrous indigestible portion of our diet, essential to the health of the digestive system. It includes oatmeal, soybeans, whole grains, and artichokes.

# Earth Science Review

Much like its name suggests, earth science deals with the origin, structure, and phenomena associated with planet Earth. But believe it or not, this includes topics that are not strictly terrestrial. It also includes studies about the atmosphere, weather, and space. This section explores all these areas.

## Geology

We start our discussion with geology, which examines Earth's physical structure. An easy way to remember this is to remember that *geo* means "Earth." Therefore, geologists are scientists who study the Earth—or, more specifically, the lithosphere (the outer portion of Earth).

Just like an onion, the Earth is made up of several layers: the crust, mantle, outer core, and inner core. The lithosphere consists of the crust and the upper mantle, and runs approximately 62 miles deep. You may think that sounds deep, but keep in mind that the core of the Earth is about 4,000 miles from the surface!

You should be familiar with a few specific concepts in this branch of science:

♦ The Earth's crust is approximately 10 miles deep and consists of several types of rock and other loose materials.

♦ The mantle lies beneath the crust and is a much larger section of the Earth. It is approximately 1,800 miles deep and represents nearly 85 percent of the Earth's total weight

and mass. The rock in this layer changes in texture from very rigid for a few miles, to soft and hot for several more miles, and then back to rigid again.

♦ The outer core is believed to run nearly 3,000 miles deep and is comprised of burning hot liquid molten rock, known as magma when it flows beneath the Earth's surface. Once it reaches topside, it's called lava. That's right, when a volcano erupts, it's bringing molten rock from the outer core all the way up to the surface. The two main elements found in the outer core are iron and nickel.

♦ The inner core, which is considered to be solid rock, is also made of iron and nickel. It extends an additional 900 miles inward.

♦ More than 3,700 known mineral rocks are present in the Earth's crust. These rocks are divided into three main categories:

   ♦ **Igneous rock.** All rocks on Earth are originally created as this type of rock; it is the result of molten lava that has cooled and hardened. These rocks are further categorized depending on where the liquid rock cooled and hardened. If the igneous rock was formed underground, it is referred to as an intrusive rock. Remember this by thinking, "*in*side the Earth, *in*trusive rock." If the lava cooled on the surface of the Earth, it is called extrusive rock.

   ♦ **Sedimentary rock.** As igneous rocks weather the elements of wind and water, they get worn down. After thousands of years, they form particles not much larger than dirt. Often they come to rest on the bottom of lakes, streams, and oceans. As these layers of rock interact with other minerals, they get heavier and more closely bonded. Eventually, they form solid layers of sedimentary rock. *Fossils* are usually found in these layers.

## def•i•ni•tion

**Fossils** are skeletons of living organisms that have been preserved over time by rock. Soft sedimentary rock, such as shale, often houses fossils.

◆ **Metamorphic rock.** Deeply entrenched in the folds of the Earth, this rock forms from igneous and sedimentary rock. The heat from Earth's interior layers basically "cooks" metamorphic rock, causing the finished product to look very different than its original version. Marble is a beautiful example of this.

◆ Rocks are often classified based on their hardness. This is determined by testing a rock's resistance to scratching and comparing the results to the Mohs scale of mineral hardness, which gives a 1 to 10 rating (1 being the softest and 10 the hardest). Soft rock, like talc or graphite, scores a 1. Minerals such as feldspar, quartz, and topaz are toward the middle (scoring 6, 7, and 8, respectively). Diamonds top the scale, at 10, as they're the hardest known mineral on Earth.

◆ The Earth is made up of various landforms, which are natural formations of rock and dirt. They vary in size and height, and include such beauties as the Grand Canyon, mountain ranges, and rolling hills. Landforms may develop as a result of glacial movement (valleys), wind (sand dunes, sandstone formations), water (canyons), weather (glaciers, ice fields), and so forth.

## Meteorology

Meteorology is arguably the category of earth science that affects our daily lives the most. This science studies atmospheric conditions, particularly as they relate to weather. Let's examine this intriguing science now that has the power to make or break weekend plans!

### Atmosphere

This is a collection of layers containing various gases that sustain life on Earth. Gases include ozone, oxygen, nitrogen, carbon dioxide, and argon. You should familiarize yourself with several layers of atmosphere:

◆ **Troposphere.** This is the layer closest to Earth and extends up into the sky where clouds form. The troposphere is the only layer of our atmosphere that can support life. Unfortunately, this is the same layer that we continue to destroy through harmful pollution.

◆ **Stratosphere.** This is the layer above the troposphere where the ozone exists. Many of us are familiar with the ozone layer, as scientists and the media frequently discuss it with regard to pollution. As harmful pollutants like chlorofluorocarbon (CFC) gasses penetrate the troposphere, they begin to damage the stratosphere. The result is that life on Earth is less protected from harmful radiation that comes from the sun. Although the stratosphere is currently much warmer than the top layers of the troposphere, depletion of the ozone could result in hot ultraviolet rays escaping into the troposphere. The effect would be a cooler stratosphere and a world that is too warm to function as it currently does.

◆ **Mesosphere.** This is the layer above the stratosphere, and it is the coldest region in the atmosphere.

♦ **Thermosphere.** This is the atmospheric layer closest to space. The temperature is very high here, with a lot of energy and fast-moving molecules. Oddly, however, there is very little heat in the thermosphere. Heat happens when energy is transferred from one atom to another. In the thermosphere, there is very little transfer of energy because the atomic molecules are so spread out.

## Barometric Pressure

You've probably heard your meteorologist talk a lot about barometric pressure. This is simply a measure of the weight of the air as it pushes down on an area of Earth. Important things to know include:

♦ High pressure generally indicates good or improving weather. Beautiful sunny days are the result of high barometric pressure.

♦ Low or falling pressure suggests poor weather is looming. Barometric pressure falls sharply just before a tornado and remains low throughout a hurricane.

## Front

This is what happens when two different types of air masses meet. Maybe you've heard of a cold front or a warm front. When your local meteorologist talks about this, it means a drastic change in temperature or weather is likely on the way.

## Clouds

Clouds are formations of gaseous water. In English, this means that when water evaporates from the Earth, it changes states from liquid to gas (see our physical science discussion). As the water reverts to a liquid state and settles in the atmosphere, clouds begin to form. Once the clouds begin to take shape, meteorologists can identify the type of cloud based on how high it is in the sky and how it looks. That's

why most clouds have two parts to their name: the first part deals with their height, the second with their appearance.

High-level clouds get the prefix *cirro*, while midlevel clouds get the prefix *alto*. Low-level clouds don't have any prefix attached to their names. The following list of identifiers typically applies to the second half of a cloud's name:

♦ Cumulus clouds are puffy and often appear in groups.

♦ Cirrus clouds are wispy and made of ice crystals.

♦ Cumulonimbus clouds are tall and thick, and often bring thunderstorms.

♦ Stratus clouds are uniform in color and density, like a blanket.

---

**Classified Intel**

Air has to be just a bit dirty for clouds to form. The water vapor needs something on which to condense, such as dirt or dust particles.

---

## Astronomy

Astronomy is the study of matter in outer space, including celestial bodies and the universe as a whole. Because Earth is a part of this, it's considered an area of focus in earth science.

Since there's a whole universe of information we could share with you about astronomy, we focus on only a few key concepts and terms, to provide a general understanding of the subject. Let's start with some general vocabulary.

## Astronomy Vocab

| Term | Definition |
| --- | --- |
| Star | An object that shines because of nuclear reactions that release energy from its core. |
| Sun | A star around which planets and other celestial objects move. |
| Planet | A celestial body larger than an asteroid that moves around and receives light from a star. |
| Solar system | The system of planets and other objects orbiting a star, such as the sun. |
| Galaxy | A group of stars, gas, and dust held together by gravity. Our galaxy is known as the Milky Way. |
| Asteroid | A rock or minor planet orbiting the Sun. |
| Meteor | Also known as a shooting star. This occurs when a particle of dust enters Earth's atmosphere. |
| Meteorite | An object from outer space, such as a rock, that falls into the Earth and lands on its surface. |
| Comet | A small, frozen mass of dust and gas revolving around the sun. |
| Constellation | Groupings of stars named by astronomers. For example, the Big Dipper is part of the Great Bear, one of the most famous constellations. |
| Astronomical unit | The distance from the Earth to the sun. |
| Light year | The distance a ray of light would travel in one year—about six trillion miles. |

| Term | Definition |
| --- | --- |
| Phases | The perceived change in the shape of the moon, Mercury, and Venus, depending on how much of the sunlit side is facing the Earth. Some examples of moon phases include crescent and full. |
| Black hole | The area around a tiny (yet massive) object that appears black. In actuality, light cannot escape this region because of an incredibly strong gravitational field. |
| Binary star | Two stars orbiting each other that look like one star. |
| Equinox | March 21 and September 22. On these dates, day and night are the same length of time all over the world. |
| Sunspots | Dark patches on the sun's surface. |

Now that you're familiar with some of the terms you may see on the ASVAB relating to astronomy, let's talk about some specific concepts you should be familiar with.

## Planets

Nine planets make up our solar system. They are most commonly listed in order, starting with the closest planet to the sun: Mercury, Venus, Earth, Mars, Jupiter, Saturn, Uranus, Neptune, and Pluto. The easiest way to memorize a list like this is to use mnemonics, like "My Very Educated Mother Just Served Us Nine Pizzas." Some other facts you should know about the planets include the following.

- Mercury is the hottest planet, and Pluto is the coldest.

- Venus is the brightest planet viewed from Earth.

- Earth spins on a vertical axis (an imaginary line that connects the north and south poles). Uranus spins on a horizontal axis.

- Jupiter is the largest planet.

- Saturn is surrounded by rings made of dust, ice, and rock.

- Mars is known as "The Red Planet" and is known for having violent dust storms.

## Kepler's Laws of Planetary Motion

Johannes Kepler, a famous astronomer, created a set of laws that have proven applicable to all planets. They include:

- The planets move in elliptical orbits, with the sun at one focus. Essentially, this means that the planets circle the sun.

- An imaginary line joining the center of a planet to the center of the sun sweeps the same amount of space all the time. Picture a compass tool that you would use in math class. You open the compass, place the sharp point on the paper, and allow the attached pencil to touch the paper as well. When you spin the compass, the pencil draws a perfect circle. Kepler's second law is based on the same concept.

- The time it takes a planet to orbit the sun is based on how far away from the sun it is.

## Eclipses

These occur when our view of one object in the sky is blocked by either another object or the Earth's shadow. Eclipses come in two types:

- **Solar.** The moon appears between Earth and the sun, temporarily casting Earth in shadow. During a total eclipse, all you can see is a beautiful ring of light surrounding a blackened moon. It is dangerous to look directly at a solar eclipse, even with sun glasses. Solar eclipses are best viewed through a pin-hole projector.

**Solar Eclipse**

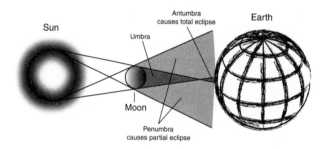

Not to scale

- **Lunar.** During this magnificent scientific event, the moon passes behind Earth, which blocks sunlight from the moon and casts it in shadow (called an umbra). Lunar eclipses can last as long as an hour and a half, and actually cause the moon to appear red. For all of you stargazers, it's perfectly safe to view, since the moon does not create its own light.

**Lunar Eclipse**

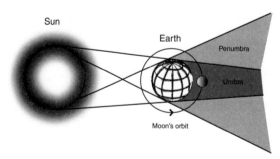

Not to scale

# Physical Science Review

Physical science examines the nonliving systems found in natural science. Two examples of this include chemistry and physics. Let's discuss a few of the basics from each of these disciplines.

## Chem Lab

Chemistry is the study of matter, which is anything that has mass and volume. Most often, chemists study substances that are considered microscopic, such as atoms, the states of matter, and chemical reactions. Consider a few basic facts regarding each of these chemistry subtopics.

### Atoms

This is the basic unit of matter. Atoms have three primary components:

◆ **Protons.** These are the positively charged particles in an atom. They actually comprise the nucleus; different atoms have different numbers of protons, which make up the atomic number or charge of the atom.

◆ **Neutrons.** Much like the root indicates in the word *neutron*, neutrons are the particles that have no charge in the atom—they are neutral. However, neutrons have a major affect on the mass and radioactivity of an atom. All atoms have neutrons (with the exception of hydrogen). An atom with the same number of protons and neutrons is called an ion.

◆ **Electrons.** These are the negatively charged particles surrounding the nucleus of an atom. They are the smallest part of the atom, and their purpose is to balance the positively charged protons.

The number of protons and neutrons an atom has determines whether it is an element (more protons than neutrons) or an isotope (more neutrons than protons).

### Element

This word describes a chemical substance that can't be separated into simpler parts by chemical means. Elements you might be familiar with include oxygen, hydrogen, copper, and aluminum. All of the known elements are listed on The Periodic Table of Elements and are classified according to atomic number and atomic weight. It's a good idea to memorize the symbols for common elements when you prep for the ASVAB. A great interactive tool for exploring elements is the Elements Database (www. elementsdatabase.com/).

### Compound

A compound is created when two or more elements are combined or bonded. For example, if you combine one atom of carbon (C) and two atoms of oxygen (O), you create the compound carbon dioxide ($CO_2$). The number of atoms is represented in the smaller number of the compound symbol.

### Molecule

Molecules are the smallest part of an element or compound. Their charge is neutral, and the atoms in a molecule are held together by chemical bonds.

### Matter

As we said earlier, matter is anything that has mass and volume. Therefore, it is all around us. Despite this all-encompassing definition, matter can be categorized into the following states:

◆ **Solid.** These are hard, closely packed molecules, capable of holding their own shape. In the case of water, an ice cube is a solid.

◆ **Liquid.** This is an in-between state of matter, between a solid and a gas. It does not hold its own shape; it takes the shape of the container in which it's placed. Water is an example of a liquid.

◆ **Gas.** Gases are random groups of atoms; they are spread out, bouncing around and full of energy. Water vapor, or steam, is an example of a gas.

◆ **Plasma.** This is similar to a gas, but different in the sense that plasma has free electrons and ions. Plasmas are super-excited and hot. You don't find plasmas occurring naturally very often (except in stars), but they are commonly found in fluorescent lightbulbs, neon signs, and most modern televisions.

◆ **Bose–Einstein Condensates.** This is a relatively new state of matter discussed in the scientific community, and may or may not be included on the ASVAB. What you should know about it is that the atoms here are incredibly unexcited and cold. When they reach the temperature "zero Kelvin," all molecular activity stops. Scientists have discovered that as they raise the temperature of the atoms by a few billionths of a degree, the separate solid atoms will clump together and become one super atom. In scientific terms, this is called a blob. Well, maybe that's not the scientific term, but it is the best description for this new state of matter.

## Chemical Reactions

These occur when two or more molecules interact and some kind of chemical change happens as a result of that interaction. Though this action may cause change (the reaction), the molecules involved remain the same. The creation of compounds is a chemical reaction. Perhaps you've heard what happens when you combine hydrogen and oxygen: with the right number of molecules, you get a substance called water!

## Physics Lab

If you're contemplating a career in the service, you've no doubt already considered a lifestyle defined by structure, rules, and laws. Physics, which is the study of force and motion, also operates by a variety of laws. This section should be a comfortable fit for you, then, scientifically speaking! Many key concepts in physical science (including Newton's laws) are further detailed in Chapter 15, but some additional ones you should familiarize yourself with include the following:

◆ **Speed.** Distance traveled in a given time period. For example, a car might travel 50 miles per hour, or 50 mph.

◆ **Velocity.** The rate of motion in a specific direction. Velocity is measured in distance (such as kilometers) per time frame (such as seconds or hours) in a given direction. For example, a car might travel 35 kilometers per hour in a northern direction (35 km/h north).

◆ **Acceleration.** The rate of change in velocity of an object. If an object changes its velocity by the same amount each second, this is known as constant acceleration. When the rate of acceleration is variable, it is known as nonconstant acceleration. Constant acceleration would take place if a car increased directional speed by 5 miles per hour every second. The acceleration would be constant at 5 mph/s.

On the other hand, if the car gradually increased speed, allowing for slow drivers and lane changes, the acceleration might vary from second to second. It would be nonconstant, with 5 mph/s the first second, 2 mph/s in the next second, 6 mph/s after that, and so forth.

◆ **Friction.** Two objects rubbing against one another, sometimes resulting in a force that holds back movement of a sliding object. For example, sandpaper on wood creates friction as it smoothes the surface of the wood. The brakes on a car apply friction to the wheels, slowing them down.

◆ **Momentum.** The mass of an object multiplied by its velocity. For example, a fire engine might have a mass of 14,000 kilograms and a velocity of 20 meters per second heading west on the interstate. The momentum of the fire truck, then, would be 280,000 kg-m/sec. Fast!

◆ **Gravity.** A force of attraction between mass and the universe. The strong force of gravity on Earth pulls everything toward the center of the planet. For this reason, no one falls off the round world as it spins and rotates.

◆ **Force.** Any influence that can cause a change in the velocity of an object. Have you ever heard someone say, "Boy, the force of the wind out there was really strong today"? Wind can be a force against a variety of things, such as a sailboat or a vehicle. Wind can cause a sailboat to change directions, slow down, or speed up. Forces are measured in Newtons using the following formula: Force = Mass × acceleration.

◆ **Work.** A force that is applied to one object and results in either the movement of that object or a transfer of energy to an object. We perform work when we lift an object, type on the keyboard, wash vegetables for dinner, and so forth. To calculate work, use the following formula: Work = Force × distance. Work is measured in joules, a basic unit of energy.

Let's say you use your strong muscles and apply a force against the leg press machine of 10 Newtons. In fact, you are so strong that you push the weights 2 whole meters! Plug these numbers into the previous formula to find that your leg press results in 5 joules of work.

We know better than anyone that all this information is a lot to take in. Heck, we wrote it! But the best way to assimilate this into your brain is to attack actual questions. Flip ahead to Chapter 17 to practice answering General Science questions.

# Chapter 12

# Electronics Skills

## In This Chapter

◆ Why you're tested on this

◆ What to expect on this section

◆ Review of key electronics concepts and theories

As we progress through the age of information technology, it has become almost essential for the average person to be computer literate, capable of telecommunication, and cyber-connected from all over the world. Modern jobs depend on these skills in both the civilian sector and the military community. Even the ASVAB exam you're prepping for is graded electronically—including the paper and pencil version!

Our world has become so dependent on electronics that we probably can't imagine a day without using something electronic, even if it's just a lightbulb. Electronic technology has enhanced the quality of our lives in many ways. Consider these interesting stats:

◆ The average American household owns 25 electronic devices, including cordless phones, cell phones, DVD players, desktop and laptop computers, and the like.

◆ Americans pay $212 billion in electrical bills every year.

◆ American homes waste more than $13 billion in energy every year.

These little tidbits of trivia remind us that electronics are an integral part of our lives. Likewise, they are a fundamental component in the modern military; your score on the electronics subtest will indicate whether a career in electronics would be a good fit for you. This chapter reviews the terms and theories often seen on the Electronics Information (EI) subtest, which will help you prepare for a variety of questions.

# Why Do I Have to Take This?

Often soldiers are portrayed as camouflage-clad warriors who crawl around in the dirt, run through jungles, and scale rough terrain in search of the enemy. Well, this depiction is certainly true—but it is only one piece of the modern soldier's composition.

These days, the military is equipped with some of the most technologically advanced equipment in the world. Infantrymen have night-vision goggles and global positioning systems, pilots have heat sensors and lasers to guide missiles, musicians have professional sound and recording equipment, and so on. There is even such a thing as an unmanned vehicle that can detect sniper location and mortar fire, and then fire back accordingly.

True enough, all this information is interesting—but what's the point? Well, here's the deal: military technology can only help accomplish the mission when the service members know how to use, maintain, and repair it. This is where people with electrical aptitudes and knowledge come in.

As with most jobs in the military, you don't have to be a civilian electrician to become one in the service. You simply have to demonstrate an initial propensity for that type of work by scoring well on the electronics subtest of the ASVAB.

Much like the correlation between civilian auto mechanics and military mechanics, electricians have skills that carry over from one sector to the other, too. This makes a military career in electrical work that much more desirable, because your marketability after service is fantastic. Plus, you'll receive training and gain experience on Uncle Sam's nickel, so to speak!

> **Classified Intel**
>
> Dozens of jobs in the electronics field require knowledge similar to that of an electrician: heating and air-conditioning technicians, refrigeration mechanics and installers, line installers and repairers, electrical and electronics installers and repairers, electronic home entertainment equipment installers and repairers, and elevator installers and repairers.

Civilian electricians perform a variety of tasks, including drilling holes; setting anchors; measuring, fabricating, and attaching conduits; creating and drawing diagrams for entire electrical systems, and more. In the military, electronics knowledge and skills are extremely valuable and offer you the opportunity to work in areas that simply aren't accessible to civilians.

Consider the following:

- With the Navy's state-of-the-art ships, highly technical submarines, advanced aircraft, and cutting-edge weapons systems, electronics are an integral part of nearly everything the Navy does.

- The Air Force uses incredibly technical equipment, performing nuclear treaty monitoring, nuclear event detection, and avionics that preserve our nation's security.

- The Army has always been a forerunner in the field of simulation-based training, offering some of the most advanced flight simulators in the world.

- The Coast Guard has used technology in their own right to save lives, enhance law enforcement techniques, and modernize telecommunications at sea.

- The Marines have advanced combat operations through the development of software-based systems that target information sharing and increase the speed of network communications.

If you decide to pursue a degree when your service is over, the coursework you completed can transfer into college credits within a network of more than 1,800 colleges nationwide. You'll also receive extensive on-the-job training with communications systems and highly sophisticated computerized equipment.

In short, scoring well on the electronics section of the ASVAB is your key to an exciting career that's loaded with military excitement and civilian job growth later.

# What to Expect

The EI subtest gives you about 30 seconds to answer each question. The CAT consists of 16 questions that must be completed in 8 minutes, and the PAP gives you 9 minutes to answer 20 questions.

But here's the good news: these questions are designed much like the questions on the science subtest—either you know the answers or you don't. There's one clearly defined right answer—nothing abstract, and no need for extensive logic or reasoning.

You'll be asked to apply your knowledge of electronic terms and concepts to questions regarding basic electricity, wiring, and electrical systems. More specifically, you should be familiar with circuits, voltage, and grounding. You'll also see questions on amplitude and frequency, sound waves, inductors, and AM radio signals.

Your best bet for excelling on this subtest is to implement one of the military's favorite phrases: attention to detail. The Army used to employ this terrific little expression as a training tool to "help" soldiers "learn" from their mistakes in basic training.

In fact, just to be sure the soldiers remembered this key piece of advice, it was drilled into them as they executed dozens of push-ups! The drill sergeant would yell, "Down!" As the soldier completed the downward motion of the push-up, he (or she) yelled, "Attention to detail!" On the up command, the punishment—er, *learning*—continued as soldiers yelled, "Teamwork is the key!"

So use this fun (but true) anecdote to your advantage. Find a buddy and study the information presented in this chapter. Pay close attention to details, remember the terminology, and look for root words on the test that you're already familiar with. Adhering to these steps will go a long way toward helping you earn the score you want on the EI subtest.

# Super-Charged Electricity Review

When it comes to the language of electronics, the following table defines a few terms you should know before you go any further.

## Must-Know Terms

| Term | Definition |
| --- | --- |
| Electricity | Flow of electrons through a conductor, such as copper or aluminum wire |
| Conductor | A material through which electricity can pass |
| Current (I) | Flow of electricity through a conductor |
| Ampere (A) | Measure of current |
| Insulator | Something through which electricity can't pass |
| Voltage | Strength with which current flows through a conductor |
| Volt (V) | Measure of voltage |
| Resistance | Hindrance to electric flow |
| Ohm (Ω) | Measure of resistance |
| Power (P) | Amount of energy transferred during a specified time |
| Watt (W) | Measure of electric power |

In the sections that follow, we break down electricity into four simple topics: current, voltage, circuits, and Ohm's law.

## Electricity 101

To explain electricity, we should really start with square one: matter, atoms, and electrons (okay, squares one, two, *and* three!). Do those terms sound familiar? They should, if you've read this book in chapter order. If not, flip back to Chapter 11 and take a minute to brush up on these concepts. They provide the foundation for basic electricity principles.

Electrons carry a negative charge with them wherever they go—you might say they never leave home without it. If a bunch of them all head out in the same direction, *bang!* You've got electricity.

> ### Classified Intel
>
> If you lined up a million electrons "shoulder to shoulder" (so to speak), they would barely stretch across the top of a pin!

Here are some interesting facts that demonstrate just how amazing electricity is:

- Electricity travels 186,000 miles per second. That's eight times around the world in a single second!

- To light a 100-watt lightbulb, it takes 6 zillion electrons.

- Water is a good conductor of electricity. The human body is made up of 60 percent water, so if you touch electricity, expect a very unpleasant reaction. At a minimum, you will probably experience a simple shock; at worst, death.

- Electricity always takes the shortest path to the ground. As a conductor of electricity, you should take care not to touch anything

connected to electricity. Touching a tree with a fallen power line resting on it could be fatal.

## A Current Affair

As electrons move together, they create something known as an electric current. To make electricity useful for human purposes, we capture the flow of negative electrons using a conductor.

> ### Heads-Up
>
> Conductors include almost any metal, such as iron, gold, silver, copper, or mercury. Most household wiring uses copper and is covered with an insulator, such as rubber, to make handling such wires possible.

To understand the concept of flow, picture two funnels. The first funnel has a very wide spout, allowing a great amount of water to pass through at one time. The second funnel has a very narrow spout, enabling only a sliver of water to pass through. If you placed the two funnels side by side and poured water into them, you would see far more water per second passing through the larger-spouted funnel than the smaller-spouted one.

Using the same concept, some household appliances require more current than other appliances. For example, hair dryers and microwaves need more current than nightlights and alarm clocks. Current is measured in amperes (or amps, for short).

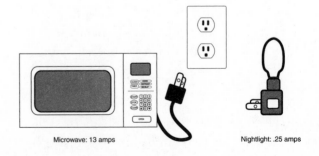

Microwave: 13 amps          Nightlight: .25 amps

## Crank Up the Voltage

If you want to know how much electrical force a power source applies, you're looking for the voltage. Think of this as the amount of force pushing the current through a conductor. If you pushed the water through the smaller funnel spout discussed earlier instead of just letting it flow naturally, you would increase the speed and force at which it exits the funnel.

Currents flowing from a power source, such as the electric company, a gas-powered generator, or a battery, operate much like the water in the funnel spout. Each produces and sends out a certain amount of voltage, which pushes current along a conductor at a certain rate.

Voltage in the United States is fairly standard for most homes. Household fixtures (such as lamps, televisions, and vacuum cleaners) typically run on 120 volts; some larger appliances, such as ranges and air conditioners, need 240 volts.

## Testing All Circuits

As electrons flow through wires or other types of conductors, the path they take is called a *circuit*.

## def•i•ni•tion

A **circuit** is a system of connected conductors that direct the path of electricity.

The circuit is functional only if a source of electricity is present to push the electrons along their path. That's why a hair dryer cord (or any other cord) is completely harmless—and useless—when it's not plugged in. Some of the most common electricity sources include batteries, wall outlets, and solar panels.

As long as electrons are able to move along their desired paths, the circuit is complete. A complete circuit may also be referred to as closed. An easy way to remember this is that *complete* and *closed* both start with the letter *c*. As soon as you turn off that hair dryer, light, or other electrical appliance, though, you have stopped the circuit. When the electrons stop moving, the circuit is called open.

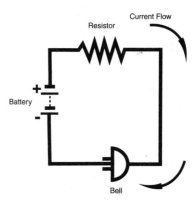

**Simple Circuit**

A basic circuit, such as the one shown, starts with a power source that generates a negative electric current, which then flows through a conductor until it meets a positive charge that closes the circuit. Along the way, it can meet resistors, loads, or other components that can change the path and properties of the energy. These can include the following:

- **Diode.** Allows current to flow in only one direction. (We discuss diodes in detail later in the chapter.)

- **Capacitor.** Acts as a filter in a circuit, either passing or blocking different voltage levels.

- **Fuse.** Prevents a circuit from overloading due to too much current.

- **Wire.** Medium through which current travels in a circuit.

- **Switch.** Opens or closes the circuit.

- **Battery.** Type of power source in the circuit.

- **Transformer.** Transfers electricity from one source to another.

- **Resistor.** Provides resistance to the current flowing through a circuit.

- **Aerial.** Produces or receives electromagnetic waves. Can also be called an antenna.

- **Amplifier.** Increases current or voltage.

- **Lamp.** Turns electrical energy into light energy.

- **Motor.** Turns electrical energy into kinetic energy.

When you see movement from positive to negative on a circuit diagram, you're seeing the flow of current. Electrons, which carry electric energy, move from negative to positive in a circuit. In other words, current and electrons actually flow in opposite directions.

But not all currents flow the same way. Alternating current (AC) and direct current (DC) describe the two types of currents that flow from sources of power. AC flows in both directions, reversing itself multiple times per second. It is commonly used by the power company for industrial and domestic customers alike. DC current travels in only one direction: from power source to destination. Batteries are a common example of DC current.

Since we're discussing direction of current, let's talk about diodes for a second. You can compare this component to the arrow signs that indicate a one-way street. Traffic responds to the sign by flowing in only one direction on a one-way street, which helps limit excess movement of cars, trucks, and other vehicles.

Likewise, a diode allows electrical current to flow in one direction but blocks it from traveling in the opposite direction. Most diodes are made of silicon and have a variety of functions. For one thing, they can be used as light sensors and emitters called light emitting diodes (LEDs).

Diodes can also convert AC current to DC current in a process known as rectification. The alternator in your car (which uses the energy produced from your engine to charge your battery) is a good example of a diode that converts AC to DC.

Now that we know *how* electric current flows through a circuit, you may be wondering *what* uses all this electricity. If you've spent any time with an electrician or if you've done electrical work yourself, you may have heard the term *load*. A load is anything that uses the electricity from a circuit. Have you ever had to replace the heating element in your oven or, better yet, changed a lightbulb? Heating elements, lightbulbs, and motors are all examples of *loads*.

## def•i•ni•tion

A **load** is part of a circuit that converts one type of energy to another (for example, electric to kinetic energy). See Chapter 15 for more information about energy.

When planning a circuit or learning how one works, schematics are usually involved. This is a technical way of mapping out all the parts in a circuit using commonly accepted symbols. The following diagram illustrates common symbols used in circuit schematics.

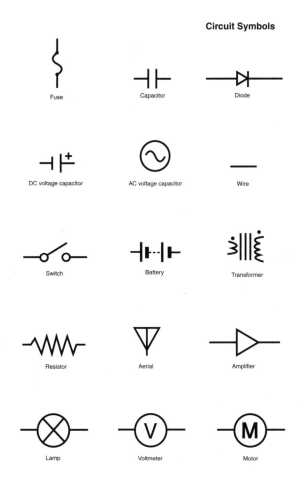

**Circuit Symbols**

Fuse · Capacitor · Diode

DC voltage capacitor · AC voltage capacitor · Wire

Switch · Battery · Transformer

Resistor · Aerial · Amplifier

Lamp · Voltmeter · Motor

For the purposes of passing the EI section of the ASVAB, you should know about these two main types of circuits, which are diagramed here using some of the symbols we just showed you:

◆ **Series.** A circuit that provides a single-flow path. Think about strings of lights in which, if one bulb goes out, the whole string does.

**Series Circuit**

◆ **Parallel.** A circuit that provides several flow paths. These are the strings of lights that don't drive you nuts when a single bulb goes out.

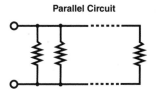

**Parallel Circuit**

Before we wrap up our discussion on circuits, we need to discuss resistance. As the name implies, resistance is anything that impedes the flow of a current.

When current moves freely, it is said to have low resistance. The amount of resistance in a wire depends on its *gauge*, length, and composition.

## def•i•ni•tion

Wire thickness is called **gauge**. Gauge is expressed in reverse of what you might expect: a large wire has a small gauge, and a small wire has a large gauge. The larger the gauge, the higher the resistance.

Good conductors of electricity offer low resistance. One example is copper, which most modern homes are wired with. Resistance causes friction, which causes heat. The higher the resistance, the hotter a wire can get.

Have you ever touched the plug on your hair dryer or portable heater after it's been in use? It's so hot that it can actually burn your skin—so we don't recommend trying this little experiment at home! Resistance is measured in ohms, which leads us to our next topic: Ohm's law.

## The Zen of Ohm's Law

With a basic understanding of voltage and current, you can understand how all of this is applied. Ohm's law is a good place to start because it defines the proportional relationship among currents, voltage, and resistance within a circuit.

Ohm's law states that electric current is directly proportional to voltage—the higher the voltage, the greater the current. It also states that electric current is inversely proportional to resistance—the higher the resistance, the lower the current. To find out how much current you have, you divide the voltage by the resistance.

You can express Ohm's law in a number of different ways. Understanding this concept will likely get you through several ASVAB questions on this subtest. Memorize these simple equations and use them to calculate any of the following.

## Related Ohm's Law Equations

| Value Sought | Equation | Translation |
|---|---|---|
| Ampere (A) | $A = \dfrac{V}{\Omega}$ | amps $=\dfrac{\text{volts}}{\text{resistance}}$ |
| Watts (W) | $W = V \times A$ | watts = volts × amps |
| Voltage (V) | $V = A \times \Omega$ | volts = amps × ohms |
| Ohms ($\Omega$) | $\Omega = \dfrac{V}{A}$ | ohms $=\dfrac{\text{volts}}{\text{amps}}$ |

Since formulas can feel a bit abstract, let's practice some ways you might apply these equations on the test, so you get a more concrete idea of what to expect.

1. You're building a circuit that has a voltage of 240. You add a resistor of 60 ohms. What is your amperage?

    (A) 4A
    (B) 6A
    (C) 8A
    (D) 10A

This question is asking you to calculate amperage. Using Ohm's law, you divide your voltage (240) by your resistance (60) and come up with answer A (4A).

2. What would your power be if you have 2 amps and 120 volts?

    (A) 40W
    (B) 120W
    (C) 240W
    (D) 360W

This question is asking you to find the wattage, which is a measure of power. If you know that your voltage is 120V and your current is 2A, you can determine that your power usage is 240W, choice C. (P = 120 × 2)

3. How many volts would you need to complete a circuit with 50 amps of current and 10 ohms of resistance?

    (A) 300V
    (B) 600V
    (C) 500V
    (D) 1,200V

Since you're being asked to find voltage, use the voltage equation here and multiply your amps by your ohms, giving you 500 volts, choice C.

Now that you understand the difference in ohms, volts, and watts, you should familiarize yourself with the following related terms. EI subtest questions asking for these definitions have been known to pop up:

◆ **Ohmmeter.** Measures resistance

◆ **Voltmeter.** Measures differences in voltage

◆ **Wattmeter.** Measures power

◆ **Ammeter.** Measures current

# Ups and Downs of Frequency and Waves

In addition to the basic concepts regarding power and electricity, the ASVAB asks questions pertaining to frequency, waves, and principles thereof. The following sections will get you up to speed in each of these areas in no time.

## Frequency Explained

Frequency is an important electronic concept that can be applied in a variety of situations. Remember our discussion a few pages back about alternating current? Well, frequency applies to electric power, because AC current has a specific number of cycles per second, known as *frequency*.

## def•i•ni•tion

> **Frequency** is a measure of any periodic event expressed as the number of complete cycles per second. This measurement applies to AC power, waves (sound, light, electromagnetic, and the like), computer clock speed, and so forth.

Frequency is measured in Hertz (Hz), after the German physicist Heinrich Hertz. He was the first scientist to prove the existence of electromagnetic waves. In the United States, our AC current has a frequency of 60Hz. When there are fewer cycles per second, the frequency is said to be lower. Other developed countries run AC power on either 50Hz or 60Hz.

To envision frequency, it may help to picture a wave that looks like the letter *S*, rotated 90 degrees. If you measure the full shape of the *S* from beginning to end, you have calculated one oscillation. This is known as 1Hz of frequency.

Another way to measure frequency is to divide the number of times an event occurs by the amount of time given. Your frequency is then

$$\frac{\text{Times Event Takes Place}}{\text{Amount of Time Elapsed}} \cdot$$

To understand frequency better, imagine the Marine Corps physical fitness test. During the abdominal crunch event, each soldier must complete as many crunches as possible (using proper form) in 2 minutes. Let's say that Private Johnny completes 100 crunches in 2 minutes, earning the maximum score possible for this event. His frequency would be 0.83Hz per second.

## Ride the Waves

A wave is a disturbance that is transmitted through space and time. It usually includes a transfer of energy as well. There are water waves in the ocean, light waves from the sun, sound waves from noise, and so forth.

Waves come in a variety of shapes and forms. The three most common types of waves include transverse, longitudinal, and surface waves:

- **Transverse waves** cause particles in the medium where the wave is located to travel in a perpendicular direction to the wave itself. Examples of transverse waves include radio, heat, and light waves.

- **Longitudinal waves** cause particles in the medium to move parallel to the wave direction. A sound wave is a good illustration of this. For example, the medium may be a room, a concert hall, an outdoor venue, or even a car in which a sound is located. The particles that vibrate in the room are air particles, and they move alongside the sound wave.

◆ **Surface waves** cause particles in the medium to move in a circular direction. Ocean waves exemplify this principle, as do certain types of seismic waves (which can cause earthquakes).

Several characteristics can be universally applied to all waves:

◆ **Reflection.** This is a change in wave direction after it strikes a reflective surface. A mirror is a good reflective surface for light waves. A reflective surface in acoustics might be a wall or a rock, which then causes echoes.

◆ **Refraction.** This is a change in wave direction because of a change in the wave's speed from entering a new medium. A good example of refraction is when you place a straw in a glass of water. Under the water, the straw appears to be broken. The water is considered the new medium, which caused the light wave speed to change once the straw entered the water.

◆ **Diffraction.** This is the bending of waves as they interact with obstacles in their path. A good example of this occurs with sound waves. If you and your friend are having a conversation outdoors and, for some reason, you step behind a tree while she is talking, you can still hear her voice.

The sound waves bend around the tree, such that if you keep backing up behind the tree, eventually the sound of her voice will be no different than if the tree wasn't even there. This is because the wavelengths begin to even out again as they get farther away from the obstacle. Diffraction also tends to be more pronounced with longer wavelengths, making it easier to hear low frequencies (such as the booming bass from a car driving by) than high frequencies (such as the guitar or vocalist in that car).

◆ **Interference.** This is when two waves come into contact with each other and collide. Have you ever tried to use a walkie-talkie or handheld radio, and you could actually hear someone else's conversation? Or maybe you had a baby monitor for a sleeping child, and you heard a lot of static coming through the speaker. These are both examples of interference in sound waves, which tend to occur when two things have the same frequency.

◆ **Dispersion.** This occurs when a wave splits up by frequency. A rainbow is a great example of dispersion of light waves. The white light is scattered into different wavelengths of various colors.

◆ **Rectilinear propagation.** This is the movement of waves in a straight line. Even if you throw a rock into a pond and bend the front of a wave, though, the wave is still moving in a generally straight line.

As we mentioned in our discussion of frequency, waves are often depicted in a never-ending letter *S* shape, rotated 90°. Three types of measurements are important to know for the ASVAB:

◆ **Wavelength.** Measures the distance from one peak or crest of a wave to the next corresponding peak or crest.

◆ **Wave speed.** Multiply the wavelength measure by the frequency.

◆ **Amplitude.** This measures the height of a wave. It's calculated by slicing a line down the middle of the *S*. You then measure from the midline to the top of a crest to determine amplitude.

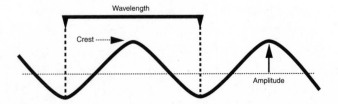

# Finishing Touches

As we wrap up our discussion on electronics, here are a few last tips for the ASVAB. Some of the questions may ask you to define acronyms that you are familiar with, even if you don't actually know what each letter stands for. After you get rid of any answer choice that does not start with the same letters as the acronym, eliminate any others that don't make sense for the subject you're working with.

**Test Tip**

Remember your root word and prefix breakdowns from Chapter 5. They still apply, even to electronics.

Also, if you're not sure about the meaning of a word or term, look to the roots of the words to get a clue about their meaning. For example, if you are asked a question about bipolar junction transistors, take the first word apart and look for prefixes or root words that you are familiar with. *Bi* means "two," as in *bicycle* (two wheels) and *biannual* (twice per year). *Polar* means "opposite," as in the north and south poles. In the case of electronics, it refers to positive and negative charges or flows of electricity.

You also know that the word *junction* refers to a place where two roads meet. In electronics, it is a place where two wires meet, or where two devices with different electrical properties meet. Thus, if all you knew was that *bi* means "two," polar means opposite, and junction is a meeting place, you could figure out this electrical definition.

You could also pick it out graphically using the same basis of knowledge. Just look for a picture that has two lines that meet and look like a sideways *T*; this represents the junction. Then look for two lines coming out of the sideways "t," one of which probably has an arrow on it. The two lines coming from

the junction will be going in different directions, representing the "bi" and "polar" aspects of the question. And there you have it!

Using the knowledge you gained through this chapter, as well as the rest of the book, should position you to do well on this portion of the ASVAB. Now flip ahead to Chapter 17 and test your knowledge on some practice questions.

# 13

# Auto Information

## In This Chapter

- ◆ Why you're tested on this
- ◆ What to expect on this section
- ◆ Basic auto systems and how they work

*"It takes 8,460 bolts to assemble an automobile and one nut to scatter it all over the road."*
*—Author unknown*

Cars are such amazing machines; they're built from hundreds of parts, all beautifully crafted and designed to work in perfect harmony with one another—until one poor decision is made by the driver, that is. That beautiful piece of machinery can suddenly become a 2,000-pound battering ram.

This is a risk the military can't afford to take, which is why the ASVAB has a section that tests aptitude for Auto Information (AI). Throughout this chapter, we discuss the function of several key systems in the modern automobile, as well as the importance of proper maintenance and repair. If you didn't start this book as an auto enthusiast or car buff, we're about to change that for you!

## Why Do I Have to Take This?

People join the military for all kinds of reasons. One of the biggest advantages to joining the service, however, is the ability to gain training and experience in the career of your choice, at no cost to you.

If you enjoy doing physical work more than sitting at a desk, the automotive field might be a good choice for you. This field has excellent transferability to similar civilian professions when your tour of duty is over, such as automotive and heavy equipment mechanics, auto and construction equipment dealers, and so forth. With automotive skills, you might also work in farm equipment companies or for state highway agencies.

The first step, though, is getting the training and experience you need in the military. To accomplish this goal, you need to score well on the Auto Information (AI) subtest of the ASVAB. As with all the technical subtests, this exam area helps recruiters determine which jobs will fit well with your particular skill set.

Auto mechanics and heavy equipment repair technicians are a critical cog in the wheel of the military. They transport the troops safely in and out of battle, ensure the replenishment of necessary supplies, and keep military operations mobile.

---

### Classified Intel

Gen. George Washington once said, "There is nothing so likely to produce peace as to be well prepared to meet an enemy." In the modern military, this means maintaining mechanized equipment so that it functions properly on a moment's notice.

---

## What to Expect

This particular subtest is designed a bit differently than the other sections of the ASVAB. First of all, it is much shorter than most of the other tests. The CAT has only 11 questions, and you'll have 7 minutes to answer them.

Secondly, the PAP combines automotive skills with the Shop Information subtest, asking you to answer a total of 25 questions on both subjects—in just 11 minutes. Regardless of which test version you take, your auto and shop skills are combined for scoring purposes under the AS category.

As in the other technical sections on the ASVAB, you'll be able to put your life experiences to the test here. Most of the questions address basic maintenance and terminology associated with cars, which means that even someone without a formal automotive education might have some basic knowledge as an owner/operator.

And there are plenty of car owners in the United States. Just a few short years ago, America had the most vehicles in total and *per capita* in the world! In 2008, we slipped a little in the rankings down to the number two spot. Still, with so many cars in the United States, most of us know something about how they work.

The other thing to keep in mind before you take the ASVAB is that some questions may not even require specific automotive knowledge. You may encounter a question or two that asks you to use a multistep process to figure out what happens next. The idea is to use logic and an understanding of the steps to arrive at a conclusion.

You will probably also find a lot more questions that use diagrams, asking you to identify parts of the illustration. Regardless of how the question is structured, though, the next few pages will help you prepare for anything that comes your way on the automotive subtest!

## Things That Make You Go Vroom

If you've read *The Pocket Idiot's Guide to the ASVAB* (see Appendix C), you may remember some of these automotive basics:

- The brakes make the car slow or stop.

- The battery supplies power for certain functions, like starting the car, using the radio, and unlocking the doors.

- The exhaust system takes excess gases from the engine and releases them into the air.

- The suspension system deals with the movement of the wheels and how the car reacts to terrain.

- The engine runs on gasoline (or diesel) and needs oil to keep all its moving parts working properly.

- The electrical system makes the lights and power systems work.

- You need coolant to keep the engine temperature at a certain level.

These are greatly simplified ways of describing a complex marriage of systems that rely on each other to make a vehicle move efficiently and safely. Automakers have radically simplified the driver's role in the maintenance, upkeep, and running of our cars. In most cases, we turn a key, fill up the tank, change the oil and tires … and that's it. That's all the labor and responsibility involved in using and enjoying our favorite 2-ton toy.

Considering how quick and painless maintaining a car nowadays is, it's quite amazing when we consider what goes on under the hood.

# Engine Basics

The engine is the heart of your car and the most important component for making it go. In fact, all of the other power-train systems, such as the ignition, electrical, fuel, and cooling systems (which we discuss in the coming sections), all work in conjunction to make sure the engine can do its job: providing the energy to propel the car forward.

Most engines and fuel systems operate using a four-stroke combustion cycle called the Otto Cycle to convert gasoline to motion. The four strokes include the following:

- Intake stroke

- Compression stroke

- Combustion or Power stroke

- Exhaust stroke

In order to explain the four-stroke combustion process, let's first consider the Army's push-up process. To properly execute a push-up, the solider must start in the "up" position. This means that the body is in a generally straight line parallel to the floor with arms extended, hands placed flat on the floor, and feet together or up to shoulder-width apart, without sagging or flexing in the middle.

When the "down" command is given, the soldier lowers his or her body until the biceps are parallel to the ground. The body must move in one fluid motion and remain in a generally straight line. It doesn't require too much muscle or effort to go down.

When the "up" command is given, the soldier must use more energy to push him- or herself back up in one fluid motion. At this point, one full push-up has been completed and the soldier is ready to do as many additional push-ups as the drill sergeant requires!

The four-stroke combustion process is very similar, but instead it takes two whole push-ups to equal the motion in one complete cycle of a four-stroke engine. Consider the following illustration of an engine.

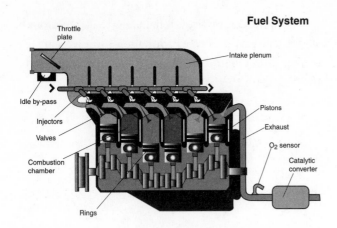

**Fuel System**

Throttle plate

Intake plenum

Idle by-pass

Injectors

Valves

Combustion chamber

Pistons

Exhaust

O₂ sensor

Catalytic converter

Rings

The *piston* starts the cycle in the top position. When the intake valve opens, the crankshaft moves the piston down so that the engine can pull a full cylinder of gas and air into the combustion chamber. This step is known as the intake stroke.

## def•i•ni•tion

**Pistons** are cylinders in an engine that fit tightly into larger cylinders and move under pressure created by the explosions in the combustion chamber.

When the crankshaft pushes the piston back up, this compresses the fuel-and-air mixture. This step is known as compression, which makes the imminent explosion more powerful. When the piston arrives all the way at the top of its stroke, the spark plug emits a spark to ignite the gasoline. Once the gasoline ignites, it explodes, which drives the piston back down. The explosion is the combustion step.

As the piston rises once again, it pushes the exhaust valve open, which enables the excess gasses to exit via the tailpipe. We explain more about this final step when we discuss the exhaust system, later in the chapter. But first, let's look at the other power-train systems that enable the engine to complete the process we just explained.

# Ignition and Starting Systems

The purpose of the ignition system is to create a spark that will ignite the fuel–air mixture in the cylinder of an engine. Timing is everything, as they say. The spark must occur at exactly the right instant, and must reoccur several thousand times per minute for each cylinder in the engine to run properly.

A simple version of an ignition system may look something like this:

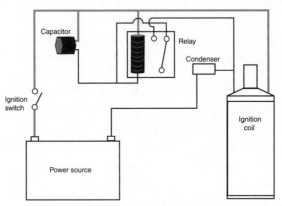

**Ignition System**

Capacitor

Relay

Condenser

Ignition switch

Ignition coil

Power source

The ignition and starting systems work together to start your car. Starting old and new cars alike involves the following steps:

1. Turning the key to the first position activates the ignition.

2. Power transfers from the battery through the ignition switch to the ignition coil, which sends power to the distributor (if present) and spark plugs.

3. When you turn the key to the next position, you engage the solenoid, a relay that powers the starter motor and turns electrical energy into mechanical energy.

4. Once engaged, the starter motor causes the fly wheel on the engine to turn, which also moves the engine's crankshaft.

5. Rods connected to the crankshaft move the pistons inside the engine up and down.

6. The piston movement draws in air and fuel (regulated by the fuel system).

7. The ignition system ignites the air–fuel mixture on the engine's combustion stroke, which we described already in the "Engine Basics" section.

Keep in mind that this overview is a very simplified version of what occurs during the ignition process. There are several other key components involved that you should be aware of, including spark plugs, the battery, the ignition coil, and the distributor (or coil pack). Depending on which ignition system your car has, these parts will vary in composition.

Modern cars use three types of ignition systems. The first of these can be found in cars that were made before 1975, called mechanical ignition systems. They did not use electronics at all and, therefore, are not installed in modern cars.

The second type of ignition system is called an electronic ignition system. This design took over for its mechanical predecessor in an attempt to respect emission control regulations in the 1970s and '80s. It also offered better control and reliability.

The third type of system (which is still in use today) is called the distributorless ignition system. As evidenced by its name, this design eliminated the use of distributor caps. It became available in the mid-1980s, and thus far, it offers the greatest reliability and the least maintenance.

## Traditional Ignition Systems

In older cars that use the mechanical or electronic ignition systems, key components include the following:

◆ **Spark plugs.** Traditionally, the spark plugs received the battery's voltage through an ignition coil. As the battery power traveled through the coil, it intensified exponentially to ignite the air–fuel mixture. In a split second, the 12 volts from the car's battery would be converted to more than 20,000 volts for the spark plugs!

---

### Classified Intel

We know that spark plugs ignite little explosions inside an engine. But did you know that it's at a rate of over 4,000 explosions per minute for a four-cylinder traveling 50 miles per hour?

---

◆ **Battery.** The battery supplied a car with the initial source of energy.

◆ **Ignition coil.** The ignition coil was essentially an electrical transformer. After the voltage was converted, it was directed to the spark plugs through the distributor.

◆ **Distributor.** The distributor, which had a replaceable cap and rotor, took the current from the ignition coil and sent it to the spark plugs within each cylinder of the engine via a spark plug wire.

## Distributorless Ignition Systems

Now let's examine a few key components to the modern distributorless system:

◆ **Spark plugs.** Newer spark plugs are made to last up to 100,000 miles and require less tension than their predecessors. They can also receive far more volts (closer to 50,000) than earlier plugs, resulting in a hotter spark.

◆ **Battery.** Batteries have changed very little over the years. Power from the battery travels to the ignition switch and is held back until you activate the ignition with your key. Then the power flows through the ignition switch to the lights, the ignition coil, the solenoid, and any electrical accessories (like your radio).

◆ **Ignition coils.** The single ignition coil has been replaced by a system of coils in newer cars.

◆ **Coil pack.** In place of the distributor, there are multiple coils; each coil serves one or two spark plugs. A typical six-cylinder engine has three coils that are mounted together in a coil "pack." Each individual coil has a spark plug wire coming out either side, connecting the coil to the appropriate spark plugs. The coil fires both spark plugs at the same time.

## The Ignition Switch Connection

Everything in your car that uses electricity to run is connected to the ignition switch. In most cars, this small device acts as an intermediary between the battery and the rest of the car's electrical components (which we tell you all about in the next section).

Once the car is started, the alternator takes over and uses the energy generated by your engine to recharge the battery. When the alternator stops working properly, the battery doesn't get charged, and what you may have suspected to be a dead battery is actually a bigger problem—bad news for your checkbook!

## Electrical System

A car's electrical system consists of a battery, starter, solenoid, alternator or generator, voltage regulator, and fuse panel (box). The purpose of this system is

to provide the initial source of power to the ignition system and to provide continuous power to all your car's accessories, such as the radio, air conditioning, headlights, defroster, windshield wipers, and the like.

**Test Tip**

Over the years, the electrical components of a car have become increasingly prevalent, sophisticated, and complex. Understanding the basics of this system is a must for the ASVAB.

Let's examine this system in more detail. Check out our diagram of a basic electrical system, and then read about its main components next.

**Electrical System**

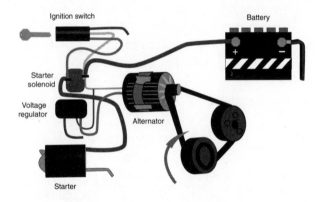

◆ **Battery.** The primary purpose of the battery is to start the engine (see our earlier discussion on starting and ignition systems). The battery also provides 12 volts of power to the electrical accessories of the car when the engine isn't running or when it's idling. Auto batteries have six cells that are stacked with positive and negative lead plates; these plates store the energy needed to accomplish all the battery's tasks.

◆ **Solenoid.** A key component in the ignition system, the solenoid is sometimes referred to as a starter relay. The reason for this nickname is that the solenoid operates much like a relay runner, whose job is to pass the baton to the next runner in the race. The solenoid receives a sizable electric current from the battery and a small electric current from the ignition switch. Upon receipt of the current from the ignition switch, the solenoid knows to pass the battery's current on to the starter.

♦ **Starter.** This small electric motor consumes the greatest amount of power in the whole electrical system. Its main job is to start the combustion process in the engine by turning the crankshaft.

♦ **Alternator.** The main role of the alternator (or generator in older vehicles) is to charge the battery. The alternator is connected to the engine by a belt, which is where it receives the necessary power to charge the battery. In so doing, it helps to power all the electrical devices in the car.

♦ **Voltage regulator.** This part does exactly what its name implies: it maintains the proper voltage level for the electrical system. It helps eliminate power surges, spikes, and brownouts, which can harm the car's electronic devices. If you've ever experienced a power surge at home, maybe during a thunderstorm, you know how damaging they can be. Many newer cars house these regulators inside the alternators, although some American models and older cars have an exterior design.

♦ **Fuse panel.** Much like the circuit breaker or fuse box in your home, the fuse box in a car helps control the function of things like headlights, dashboard lights, radios, clocks, and so forth. Fuse boxes are usually located near the bottom of the dashboard or under the hood.

## Fuel System

This is undoubtedly the system that the average driver deals with the most often. Every time we fill up the gas tank, we are working with a key component in the fuel system: gas. The main purpose of this system is to store and supply fuel to the combustion chamber in the engine, where it combines with air, vaporizes, and then burns to give the engine energy.

**Heads-Up**

If this is starting to sound familiar, we've already described some of this in our "Engine Basics" section. Make sure you go back and review the diagram in that section when studying the fuel system.

Until the day that cars are completely free of fuel requirements, though, it is important to understand how this system works. A few key components you should become familiar with include fuel, fuel pumps, fuel filters, and fuel injectors (or carburetors in older cars).

## Fuel

This usually comes in two forms: gasoline or diesel. Fuel gives the car motion. Cars are typically equipped with one of two engine types: a diesel engine, which uses diesel fuel; or an internal combustion engine, which uses gasoline.

Both engines are considered internal combustion engines, which means that the fuel is burned inside the engine. When the fuel is ignited inside the engine, an incredible amount of energy is released in the form of expanding gas. The two main types of fuel include:

♦ **Gasoline.** A complex blend of hydrogen and carbon, with additives mixed in to improve performance. It burns more cleanly than diesel fuel, but gas engines are typically less efficient than diesel engines.

◆ **Diesel fuel.** This is also a combination of carbon and hydrogen compounds that requires additives for performance. However, diesel fuel vaporizes at a much higher temperature than gasoline, gets better gas mileage, and is more dense than gasoline.

Fuel is stored in a tank, where it stays until the fuel pump siphons it out and brings it to where it's needed.

## Fuel Pump

Older engines were often built without this key component, relying on gravity to carry the fuel to the engine via a hose. However, in designs that don't utilize gravity, fuel pumps are essential.

These pumps feed fuel to the engine from the fuel tank. In older cars that used carburetors, the fuel pump had a mechanical design and was usually mounted outside the fuel tank. In newer cars with the higher-pressure fuel injection system, the fuel pumps tend to be electric and are mounted inside the fuel tank.

## Fuel Filter

These devices filter out dirt and rust particles in the fuel before they reach the engine. They are usually made of cartridges with filter paper inside, similar to the paper used in coffee filters. Fuel filters are found in most modern vehicles; they improve engine performance by allowing it to burn cleaner fuel.

## Fuel Injector

This part consists of a nozzle and a valve; it mixes fuel with air inside the internal combustion engine. Unlike carburetors, which use a low-pressure system to mix fuel with intake air, fuel injectors forcibly pump fuel through a small space under high pressure. Fuel injectors began replacing carburetors in the late 1980s.

## Exhaust System

The purpose of the exhaust system is to direct exhaust gas away from the controlled combustion inside the engine. It is also designed to reduce the noise of the engine, maintain performance, and reduce or eliminate harmful emissions.

Whew! That's quite a job description! The exhaust "team" has a few key "players," which vary depending on the size and style of the vehicle. A basic exhaust system may look something like this:

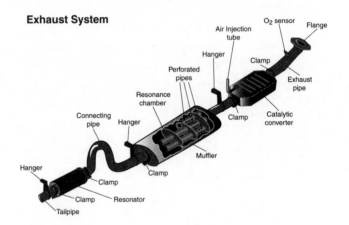

Some of the most common parts include an assortment of pipes, a muffler, a resonator, and a catalytic converter.

## Pipes

Many pipes carry out exhaust functions. Some of these include the following:

◆ **Exhaust pipe.** The exhaust pipe transports the gases and vapor away from the engine farther down the exhaust system.

◆ **Intermediate pipe.** This connects the exhaust pipe with the muffler or resonator, whichever comes first. The main function is to help silence exhaust noise, but not all cars have this pipe. Sometimes this pipe is referred to as an extension pipe or connecting pipe.

- **Tailpipe.** This is the last step in the exhaust process, guiding gases out and away from the vehicle. It's usually at least a foot long (if not longer), to help prevent gases from reentering the inside of the car.

## Muffler

The main job of the muffler is to silence exhaust gas noises. Essentially, it absorbs and dissipates noises while continuing to move the exhaust gases on their way out the tailpipe. Mufflers are typically located near the rear of the vehicle and tend to be round, oval, or even custom shaped.

## Resonator

This is a second silencing part that may be found on some cars. It is usually used when a standard muffler won't fit on the undercarriage of the car. If a smaller muffler doesn't adequately control noise, another silencer is added to "finish the job."

## Catalytic Converter

This is a simple device created in the 1970s to control the emissions of a car. Cars mostly emit nitrogen gas, carbon dioxide, and water vapor. Most modern cars are built with three-way catalytic converters to help control emissions of all three of these gases.

## Cooling System

Although many of the systems in our cars have changed over the years (particularly through the age of technology), the cooling system has evolved very little from the original design used in Ford's Model T.

Almost 100 years later, most cooling systems still circulate liquid coolant through the engine and back out to the radiator, where it is cooled by the air blowing through the front grill of the vehicle.

There are actually two types of cooling systems used in cars: liquid cooled and air cooled. The latter of these is less common and is occasionally found in older vehicles. For the purpose of this exam, we discuss the liquid-cooled systems.

---

### Classified Intel

The inside of an engine's combustion chamber can reach temperatures that exceed 4,500° Fahrenheit. No wonder engines need a cooling system to keep things from overheating!

---

Several key components allow the cooling system to do its job, including a water pump, the engine passages through which the liquid travels, a radiator, a radiator cap, and a thermostat. These components help maintain homeostasis in the engine, regardless of the outside air temperatures. (Remember the term *homeostasis* from Chapter 11?)

- **Water pump.** The water pump provides the pressure needed to circulate coolant through the cavities of the engine.

- **Passages in the engine.** Liquid coolant travels through the engine block and heads, picking up heat from the engine. As it exits the hot engine, the coolant travels through a rubber hose connected to the radiator.

- **Radiator.** The radiator reduces the temperature of the coolant after it exits the engine. It consists of a parallel network of small tubes through which the hot fluid flows. This fluid faces the front grill and a fan system that forces cool air through the radiator, helping to cool the fluid.

- **Radiator cap or pressure cap.** As the coolant picks up heat from a 4,500°F engine, it becomes very hot and expands. If the coolant gets too hot, it runs the risk of boiling; the radiator cap is therefore needed to maintain pressure in the cooling system, which raises the boiling point of the water. The excessively hot liquid takes up more space than the system can hold, so it is released into a reserve tank until it is cool enough to return to the engine. This mechanism helps keep the pressure within the system at the right level, prevents hoses and other parts from bursting, and is known as a closed cooling system.

♦ **Thermostat.** Much like your home has a thermostat to control the air temperature, a vehicle has a thermostat to help control the temperature of the engine. It is located between the engine and the radiator, and it functions by opening and closing a valve to regulate the flow of coolant to the engine. Ideally, the thermostat doesn't allow too much coolant through, so the engine can heat up sufficiently for the vehicle to function properly; at the same time, it pushes enough coolant through so that the engine doesn't overheat.

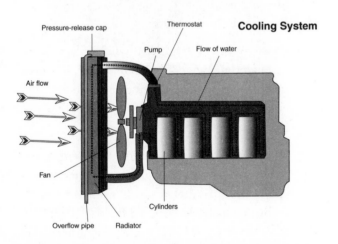

**Cooling System**

Pressure-release cap
Thermostat
Pump
Flow of water
Air flow
Fan
Cylinders
Overflow pipe
Radiator

Now that we've taken you through each of the main systems that support your car's vital functions, it's time to move on to the systems that keep everything together.

# Brakes

In the 1970s and 1980s, a lot of detective shows on television featured an episode in which the villain tampered with the hero's brakes. The result was usually a nearly fatal accident, which made for good drama.

Fortunately, the reality is that brake failure accounts for only about 5 percent of motor vehicle fatalities in the United States each year. Still, many of us tend to take for granted the fact that our brakes will work whenever we need them.

Generally, modern cars are designed with front-wheel disc brakes and rear-wheel drum brakes, so it's important to know how both work.

## Disc Brakes

This type of brake relies on friction and heat to slow a vehicle. Although the same principle applies to drum brakes, disc brakes are considered superior in design and operation. They have a reduced chance of overheating, tend to be more responsive than drum brakes when applied hard, and offer better performance in wet weather. These advantages come at a cost, though.

Disc brakes are more expensive than drums. Let's take a moment to examine their components: brake pads, rotors, and calipers.

♦ **Brake pads.** These are metallic blocks that apply friction to both sides of the disc brake. (Newer-style pads can also be made from ceramics and other materials.) Brake pads have a little metal clip that scrapes against the rotor when the pads are getting worn and need to be replaced. The sound of metal scraping on metal is an easy indication that it's time to perform maintenance on the brake system.

◆ **Rotors.** These are made of machined steel and are mounted to the hub. The hub allows the car to turn and the wheels to spin.

◆ **Calipers.** This is the part that houses the brake pads; they are mounted so that they straddle the rotor. The caliper contains at least one piston. When you press the brake pedal, hydraulic pressure (fluid power) is exerted on the piston, which then forces the pad against the rotor. Friction between the pads and the rotors (which are sometimes referred to as discs) causes the car to slow down.

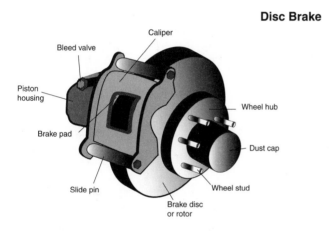

**Disc Brake**

## Drum Brakes

These brakes function similarly to disc brakes, even though they tend to be slightly less effective. The parts of a drum brake include a backing plate, brake shoes, a brake drum, and a wheel cylinder.

◆ **Backing plate (or mounting plate).** This is where each of the drum elements is attached.

◆ **Brake shoes.** These can be functionally compared to the brake pads from the disc system. The main difference is that, whereas the brake pads are flat, the shoes are curved and push out instead of in. Like disc brakes, drum brakes have a small metal clip to alert the driver that the shoes are getting worn and should be replaced.

◆ **Brake drum.** This is a hollow metal cylinder that's attached to the wheel. It fits snugly around the brake shoes so that when the shoes press against it, the resulting friction slows the vehicle.

◆ **Wheel cylinder.** This is located at the top of the backing plate. It houses two pistons, one on either side. When you step on the brake, hydraulic fluid forces each piston out of the cylinder.

The pistons are slotted at the end so that the shoe fits into their groove. When you take your foot off the brake, they are then retracted by a set of springs into the cylinder so that they're ready to perform the whole process all over again.

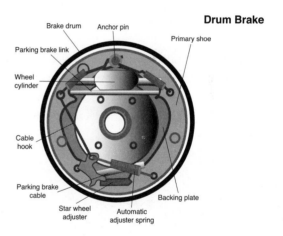

**Drum Brake**

## The Emergency Brake

The emergency brake (or parking brake) controls the rear brakes through a series of steel cables that the driver operates via a hand lever or foot pedal. Emergency brakes are considered secondary braking devices in terms of design and safety. That is, if the *hydraulic system* of the front and rear wheels fails, a mechanical emergency brake can bypass the failed system to stop the vehicle.

Visit science.howstuffworks.com/hydraulic.htm for an animated explanation of hydraulic systems.

# def•i•ni•tion

Hydraulic system refers to the transfer (and often the increase) of force between points via some type of fluid that can't be compressed. Oil is a common fluid used in hydraulics.

Drum emergency brakes have two main components:

- **Braking cable.** This circumvents the wheel cylinder and controls the brakes directly by pushing the rear shoe against the drum.

- **Rear shoe.** This is quite a bit larger than the front shoe in the drum brake. It engages the drum and eliminates its ability to turn.

Cars with disc brakes on the rear wheels have additional components in an emergency brake and are designed in one of two ways:

- Using an existing rear-wheel caliper, a lever is added to a mechanical corkscrew device inside the caliper piston. When the driver engages the parking brake, the brake cable pulls on the lever. The corkscrew device then pushes the piston against the pads, thereby stopping the vehicle mechanically.

- The other emergency brake system for rear-wheel disc brakes uses a mechanical drum brake unit that is mounted inside the rear rotor. Here the brake shoes are connected to a lever that is pulled by the parking brake cable. Once again, the vehicle is able to stop mechanically rather than hydraulically as the lever pushes the shoes against the drum unit.

Often drivers choose not to use parking brakes on vehicles with automatic transmissions. The problem with this is that lack of use can cause the parking brake cables to become corroded and eventually inoperable. Occasional use helps the cables stay clean and functional.

# Suspension

The suspension system includes the various components that connect a vehicle to its wheels. A lot of people talk about suspension when they talk about how well a car rides. A good system does the following:

- Makes for a smooth ride by minimizing road noise, bumps, and vibrations

- Contributes to the car's handling and braking

- Protects the car from damage and wear and tear

To accomplish all these goals, automakers have to strike just the right balance within the various components of the system. One of the ways they accomplish this is by maximizing the friction between the tires and the road surface. When your car hits a bump, the wheel that hit the bump experiences vertical acceleration as it moves up and down.

Without suspension, the wheel can lose contact with the road completely, only to slam back down moments later because of gravity. Suspension helps absorb the energy of the vertically accelerated wheel, maximizing tire friction on the road and minimizing passenger discomfort.

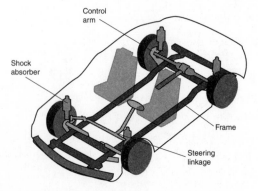

**Car Suspension**

Control arm

Shock absorber

Frame

Steering linkage

Let's take a moment to discuss some of the main components found in a suspension system:

- **Shock absorber or damper.** As the name implies, the shock absorber helps smooth the jolt of a bump and absorbs the energy created by that bump.

- **Control arm.** Triangular in shape, the control arm pivots in two places, to manage the motion of the wheels.

- **Frame.** This supports the car's engine and body and is a key structural element of the car.

- **Steering linkage.** This is a series of arms, rods, and ball sockets that allow the wheels to swivel when the driver turns the steering wheel. As a result, the car is able to turn.

- **Springs.** There are several different types of springs in the suspension system, including coil springs, leaf springs, torsion bars, and air springs. Generally, their purpose is to absorb the motion of the wheels.

- **Antisway or stabilizer bars.** These help prevent a car from rolling during a sharp turn.

## Types of Suspension Systems

There are two main types of suspension systems: front wheel and rear wheel. Each of these can be further categorized as dependant or independent.

- **Front wheel dependent.** In this design, the front wheels are connected by an inflexible axle, forcing them to move in unison. Although these are still commonly found in trucks, they haven't been used on cars in decades.

- **Front wheel independent.** This design was developed in 1947 and allows the wheels to move *independently* of one another—hence the name. This is the most common front-wheel suspension system for cars.

- **Rear wheel dependent.** Similar to the dependent front-wheel suspension system, a solid axle connects the rear wheels in this design.

- **Rear wheel independent.** This construct is similar to that of the front wheel independent system, but it is a simplified version. In rear wheel independent systems, there is no steering rack. (The steering rack enables the wheels to turn from side to side and is unnecessary in the back.)

Some cars have specialty suspension systems, such as Formula One racers, hot rods (built between the 1940s and 1960s), Volkswagen Baja Bugs, and so forth.

Cars are incredibly complex, intricate machines that you could spend months—even years—studying. Hopefully, however, our condensed review has simplified a few of the major systems every car has. For more information, see *The Complete Idiot's Guide to Auto Repair* (see Appendix C), and don't forget to check out the practice questions in Chapter 17.

Chapter **14**

# Shop Skills

## In This Chapter

- Why you're tested on this
- What to expect on this section
- Review of basic tools

Have you ever toyed with the idea of woodworking or carpentry? What about some minor home repairs or decorating projects? If any of these ideas have ever struck your fancy, here are a few fun facts about carpentry that you might get a kick out of:

- The word *carpenter* originates from the Latin word *carpentrius*, which means "maker of a carriage."
- Carpenter frogs were so named because of the hammerlike sound of their call.
- British and Australian carpenters are sometimes referred to as "chippies."
- Carpenter ants are very social, strong, hard-working creatures.
- The German word for *carpenter* is *zimmermann*, which literally means "room man." More loosely translated, it means "room-maker."

All fun aside, this chapter is designed to cover some shop basics so that you'll be well prepared for the ASVAB. Take a few minutes to familiarize yourself with the terms in this chapter, and you'll be on your way to an excellent technical score for this subtest!

## Why Do I Have to Take This?

If you've spent any time in the civilian workforce, chances are, you've read a job announcement or two. Perhaps you've seen one that looks something like the following.

Local company seeks a full-time carpenter for its business. Duties include general carpentry work, including cabinetry installation, laminate countertop repairs, ceramic tile, drywall, door repair, and minor painting. Must be willing to assist in other general carpentry work. Possible temporary-to-hire position. Full-time hours. Must have 5+ years of carpentry experience and high attention to detail.

No matter how tight the job market is at any given time, you can usually be sure that employers will want a few years of experience. If that's not enough, the qualifications keep expanding, the requirements for each job are loaded, and there is little job security.

But here's the good news: there is one employer with locations all over the world who wants to hire people with *no* experience, pay a reasonable salary, offer incredible benefits, and train employees to do the kind of work they enjoy! This is no joke—we're talking about the U.S. Armed Forces, of course.

While it's certainly true that there are sacrifices and great commitments required of military service members, the opportunities are vast. Using the same example of the carpentry field, check out the job description for a Carpentry and Masonry Specialist in the Army:

As a Carpentry and Masonry Specialist, you'll perform general heavy carpentry, structural steel, and masonry duties. Some of your duties as a Carpentry and Masonry Specialist may include:

- Fabricating, erecting, maintaining, and repairing rigging devices, trusses, and other structural assemblies

- Replacing in building layout, framing, sheathing, fabricating and roofing structures

- Performing basic carpentry and masonry skills

- Repairing and constructing all types of structures

- Assisting in the performance of combat engineer missions

- Constructing concrete form work for slabs, walls, and columns

Job training for a Carpentry and Masonry Specialist requires nine weeks of Basic Training, where you'll learn basic soldiering skills, and nine weeks of Advanced Individual Training and on-the-job instruction. Part of this time is spent in the classroom and part in the field. Some of the skills you'll learn are basic concrete technology, concrete materials and proportioning, concrete control tests, proper use of finishing tools, placing, consolidation and finishing, edging, jointing, curing and protection, basic structure forming, basic roofing, and basic flooring.

Helpful attributes include a preference for working outdoors, an ability to use hand tools, a preference for doing physical work, and an interest in science and math.

The skills you learn as a Carpentry and Masonry Specialist will help prepare you for a civilian career in commercial and residential construction. You'll be able to consider a future as a mason, carpenter, cement mason, concrete finisher, drywall installer, or ceiling tile installer (www.goarmy.com).

Did you notice the similarities between the two jobs? Many of the tasks were the same, and there was quite a bit of variety in both jobs.

The differences were also fairly obvious. The military is looking for people who have an interest in carpentry, not necessarily an acquired skill. That's why it's important to brush up on the technical skill sections of the ASVAB. Scoring well on the technical subtests is the first step in securing the job of your choice in the military.

More specifically, a good score on the Shop subtest is critical if your dream job involves any type of hands-on building or repair work. In this chapter, we "talk shop"—literally, that is. If either of the previous job announcements caught your interest, this is definitely a chapter you'll want to spend some extra time with.

## What to Expect

The Shop Information subtest won't take up too much of your time on the CAT version of the ASVAB. You'll be asked only 11 questions, and you'll have 6 minutes to choose your answers. The score you receive from this section is called Shop Information, or SI.

Once you've completed the entire ASVAB, your SI score is combined with your Auto Information (AI) score. On your score report, your line score will be labeled AS, which indicates your combined Auto and Shop scores.

On the PAP, the Shop and Auto subtests are already combined in one section, giving you the combination AS score right off the bat. Because the two subtests are already joined on the PAP, you will have a total of 11 minutes in which to answer 25 questions about both subjects.

The great part about this subtest is that you can rely heavily on practical knowledge rather than book knowledge alone. Even if you're not a carpenter by trade, you may have performed some minor home improvement projects, such that you have a basic awareness of shop tools. Or maybe you've watched someone else do this kind of work enough to be familiar with some fundamental terms, like a

Phillips head screwdriver, a circular saw, or a drill. Either way, some of the information the ASVAB tests will likely be familiar to you, especially if you're a do-it-yourselfer.

You will also find that diagrams are sometimes used to communicate test material, which is particularly helpful if you are a visual learner. You will see similar diagrams throughout this chapter. Let's begin our review of some basic hand tools and power tools now.

## Basic Hand Tools Review

Hand tools have been around since the dawn of civilization. In fact, archeologists in Kenya have found tools that are estimated to be more than 2.6 million years old! If time is a testament to quality, it's safe to say that hand tools have proven their worth over the millennia.

Here's a brief list of some popular categories of tools that have made their way to some ASVAB exams.

> **Test Tip**
>
> If you'd like to get real-life examples of any of the tools described in the following sections, visit the Agricultural Technology Information Network website at www.atinet.org/atinetscripts/slides/ShowAll.asp?ShowID=5, for a comprehensive list of shop tools, descriptions, and photographs.

### Shaping Tools

These tools are used to contour objects, usually wood or metal. They are designed to make curves, incisions, scores, and other intricate forms. Consider a few examples of some of the most common shaping tools.

◆ **Plane tools.** Plane tools are used to flatten, smooth, and narrow the width of wood. Two specific types of planes are the jack and block planes. A jack plane is typically used for smoothing the edge of wood and/or reducing its size. When the jack plane is used on the edge of wood, it tends to have a curved blade.

Conversely, a straight-bladed jack plane is generally selected for smoothing wood joints. A block plane is an ideal general-purpose type of plane. It is small, can fit into tight spaces, and is used to trim wood edges and joints as well. The versatility of this tool makes it useful for home improvement projects and carpenter's work alike.

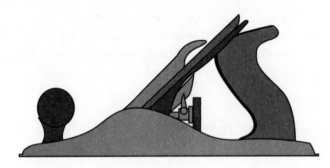

Jack plane

◆ **Chisels.** These tools are highly versatile and do not have a comparable counterpart with power. They are essential in joint making, boat building, timber framing, and dozens of other applications. Although there are numerous different styles of chisels, the basic design remains the same for all: on one end of the chisel is a wood or metal handle that the operator holds on to when shaping the wood. The other end of the chisel has a formed cutting edge with a blade.

The person using the chisel either uses the strength of his or her own hand to push the chisel into the wood, or uses a mallet of some kind to strike the handle end of the chisel. With each pound, the blade of the chisel cuts into the wood.

Two examples of popular chisels include the wood chisel and the cold chisel. The wood chisel ranges in size from $\frac{1}{4}$ inch to 2 inches wide and is often used in such capacities as creating pockets for door hinges. The cold chisel, on the other hand, is generally used when cutting cold metals to remove waste metal. It is made of tempered steel and is not used in conjunction with torches or other heating devices—hence the name "cold" chisel.

◆ **File.** A file functions similarly to a nail file, even if the design is a bit different. Files can be used on wood, metal, or plastic and are employed to shape, trim, and smooth surfaces. Basically, a file is a hand-held steel bar that is covered with tiny ridgelike grooves. It is used after a saw to smooth out the rough edges, but before the sandpaper because it is not that fine of an instrument.

◆ **Rasp.** A rasp is similar to a file but is designed strictly for wood. Rasps are generally larger than files, too, with more pointed ridges. These ridges are often referred to as "teeth" because of their size and sharpness. It, too, should be used in between the saw and the sandpaper steps.

## Saws

These are thin pieces of metal with jagged edges, used to cut through wood or metal. They usually have a wood or metal handle and can be operated using a back-and-forth motion. Numerous different types of saws exist, and while many people prefer power tools these days, hand saws still have a lot of value for woodworkers and carpenters. Some examples of common hand saws include the following:

◆ **Hack saw.** This tool is most commonly used for cutting metal or bone. It is designed such that a fine-toothed blade is held in place using tension and an arched metal frame. The handle is usually shaped like the grip of a pistol, and the blade is able to cut on both push and pull strokes.

- **Crosscut saw.** This type of saw is best used for cutting wood against the grain, and is comprised of a blade and a handle. The blade usually has 8 to 15 teeth per inch, with alternating cutting edges. There are two common tooth styles found on the crosscut saw—one is known as the Tuttle style, and the other is called the Champion. Generally, the Tuttle style works best on hardwoods because of the tooth design. The Champion, on the other hand, is ideal for cutting softwoods.

- **Miter saw.** Although there are some exceptional powered miter saws, this hand tool still brings a lot to the table. Also known as a miter box, this saw is ideal for making angled cuts, such as those on a picture frame. It consists of a small hack saw that is guided and steadied by a framework that helps the user make a perfect cut at the desired angle. Using a miter box is not only simple and efficient, but also less expensive than using its electric counterpart.

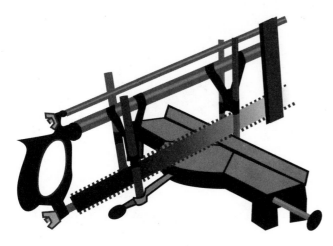

Miter saw

## Hammers

The hammer may be the most basic household necessity in terms of tools and is extremely versatile. What you may not have realized, however, is the vast number of hammer variations. Consider some of the most common hammer types:

- **Rubber mallet hammer.** The beauty of this tool is that it is able to withstand the effects of both water and oil, giving the user more freedom of application. The rubber mallet features a nonmarring rubber head, making it ideal in situations when a steel-head could damage the material being hammered into. It may be used on sheet metal, upholstery, plasterboard, and even toys!

- **Curved claw hammer.** When you think of a hammer, this is likely what you picture, as it's arguably the most common hammer. It consists of a rounded metal head on one side and a curved claw on the other that can be used for pounding *and* pulling nails in or out of wood. It is best used in conjunction with finishing nails, and generally ranges in weight from 10 to 24 ounces. Curved claw heads usually are made of carbon or cast steel, and feature handles made of wood, fiberglass, graphite, or steel.

- **Ball pein hammer.** This hammer looks similar to the curved claw hammer, minus the claw. In its place is a ball-shaped sphere of steel, as depicted in the hammer's name. It is most commonly used in construction projects, woodworking, and auto repairs. The spherical pein end of the hammer is sometimes used in conjunction with chisels or metal shaping.

Ball pein hammer

◆ **Engineer's hammer.** Some people refer to this hammer as a baby sledge, as it looks quite similar to the sledge, but smaller. It is usually used for demolition and weighs between 1 and 5 pounds. Because it is lighter and smaller than a sledge, it can be used in more confined spaces and offers better versatility. However, its weight enables the hammer to perform tasks that would be unwieldy for the smaller carpenter's hammer.

◆ **Tinner's hammer.** This type of hammer is designed for machinists to drive rivets into sheet metal. The face of the hammer head is usually flat and octagonal in shape, while the pein across from the head tends to have a sharp, beveled edge. In fact, the cross pein almost resembles the end of a chisel. Handles are usually made of wood, for a comfortable grip.

## Screwdrivers

These common shop tools come in many different shapes, sizes, and styles. A screwdriver is used to manually twist a screw into a piece of wood, plastic, or metal. Generally, the purpose is to fasten two materials to one another. There are two types:

◆ **Phillips head screwdriver.** This tool is a staple in most homes and in most industrial workshops. Why? Its pointy, tapered end with an *X* shape at the bottom makes it easier to connect the tip of the screwdriver with the head of the screw, particularly at awkward angles. The *X* shape provides more stability to the connection between screw and screwdriver, and makes turning the screw much easier. Therefore, Phillips head screwdrivers can only be used with Phillips head screws, which also has an *X* shape on top.

◆ **Flathead screwdriver.** This type of screwdriver has a single, flat end that fits into a slotted screw. On top of a flathead screw is a single groove into which the screwdriver fits. Unlike with the Philips head screws, connecting the tip of a flathead screwdriver in the proper spot on the screw can be difficult and the screwdriver can slip easily.

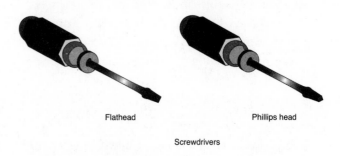

Flathead                          Phillips head

Screwdrivers

## Drills and Drill Bits

A drill is a tool with a rotating bit that is used for boring holes into certain materials. Although the power drill has largely replaced the hand drill, many woodworkers prefer to use a hand drill. Hand drills require very little maintenance but offer the operator total control.

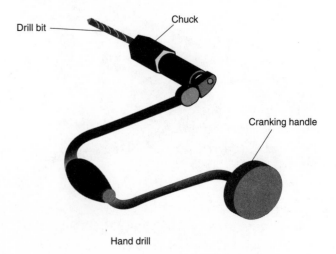

Drill bit          Chuck

Cranking handle

Hand drill

The three main parts of a hand drill include the chuck, the cranking handle, and the drill bit. The chuck is a clamping device that holds the drill bit in place; if it is too loose, the bit could slide out of the drill. The cranking handle turns the main shaft of the hand drill, to which the chuck and drill bit are attached. When the cranking handle is operated, the drill bit rotates and bores into the material that needs a hole.

The drill bit is a removable component that slides into the chuck and actually does the cutting. It comes in a variety of different sizes, depending on the size of the hole that's needed.

There are several different types of drill bits:

◆ **Auger bit.** This bit is specifically made for drilling large, deep holes in wood. Furthermore, it is best used in conjunction with the hand drill. The center point of the bit has small threads that help pull the bit into the wood. The rest of the bit has a spiral shape with chisel-like edges that cut the wood as the bit rotates.

◆ **Spade bit.** Typically, you use this bit when you need to make a larger hole than a twist bit will allow. The shape resembles a flat shovel with a point at the end. These bits may also be known as flat wood bits and, as evidenced by their pseudonym, are mostly used on wood.

◆ **Carbide-tipped masonry bit.** This type of bit is designed for use with brick, stone, quarry tile, or concrete. Because of the hardness of the surface that is being drilled, the masonry bit is rarely used in hand drills anymore. However, the tip of the bit is prone to overheating, so the slow rotational speed of a hand drill is sometimes more suitable for this type of bit.

◆ **Twist bit.** This is undoubtedly the most common type of drill bit for the average handyman or do-it-yourselfer. Twist bits are great for use on wood, metal, and plastics, and are generally made of high-speed steel or carbon steel. They can also be found less often in titanium nitride. Twist bits cut using the front edges of the bit and withdraw waste via the spirals.

◆ **Countersink.** This is used to create a hole in which the top part of the hole is enlarged. The purpose is to allow the head of a screw or bolt to lie flush with (or slightly below) the surface of the wood or metal.

## Wrenches

A wrench is designed to provide torque to tighten or loosen things like screws, nuts, and bolts. Wrenches come in a variety of types:

◆ **Open-end wrench.** This wrench is one that is most often depicted to symbolize tools of all kinds. It has an open end that is nonadjustable and fits around the right-size nuts and bolts. Because nuts and bolts come in so many different sizes, open-end wrenches come in a variety of sizes as well. This wrench design is quite versatile, though it sometimes causes slippage if the tool isn't exactly the right size for the job.

◆ **Combination-end wrench.** This wrench has an open design at one end with a box design at the other end. The box construct at the other end of the wrench is designed to slip vertically over the fastener, which means the wrong-size wrench won't fit. This reduces slippage and is an improvement over the side-access design of the open-end wrench.

◆ **Adjustable-end wrench.** Much like the name implies, the adjustable wrench is designed with a set of clamps at one end that can expand and contract with a simple screw adjustment. The wrench itself comes in many different sizes, ranging from 4 to 24 inches. It is the ideal tool for most bicycle repairs, as well as many other household and shop projects. The adjustable wrench should be operated using a pulling rather than pushing action, so as not to damage your hands or the edges of the nut to which the tool is clamped.

---

### Classified Intel

Adjustable wrenches are also sometimes referred to as crescent or spanner wrenches.

---

- **Pipe wrench.** This is actually considered a form of the adjustable wrench, but it is more specific in terms of its abilities and applications. This is a popular tool for mechanics, plumbers, and handymen, with adjustable claws on one end that allow it to grip different-size objects.

- **Allen wrench.** This is an L-shaped bar with a hexagonal head. It is used to turn Allen screws, which are commonly found in ready-to-finish or -assemble furniture.

- **Socket wrench.** Also known as a ratchet, this wrench uses separate, removable sockets to tighten different sizes of nuts and bolts. These wrenches are used in automotive repairs, as well as other household projects.

Adjustable wrench  Pipe wrench  Socket wrench  Allen wrench

Wrenches

## Clamps

These are very useful tools that are used to fasten an item in place or hold two objects together to prevent movement. There are several different types of clamps:

- **Hand screw.** Quite simply, this type of clamp tightens around an object using two long screws. The screws are rotated by hand, causing the jaws of the clamp to apply inward pressure to the object being held.

- **Pipe clamp.** This clamp holds a pipe in place so that the pipe may be cut, threaded, lifted, or suspended. The clamp itself is a metallic strap or band, and it is also used to stop leaks.

- **Bar clamp.** This clamp has adjustable jaws that are attached to a long bar. A screw mechanism tightens the large jaws, which are often used for wide-width projects.

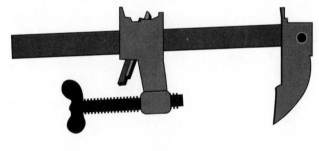

Bar clamp

- **Vise grip.** This is basically a large version of locking pliers. A screw or lever opens the large jaws, which are used in woodworking and carpentry projects.

## Power Tools Review

The military is a big proponent of the saying, "Work smart, not hard." In many instances, power tools have fit the bill with this old adage. Power tools are powered by an electric motor, a compressed-air motor, or, in rare cases, a gasoline engine.

Many of the tools we've discussed, such as wrenches and hammers, can only be found in the hand tool section of your hardware store. However, some shaping tools and saws have power counterparts:

- **Router.** This power tool cuts the surface of metal or wood and is usually used in the finishing stages of a project. It can smooth rough edges, buff surfaces, and sand wood.

- **Lathe.** Like a router, a lathe is a power shaping tool that can be used with either metal or wood. The item being cut rotates on the axis of the lathe, while the edge that needs shaping is pressed against a fixed cutting or abrading tool (often a chisel or sandpaper).

- **Power saws.** All kinds of power saws are on the market today, depending on the type of cut needed. Two examples of popular power saws include these:

    - **Circular saw.** This is one of the most common saws in use today. Depending on the blade it's equipped with, it can cut wood, steel, masonry, or ceramic tile. Its primary function is to make straight, continuous cuts.

    - **Jigsaw.** This type of saw does just the opposite of the circular saw. It is designed to make cuts in different directions and shapes. It has a narrow blade that moves vertically in a reciprocating motion and can make intricate cuts and curves.

- **Power drill.** Like the hand drill, power drills cut holes, but with far less effort than their nonelectric counterparts. Power drills also use removable bits in a variety of widths, depending on the size needed for the hole. Different kinds of drills include these:

- **Pistol grip.** Probably the most common, the pistol grip can be found in both corded and cordless varieties. It's typically used for standard projects, such as drilling holes in drywall to hang pictures, drilling through wood, and so on.

- **Hammer drill.** This drill uses an action similar to its namesake and is used most frequently in drilling masonry. A jackhammer is an example of a hammer drill.

- **Drill press.** This is a fixed tool that is typically either mounted to a workbench or bolted to the floor. Its main advantages are that it takes less human effort to operate, and the project can be more securely held in place during the drilling process.

Hundreds of tools out there can really make or break even the smallest project. Tools have not only simplified our lives, but they have also created the products we use every day. Understanding some basic hand and power tools will help you succeed not only on the ASVAB, but also at home. To test your knowledge of shop tools, turn to Chapter 17 for practice questions, answers, and explanations.

# Chapter 15

# Mechanical Comprehension

## In This Chapter

◆ Why you're tested on this

◆ What to expect on this section

◆ Review of basic mechanics

If you like solving problems, enjoy tinkering with broken appliances, or have ever had an inkling to become an engineer, you'll really find your stride with the Mechanical Comprehension (MC) section of the ASVAB. If not, hang in there anyway! Remember, military jobs are made up of a combination of ASVAB scores. You want to score as high as possible on every technical subtest so that you have the largest pool of jobs available to you. In this chapter, we help you review basic mechanical principles, theories, and applications that will help you get the score you're looking for.

## Why Do I Have to Take This?

As you are no doubt aware, the military has become increasingly reliant on electronic systems as the primary mode of doing business—even on the battlefield. As we discussed in Chapter 12, each branch of service needs skilled technicians to operate, maintain, and repair these systems.

Since the military is willing to train individuals to do a job, it's in their best interest to select the right personnel. In this case, that includes individuals who have the ability to learn the technical pieces of the job, as well as an ability to see the bigger picture in the absence of textbook methods or clearly assigned directives. This is where the MC section of the ASVAB comes in.

# What to Expect

One of the main reasons the ASVAB wants to test your mechanical comprehension knowledge is to determine whether you're capable of locating and repairing faults in electronic control systems. This is accomplished via fault-diagnosis questions, which tend to be abstract in nature. They require logic and an awareness of principles rather than straight mathematical calculations.

This skill is needed because electronic systems often provide very little physical evidence of the reason they are malfunctioning. In such a case, the process of elimination combined with logic is the best way to go.

The other tool that will help you ace this section of the test is basic terminology knowledge. All the mechanical intuition in the world won't help you if you don't know the language. We provide many of the fundamentals for you in this chapter.

The important point is not to feel intimidated or overwhelmed by the prospect of learning (or relearning) a few vocabulary words. You'll be required to learn a whole new language when you join the military anyway, so consider this practice for the real thing!

And keep in mind that if you're taking the CAT, you'll have to answer 16 questions in 20 minutes. On the PAP, you'll have 19 minutes to answer 25 questions. Let's get started with some of those mechanical terms now.

# Mechanical Basics

Like the military (and many of the subject areas you've already read about in this book), mechanical science has a language all its own. Some of these terms are quite simple, and even someone with no

scientific background would be able to identify them: *pounds, motion, speed, acceleration, force, energy, work, pressure,* and so on.

Familiarize yourself with the following terms:

## Must-Know Terms

| Term | Definition |
| --- | --- |
| Mass | The amount of matter an object has. Can be measured in kilograms. |
| Matter | Anything that occupies space and has mass. |
| Motion | Any object that changes distance over a period of time. |
| Speed | How fast an object is moving. |
| Velocity | Speed plus the direction of motion. |
| Acceleration | The rate of change in velocity; can be positive or negative. |
| Work | Transfer of energy through force over a distance. |
| Force | Something that changes an object at rest into an object in motion. |
| Energy | The amount of work a force can produce. |
| Potential energy | Stored energy; an object with the potential to do work. |
| Kinetic energy | Energy of motion. |

Now that you have a general idea of the topics we'll be discussing, let's dive into specifics.

# Energy Review

Energy has numerous forms, including kinetic, potential, gravitational, electromagnetic, chemical, elastic, thermal, sound, and light.

Whew! That's a long list, and it doesn't stop there! But don't panic: you only need to know the basics for the ASVAB. Besides, a few of the energy forms should sound familiar from our electronics discussion in Chapter 12. Let's take a look at two types of energy often seen on the ASVAB: potential and kinetic.

## Potential Energy

If you know what the word *potential* means, you're already halfway there when it comes to understanding this concept. *Potential* means having a latent possibility, a capacity to develop, or the ability to become something. Therefore, if an object has *potential energy*, it has the possibility and capability of becoming another kind of force, usually motion energy.

## def•i•ni•tion

> **Potential energy** is energy that is stored in an object. When it's released, potential energy converts to kinetic—or motion—energy.

The simplest example of potential energy occurs when you stretch a rubber band. If you hold the rubber band in the stretched position, it has potential energy, or the ability to do work. (We get to this later in this chapter.) When you release the rubber band, it goes flying across the room using motion energy.

A rubber band is also said to have elastic energy. Elastic energy is found in objects that can rearrange themselves and then restore their shape later. A spring is another example of elastic energy.

Another way of describing potential energy is as follows: it exists in any object with mass that's located in a force field. One example of a force field is a gravitational field.

Gravity is the force that makes objects fall to the ground. For example, the Earth exerts a natural force of attraction between it and objects near its surface, drawing them toward the ground like a magnet. With this in mind, you're now prepared to measure potential energy.

One way to determine the gravitational potential energy of an object is to multiply its mass ($m$) by the gravitational force ($g$) exerted on it and its height ($h$) above the Earth's surface: PE = $mgh$.

Keep in mind that gravitational force is always represented as 9.8 meters per second squared, or $9.8\frac{m}{s^2}$. Now consider this example:

If you have an object with a mass of 10 kilograms located 15 meters above the Earth, what is the object's potential energy?

Plug the numbers into the formula as follows:

$$PE = 10 \times 9.8 \times 15$$

$$PE = 1{,}470 \text{ joules}$$

You just calculated gravitational potential energy!

## Kinetic Energy

As we mentioned earlier, kinetic energy is also known as motion energy. Whenever an object is in motion, it is said to have kinetic energy.

Everything that we see moving has kinetic energy, as a matter of fact. A good example of kinetic energy involves hypothetically positioning a large rock at the top of a hill and giving it a shove. As soon as the rock started rolling downhill, it would begin converting its potential energy into kinetic energy. If the rock ran over some flowers, it would be "doing work" on the flowers by flattening them.

> ### Classified Intel
>
> To gain kinetic energy, you generally have to convert another form of energy to it. For example, if you go swimming in a pool, you're converting chemical energy to kinetic energy in order to achieve the swimming motion. This is because our bodies are powered by chemical nutrients known as chemical energy.

Kinetic energy, potential energy, and work are all measured in units called joules. To measure kinetic energy, you multiply the object's mass (in kilograms) by the square of its velocity ($v$), and then multiply that value by $\frac{1}{2}$:

$$KE = \frac{1}{2}mv^2$$

We discuss velocity in greater detail when we review motion. For the purposes of this equation, though, you should know that velocity is a measure of the speed and direction in which an object is moving.

Let's practice measuring kinetic energy using the following example:

Suppose you have a vehicle that weighs 200 kilograms. If the vehicle is traveling at a speed of 10 meters per second, how much kinetic energy does it possess?

The answer to this question can be computed as follows:

$$KE = \frac{1}{2} \times 200 \times 10^2 \text{ joules}$$

$$KE = \frac{1}{2} \times 200 \times 100 \text{ joules}$$

$$KE = \frac{1}{2} \times 20,000 \text{ joules}$$

$$KE = 10,000 \text{ joules}$$

Now consider this:

If you have another vehicle that weighs 300 kilograms moving at a speed of 6 meters per second, which vehicle has more kinetic energy? Use the same formula to determine the second vehicle's kinetic energy using the figures supplied in the example.

$$KE = \frac{1}{2} \times 300 \times 6^2$$

$$KE = \frac{1}{2} \times 300 \times 36$$

$$KE = \frac{1}{2} \times 10,800$$

$$KE = 5,400 \text{ joules}$$

Subtract the totals and you'll see that the first vehicle has more kinetic energy than the second.

# Work Review

Work and energy are inextricably intertwined. It should come as no shock, then, to hear that work is actually defined as a transfer of energy. More specifically, work is the amount of energy that is transferred through force over a distance.

To visualize the transfer of energy through force and distance, picture a tennis game. If you've ever played tennis, you know this is a good example of hard work!

The tennis player does work on the racket by swinging it. The energy is transferred from the athlete to the racket. Next, the racket does work on the ball and transfers energy to it. If the tennis player did enough work to start with, the ball will go flying over the net with enough force that the opponent will miss it!

If you want to measure work, you need to multiply force by distance: $W = fd$.

Let's use a simple example we're all familiar with to calculate this formula. Suppose you have to carry two heavy grocery bags from your car up to your apartment, which is 15 meters above ground level. If the bags weigh 20 kilograms each and the distance up to the apartment is 15 meters, then you are doing 600 joules of work:

$W = (20 + 20)(15)$

$W = (40)(15)$

$W = 600$ joules

What if you had only one grocery bag in your hand? With only one bag, your work would be cut in half:

$W = (20)(15)$

$W = 300$ joules

Likewise, the amount of work you perform is directly proportionate to the distance you have to travel. If your house is 30 meters above ground level and you are carrying one bag at a time, you'll be performing 600 joules of work:

$W = (20)(30)$

$W = 600$ joules

Even though you reduced your load by half from the original example, you still had to do the same amount of work because your distance doubled. Anyone who has ever carried heavy suitcases or bags a given distance can attest to this principle!

**Heads-Up** _____

Keep in mind that the examples we've used to calculate work are in the simplest form. Work is affected by a variety of other factors, including gravity, wind resistance, incline, and so forth. This formula should get you through most work examples you'll see on the ASVAB, though.

# Motion Review

Motion is simply movement of any kind. It could be something as large as a jet soaring through the sky or as small as a vibration generated by a single voice. To fully grasp the concept of motion, you need some knowledge of the law—Newton's law, that is!

Sir Isaac Newton is known to many as the greatest scientist in the history of the world—even greater than Albert Einstein! Born in the mid-1600s, Newton is also credited with completely initiating classical mechanics, optics, and even mathematics. But he's most well known for his laws of motion.

## Newton's First Law

Newton's first law is also known as the law of inertia. It states that objects tend to resist changes in motion. An object in motion tends to stay in motion, and an object at rest tends to stay at rest, unless a force is exerted upon it.

It's important to understand the difference between mass and weight. Weight, although similar to mass, measures the amount of gravitational force exerted on an object. If that force is altered—say, by going to the moon—weight changes. The mass of an object, however, is the same anywhere in the universe, regardless of gravitational pull.

To figure out the mass of an object, you multiply its volume ($v$) by its density ($d$): Mass = $dv$. To calculate weight, you multiply the mass ($m$) of the object by the _gravitational acceleration_ ($g$) exerted on the object: Weight = $mg$.

## def•i•ni•tion _____

Gravitational acceleration is the scientific name for what we think of as the force or pull of gravity. On Earth, it is always equal to $9.8 \frac{m}{s^2}$ or $32.2 \frac{ft}{s^2}$.

Mass is expressed in metric units, usually kilograms or variations thereof. Though in the United States we tend to use our own system of measurement, most of the world uses metric. This is why most units of measure in math and science are metric.

In the United States, weight is usually expressed in pounds. The metric system expresses weight in Newtons. Most people in other areas of the world measure an object's mass, not its weight. That's why you hear the term *kilograms* more often than *Newtons*.

## Newton's Second Law

This law of motion states that the acceleration of an object is directly proportional to the net force acting on the object. It also states that an object accelerates in the direction of the net force acting on it.

Basically, this law is all about how a force influences the speed of an object. To calculate force, you multiply the mass (*m*) of the object by its acceleration (*a*): $F = ma$.

Consider this example:

> If you are trying to close an overstuffed suitcase and you push the lid down, in what direction will the lid move?

No, this is not a trick question. You're right— the lid moves in a downward motion as you easily guessed. That's because an object moves in the direction of the force acting upon it. Now for part two of the question:

> As you try to close the suitcase with one hand, you realize that you're getting nowhere, so you switch to two hands. By exerting twice as much pressure, the lid accelerates downward:

(A) Slightly
(B) Not at all
(C) Twice as much
(D) Three times as much

Again, the answer is probably fairly obvious—it's letter C. Twice the force causes an object to accelerate twice as fast. Here's the last part of the question:

> You finally get the frustrating lid closed on the overstuffed suitcase, but by now you are so aggravated that you decide to give it a good shove. In fact, you're so steamed that you also shove the suitcase next to it (even though it closed without a problem). The overstuffed suitcase is five times as large as the other piece you pushed. How quickly does the bursting luggage accelerate, compared to the lighter piece next to it?

The correct answer is one fifth as fast. When an object has five times the mass of another object, it will accelerate one fifth as fast. Acceleration, therefore, is directly proportionate to force and inversely proportionate to mass.

> **Classified Intel**
>
> When there is no acceleration, an object is said to be in mechanical equilibrium.

## Newton's Third Law

The law of reciprocal action is pretty straightforward and very famous: "For every action, there is an equal and opposite reaction." Chances are, you heard about this as a kid. It means that every motion results in the creation of another motion that runs in the opposite direction. For example, when you do a 5-mile march, your feet push against the ground with every step you take. What you don't feel is that the ground is simultaneously pushing against you (which is partially the reason why your feet ache when you're done).

Now if you strap on "full battle rattle" (as soldiers sometimes call it) and head underwater for training exercises, the force you exert is countered by the force of the water all around you—not just what's under your feet. Though your weight is much lighter in this environment, you feel the force everywhere.

## Speed

Now that we've discussed the basics of motion, let's look at some of the tools used to measure it. We'll start with speed, the rate at which an object moves. If you've ever driven a car, you are familiar with the formula for calculating speed:

$\text{Speed} = \dfrac{\text{Distance}}{\text{Time}}$. This means that if you drive 20 miles per hour, your speed will take your car 1 mile every 3 minutes.

Consider another example. Let's say Private Snuffy fails to make his bed one morning, and you want to measure the speed of Drill Sergeant Joe's wrath. As Drill Sergeant Joe comes running out of the barracks, he covers about 50 meters in 5 seconds, headed in a straight line for Private Snuffy. What is Drill Sergeant Joe's speed?

Using the formula for speed, you can determine that this swift (and angry) drill sergeant will cover about 10 meters every second.

## Velocity

Velocity is a measure of both the speed and direction an object moves. If Drill Sergeant Joe ran at the same rate of speed and in a straight line to Private Snuffy, we would say he maintained constant velocity. Speed and direction have to be unchanging for constant velocity to occur.

However, if Drill Sergeant Joe had to run around some obstacles to get to Private Snuffy, his direction would no longer be constant. So even if his speed never wavered, the velocity would not be considered constant anymore.

## Acceleration

Speaking of change, what happens when an object speeds up (increases velocity)? In general, this change is known as acceleration ($a$) and is calculated by subtracting the initial rate of velocity ($vi$) from the final rate of velocity ($vf$), and dividing that value by the length of time ($t$) in which the change occurs: $\text{Acceleration} = \dfrac{vf - vi}{t}$.

Imagine how it feels when an airplane prepares for takeoff. Usually, the pilot positions the plane at the beginning of the runway, pauses for a few seconds, and then hits the gas (so to speak). Your body presses into the seat as the plane accelerates rapidly down the runway.

Now, if the plane goes from 4 miles per second to 10 miles per second in 2 seconds, you would say the plane is accelerating 3 miles per second per second ($3\dfrac{\text{mi}}{\text{s}^2}$).

Likewise, when the plane comes in for a landing and hits the brakes, this is known as negative acceleration. The same principles apply.

If the pilot slows the plane from 300 miles per hour to 20 miles per hour over the course of 7 hours, you could determine that his negative acceleration was $40\dfrac{\text{mi}}{\text{h}^2}$. The change in velocity was 280 miles per hour, divided by a time interval of 7 hours.

## Gravitational Acceleration

When an object is allowed to fall with only the force of gravity acting on it (we call this freefalling), the ratio of weight to mass is constant. This means that, in theory, a car and a paper clip dropped in an environment with no air friction would both hit the ground at the same time; the ratio of weight to mass is the same for both the heavy object and the light object.

Now apply this knowledge to the following question. Will a car and a paper clip fall at the same speed when dropped from a tall building? The answer is, not quite. Though the car may have more than 500 times the mass of a paper clip, it also has 500 times the force against it, which would theoretically cause them to fall at the same speed. However, air friction and wind resistance can make for some deviation from this rule.

Although it's often safe to ignore air friction in calculating equations on paper, it can make quite a difference in reality, as any paratrooper will tell you.

## Centripetal and Centrifugal Force

Another term you should familiarize yourself with is *centripetal force*, which is what happens when an object gets pulled into a circular path. Basically, it's an inward force that causes an object to turn.

Have you ever gone to a carnival and ridden on the swings? The swings are attached to long chains that are likewise attached to arms connected to a base that turns. This construction causes the swings to travel in a circular motion (once the ride begins) because of centripetal force. Conversely, when the swings move outward from the center, centrifugal force is at work. This is an outward motion that results from a rotating motion.

## Gear Review

Because gears are used in so many mechanical devices, they are an essential concept for you to review. Gears are small wheels with teeth that mesh with other toothed wheels to do one of the following: (1) change the speed of a mechanism, (2) change the motion of a device, or (3) change the direction of the machinery.

When gears reduce the speed of machinery, this is known as gear reduction. The motor or mechanism slows down so that it can produce a more forceful output. In other words, more work gets done, even though it takes longer to do it. The reason gears are used to reduce the speed of a mechanism is to achieve something called mechanical advantage, which enables people to exert less force by allowing simple machinery to do work for them. We discuss this in more detail in the following section.

Several different types of gears exist, each with its own function. Here's a list of some of the most popular gears being used today:

- **Spur gears.** These are the most common category of gears, with straight teeth (see the following diagram). Spur gears are mounted on parallel shafts and are often found in washing machines, clothes dryers, and electric screwdrivers. They provide a great deal of gear reduction.

- **Helical gears.** This type of gear operates very smoothly and quietly, due largely in part to the shape of its teeth. The teeth are angled inward so that, as each tooth interlocks with another helical gear, the contact slowly spreads across the full length of the teeth on the second helical gear. They are most commonly found in car transmissions. These gears are more versatile than spur gears because they can be mounted on parallel or perpendicular shafts.

◆ **Bevel gears.** These mechanisms are generally mounted on perpendicular shafts and feature several different teeth styles. Their main function is to change the direction of rotation, such as when you put your car in reverse or when you remove a screw using the reverse function of an electric screwdriver. They are primarily used in car differentials, which basically allow the rear wheels to be driven at different speeds when the car is turning.

◆ **Worm gear.** This style is used when a very high gear reduction is needed. The teeth on this gear mesh with a partially threaded shaft instead of just another gear. They are found most commonly on conveyor systems or in certain high-performance car differentials.

A driving gear is one that is motorized by some force. When its teeth interlock with another gear, the motion from the driving gear turns the second gear in the opposite direction. Take a look at the following figure:

If the small gear in the middle is the driving gear, it causes the other gears to move based on the force of its motion. Because it turns to the left, the other gears it propels turns to the right.

Before we wrap up our discussion on gears, let's take a moment to cover one more concept that you'll likely see on the ASVAB: gear ratio. To understand the idea behind gear ratio, picture a

10-speed bike. When the bike is in its lowest gear, you have a 1:1 ratio, meaning every full turn of your bike pedals results in one full turn of the bike wheels.

If you're going uphill, it takes a lot of effort to pedal using the 1:1 ratio. As you begin shifting gears to get the bike uphill with less effort, you are lowering the gear ratio. Eventually, you may settle on a gear that allows you to turn the pedals three full rotations for one full wheel rotation, or 3:1. The advantage here is that the gears are taking on more of the work so you can expend less energy pedaling.

One easy way to determine the ratio of two gears is to count their teeth. Look at the following figure:

In the figure, the gear on the left has 12 teeth, while the gear on the right has 6 teeth. This makes the gear ratio 12:6, or 2:1.

As described in the bike example, gear ratio directly influences the rate at which the two gears turn. Therefore, if we have a gear ratio of 2:1, we know that for every one turn the larger gear makes, the smaller gear turns twice. See Chapter 8 for more information on ratios and reducing fractions.

# Pulley Review

Pulleys are simple machines that make heavy work a lot easier. A pulley is made up of a grooved wheel attached to an axle that allows the wheel to turn. If you run a rope through the groove and attach the rope to an object, lifting that object becomes easier. This is called mechanical advantage. Here's how it works:

1. In a simple one-wheeled pulley system, the only real advantage is changing the direction of force you use to lift the weight. If you have to lift a 100-pound object a distance of 4 meters, a pulley does not change that. However, instead of having to push the weight straight up in the air, the pulley allows you to use a downward pulling motion, which may feel easier.

2. In a basic two-wheeled pulley system, there is a force-distance trade-off, causing a distinct mechanical advantage. By inserting a second pulley into the system, you now have the ability to disperse the weight of the object between the two pulleys.

   A 100-pound object now feels like 50 pounds when you pull the rope. However, to move the object 4 meters, you must now pull the rope twice as far, or 8 meters in this example. You have to pull the rope a longer distance, but you have a lesser force to deal with.

3. If you add two more pulleys, for a total of four pulleys, you have made your task even easier. The same concept applies with the force and distance ratio—you have half the force to move, but twice the distance to pull the rope. Your object now feels like a mere 25 pounds because of the number of pulleys you can use to distribute the weight. However, you have to pull the rope 16 meters now just to raise the object the original 4 meters! This process continues with the addition of pulleys.

There are three main types of pulleys:

- **Fixed.** The axle is connected to a stationary object, such as a hook or wall. A clothesline is a good example of a fixed pulley. The mechanical advantage with a fixed pulley is 1. This simple machine changes the direction of force, though, which makes it *feel* easier to move an object; in fact, you actually have to apply *more* effort than the load just to move it.

- **Compound.** This pulley system blends several fixed or movable pulleys to maximize mechanical advantage. A block and tackle is a common type of compound pulley, often used in the shipping industry. Mechanical advantage increases with the number of additional pulleys added to the system.

- **Movable.** The axle here is not attached to anything except the pulley wheel, meaning that the pulley actually moves with the load. These are commonly found in weightlifting machines. With this system, you have a mechanical advantage of 2; this means you can apply half the force of the object to move it. You do, however, have to pull or push the pulley up and down.

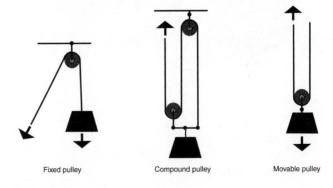

Fixed pulley          Compound pulley          Movable pulley

# Lever Review

Much like pulleys, *levers* also make life easier in terms of lifting heavy objects.

## def•i•ni•tion

> A **lever** is a simple machine with a rigid bar that pivots on a fixed point. The purpose is to move an object that is resting on one end of the bar by pushing down on the other end of the bar.

The object on which a lever pivots is called a fulcrum. To better envision a lever-and-fulcrum combination, picture a seesaw (or teeter totter) from your childhood days. You sat on one end, and the force of your weight pushed that end of the seesaw down to the ground. Then your friend had to try to climb onto the opposite end. (This was always difficult because that end was sticking up high in the air, due to your weight at the other end!)

If your friend weighed more than you, you shot up into the air. If your friend weighed less than you, you remained on the ground and had to push up with your leg muscles to get the seesaw moving. If your friend weighed about the same as you, this was ideal, because you could take turns going up and down with little effort.

The fulcrum was the object in the middle of the seesaw that anchored it to the ground. On a classic seesaw, the fulcrum was positioned in exactly the midpoint of the lever. However, this is not necessarily the case with all levers. Take note of the variance in fulcrum location with each class of lever:

- ◆ **1st-class lever.** The fulcrum is located between the load and the effort. Good examples include a seesaw, scissors, a hammer claw, and a wheel and axle.

- ◆ **2nd-class lever.** The load is between the effort and the fulcrum. Good examples include a nutcracker, a wheelbarrow, a wrench, and a springboard diving board.

- ◆ **3rd-class lever.** The effort is between the fulcrum and the load. For this type of lever to work properly, the fulcrum is usually attached to the lever. Good examples include tongs, tweezers, and a stapler.

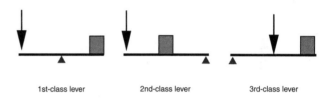

1st-class lever     2nd-class lever     3rd-class lever

Once you understand how levers and fulcrums work, you can begin applying numbers and weights to these diagrams. Let's examine a few basic equations now.

In a 1st-class lever situation, such as a seesaw, you have the following variables: the distance from the fulcrum ($d_1$) to weight number 1 ($w_1$), and the distance on the other side of the fulcrum ($d_2$) to weight number 2 ($w_2$).

The lever just shown is balanced as follows:

$$w_1 \times d_1 = w_2 \times d_2$$

To better understand how to apply this equation to a word problem you may see on the ASVAB, consider this scenario.

Little Isabella weighs 45 pounds. She wants to play on the seesaw with her friend, Sarah. Sarah also weighs 45 pounds. They both sit equidistant from the pivot point (or fulcrum) on the seesaw, which is 2 meters. Is the lever balanced?

The answer is yes, the lever is balanced, because $45 \times 2 = 45 \times 2$. If Sarah weighed less than Isabella (or vice versa), the lever would not be balanced.

Here's another situation you may encounter with a lever:

Thomas weighs 55 pounds, but his twin sister Sarah weighs only 45 pounds. If they are sitting 20 feet away from each other on a very large seesaw, how far away should the fulcrum be placed from each child?

First of all, let's put Thomas on the left side of the seesaw and call the distance between him and the fulcrum $x$. On the right side of the seesaw, we will place Sarah. The distance between her and the fulcrum will be known as $20 - x$. (Remember, 20 is the full distance between the two children, which is where that number came from in this word problem.)

Now we multiply Thomas's weight by $x$. This is equated to Sarah's weight multiplied by $20 - x$. See the following equation with the numbers plugged in:

$55x = 45 (20 - x)$

Now solve for $x$:

$55x = 900 - 45x$

$+45x = +45x$

$100x = 900$

$x = 9$

Now that we know $x$ equals 9, we know that Thomas should be placed 9 feet from the fulcrum on the seesaw. As for Sarah, we said she should sit $20 - x$ feet away from the fulcrum. In this case, that means she needs to be 11 feet away from the fulcrum. Her lower body weight is now properly offset by Thomas's greater body weight because of the variance in distances to the fulcrum.

For more help with lever word problems, check out www.psychometric-success.com/faq/faq-mechanical-comprehension-tests.htm. The main thing to remember for this section of the ASVAB is to think outside the box. This section is testing your ability to solve problems more than just reiterate a bunch of memorized facts. Be sure to practice some of these word problems in Chapter 17, too.

# Chapter 16

# Assembling Objects

### In This Chapter

- ◆ Why you're tested on this
- ◆ What to expect on this section
- ◆ How to solve the puzzles

Did you know that you use your visual intelligence every day? This skill comes in handy whenever you read a map, pack your groceries in your car, or even play games like Tetris or Snoodoku (a version of the popular puzzle game Sudoku that uses faces instead of numbers). By using your sense of sight and analytical skills, you gain information about the world around you and figure out the relationship between objects and their surroundings.

These skills are very important in the military, which is why the Assembling Objects (AO) test was added to the ASVAB several years ago. This chapter introduces you to this one-of-a-kind subtest and walks you through how to approach the questions.

## Why Do I Have to Take This?

Believe it or not, figuring out how objects are connected measures your *spatial intelligence* and problem-solving abilities.

By gauging your spatial intelligence, the military gets an idea of how you might perform a multitude of tasks, including these:

- ◆ Estimating distance
- ◆ Strategizing an attack
- ◆ Repairing machinery
- ◆ Navigating military transports
- ◆ Executing missions
- ◆ Conducting accurate reconnaissance

# def•i•ni•tion

Spatial intelligence refers to a person's ability to think visually or in abstract ways. Mastery of this type of task requires good analytical skills, creativity, and (typically) communication skills.

Many jobs in each branch of the Armed Forces require good visualization and spatial perception. Yet as of this writing, the Navy is the only service that requires scores from the AO subtest for job eligibility. Sources from the Official ASVAB Enlistment Testing Program, however, say that other branches of the Armed Forces may include AO scores in their job eligibility criteria in the near future.

Even if you're not planning to enlist in the Navy, your chosen service may look at your AO score anyway, to gain some more insight into your potential. Any way you slice it, doing well on this section is a good idea.

## What to Expect

Regardless of which version of the ASVAB you take, you'll have the AO subtest as your last hurdle to jump before completion. On the CAT, expect to see 16 questions for which you'll have 16 minutes to record your answer. On the PAP, you'll get 9 more questions to answer and 1 less minute in which to answer, for a grand total of 25 questions in 15 minutes on this version of the test.

So what exactly will you have to do in this section? In a nutshell, the AO subtest is all about solving puzzles—literally. Each question will have a sample drawing that depicts one of two scenarios: two shapes with connection points or a series of shapes that fit together in a certain way.

Following the sample are four answer choices, which will be some iteration of what's in the sample.

Depending on the question, you will be required to either (1) choose the answer choice that accurately shows how the two shapes will be joined if a straight line connected the two points in the example, or (2) determine how the pieces in the example would fit together to make a whole.

The best approach to all these questions is the process of elimination, which means discarding prospective answer choices that clearly don't work. We get into specifics of what to look for in the next two sections, which detail how to approach the two types of AO puzzles you'll see on the ASVAB.

# The Right Connections

Connector questions are very straightforward and look something like this:

In the following diagram, which figure best shows how the objects in the first box would touch if points A and B were connected?

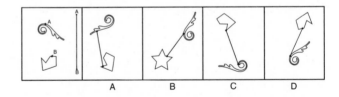

The first box is the sample. It shows a curvy, flourished shape and one that has sharp angles. Point A is marked as a dot where the curled end meets the straight part of the flourish. Point B is right next to the left side of the flat portion at the top of the jagged shape.

The shapes are repeated in various positions in boxes A through D. You're looking for the answer choice that has the two points connecting at the exact same place as shown in the sample. Look at the points in each choice and determine if they match up with the example.

(A) The points are at different places on both shapes.

(B) A star replaces the jagged shape, so obviously it doesn't match.

(C) Again, the points are at different places on both shapes.

(D) The points do match in the same places shown in the sample.

Using process of elimination, the correct answer is clearly D.

**Test Tip**

Notice that point B in the sample drawing in the previous example has a small line extending from the dot marking its place. This tells you that the correct answer will have the line connecting with the dot at this exact angle. Not every connector question will have one, but knowing the reason that little line is there can help you eliminate answer choices.

Feeling good about connectors? You should. They're pretty easy to figure out once you get used to them and know what you're looking for in a correct answer. Some of the most common reasons you'll find to eliminate a choice on an AO question include these:

♦ The points don't match up with those shown in the sample.

♦ One or more shapes have been changed from those shown in the sample.

♦ One or more shapes have been "mirrored," or changed into a mirror image of themselves. Mirror images may look exactly the same, but they're not.

♦ The connecting line is not coming into the point at the correct angle.

Let's try another question and see what we can eliminate based on these reasons.

In the following diagram, which figure best shows how the objects in the first box would touch if points A and B were connected?

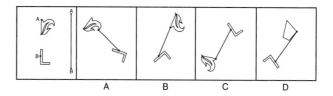

In this question, we have a leaflike flourish and what looks like an *L*. Point A is shown at the tip of one of the leaf's points, and point B is shown toward the middle of the vertical line in the *L*. Now let's look at the answer choices:

(A) Two issues here. First, the placement of point A is different from the sample. Second, the *L* is mirrored.

(B) Although the points appear to be in the same spots on both shapes, the shapes themselves are mirrored.

(C) Although both shapes are rotated, the points connect at the correct places on both shapes. If answer D doesn't have any obvious flaws, this is most likely the answer that will get you the points.

(D) A quadrilateral is shown in this choice instead of the leaf, making it an incorrect answer.

The best answer is C.

Even if this type of visualization is difficult initially (or just plain weird), a little practice will get you in ship shape in no time. In addition to working with the more than 100 AO problems in this book, you can help build the skills you need to ace connector questions by reading maps or doing some simple sketching. This type of work has proven useful in enhancing a person's visual-spatial skill set.

# Making the Pieces Fit

If you're good at figuring out how to best organize your kitchen cupboards or you like to curl up on rainy Sundays and do jigsaw puzzles, you'll love this type of AO question.

As like with connector questions, puzzle questions give you a sample box with several shapes. Your task this time is to figure out how they fit together. Some answer choices will form a complete shape. Others will simply show the shapes touching in some way.

Either way, you should approach these questions the same way you would a connector question. Furthermore, you should use the same common reasons to eliminate answer choices—looking for connection points being the obvious exception.

Let's take a look at an AO puzzle question:

Which answer choice best shows how the objects in the first box would appear if they were fitted together?

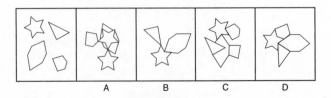

The sample has four shapes: a star, a triangle, a six-sided figure, and a five-sided figure. Now go through the answer choices and look for reasons to eliminate some:

(A) Two of the shapes are layered, which may make it difficult to discern what shape is in the back. However, there is a more obvious error here; there are two stars instead of one. This is not a match.

(B) We're looking for a puzzle with four shapes. This one has only three.

(C) This answer has too many shapes! Although all the sample shapes are there and in the correct proportion, a quadrilateral has been added, which eliminates this answer.

(D) This answer shows all the shapes in the right size and number.

The correct choice is D.

Let's try another one:

Which answer choice best shows how the objects in the first box would appear if they were fitted together?

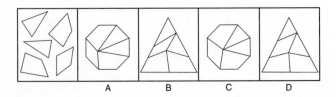

This question gives us five shapes, but this time they make up a whole object. Since all of them are angular and look similar, we need to look carefully at how each of the answer choices is constructed. All we need is one piece that doesn't match the sample to eliminate the answer choice:

(A) The diamond shape in the sample is less proportionate than the one in this answer, which also affects the sizes of the other shapes in the choice.

(B) None of the shapes in this answer choice match up in size or shape with those in the sample.

(C) The diamond shape in this choice matches the one in the sample, as do the rest of the shapes within. So far, this is the best choice.

(D) The same issues in answer B apply here. The shapes are way off.

The best choice is C.

Even if you weren't sure that the shapes in answer C matched the sample perfectly, there were enough more noticeable reasons to eliminate the other answer choices. Using this approach can help you turn a tough AO puzzle into something more manageable.

To help sharpen your skills at putting shapes together, try computer games like Tetris, in which you fit shapes together to make whole lines, or Snoodoku, a version of the math puzzle game in which the numbers are replaced with wacky Snood characters. If you prefer to work offline, try any of the following:

♦ Putting together classic jigsaw puzzles

♦ Searching for hidden pictures, such as those found in *Highlights* magazine

♦ Scrutinizing the *I Spy* or *Where's Waldo?* books to locate a specific object

# Chapter 17

# Technical Skills Workout

## General Science

1. Biology is the study of
    (A) life and living organisms.
    (B) origin, structure, and phenomena associated with planet Earth.
    (C) nonliving systems found in natural science.
    (D) matter.

2. Genes are located on
    (A) dominant alleles.
    (B) recessive alleles.
    (C) chromosomes.
    (D) proteins.

3. Which biological classification can be found between phylum and order?
    (A) family
    (B) class
    (C) genus
    (D) species

4. Mushrooms and molds are part of the kingdom
    (A) protista.
    (B) animalia.
    (C) plantae.
    (D) fungi.

5. Where are chloroplasts located?
    (A) gametes
    (B) chromosomes
    (C) plant leaves
    (D) carbon dioxide

6. A habitat is
    (A) an environment in which an organism or group of organisms normally live.
    (B) a region in the Northern Hemisphere that has cone-bearing trees.
    (C) the study of the environment.
    (D) a home for multiple biomes.

7. Deciduous trees

    (A) are known as evergreens.

    (B) have leaves that change colors in the fall.

    (C) shed foliage at the end of the growing season.

    (D) Both B and C.

8. A family of cells that live close together is defined as a(n)

    (A) organ.

    (B) tissue.

    (C) system.

    (D) body.

9. Newly formed proteins mature in the

    (A) mitochondria.

    (B) nucleus.

    (C) golgi.

    (D) lysosome.

10. Which cells do NOT undergo mitosis?

    (A) skin cells

    (B) hair cells

    (C) fingernail cells

    (D) sex cells

11. In meiosis, the number of chromosomes in gamete cells is

    (A) doubled.

    (B) the same as in all other cells.

    (C) halved.

    (D) dependent on DNA composition.

12. Spores are created by

    (A) bacteria, plants, and algae.

    (B) animals and humans.

    (C) genes and chromosomes.

    (D) the excretory system.

13. The system that oxygenates blood is the

    (A) circulatory system.

    (B) respiratory system.

    (C) digestive system.

    (D) excretory system.

14. Overhydration is a problem because

    (A) the body doesn't have enough water.

    (B) sugar levels become unbalanced with water levels.

    (C) water intake is too fast for the respiratory system.

    (D) salt levels become unbalanced with water levels.

15. What percent of the body is comprised of water?

    (A) less than 30 percent

    (B) more than 80 percent

    (C) less than 50 percent

    (D) more than 60 percent

16. Vitamin D can be found in which foods?

    (A) spinach and parsley

    (B) fish oil and leafy veggies

    (C) cheese and eggs

    (D) citrus fruits and tomatoes

17. Earth's crust is approximately how many miles deep?

    (A) 10

    (B) 180

    (C) 1,800

    (D) 3,000

18. Clouds that are puffy and often found in groups are called

    (A) cirrus.

    (B) cumulus.

    (C) stratus.

    (D) cumulonimbus.

19. The smallest part of an element is

    (A) compound.
    (B) matter.
    (C) proton.
    (D) molecule.

20. Which state of matter is commonly found in stars, fluorescent lightbulbs, and neon signs?

    (A) Bose–Einstein Condensate
    (B) plasma
    (C) gas
    (D) liquid

# Answers and Explanations

1. **A.** Answer B is the definition of earth science, answer C is the definition of physical science, and answer D is the definition of chemistry.

2. **C.** Choices A and B refer to specific types of traits, such as those used in determining eye color, hair color, and the like. Choice D is wrong because proteins are organic compounds found in cells that are designed to assist in the digestive process.

3. **B.** Remember taxonomy order using the mnemonic device "Keen People Can Often Find Good Sales."

4. **D.** The protista group includes slime molds and some algae. The animalia group includes animals, vertebrates, and invertebrates.

5. **C.** Gametes are sexual reproductive cells. Chromosomes are threadlike strands of DNA located in the nucleus of cells. Carbon dioxide is one of the elements in photosynthesis that gets converted to sugar and oxygen.

6. **A.** Choice B describes a coniferous forest. Choice C is the definition of ecology. Choice D is wrong because biomes are major regional biological communities, such as a forest or

desert. Habitats are located within a *single* biome, rather than multiple biomes living within a habitat.

7. **D.** Choice A is wrong because cone-bearing trees define the term *coniferous*. Both B and C are correct descriptions of deciduous trees.

8. **B.** Choice A is wrong because an organ is a group of tissues working together. Choice C is wrong because a system is a group of organs working together. Choice D is wrong because a body is multiple systems working together.

9. **C.** Choice A is wrong because mitochondria convert nutrients to energy. Choice B is wrong because the nucleus is the "command center" of the cell. Choice D is wrong because lysosomes contain the necessary digestive enzymes for the cell.

10. **D.** Sex cells are the only ones listed that do not undergo mitosis.

11. **C.** Refer to our discussion on meiosis for additional information about sexual reproduction in animal cells.

12. **A.** Spores are the reproductive structure produced by bacteria, plants, algae, fungi, and some protozoans.

13. **B.** Choice A is wrong because the circulatory system controls the flow of blood, but it doesn't supply it. Choice C is wrong because the digestive system converts food to energy. Choice D is wrong because the excretory system regulates the chemical composition of the body.

14. **D.** Choice A is wrong because it describes *de*hydration, not *over*hydration. The other selections have nothing to do with overhydration.

15. **B.** Up to 80 percent of the human body can be made of water, depending on size.

16. **C.** Choice A is wrong because it describes vitamin K. Choice B is wrong because it describes vitamin A. Choice D is wrong because it describes vitamin C.

17. **A.** Choice B is simply wrong, while choices C and D describe the depth of the mantle and the outer core, respectively.

18. **B.** Choice A is wrong because cirrus clouds are wispy and made of ice crystals. Choice C is wrong because stratus clouds are uniform in color and density. Choice D is wrong because cumulonimbus clouds are tall and thick.

19. **D.** Choice A is wrong because a compound is created when two or more elements combine. Choice B is wrong because matter is anything with mass and volume. Choice C is wrong because a proton is a positively charged particle inside an atom.

20. **B.** Choice A is wrong because Bose–Einstein Condensates are incredibly cold, unlike the matter in stars and lights. Choice C is wrong because gases don't have the free electrons and ions that plasmas have. Choice D is wrong because liquids cannot hold their own shape, while a star clearly does hold its shape.

# Electronics Skills

1. Current is defined as

    (A) the flow of air through a conductor.

    (B) the flow of electricity through a conductor.

    (C) the strength with which current flows through a conductor.

    (D) the amount of energy transferred during a specified time.

2. Ohms measure

    (A) voltage.

    (B) current.

    (C) electric power.

    (D) resistance.

3. Household wiring is most commonly made of

    (A) copper.

    (B) iron.

    (C) mercury.

    (D) silver.

4. Which of the following is NOT an example of a power source?

    (A) electric company

    (B) wall outlet

    (C) gas-powered generator

    (D) battery

5. A circuit is

    (A) a system of connected conductors that direct the path of electricity.

    (B) a material through which electricity passes.

    (C) something through which electricity cannot pass.

    (D) a measurement of electrical pressure.

6. A circuit is complete when it is

    (A) closed.

    (B) open.

    (C) full.

    (D) hot.

7. Alternating current (AC) travels

    (A) to the source of power only.

    (B) from the source of power only.

    (C) to and from the source of power.

    (D) to and from the diodes.

8.  A bulb in your strand of Christmas lights goes out, which causes them all to go out. What type of circuit do these lights operate on?

    (A) parallel

    (B) LED

    (C) switch

    (D) series

9.  The thickness of a 12-gauge wire is _____ than a 3-gauge wire.

    (A) more thick

    (B) less thick

    (C) the same

    (D) not enough information to tell

10. You have a 100-watt lightbulb and 20 volts of electrical pressure. How many amps of current do you have?

    (A) 5

    (B) 2,000

    (C) 200

    (D) 6

11. If you have 6 ohms of resistance and 2 amps of power, how many volts do you have?

    (A) 3

    (B) 12

    (C) 18

    (D) 2

12. Suppose you have 15 volts of pressure and 5 ohms of resistance. How many amps do you have?

    (A) 75

    (B) .33

    (C) 3

    (D) 750

13. Frequency is measured in

    (A) ammeters.

    (B) Hertz.

    (C) AM.

    (D) FM.

14. The number of complete cycles per second in any given periodic event is called

    (A) wave.

    (B) refraction.

    (C) frequency.

    (D) dispersion.

15. Suppose you are trying to earn the world record for bouncing a Ping-Pong ball on the paddle without dropping it. If you bounce it 2,500 times over the course of 300 minutes, what is your frequency?

    (A) .14 Hertz

    (B) 750,000 Hertz

    (C) .12 Hertz

    (D) 50 Hertz

16. Particles in the medium move parallel to the wave direction in a

    (A) transverse wave.

    (B) longitudinal wave.

    (C) surface wave.

    (D) seismic wave.

17. The bending of waves as they interact with obstacles in their path is

    (A) dispersion.

    (B) rectilinear propagation.

    (C) diffraction.

    (D) reflection.

18. Amplitude measures the

    (A) height of a wave.

    (B) speed of a wave.

    (C) distance from one wave peak to another.

    (D) intensity of a wave.

19. Which device is used to measure power?

    (A) ohmmeter

    (B) voltmeter

    (C) wattmeter

    (D) ammeter

20. Radio, heat, and light waves are

    (A) longitudinal.

    (B) surface.

    (C) parallel.

    (D) transverse.

# Answers and Explanations

1. **B.** Choice A is wrong because air has nothing to do with current. Choice C is wrong because it describes voltage. Choice D is wrong because it describes power.

2. **D.** Choice A is wrong because voltage is measured by volts. Choice B is wrong because current is measured by amperes. Choice C is wrong because electric power is measured by watts.

3. **A.** The other choices depict other common conductors of electricity, but they are not found in household wiring.

4. **B.** Power is not generated from the wall outlet, although it's often part of an electric circuit.

5. **A.** Choice B is wrong because it describes a conductor, choice C describes an insulator, and choice D describes voltage.

6. **A.** An open circuit is not complete because the electrons have stopped moving, so choice B is wrong. Choices C and D are also wrong.

7. **C.** Choice A is not only wrong, but it is impossible. Current has to come from a power source of some kind. Choice B is wrong because it describes direct current (DC). Choice D is wrong because current doesn't come from a diode; a diode directs the flow of current in some situations.

8. **D.** Choice A is wrong because, on a parallel circuit, there are enough paths for the current to flow so that one malfunctioning light won't cause the whole strand to go out. Choice B is wrong because LED stands for light emitting diodes and is not a type of circuit. Choice C is wrong because a switch is not a type of circuit, either.

9. **B.** Thick wire has a small gauge; thin wire has a larger gauge.

10. **A.** To determine amps when you know volts and watts, use the following formula: $W = V \times A$.

11. **B.** To determine volts, multiply amps by ohms.

12. **C.** To determine amps, divide volts by ohms.

13. **B.** Choice A is wrong because an ammeter is a device used to measure current. Choice C is wrong because AM stands for amplitude modulated and is a carrier signal for radio waves. Choice D is wrong for the same reason, although it stands for frequency modulated.

14. **C.** Choice A is wrong because a wave is a disturbance that is transmitted through space and time. Choice B is wrong because refraction is a change in wave direction because of a change in wave speed as it enters a new medium. Choice D is wrong because dispersion occurs when a wave is split up by frequency.

15. **A.** To determine frequency, divide the number of occurrences by the total time.

16. **B.** Choice A is wrong because transverse waves cause particles to move in a perpendicular direction to the wave. Choice C is wrong because surface waves cause particles to move in a circular direction to the wave. Choice D is wrong because seismic waves are a type of surface wave.

17. **C.** Choice A is wrong because dispersion occurs when a wave is split up by frequency. Choice B is wrong because rectilinear propagation is the movement of waves in a straight line. Choice D is wrong because reflection is the change in wave direction after it strikes a reflective surface.

18. **A.** Choice B is wrong because it describes wave speed. Choice C describes wavelength, and choice D is simply wrong because, depending on what type of wave you are trying to measure, there are different methods of calculating intensity.

19. **C.** Choice A is wrong because it measures resistance, choice B is wrong because it measures the difference in voltage, and choice D is wrong because it measures current.

20. **D.** Choice A is wrong because longitudinal waves include sound waves, for example. Choice B is wrong because surface waves include ocean waves, for example. Choice C is wrong because parallel is a direction of particle movement within a wave medium, not a type of wave.

# Automotive Skills

1. The Otto Cycle is
   (A) part of the brake system.
   (B) the four-stroke combustion process.
   (C) part of the solenoid.
   (D) the five-step cooling process.

2. Pistons are
   (A) solid cylinders or discs in an engine that move under fluid pressure.
   (B) suppliers of the initial source of energy for the car.
   (C) electrical transformers.
   (D) devices that take current from the ignition coil and send it to the spark plugs.

3. Newer spark plugs
   (A) produce cooler, faster sparks.
   (B) must be changed more frequently than their predecessors.
   (C) receive more volts and hotter spark.
   (D) require more tension than older plugs.

4. Which components comprise a car's electrical system?
   (A) spark plugs, battery, ignition coils, coil pack
   (B) pipes, resonator, catalytic converter
   (C) water pump, radiator, pressure cap, thermostat
   (D) battery, starter, solenoid, alternator

5. How many volts of power does the battery provide to electrical accessories in the car?
   (A) 6
   (B) 6,000
   (C) 120
   (D) 12

6. What component does a coil pack replace in modern vehicles?
   (A) distributor
   (B) ignition coil
   (C) starter
   (D) generator

7. The voltage regulator

   (A) converts battery voltage.

   (B) helps eliminate power surges.

   (C) regulates voltage in the cooling system.

   (D) times spikes so they will coincide with brownouts, to cancel each other out.

8. An engine that uses gasoline is called a(n)

   (A) diesel engine.

   (B) external combustion engine.

   (C) gas turbine engine.

   (D) hydrogen engine.

9. What did older engines rely on to carry fuel to the engine?

   (A) gravity

   (B) fuel pump

   (C) fuel injectors

   (D) electric filters

10. Which of the following is NOT a function of the exhaust system?

    (A) reduce the noise of an engine

    (B) filter out dirt and rust particles in the fuel

    (C) maintain performance

    (D) reduce or eliminate harmful emissions

11. The pipe that connects the exhaust pipe to the muffler is the

    (A) tailpipe.

    (B) resonator pipe.

    (C) intermediate pipe.

    (D) X-pipe.

12. Three-way catalytic converters most commonly control emissions of

    (A) nitrogen, carbon dioxide, and water vapor.

    (B) nitrogen, carbon monoxide, and hydrogen.

    (C) hydrogen, water vapor, and helium.

    (D) carbon monoxide, hydrogen, and sulfur.

13. The thermostat

    (A) prevents coolant from boiling.

    (B) picks up heat from the engine.

    (C) provides pressure needed to circulate coolant through the engine cavities.

    (D) controls the temperature of the engine.

14. What do disc brakes rely on to slow a vehicle?

    (A) backing plate

    (B) brake shoes

    (C) heat and friction

    (D) liquid coolant

15. Brake shoes can be compared to which disc brake component?

    (A) brake pads

    (B) rotors

    (C) calipers

    (D) wheel cylinder

16. Emergency brakes are considered a

    (A) primary braking device.

    (B) secondary braking device.

    (C) hydraulic braking device.

    (D) fluid braking device.

17. The suspension system connects the

    (A) fuel system to the exhaust system.

    (B) shock absorber to the steering linkage.

    (C) vehicle to its wheels.

    (D) dependent to the independent wheel systems.

18. Which wheel design hasn't been used on cars in decades?

    (A) front wheel independent

    (B) front wheel dependent

    (C) rear wheel independent

    (D) rear wheel dependent

19. A wheel system that uses a solid axle to connect rear wheels is called

    (A) front wheel independent.

    (B) front wheel dependent.

    (C) rear wheel independent.

    (D) rear wheel dependent.

20. Which element of the electrical system uses the most power?

    (A) solenoid

    (B) starter

    (C) alternator

    (D) voltage regulator

# Answers and Explanations

1. **B.** The Otto Cycle's main function is to convert gasoline to motion. Choices A and D have nothing to do with the engine's fuel system. Choice C talks about a solenoid, which is part of the electrical system.

2. **A.** Choice B is wrong because it describes a battery. Choice C is wrong because it describes an ignition coil. Choice D is wrong because it describes the distributor.

3. **C.** Choice A is wrong because newer spark plugs have a hotter spark. Choices B and D describe the exact opposite features of newer spark plugs.

4. **D.** Choice A is wrong because it describes a distributorless ignition system. Choice B is wrong because it describes the exhaust system. Choice C is wrong because it describes the coolant system.

5. **D.** Choice A refers to the number of cells in a battery. Choice B is a random number. Battery power does, however, get converted by the ignition coil to thousands of volts of power during the ignition process. Choice C was another random number.

6. **A.** Choices B and C are still found in modern cars. A generator (as in choice D) has been replaced by an alternator in modern cars.

7. **B.** Choice A is wrong because the ignition coil converts voltage. Choice C is wrong because voltage is regulated by the electrical system, not the cooling system. Choice D is wrong because voltage regulators try to eliminate spikes and brownouts, not time them to occur simultaneously.

8. **C.** Choice A is wrong because a diesel engine uses diesel fuel. Choice B is wrong because gas is used by *in*ternal combustion engines, not *ex*ternal. Choice D is wrong because hydrogen isn't a type of engine; it is one of the main elements in gasoline fuel.

9. **A.** Choice B is wrong because fuel pumps are used in newer cars to carry fuel to the engine, not older cars. Choice C is wrong because a fuel injector forcibly pumps fuel under high pressure in newer cars. Choice D is wrong because there is no such thing as an electric filter in cars.

10. **B.** Choice B is a function of the fuel filter in the fuel system. All other choices relate to the exhaust system.

11. **C.** Choice A is wrong because the tailpipe is the last piece of tubing in the exhaust process. Choice B is wrong because a resonator is not a pipe. It is a second silencing mechanism that may be used when standard mufflers don't adequately control noise. Choice D is wrong because an X-pipe describes a specially shaped piping system used to equal the pressure in a dual exhaust system.

12. **A.** None of the other answers have the correct combination of gases controlled by catalytic converters.

13. **D.** Choice A refers to a radiator cap, or a pressure cap. Choice B refers to the passages in the engine through which liquid coolant travels, and choice C refers to a water pump.

14. **C.** Choices A and B describe components of drum brakes. Choice D uses a term from the cooling system, not the elements disc brakes use for stopping.

15. **A.** Choices B and C refer to other elements of disc brakes. Neither of these function similarly to the brake shoes of drum brakes. Choice D is wrong because it describes another component of the drum brake system.

16. **B.** Choice A is wrong because disc and drum brakes are the primary system used for braking. Choice C is wrong because emergency brakes rely on a mechanical system, whereas the primary brakes use hydraulics. Choice D is just wrong.

17. **C.** Choice A doesn't make sense and has nothing to do with the suspension system. Choice B refers to components of the suspension system, and choice D refers to two separate types of suspension systems.

18. **B.** All of the other designs are still in use.

19. **D.** Choices A and B refer to the front wheels, so they are wrong. Choice C uses a flexible system to connect rear wheels.

20. **B.** Each choice represents an element of the electrical system, but only the starter uses an exorbitant amount of power in that system.

# Shop Skills

1. Which of the following is NOT a function of shaping tools?

    (A) contour objects

    (B) make curves

    (C) make incisions

    (D) cut large sections of wood or metal

2. A cold chisel is used for

    (A) creating pockets for door hinges.

    (B) cutting cold wood.

    (C) cutting cold metal.

    (D) boat building.

3. Rasps are generally used on

    (A) wood.

    (B) metal.

    (C) plastic.

    (D) all of the above.

4. A hand saw used for cutting metal or bone is a

    (A) crosscut saw.

    (B) hack saw.

    (C) miter saw.

    (D) circular saw.

5. A Tuttle saw works best on

    (A) soft wood.

    (B) any wood.

    (C) hard wood.

    (D) old wood.

6. What types of projects usually require the use of a ball pein hammer?

    (A) anything with upholstery

    (B) something with toys or plaster board

    (C) one that requires the removal of nails

    (D) some auto repairs and woodworking tasks

7. Which type of hammer is often referred to as a baby sledge?

    (A) tinner

    (B) engineer

    (C) ball pein

    (D) curved claw

8. The end of a Phillips head screwdriver looks like a(n)

    (A) *x*.

    (B) narrow slot.

    (C) star.

    (D) hexagon.

9. Which of the following is NOT one of the three main parts of a hand drill?

    (A) chuck

    (B) cranking handle

    (C) crankshaft

    (D) drill bit

10. An auger bit is used to

    (A) drill large, deep holes in wood.

    (B) make a larger hole than a twist bit will create.

    (C) make a hole where the top part of the hole is enlarged.

    (D) make holes in stone or quarry.

11. Which tool should you use to loosen nuts and bolts?

    (A) plane tool

    (B) wrench

    (C) screwdriver

    (D) clamp

12. A wrench ideal for bicycle repairs is a(n)

    (A) open-end wrench.

    (B) combination-end wrench.

    (C) Allen wrench.

    (D) adjustable-end wrench.

13. Crescent, spanner, and pipe wrenches are all forms of

    (A) socket wrenches.

    (B) open-end wrenches.

    (C) adjustable-end wrenches.

    (D) Allen wrenches.

14. What type of clamp uses two long screws to force the clamp jaws toward one another, thereby holding an object in place?

    (A) hand screw

    (B) pivot screw

    (C) jack screw

    (D) vise screw

15. Which type of clamp is similar to a version of locking pliers?

    (A) pipe clamp

    (B) bar grip

    (C) vise grip

    (D) power clamp

16. Which of the following is NOT a function of a router?

    (A) contour plastic

    (B) smooth rough edges

    (C) buff surfaces

    (D) sand wood

17. A fixed cutting tool often used in conjunction with a powered lathe is a

    (A) circular saw.
    (B) jigsaw.
    (C) chisel.
    (D) rasp.

18. The most common type of power drill is the

    (A) hammer drill.
    (B) pistol grip.
    (C) drill press.
    (D) crank drill.

19. A saw with a narrow blade that moves in a vertical and reciprocating motion is a

    (A) circular saw.
    (B) miter saw.
    (C) table saw.
    (D) jigsaw.

20. What type of general-purpose plane tool can fit into tight spaces and is used to trim wood edges and joints?

    (A) chisel.
    (B) jack plane.
    (C) router.
    (D) block plane.

# Answers and Explanations

1. **D.** Cutting large sections of an object is the job of a saw, not a shaping tool. All the other choices were functions of shaping tools.

2. **C.** Choice A describes a wood chisel. Choices B and D are wrong because cold chisels are used specifically to cut cold metals, not wood.

3. **A.** The other surfaces can be used with a file, but not a rasp.

4. **B.** Choice A is wrong because a crosscut saw is used for cutting wood against the grain. Choice C is wrong because a miter saw is used for making angled cuts, often for picture frames. Choice D is wrong because it is not a hand saw.

5. **C.** Choice A is wrong because champion saws usually work best on soft woods. Choices B and D are wrong because Tuttle saws work best on hard woods.

6. **D.** Choices A and B describe a rubber mallet hammer. Choice C describes a curved claw hammer.

7. **B.** An engineer's hammer is called a baby sledge because it looks similar to the sledge, but smaller. It generally weighs between 1 and 5 pounds.

8. **A.** Choice B describes a flathead. Choice C, describes a seldom-used tool called a Torx screwdriver, which is sometimes used in some seatbelt systems. Choice D describes an Allen wrench.

9. **C.** Crankshafts are found in automobiles, not a hand drill.

10. **A.** Choice B is wrong because it describes a spade bit. Choice C is wrong because it describes a countersink. Choice D is wrong because it describes a carbide-tipped masonry bit.

11. **B.** Choice A is wrong because plane tools are used to flatten, smooth, and narrow the width of wood. Choice C is wrong because screwdrivers are used in conjunction with screws, not nuts and bolts. Choice D is wrong because clamps are used to fasten an item in place.

12. **D.** Choice A is wrong because it may cause slippage if it's not the right tool for the job, which can cause some bloody knuckles in a bicycle repair. Choice B is not the *best* tool to use for this type of work, and choice C is most commonly used in furniture assembly.

13. **C.** Crescent, spanner, and pipe wrenches all have specific functions as adjustable wrenches.

14. **A.** When the screws of a hand screw are rotated, they cause the jaws of the clamp to apply inward pressure, holding an object in place.

15. **C.** Choice A is wrong because a pipe clamp is used to hold a pipe in place for cutting, threading, lifting, or suspending. Choice B is wrong because a bar clamp uses a screw mechanism to tighten its large jaws. Choice D is wrong because a power clamp does not resemble locking pliers. It may be used in welding projects and is often made of cast aluminum.

16. **A.** Routers are used with metal and wood, not plastic.

17. **C.** Lathes are used to shape metal or wood by rotating the item on the axis of the lathe. The edge of the item needing to be cut is pressed against a fixed cutting object, like a chisel or sandpaper.

18. **B.** Choice A is usually used for drilling masonry—a jackhammer is a good example of this type of drill. Choice C is wrong because a drill press is a fixed tool mounted to a workbench or the floor. Choice D is wrong because a crank drill is what people sometimes call a hand drill. None of these are as popular as the pistol grip power drill.

19. **D.** Choices A and C are wrong because they both have circular blades. Choice B is wrong because miter saws have straight horizontal or circular blades, too.

20. **D.** Choices A and C are wrong because they are not plane tools. Choice B is wrong because it cannot easily fit into tight spaces and isn't considered general purpose like the block plane.

# Mechanical Comprehension

1. Transferring energy through force over a distance is called

   (A) potential energy.

   (B) kinetic energy.

   (C) work.

   (D) motion.

2. When an object can rearrange itself and then restore its original shape later, it has

   (A) elastic energy.

   (B) spring energy.

   (C) gravitational energy.

   (D) chemical energy.

3. The formula for gravitational potential energy is

   (A) $PE = \dfrac{mg}{h}$.

   (B) $PE = mgh$.

   (C) $PE = \dfrac{m}{gh}$.

   (D) $PE = \dfrac{mh}{g}$.

4. If a sailor who weighs 64 kilograms is running at a rate of 8 meters per second, what is his kinetic energy?

   (A) 4,096 joules

   (B) 131,072 joules

   (C) 256 joules

   (D) 2,048 joules

5. Work is

   (A) force times distance.

   (B) force times distance multiplied by one half.

   (C) force divided by distance squared.

   (D) force divided by distance.

6. What unit is used to measure work?

   (A) Newtons

   (B) joules

   (C) meters

   (D) kilograms

7. Gravitational pull on Earth is

   (A) $\dfrac{9.8 \text{ m}}{\text{s}^2}$.

   (B) $\dfrac{32.2 \text{ m}}{\text{s}^2}$.

   (C) $\dfrac{9.8 \text{ m}^2}{\text{s}}$.

   (D) $\dfrac{98 \text{ m}}{\text{s}}$.

8. Newton's second law of motion states that

   (A) an object in motion tends to stay in motion.

   (B) an object at rest tends to stay at rest.

   (C) the acceleration of an object is directly proportionate to the net force acting on it.

   (D) for every action, there is an equal and opposite reaction.

9. If you run 6.2 miles in 31 minutes, what is your speed?

   (A) 1 mile every 4 minutes

   (B) $\dfrac{2}{10}$ of a mile every minute

   (C) 2 miles every 6 minutes

   (D) $\dfrac{6}{10}$ of a mile every 2 minutes

10. When you are driving due north at 60 miles per hour, what type of motion do you use?

    (A) constant acceleration

    (B) gravitational acceleration

    (C) constant negative speed

    (D) constant velocity

11. If an elephant and a chipmunk both jump off a ledge that exists in a vacuum, who will hit the ground first?

    (A) the elephant

    (B) the chipmunk

    (C) both will hit at the same time

    (D) there's no way to tell

12. When an object gets pulled into a circular path, this is known as what?

    (A) centripetal force

    (B) centrifugal force

    (C) circular force

    (D) constant force

13. The most common type of gear is the

    (A) helical gear.

    (B) bevel gear.

    (C) worm gear.

    (D) spur gear.

14. When a driving gear engages with another gear, in which direction does the second gear turn?

    (A) the same as the driving gear

    (B) the opposite of the driving gear

    (C) depends on what type of driving gear you have

    (D) depends on the size of the driving gear

15. This simple machine is made of a grooved wheel attached to an axel. Often a rope is run through the wheel to make lifting heavy things easier. What type of machine is this?

    (A) gear

    (B) lever

    (C) pulley

    (D) fulcrum

16. A clothesline is an example of a

    (A) fixed pulley.

    (B) moveable pulley.

    (C) compound pulley.

    (D) level pulley.

17. A seesaw is an example of a

    (A) gear.

    (B) pulley.

    (C) lever.

    (D) mechanical advantage.

18. In a 3rd-class lever, the effort is between the _____ and the _____:

    (A) fulcrum, load

    (B) load, lever

    (C) fulcrum, gear

    (D) middle, end of the lever

19. In a 1st-class lever, the distance between the fulcrum and the load on the right side of the lever is the same as that on the left side. The distance between the fulcrum and the right-side load is 10 meters, while the distance between the fulcrum and the load on the left side is 11 meters. Is the lever balanced?

    (A) yes

    (B) no

    (C) not enough information

    (D) yes, as long as the load on the left side is wider than the load on the right side

20. The force that makes objects fall to the ground is

    (A) centripetal.

    (B) gravity.

    (C) joules.

    (D) kinetic.

# Answers and Explanations

1.  **C.** Choice A is wrong because potential energy is defined as stored energy or an object with the potential to do work. Choice B is wrong because kinetic energy is the energy of motion. Choice D is wrong because motion is defined as any object that changes distance over a period of time.

2.  **A.** Choice B is wrong because a spring is an example of elastic energy. Choice C is wrong because gravitational energy is energy associated with a gravitational field. Choice D is wrong because chemical energy is a form of potential energy related to the molecular structure of atoms.

3.  **B.** Potential energy is measured by multiplying mass ($m$) by gravitational force ($g$) by height above Earth's surface ($h$).

4.  **D.** The formula for kinetic energy is: $KE = \frac{1}{2}mv^2$.

5.  **A.** None of the other formulas represent work.

6.  **B.** Joules are used to calculate work and energy.

7.  **A.** Gravitational acceleration, also known as gravitational pull, is always represented by the same mathematical figure (on Earth).

8.  **C.** Choices A and B are wrong because they express Newton's first law of motion. Choice D is wrong because it expresses Newton's third law of motion.

9.  **B.** Speed is calculated using the following formula: $\text{Speed} = \frac{\text{Distance}}{\text{Time}}$.

10. **D.** Constant velocity means that speed and direction are both unchanging.

11. **C.** If two objects fall at the same time, the ratio of weight to mass is the same for both heavy and light objects. In a vacuum that has no wind resistance or air friction, both would hit the ground at the same time because of this concept.

12. **A.** Choice B is wrong because centrifugal force occurs when outward force is placed on a body that is traveling in a circular direction.

13. **D.** Spur gears are found in such common appliances as washing machines, clothes dryers, electric screwdrivers, and the like.

14. **B.** The motion from the driving gear, which is motorized by some force, causes the second gear to turn in the opposite direction.

15. **C.** Choice A is wrong because a gear is a small wheel with teeth that meshes with other toothed wheels. Choice B is wrong because a lever is a rigid bar that pivots on a fixed point. Choice D is wrong because a fulcrum is the pivot on which a lever turns.

16. **A.** Choice B is wrong because a moveable pulley is not attached to anything except the pulley wheel, which would make hanging clothes rather difficult! Choice C is wrong because a compound pulley is far more involved than a simple clothesline system. Choice D is wrong because a level is not a type of pulley.

17. **C.** A seesaw uses a lever and a fulcrum. Choices A and B are wrong because no gears or pulleys are involved with a seesaw. Choice D is wrong because mechanical advantage is the reason simple machines are used; it is not a specific type of machine.

18. **A.** Examples of 3rd-class levers include tongs, tweezers, and staplers.

19. **B.** 1st-class levers are balanced only when the loads weigh the same on both sides of the fulcrum *and* when they are equidistant from the fulcrum.

20. **B.** Choice A is wrong because centripetal force occurs when an object gets pulled in a circular path. Choice C is wrong because a joule is the unit used to measure work and energy. Choice D is wrong because kinetic is the energy of motion.

# Assembling Objects

1. Which answer choice best shows how the objects in the first box would appear if they were fitted together?

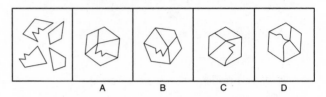

2. Which answer choice best shows how the objects in the first box would appear if they were fitted together?

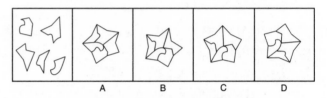

3. In the following diagram, which figure best shows how the objects in the first box would touch if points A and B were connected?

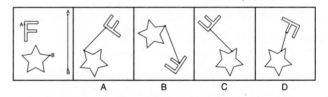

4. Which answer choice best shows how the objects in the first box would appear if they were fitted together?

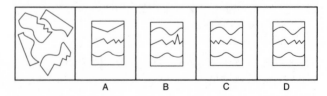

5. In the following diagram, which figure best shows how the objects in the first box would touch if points A and B were connected?

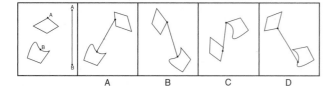

6. Which answer choice best shows how the objects in the first box would appear if they were fitted together?

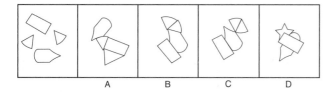

7. In the following diagram, which figure best shows how the objects in the first box would touch if points A and B were connected?

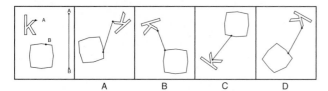

8. Which answer choice best shows how the objects in the first box would appear if they were fitted together?

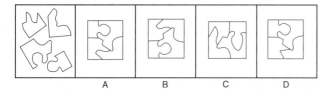

9. Which answer choice best shows how the objects in the first box would appear if they were fitted together?

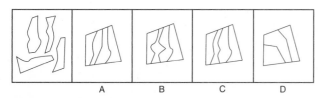

10. In the following diagram, which figure best shows how the objects in the first box would touch if points A and B were connected?

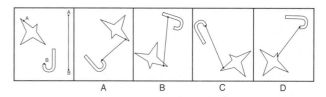

11. In the following diagram, which figure best shows how the objects in the first box would touch if points A and B were connected?

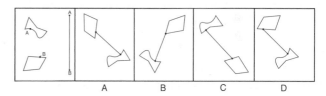

12. Which answer choice best shows how the objects in the first box would appear if they were fitted together?

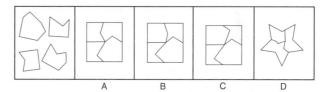

13. In the following diagram, which figure best shows how the objects in the first box would touch if points A and B were connected?

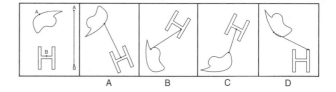

14. Which answer choice best shows how the objects in the first box would appear if they were fitted together?

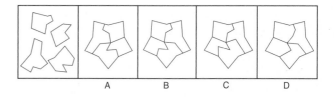

15. In the following diagram, which figure best shows how the objects in the first box would touch if points A and B were connected?

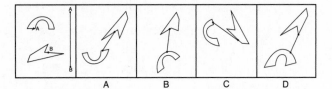

16. Which answer choice best shows how the objects in the first box would appear if they were fitted together?

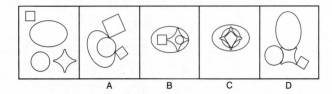

17. In the following diagram, which figure best shows how the objects in the first box would touch if points A and B were connected?

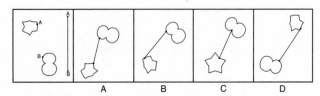

18. Which answer choice best shows how the objects in the first box would appear if they were fitted together?

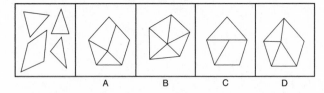

19. In the following diagram, which figure best shows how the objects in the first box would touch if points A and B were connected?

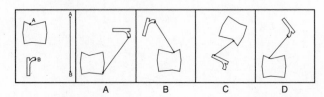

20. Which answer choice best shows how the objects in the first box would appear if they were fitted together?

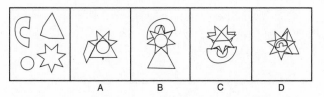

# Answers and Explanations

1. **B.** One of the pieces in answer A is mirrored. Two of the shapes in answer C have been changed from the sample. In answer D, only one shape has not been changed.

2. **C.** The shapes in answer A are elongated. Some of the shapes in answer B have been altered. Answer D is completely mirrored.

3. **A.** Answer B has the A connection on the wrong part of the *F*. Both connection points are in the wrong places in answers C and D.

4. **D.** The several shapes in answers A and B don't match the sample. Answer C has mirrored shapes.

5. **B.** Answers A and C have the A connection in the wrong place on the diamond shape. Answer D has the B connection in the wrong place.

6. **C.** In answer A, one of the pie pieces is now a larger triangle. The large piece with the curved angle tip in answer B has one side that is not curved anymore. Answer D doesn't have the two pie pieces.

7. **D.** The angle at which the line connects to the A point on the *k* in answer A doesn't match the diagram. The point on the four-sided figure in answer B is on the corner instead of toward the middle, and the connection point on the *k* in answer C doesn't match the sample.

8. **A.** The pieces in answer B are mirrored. Some of the shapes in answers C and D don't match the sample.

9. **C.** The shapes in answers A and B are different from those in the sample. Answer D has only three shapes, whereas the sample has four.

10. **C.** The *J* in answer A is mirrored. The connection point on the *J* in answer B is in the wrong place, while the connection point on the star in answer D is in the wrong place.

11. **A.** The connection points on the four-sided figure in answers B and C don't match the sample. In answer D, the connection on the four-sided figure is in the right place, but the angle it connects from is wrong.

12. **A.** Some of the shapes in answers B and C are different from those in the sample. Answer D has only three shapes, whereas the sample has four.

13. **A.** The connection points on the rounded figures in answer B and C are in the wrong places. The connection point on the *H* in answer D is also in the wrong place.

14. **B.** Answer A is completely mirrored. The angles in the shapes in answers C and D don't match the sample.

15. **A.** The connection points on the rainbow shape in answers B and D don't match the sample. The connection point on the angled figure in answer C doesn't match the sample.

16. **D.** The star shape in answer A is now a square. The circle in answer B is much smaller than in the sample. The small square in answer C has been turned into a diamond.

17. **B.** The A connections in answers A and D are off. The eight-sided figure in answer C has been replaced with a star.

18. **D.** The overall shape of answer A is right, but the pieces that make it up are off. Answer B has an extra piece. Answer C has only three pieces, whereas the sample has four.

19. **D.** The connection point on the four-sided figure in answer A doesn't match the sample. The four-sided figure in answers B and D has been mirrored.

20. **B.** There is no rainbow shape in answer A, and there is now a four-sided shape in its place. The circle in answer C has been replaced with a triangle. In answer D, the size of the rainbow shape has been reduced.

# Part 5

# After Action Review: Practice Tests

Now that you've learned everything you've ever wanted to know about vocabulary, reading, reasoning, math, science, and visual intelligence—and much, much more—it's time to prep for the real thing.

This part offers you three complete practice ASVAB tests, along with an additional AFQT practice test to help you test your knowledge, speed, and accuracy. Attempting practice questions under the same conditions as the real ASVAB is a crucial part of preparing for the exam. Trial and error, plus answers and detailed explanations for every question, can be even more of an effective learning tool than straight studying.

# General Science

**Time:** 11 Minutes

**Questions:** 25

**Directions:** This section tests your general knowledge in the area of science. Carefully read each question and choose the answer choice that best answers the question.

1. If a car is traveling at "constant velocity," what is the car doing?

    (A) maintaining constant speed with no change in direction
    (B) maintaining constant speed on a circular track
    (C) maintaining constant direction at varying speeds
    (D) driving too fast on a circular track

2. Which planet is farthest from the sun?

    (A) Mercury
    (B) Earth
    (C) Neptune
    (D) Pluto

3. Which of the following are the three states of matter?

    (A) liter, milliliter, gram
    (B) proton, electron, neutron
    (C) solid, liquid, gas
    (D) hydrogen, oxygen, carbon

4. Rock that is heated melts to become

    (A) oxide.
    (B) carbonate.
    (C) magma.
    (D) granite.

5. The majority of elements on the periodic table are

    (A) metals.

    (B) nonmetals.

    (C) metalloids.

    (D) alkali metals.

6. The process that allows the skin to grow back after you get a cut is called

    (A) homeostasis.

    (B) mitosis.

    (C) stem cell reproduction

    (D) collagen.

7. Human DNA has how many chromosomes?

    (A) 22

    (B) 36

    (C) 46

    (D) 43

8. The hardest material on Earth is

    (A) topaz.

    (B) quartz.

    (C) diamond.

    (D) calcite.

9. The system that regulates growth, hormones, and metabolism is the

    (A) musculoskeletal system.

    (B) nervous system.

    (C) digestive system.

    (D) endocrine system.

10. The moon shines because

    (A) it reflects the light of the sun.

    (B) it is a giant ball of fire.

    (C) there is no gravity on the moon.

    (D) it is reflecting the light of the Earth.

11. A substance made up of one type of atom is called a(n)

    (A) nucleus.

    (B) microscopic.

    (C) compound.

    (D) element.

12. Olfaction refers to the sense of

    (A) sight.

    (B) smell.

    (C) hearing.

    (D) touch.

13. The mineral needed to make bone is

    (A) calcium.

    (B) iron.

    (C) iodide.

    (D) fluoride.

14. Which of the following words does NOT describe a form of water condensation near the surface of the Earth?

    (A) dew

    (B) frost

    (C) fog

    (D) rain

15. Dense connective tissue usually found in joints is

    (A) cartilage.

    (B) muscle.

    (C) tendon.

    (D) ligament.

16. Most metal in the Earth's crust is

    (A) aluminum.

    (B) oxygen.

    (C) iron.

    (D) calcium.

17. The most extensive part of digestion occurs in the

    (A) stomach.
    (B) small intestine.
    (C) large intestine.
    (D) pancreas.

18. Clouds that are low, appear uniformly gray, and often cover the whole sky are called

    (A) stratus.
    (B) cirrus.
    (C) cumulus.
    (D) cirrocumulus.

19. Mass is measured in

    (A) Newtons.
    (B) Centigrade.
    (C) Celsius.
    (D) kilograms.

20. The contact zone between two different air masses is called a(n)

    (A) cyclone.
    (B) orographic lifting.
    (C) front.
    (D) thunderstorm.

21. Unreactive gases on the periodic table of elements, called noble gases, tend to do which of the following?

    (A) react mostly with transition metals
    (B) combine with most other gases
    (C) not react to other elements
    (D) explode

22. A key source of energy for the human body is

    (A) insulin.
    (B) enzymes.
    (C) carbohydrates.
    (D) cholesterol.

23. When rock weathers, it breaks down and produces

    (A) sediment.
    (B) glaciers.
    (C) coral reefs.
    (D) fossils.

24. How long does it take the Earth to orbit the sun?

    (A) 1 day
    (B) 365 days
    (C) 7 days
    (D) 88 days

25. What type of storm causes clouds to become electrically charged?

    (A) tornadoes
    (B) thunderstorms
    (C) tsunamis
    (D) snowstorms

# Arithmetic Reasoning

**Time:** 36 Minutes

**Questions:** 30

**Directions:** This section tests your ability to reason through mathematical problems using basic arithmetic. Carefully read each question and choose the answer choice that best answers the question.

1. A real estate agent completes the sale of a $2.2 million home. She will get a 6% commission. Of that amount, she has to give 40% to the firm she works for. About how much money will she actually take home from the sale?

   (A) $50,000
   (B) $80,000
   (C) $95,000
   (D) $135,000

2. On Election Day, 5,500 people voted for two candidates. If Candidate A received 3,080 votes, by what percentage did Candidate B lose the election?

   (A) 7%
   (B) 10%
   (C) 12%
   (D) 44%

3. 5!

   (A) 55
   (B) 100
   (C) 120
   (D) 123

4. The senior center has 145 members. If 29 are men and the rest are women, what is the ratio of men to women?

   (A) $\frac{2}{3}$
   (B) $\frac{5}{10}$
   (C) $\frac{5}{8}$
   (D) $\frac{1}{4}$

5. If you travel from point A at 60 miles per hour to point B 120 miles away, how long will you be on the road?

   (A) 1.5 hours
   (B) 2 hours
   (C) 2.25 hours
   (D) 3 hours

6. If you make a 15% down payment on a $23,462 car, how much money do you have left to pay?

   (A) $19,942.70
   (B) $22,733.21
   (C) $43,000.00
   (D) $86,000.00

7. Kelly purchased a book for $3.45 at an online store. She did not have to pay tax, but she did have to pay $7.32 in shipping charges. How much did her total purchase cost?

    (A) $9.22
    (B) $10.47
    (C) $10.77
    (D) $11.82

8. Farmer Joe harvested enough hay over the last four years to make 22, 30, 35, and 32 bales of hay, respectively. If Joe sold each bale for $25, what's the average amount of money he took in over the last four years?

    (A) $650.22
    (B) $743.75
    (C) $1,572.64
    (D) $2,975.75

9. If the value of a bond increases by .25 dollars per week, how much will a $25 bond be worth after seven years?

    (A) $13
    (B) $43
    (C) $91
    (D) $116

10. $\sqrt{81}$ =

    (A) 9
    (B) 10
    (C) 11
    (D) 12

11. You have to buy pencils, markers, erasers, and paper to get ready for the upcoming school year. The local stationery store sells packages of pencils for $1.25, markers for $1.75, erasers for 50¢, and paper for $2.50. If you buy one package of each for each of your three children, how much will all your school supplies cost?

    (A) $17
    (B) $18
    (C) $19
    (D) $20

12. When school lets out for the summer, 75% of the students in Miss George's class said they would start camp within the week. The rest were going on vacation. If Miss George had 28 students in her class, what is the ratio of students who were going to camp versus those going on vacation?

    (A) 1:3
    (B) 3:1
    (C) 4:5
    (D) 5:4

13. Your test scores are 89, 63, 75, 80, 85, and 92. What is your average test grade?

    (A) 68.9
    (B) 73.7
    (C) 78.2
    (D) 80.6

14. A class of 126 students fills out surveys about their future plans. Every student responds: 36 women and 90 men. If $\frac{3}{4}$ of the women and $\frac{5}{6}$ of the male respondents said they were going to college, about how many total students said they are pursuing other options?

    (A) 15
    (B) 22
    (C) 24
    (D) 102

15. A cookie jar has four chocolate chip cookies, two oatmeal cookies, five sugar cookies, and two gingerbread cookies. If you close your eyes and pick a cookie at random, what are the chances that you'll take out any other cookie besides an oatmeal one?

    (A) 6/7
    (B) 2/14
    (C) 1/7
    (D) 5/14

16. Sabrina is three years older than Draydon, who is $\frac{1}{3}$ Blake's age. If Blake just turned 18, how old is Sabrina?

    (A) 7
    (B) 8
    (C) 9
    (D) 10

17. Addie is planning a road trip to Las Vegas. If she lives 426 miles away, about how fast would she have to drive if she wanted to make it there in six hours?

    (A) 70 mph
    (B) 71 mph
    (C) 75 mph
    (D) 80 mph

18. If your boss gives you $67 from a sale that you rang up as $342.50, what percentage of commission did you get?

    (A) 19.6
    (B) 20.9
    (C) 22.8
    (D) 25.4

19. You want to tile your kitchen floor, which is 6.5 ft by 12.5 ft. How many whole 2 × 2-ft tiles will you need to buy to cover the entire floor?

    (A) 18
    (B) 19
    (C) 20
    (D) 21

20. What is three fifths of 185?

    (A) 101
    (B) 105
    (C) 111
    (D) 220

21. The widget factory can make 45 widgets in two hours. If it ran six hours a day, how many widgets could it make in half of a seven-day week?

    (A) 427.5
    (B) 472.5
    (C) 574.2
    (D) 752.4

22. If a car costs $3,985, how much money would you owe if you made a down payment of $\frac{2}{3}$ the price?

    (A) $1,328.33
    (B) $1,458.60
    (C) $1,574.80
    (D) $1,628.90

23. It takes Jim 45 minutes to walk 2.5 miles. If he has to meet Casey at a park seven miles away at 12:30 P.M., what time would he have to start walking to make it there on time?

    (A) 10:14 P.M.
    (B) 10:14 A.M.
    (C) 10:24 P.M.
    (D) 10:24 A.M.

24. You make 30 bracelets and bring them to school. One third of the class wants one bracelet each. If you have 24 bracelets left at the end of the day, how many students did you give bracelets to?

    (A) 3
    (B) 6
    (C) 9
    (D) 12

25. Say you need to earn an extra $3,689 this year to afford a cruise to Aruba this summer. You get a part-time job that pays $8.49 per hour. How many hours will you have to work to earn enough money to pay for the trip?

    (A) 226.89
    (B) 368.20
    (C) 434.51
    (D) 552.28

26. If you draw a chalk circle on your driveway with a diameter of 22 feet, what is its radius?

    (A) 11 feet
    (B) 22 feet
    (C) 44 feet
    (D) 66 feet

27. A bag holds four red beads, three blue beads, and eight black beads. If you reach into the bag, what is the probability you will draw a blue bead?

    (A) $\dfrac{1}{5}$

    (B) $\dfrac{3}{16}$

    (C) $\dfrac{4}{15}$

    (D) $\dfrac{8}{15}$

28. If 17 of the 132 English faculty on a community college campus has a doctorate degree, about what percentage of the total faculty does NOT?

    (A) 24%
    (B) 56%
    (C) 82%
    (D) 87%

29. Your favorite band is playing at the stadium near your house. When you call to get tickets, you find out that only 38% of the seats have been sold. If the stadium has 1,500 seats, how many are still available?

    (A) 390
    (B) 570
    (C) 930
    (D) 1,280

30. Nora plays racquetball twice a week with Jan and three times a week with Blaine. If she has to pay $3.75 for each player, including herself, how much money does she spend on racquetball games per week?

    (A) $7.50
    (B) $11.25
    (C) $18.75
    (D) $37.50

# Word Knowledge

**Time:** 11 Minutes

**Questions:** 35

**Directions:** This section tests your knowledge of and ability to use vocabulary. Read each question and choose the answer choice that most nearly means the same as the underlined word.

1. The police needed <u>concrete</u> evidence that showed the woman committed the crime before they could make an arrest.

   (A) inconsistent
   (B) tangible
   (C) merited
   (D) difficult

2. <u>Expectant</u> most nearly means

   (A) anticipative.
   (B) incorrect.
   (C) beloved.
   (D) normal.

3. Her <u>inventive</u> ideas were what won the team high marks for creativity in the competition.

   (A) frigid
   (B) optimal
   (C) clever
   (D) dispassionate

4. <u>Opulent</u> most nearly means

   (A) simple.
   (B) advanced.
   (C) meager.
   (D) luxuriant.

5. <u>Omnipotent</u> most nearly means

   (A) encompassing.
   (B) supreme.
   (C) panoramic.
   (D) interesting.

6. <u>Germane</u> most nearly means

   (A) suited.
   (B) foreign.
   (C) harsh.
   (D) benign.

7. <u>Meander</u> most nearly means

   (A) navigate.
   (B) attack.
   (C) zigzag.
   (D) forgive.

8. <u>Atrocious</u> most nearly means

   (A) horrible.
   (B) unmoving.
   (C) excited.
   (D) lonely.

9. The <u>intrepid</u> warrior stood vigil over the sleeping camp throughout the night, never taking his eyes away from the path where enemies could approach.

   (A) outgoing
   (B) meek
   (C) gutsy
   (D) arrogant

10. Succinct most nearly means

    (A) amuse.

    (B) match.

    (C) heavy.

    (D) blunt.

11. Vociferous most nearly means

    (A) loud.

    (B) singular.

    (C) decision.

    (D) selective.

12. Frugal most nearly means

    (A) open.

    (B) cheap.

    (C) fortunate.

    (D) easy.

13. Judicious most nearly means

    (A) intuitive.

    (B) instructive.

    (C) judgmental.

    (D) prudent.

14. Even though Mary said she was happy, her mother's astute senses alerted her that there was something her daughter was worried about.

    (A) dull

    (B) buried

    (C) sharp

    (D) clouded

15. Her tendency to say what she thought whenever she liked made most people view her as abrasive.

    (A) incredulous

    (B) tactless

    (C) available

    (D) instinctive

16. Incorrigible most nearly means

    (A) calm.

    (B) sincere.

    (C) respectful.

    (D) unruly.

17. Stringent most nearly means

    (A) mainstream.

    (B) severe.

    (C) offensive.

    (D) wicked.

18. After an immense search effort that encompassed hundreds of miles, the man was not able to locate a source of water for the village.

    (A) heroic

    (B) fortuitous

    (C) intimate

    (D) tremendous

19. Potent most nearly means

    (A) eligible.

    (B) strong.

    (C) makeshift.

    (D) irritating.

20. Bigotry most nearly means

    (A) antagonism.

    (B) admiration.

    (C) chauvinism.

    (D) transcendence.

21. I didn't mean to belittle the club's generous financial contribution to the charity by suggesting we aim for a higher goal next year.

    (A) demean

    (B) praise

    (C) insist

    (D) exclaim

22. <u>Opponent</u> most nearly means

    (A) acquaintance.

    (B) friend.

    (C) catalyst.

    (D) antagonist.

23. <u>Eloquent</u> most nearly means

    (A) elegant.

    (B) articulate.

    (C) mumbled.

    (D) relatable.

24. <u>Florid</u> most nearly means

    (A) short.

    (B) ornate.

    (C) simple.

    (D) exponential.

25. <u>Dialogue</u> most nearly means

    (A) insist.

    (B) argue.

    (C) chat.

    (D) accuse.

26. One of Anne's favorite weekend activities was going to the bookstore to <u>peruse</u> the new titles released that week.

    (A) examine

    (B) interact

    (C) eliminate

    (D) sanctify

27. The car that tapped my rear bumper caused only <u>superficial</u> damage.

    (A) significant

    (B) internal

    (C) external

    (D) permanent

28. <u>Mischievous</u> most nearly means

    (A) playful.

    (B) obedient.

    (C) forgiven.

    (D) uninitiated.

29. It took nearly two years of physical therapy, but Liam was able to <u>recuperate</u> from having both legs broken in a car accident.

    (A) respond

    (B) reconstitute

    (C) relive

    (D) recover

30. <u>Reticence</u> most nearly means

    (A) openness.

    (B) intelligence.

    (C) historic.

    (D) reserve.

31. Having already been through a bad divorce, Ted was <u>averse</u> to the idea of getting married again.

    (A) affectionate

    (B) resistant

    (C) perplexed

    (D) efficient

32. <u>Predecessor</u> most nearly means

    (A) instigator.

    (B) infiltrator.

    (C) ancestor.

    (D) substitute.

33. <u>Procrastinate</u> most nearly means

    (A) delay.

    (B) force.

    (C) retaliate.

    (D) pursue.

34. Mary chose a fast-paced, inspiring story to <u>uplift</u> the students' mood in her early morning class.

    (A) moisten
    (B) entrance
    (C) forego
    (D) elevate

35. <u>Militant</u> most nearly means

    (A) instinctive.
    (B) revolutionary.
    (C) proper.
    (D) reserved.

# Paragraph Comprehension

**Time:** 13 Minutes

**Questions:** 15

**Directions:** This section tests your ability to read and understand written information, as well as come to logical conclusions based on a text. Read each passage and answer the questions that follow. Choose the answer choice that best answers the question.

(1) Organic foods and other natural products should be more accessible to the general consumer. (2) Too often they are only found online, which requires shipping, or in specialty shops in remote areas. (3) Being able to purchase a variety of organic foods at your local grocery store would make it easier for consumers to live healthy lifestyles. (4) It would also stimulate sales for this growing industry.

1. The main idea of this passage is stated in which sentence?

    (A) 1
    (B) 2
    (C) 3
    (D) 4

*Use the following passage to answer questions 2–3:*

The Louisiana Purchase was a strategic political move for President Thomas Jefferson. Since 1762, this 828,800-square-mile expanse of land between the East and West Coasts had been controlled by the Spanish and French. By purchasing the Louisiana Territory from Napoleon in 1803, Jefferson was able to secure trade access to the port of New Orleans and greatly increase the United States' standing as a formidable country.

2. The Louisiana Purchase was

(A) a significant part of American history.

(B) a strategic move for Spain.

(C) a way to antagonize Canada.

(D) insignificant in comparison to the wars going on in Europe at the time.

3. The main idea of the passage is that

(A) no forethought went into the consequences of the Louisiana Purchase.

(B) without the Louisiana Purchase, Jefferson would not have been reelected.

(C) the Louisiana Purchase was not supported by American allies.

(D) the Louisiana Purchase was a strategic move to improve America's economic and political standing in the world.

*Use the following passage to answer questions 4–6:*

Deforestation is a serious issue that more people should take an active part in preventing. Not only does the decline of vegetation and trees in certain sections of Earth contribute to global warming, but habitats for myriad species are also being destroyed. As a result, these species are facing certain extinction.

If too many types of plants and animals no longer exist on Earth, serious ecological consequences may occur. These include increased populations of insects and pests, interruptions in the food chain that can lead to famine and pestilence worldwide, the breakdown of entire ecosystems, and an increase in the speed of global warming. It is every citizen's responsibility to educate themselves about the dangers of deforestation and how they can do their part in slowing down its progress.

4. The author would most likely support

(A) legislation approving the building of housing developments on nature preserves.

(B) a community education program that teaches people how they can contribute to reforestation efforts.

(C) increased imports from South American farms that have recently expanded into the rainforest.

(D) efforts to support a boost in the timber industry.

5. In the passage, <u>myriad</u> most nearly means

(A) a finite amount.

(B) a disproportionate amount.

(C) many types of.

(D) interesting.

6. The tone of this passage can best be described as

(A) contemplative.

(B) persuasive.

(C) dispassionate.

(D) lazy.

*Use the following passage to answer questions 7–8:*

> Coffee beans are not actually beans, but rather roasted seeds of coffee berries. After the seeds are separated from the berries, they're fermented, cleaned, and air dried. Now called green coffee beans, they must be roasted before they are consumed. The internal temperature must be raised to at least 205° Celsius to produce caffeol oil, which produces the flavor commonly associated with coffee.

7. What is produced when the internal temperature of a coffee bean reaches at least 205° Celsius?

    (A) caffeine

    (B) caffeol oil

    (C) dark coloring

    (D) extra flavor

8. According to the paragraph,

    (A) coffee beans can be eaten directly from the plant.

    (B) coffee beans taste like berries.

    (C) coffee beans must be cleaned before they are fermented.

    (D) coffee beans are seeds.

*Use the following passage to answer questions 9–10:*

> The U.S. Constitution mandates that the federal government take a national census every 10 years. The data is used to calculate how many congressional seats need to be appointed per state, to determine the number of electoral votes each state gets, and to set state and municipal funding. Census data also gives comprehensive demographic information about the population.

9. In this paragraph, the word <u>mandates</u> most nearly means

    (A) enlists.

    (B) believes.

    (C) requires.

    (D) restricts.

10. The purpose of this passage is to

    (A) inform.

    (B) persuade.

    (C) incite.

    (D) evaluate.

*Use the following passage to answer questions 11–12:*

> Vitamin C is an essential nutrient for maintaining good health. It helps boost the immune system, acts as a natural antihistamine, and can help wounds heal faster. While citrus fruits, such as oranges and lemons, are the foods most often associated with vitamin C, many other fruits and vegetables are rich in this nutrient. Red peppers, cantaloupe, strawberries, kiwi, and mangoes are all good choices for someone looking to increase the amount of vitamin C in their diet.

11. According to the passage, vitamin C would be something a person should add to their diet if they

    (A) were preparing for a test.

    (B) were looking to run faster.

    (C) had a paper cut.

    (D) needed to sleep better.

12. A good title for this passage would be

    (A) How to Live a Healthy Life

    (B) Simple Homeopathic Remedies

    (C) Nutrients and Your Health

    (D) The Health Benefits of Vitamin C

*Use the following passage to answer questions 13–15:*

Everyone should take an interest in their local government. Not enough people attend their local town council meetings and are not informed about the decisions their leaders are making about laws that can affect their lives. It's our responsibility as American citizens to monitor the actions of our elected officials and hold them accountable. If we don't, then who will?

13. According to the passage, the average citizen

   (A) is not informed about the actions of their local government.

   (B) attends town council meetings regularly.

   (C) has a good understanding of how local government works.

   (D) pays attention to their surroundings.

14. In the passage, <u>accountable</u> most nearly means

   (A) is interested in an outcome.

   (B) has assets at stake.

   (C) is responsible for one's actions.

   (D) is informed about circumstances.

15. The author of this passage would most likely agree with which of the following statements?

   (A) Too many people come to council meetings.

   (B) Elected officials must answer to the public.

   (C) Council meetings are the best place to air a grievance about the community.

   (D) Town councils should recognize citizens more often.

# Mathematics Knowledge

**Time:** 24 Minutes

**Questions:** 25

**Directions:** This section tests your knowledge of basic mathematics, algebra, and geometry. Carefully read each question and choose the answer choice that reflects the best answer.

1. $(a + 5) (a + 8)$

    (A) $a^2 + 3a + 40$
    (B) $a^2 + 13a + 40$
    (C) $a^3 + 3a + 40$
    (D) $a^3 + 13a + 40$

2. If $b = 4$, then $5 \times b^3 + \dfrac{3b}{2} =$

    (A) 326
    (B) 345
    (C) 425
    (D) 623

3. $y^2 \times y^3 \times y^4 \times y^5 =$

    (A) $y^1$
    (B) $y^{-10}$
    (C) $y^{14}$
    (D) $y^{120}$

4. A vertex is

    (A) the space an object occupies.
    (B) a single number or variable, or combinations of them.
    (C) action you need to take with a value.
    (D) the point where the two lines that make up an angle intersect.

5. Solve for $x$: $4x - 3 < 5 + 2y$

    (A) $x < 2 + 2y$
    (B) $x < \dfrac{8 + 2y}{4}$
    (C) $x > 2 - 2y$
    (D) $x > \dfrac{8 - 2y}{4}$

6. $32.6\overline{)4}$

    (A) .122
    (B) .123
    (C) .124
    (D) .125

7. Solve for $y$: $x + 2y - 4x + 6 = 2$

    (A) $y = -2 + \dfrac{3x}{2}$
    (B) $y = -2 + 3x$
    (C) $y = 4 - \dfrac{3x}{2}$
    (D) $y = 2 + \dfrac{3x}{2}$

8. If a rectangular solid has a length of 3 meters, a height of 5 meters, and a width of 10 meters, what is its total surface area?

    (A) 30 m²
    (B) 60 m²
    (C) 150 m²
    (D) 190 m²

9. $12.475 \times 20.2 =$

    (A) 25.19950

    (B) 251.9950

    (C) 2519.950

    (D) 25199.50

10. $6\frac{1}{4} \div \frac{5}{8} =$

    (A) $5\frac{5}{24}$

    (B) 8

    (C) 10

    (D) $5\frac{6}{24}$

11. Solve for $x$: $3x + 5^2 \neq 7 - 12$

    (A) 7

    (B) 10

    (C) 11

    (D) 16

12. Factor: $b^2 - 14b + 24$

    (A) $(b + 2)(b + 12)$

    (B) $(b - 2)(b + 12)$

    (C) $(b + 2)(b - 12)$

    (D) $(b - 2)(b - 12)$

13. A quadrilateral with two parallel sides is called a

    (A) parallelogram.

    (B) polygon.

    (C) trapezoid.

    (D) rhombus.

14. If side $a$ in a right triangle equals 6 and the hypotenuse equals 7.8, the value of side $b$ equals

    (A) 24.84

    (B) 60.84

    (C) $\sqrt{24.84}$

    (D) $\sqrt{60.84}$

15. $[(6 + 4)^2 + (14 - 8)] - \frac{2}{3} \times \frac{9}{2} =$

    (A) 52

    (B) 54

    (C) 103

    (D) 106

16. Solve for $a$: $\frac{3}{6} = \frac{a}{12}$

    (A) 6

    (B) 8

    (C) 12

    (D) 15

17. In the following diagram, the value of side $b$ is proportional to the value of side

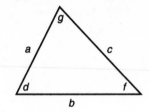 

    (A) $x$

    (B) $y$

    (C) $z$

    (D) $d$

18. What is 16,597,000,000 equal to in scientific notation?

    (A) $1.6597 \times 10^9$

    (B) $1.6597 \times 10^{10}$

    (C) $1.6597 \times 10^{11}$

    (D) $1.6597 \times 10^{12}$

19. $2\frac{4}{5} - \frac{7}{8} =$

    (A) $\frac{40}{37}$

    (B) $\frac{37}{40}$

    (C) $1\frac{23}{40}$

    (D) $1\frac{37}{40}$

20. In an isosceles right triangle, two sides are

    (A) divisible.

    (B) equal.

    (C) unequal.

    (D) complimentary.

21. The following shape is a

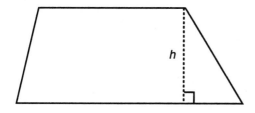

    (A) rhombus.

    (B) hexagon.

    (C) trapezoid.

    (D) chord.

22. $8! =$

    (A) –20

    (B) 36

    (C) 22,961

    (D) 40,320

23. Factor: $c^2 - 121$

    (A) $(c + 11)(c - 11)$

    (B) $(c - 11)(c + 11)$

    (C) $(c + 11)(c + 12)$

    (D) $(c + 11)(c - 12)$

24. Two angles that share a common side are

    (A) adjacent.

    (B) congruent.

    (C) similar.

    (D) straight.

25. One side of a square is 15.2 ft. What is the area of the square?

    (A) 30.4 ft$^2$

    (B) 60.8 ft$^2$

    (C) 121.6 ft$^2$

    (D) 231.04 ft$^2$

# Electronics Information

**Time:** 9 Minutes

**Questions:** 20

**Directions:** This section tests your knowledge of basic electronics principles and applications. Carefully read each question and choose the answer choice that reflects the best answer.

1. In what direction does current flow on a circuit diagram?

    (A) positive to negative
    (B) positive to neutral
    (C) negative to positive
    (D) negative to neutral

2. Insulators are often made from

    (A) copper.
    (B) plastic.
    (C) rubber.
    (D) iron.

3. The following is the symbol for a

    (A) fuse.
    (B) wire.
    (C) capacitor.
    (D) diode.

4. If you have 15 volts and 180 watts of power, how many amps do you have?

    (A) 10
    (B) 12
    (C) 270
    (D) 280

5. What type of power source is represented in the following diagram?

    (A) gas-powered generator
    (B) circuit
    (C) diode
    (D) battery

6. What pushes electrons along their path in a circuit?

    (A) protons
    (B) electricity
    (C) ohms
    (D) amps

7. Heating elements, lightbulbs, and motors are all examples of

    (A) conductors.
    (B) switches.
    (C) loads.
    (D) circuits.

8. If you have a wave whose speed is 20m/s and length is 2 meters, its frequency is

    (A) 40Hz.
    (B) 22Hz.
    (C) 18Hz.
    (D) 10Hz.

9. The following is the symbol for a(n)

   (A) transformer.
   (B) resistor.
   (C) battery.
   (D) aerial.

10. If you have 50 volts and 10 ohms, how many amps do you have?

   (A) 5
   (B) 500
   (C) .20
   (D) 25

11. Resistance causes

   (A) friction.
   (B) power surges.
   (C) circuit malfunction.
   (D) electric shock.

12. The type of frequency easiest to hear is

   (A) low.
   (B) high.
   (C) midrange.
   (D) none of the above—they are all equal.

13. If you have 15 volts and 5 amps, how many ohms do you have?

   (A) 75
   (B) 10
   (C) 20
   (D) 3

14. This device is used to measure power:

   (A) ohmmeter
   (B) voltmeter
   (C) wattmeter
   (D) ammeter

15. What is used to measure alternating current?

   (A) frequency
   (B) direct current
   (C) electromagnetic
   (D) amplitude modulated

16. What is the purpose of the following diagram?

   (A) to convert AC to DC power
   (B) to smooth and increase DC voltage
   (C) to supply DC power to electronic circuits
   (D) to convert main AC supply to low-voltage AC

17. When two things have the same frequency, the result is

   (A) scattered wavelengths.
   (B) interference.
   (C) rectilinear propagation.
   (D) waves bending.

18. If you have 15 volts and 1 ohm of resistance, how many amps do you have?

   (A) 16
   (B) 14
   (C) 15
   (D) 1

19. If you have a wave whose wavelength is 4 meters and a frequency of 3 Hz, what is the wave speed?

    (A) 7 meters per second

    (B) .75 meters per second

    (C) 12 meters per second

    (D) 1 meter per second

20. Good conductors of electricity offer _____ resistance:

    (A) high

    (B) 5 ohms of

    (C) 10-gauge

    (D) low

# Automotive and Shop Information

**Time:** 11 Minutes

**Questions:** 25

**Directions:** This section tests your knowledge of automotive components and principles, as well as general shop tools and applications. Carefully read each question and choose the answer choice that reflects the best answer.

*Refer to the following diagram to answer questions 1–3:*

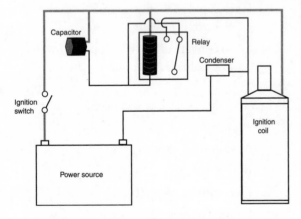

**Ignition System**

1. The battery transfers power through the _____ to the _____ after you turn the key.

    (A) ignition switch, ignition coil

    (B) capacitor, relay

    (C) condenser, ignition coil

    (D) relay, power source

2. The solenoid is another word for which part pictured in the diagram?

    (A) capacitor

    (B) relay

    (C) condenser

    (D) ignition coil

3. In what position is the ignition switch as illustrated in the diagram? Is power being passed through the circuit?

    (A) open; yes, power is being passed through the circuit

    (B) closed; yes, power is being passed through the circuit

    (C) open; no, power is not being passed through the circuit

    (D) closed; no, power is not being passed through the circuit

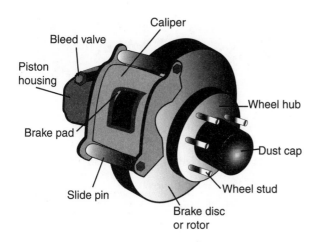

*Use the previous diagram to answer questions 4–6.*

4. Which type of brake is pictured?

   (A) drum brake

   (B) disc brake

   (C) emergency brake

   (D) secondary brake

5. Which of the parts pictured in the diagram houses the brake pads?

   (A) slide pin

   (B) wheel hub

   (C) rotor

   (D) caliper

6. After pressing on the brake pedal, hydraulic pressure is exerted on what?

   (A) bleed valve

   (B) brake pad

   (C) piston

   (D) dust cap

7. When can a resonator be found on an exhaust system?

   (A) when a standard muffler won't fit on the undercarriage of the car

   (B) when a catalytic converter won't fit on the undercarriage of the car

   (C) when the air injection tube won't fit on the undercarriage of the car

   (D) when there isn't room for a dual exhaust system on the undercarriage of the car

8. Which part is used to control the emissions of the car?

   (A) tailpipe

   (B) catalytic converter

   (C) exhaust pipe

   (D) muffler

9. Which part of the exhaust system is the last to guide gases out and away from the vehicle?

   (A) exhaust pipe

   (B) catalytic converter

   (C) hanger

   (D) tailpipe

10. When gasoline is converted to motion, what is the second stroke in the four-stroke process?

   (A) combustion stroke

   (B) intake stroke

   (C) compression stroke

   (D) exhaust stroke

11. The piston starts the Otto Cycle in which position?

    (A) up
    (B) down
    (C) open
    (D) closed

12. What is the purpose of the ignition system?

    (A) to stop the car
    (B) to provide the initial source of power to the suspension system
    (C) to keep the engine cool
    (D) to create a spark that will ignite the fuel–air mixture in the cylinder of the engine

13. Carburetors have been replaced by what component of the fuel system in modern cars?

    (A) fuel injector
    (B) fuel filter
    (C) fuel pump
    (D) alternator

14. The radiator consists of a network of _____ that cools hot fluid from the engine.

    (A) pumps
    (B) calipers
    (C) pistons
    (D) tubes

15. A brake drum is _____.

    (A) solid
    (B) hollow
    (C) full of brake fluid
    (D) attached to the calipers

*Use the previous diagram to answer questions 16–17.*

16. What type of hammer is pictured?

    (A) rubber mallet
    (B) ball pein
    (C) engineer's
    (D) tinner's

17. What type of work is the hammer NOT suited for?

    (A) metal shaping
    (B) construction projects
    (C) auto repairs
    (D) driving rivets into sheet metal

*Use the previous diagram to answer questions 18–19.*

18. What type of tool is pictured?

    (A) hand drill
    (B) Allen wrench
    (C) auger bit
    (D) bar clamp

19. Why would a woodworker prefer the pictured tool over its powered counterpart?

    (A) It is easier to use.

    (B) It can bore larger holes.

    (C) It is faster to use.

    (D) It offers total control.

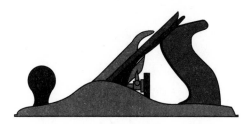

*Use the previous diagram to answer questions 20–22.*

20. What type of tool is pictured?

    (A) pipe clamp

    (B) hand screw

    (C) jack plane

    (D) block plane

21. What is the purpose of the pictured tool?

    (A) smooth out wood joints

    (B) trim wood edges in tight spaces

    (C) apply inward pressure to an object

    (D) hold a pipe in place for cutting or threading

22. Which category does the tool pictured fit into?

    (A) cutting tools

    (B) shaping tools

    (C) clamping tools

    (D) power tools

23. Which of the following is NOT a common type of saw?

    (A) hack

    (B) miter

    (C) chisel

    (D) crosscut

24. Which type of power drill is generally bolted to a workbench or the floor?

    (A) pistol grip

    (B) hammer drill

    (C) drill press

    (D) jigsaw drill

25. What type of tool has tiny, ridgelike grooves used to smooth out rough edges of wood, metal, or plastic?

    (A) file

    (B) rasp

    (C) chisel

    (D) crosscut saw

# Mechanical Comprehension

**Time:** 19 Minutes

**Questions:** 25

**Directions:** This section tests your knowledge and application of basic mechanical principles. Carefully read each question and choose the answer choice that reflects the best answer.

1. Suppose your son is playing tee ball, and he strikes the ball with the bat. The ball rolls along the ground all the way down the first baseline. Which of the following is NOT an example of work being done in this scenario?

   (A) Your son does work on the bat.

   (B) The bat does work on the ball.

   (C) The ball does work on the bat.

   (D) The ball does work on the ground.

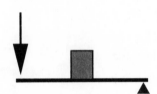

2. Which type of lever is pictured above?

   (A) 1st class

   (B) 2nd class

   (C) 3rd class

   (D) 4th class

3. Suppose you are trying to balance stacks of books on a 1st-class lever. One stack weighs 25 pounds, and the other stack weighs 50 pounds. If the books are placed 15 meters from one another on the lever, how far should each stack be from the fulcrum?

   (A) The 50-pound stack should be 5 meters from the fulcrum, while the 25-pound stack should be 10 meters from the fulcrum.

   (B) The 50-pound stack should be 10 meters from the fulcrum, while the 25-pound stack should be 5 meters from the fulcrum.

   (C) The 50-pound stack should be 15 meters from the fulcrum, while the 25-pound stack should be 15 meters from the fulcrum.

   (D) The 50-pound stack should be 25 meters from the fulcrum, while the 25-pound stack should be 50 meters from the fulcrum.

4. A nutcracker, wheelbarrow, and wrench are all example of which type of lever?

   (A) 2nd class

   (B) 3rd class

   (C) 1st class

   (D) 4th class

5. Mechanical advantage _____ with each additional pulley.

    (A) decreases

    (B) remains the same

    (C) changes, depending on what size the pulleys are

    (D) increases

6. What is the formula that is used to demonstrate a balanced load on a 1st-class lever?

    (A) $w_1 \div d_1 = w_2 \times d_2$

    (B) $w_1 \times d_2 = w_2 \div d_2$

    (C) $w_1 \times d_1 = w_1 \div d_2$

    (D) $w_1 \times d_1 = w_2 \times d_2$

7. If you have a 40-pound object that is being lifted 8 meters on a fixed pulley, what is your mechanical advantage?

    (A) 1

    (B) 2

    (C) 3

    (D) 4

8. Suppose you have two gears. For each circle the larger gear makes, the smaller gear makes four circles. What is the gear ratio?

    (A) 1:1

    (B) 4:1

    (C) 1:4

    (D) 4:4

9. Suppose you have two gears. One has 200 teeth, and the other has 40 teeth. What is the gear ratio?

    (A) 1:1

    (B) 200:1

    (C) 5:1

    (D) 40:1

10. Which of the following is NOT a purpose for gears?

    (A) change the speed of a mechanism

    (B) change the weight of an object

    (C) change the motion of a device

    (D) change the direction of machinery

11. When an object falls with only the force of gravity acting on it, we call this

    (A) friction.

    (B) acceleration.

    (C) speed.

    (D) freefalling.

12. If you are traveling at a rate of 60 kilometers per hour and you decrease your speed to 45 kilometers per hour over the course of 5 seconds, what is your negative acceleration?

    (A) 3 kilometers per hour per second

    (B) 15 kilometers per second per second

    (C) 5 seconds per mile per second

    (D) 15 miles per second per mile

13. What does velocity measure?

    (A) the change in speed during a given time

    (B) the speed and direction of an object

    (C) the direction and friction of an object

    (D) the gravitational pull on an object

14. The law of reciprocal action states what?

     (A) For every action, there is an identical reaction.

     (B) For every motion, there is an unequal and similar reaction.

     (C) For every action, there is an equal and opposite reaction.

     (D) For every acceleration, there is an identical velocity.

15. Which type of lever is pictured above?

     (A) 1st class

     (B) 2nd class

     (C) 3rd class

     (D) 4th class

16. Newton's second law states that an object accelerates in the direction of what?

     (A) the net force acting on it

     (B) the electromagnetic pressure around it

     (C) the gravitational pull exerted on it

     (D) none of the above

17. What is the formula for force?

     (A) Force = Mass × velocity

     (B) Force = Mass × acceleration

     (C) Force = Acceleration × velocity

     (D) Force = Acceleration × density

18. Suppose that you kick a box that weighs 1 pound, and then you kick another box that weighs 10 pounds. Assume that you kick both with the same amount of effort. How far will the lightweight box move compared to the heavy one?

     (A) the same distance

     (B) 10 times as far

     (C) one tenth as far

     (D) twice as far

19. How is weight expressed in the metric system?

     (A) pounds

     (B) kilograms

     (C) joules

     (D) Newtons

20. How do you determine the mass of an object?

     (A) Volume × Density

     (B) Weight × Height

     (C) Speed × Velocity

     (D) Width × Acceleration

21. Movement of any kind is called what?

     (A) mass

     (B) speed

     (C) acceleration

     (D) motion

22. Suppose you apply 20 kilograms of force against an object for 10 meters. How much work have you done?

     (A) 20 joules

     (B) 10 joules

     (C) 200 joules

     (D) 30 joules

23. Suppose an object weighs 50 kilograms, and it travels at a rate of 5 meters per second. What is the object's kinetic energy?

   (A) 625 joules

   (B) 250 joules

   (C) 1,250 joules

   (D) 55 joules

24. Suppose an object weighs 80 kilograms, and you move it 2 meters. How much work have you done?

   (A) 82 joules

   (B) 160 joules

   (C) 320 joules

   (D) 78 joules

25. Suppose you have two balanced objects on a 1st-class lever, but you know the mass of only one of them. Object #1 weighs 18 kilograms. It is clearly heavier than object #2. If you set the objects 30 feet apart on the lever, with object #1 sitting 10 feet from the fulcrum, how heavy is object #2?

   (A) 9 kilograms

   (B) 10 kilograms

   (C) 11 kilograms

   (D) 12 kilograms

# Assembling Objects

**Time:** 15 Minutes

**Questions:** 25

**Directions:** This section tests your ability to visualize how objects fit together. Carefully read each question and choose the answer choice that reflects the best answer.

1. In the following diagram, which figure best shows how the objects in the first box would touch if points A and B were connected?

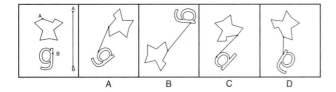

2. Which answer choice best shows how the objects in the first box would appear if they were fitted together?

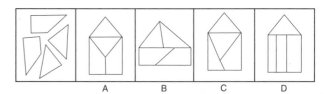

3. In the following diagram, which figure best shows how the objects in the first box would touch if points A and B were connected?

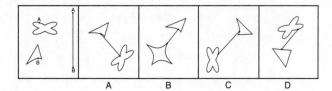

4. Which answer choice best shows how the objects in the first box would appear if they were fitted together?

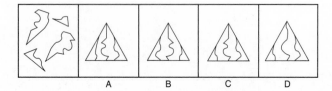

5. In the following diagram, which figure best shows how the objects in the first box would touch if points A and B were connected?

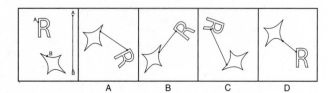

6. Which answer choice best shows how the objects in the first box would appear if they were fitted together?

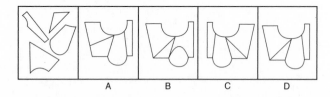

7. In the following diagram, which figure best shows how the objects in the first box would touch if points A and B were connected?

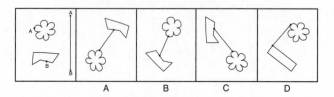

8. Which answer choice best shows how the objects in the first box would appear if they were fitted together?

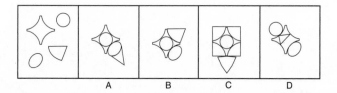

9. Which answer choice best shows how the objects in the first box would appear if they were fitted together?

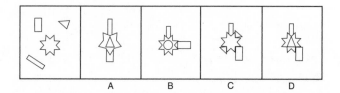

10. In the following diagram, which figure best shows how the objects in the first box would touch if points A and B were connected?

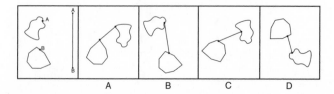

11. In the following diagram, which figure best shows how the objects in the first box would touch if points A and B were connected?

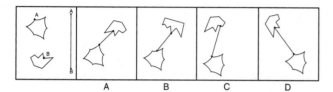

12. Which answer choice best shows how the objects in the first box would appear if they were fitted together?

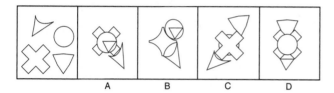

13. In the following diagram, which figure best shows how the objects in the first box would touch if points A and B were connected?

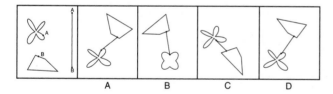

14. Which answer choice best shows how the objects in the first box would appear if they were fitted together?

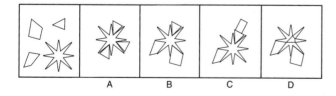

15. In the following diagram, which figure best shows how the objects in the first box would touch if points A and B were connected?

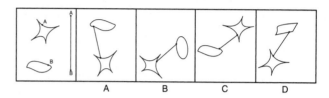

16. Which answer choice best shows how the objects in the first box would appear if they were fitted together?

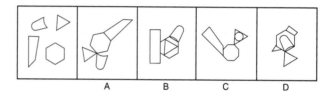

17. In the following diagram, which figure best shows how the objects in the first box would touch if points A and B were connected?

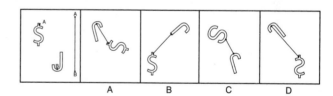

18. Which answer choice best shows how the objects in the first box would appear if they were fitted together?

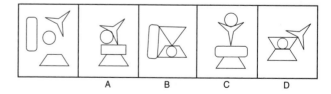

19. In the following diagram, which figure best shows how the objects in the first box would touch if points A and B were connected?

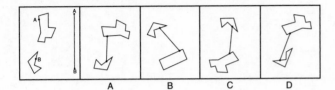

20. Which answer choice best shows how the objects in the first box would appear if they were fitted together?

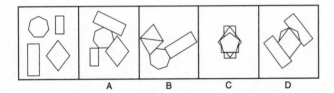

21. In the following diagram, which figure best shows how the objects in the first box would touch if points A and B were connected?

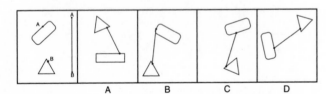

22. Which answer choice best shows how the objects in the first box would appear if they were fitted together?

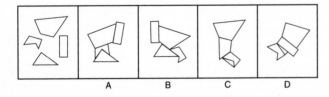

23. In the following diagram, which figure best shows how the objects in the first box would touch if points A and B were connected?

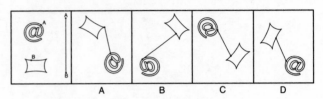

24. Which answer choice best shows how the objects in the first box would appear if they were fitted together?

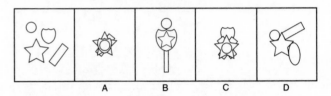

25. In the following diagram, which figure best shows how the objects in the first box would touch if points A and B were connected?

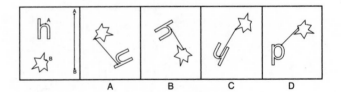

# Answers and Explanations

## General Science

1. **A.** Eliminating answer choices here is a good idea. Because we're dealing with *constant* velocity, we can assume that any answer choice that suggests variation is wrong. That gets rid of C. There is no suggestion of circular tracks in the name. You can infer that you're looking for an answer choice that's all about speed and direction remaining the same, or "constant."

2. **D.** The planets in order from the sun are Mercury, Venus, Earth, Mars, Jupiter, Saturn, Uranus, Neptune, and Pluto.

3. **C.** Hydrogen, oxygen, and carbon are elements. Protons, electrons, and neutrons are parts of an atom. Liter, milliliter, and gram are metric measurements that you have probably seen on soda bottles and other food products.

4. **C.** Magma, by definition, is melted rock. Carbonate and oxide are not types of rock, and granite is a solid rock.

5. **A.** Ninety-two out of 117 elements are metals. There are only 12 non-metals and 5 metalloids. Alkali metals are not a separate category on the periodic table; they fall under the metals category.

6. **B.** Mitosis is the process of dividing one cell nucleus into two nuclei. Answer A is wrong because homeostasis refers to the body maintaining equilibrium or a stable state internally, despite external conditions. Answer C is wrong because stem cells are known for their ability to renew themselves through mitosis. Answer D is wrong because collagen is a protein found in connective tissue.

7. **C.** Human DNA has 23 pairs of chromosomes for a total of 46. Each chromosome contains a strand of DNA and many of our genes, which is the basic way we inherit traits from our ancestors.

8. **C.** Diamond rates a 10 on the Mohs scale of mineral hardness and is considered the hardest substance on Earth. Quartz is 7, topaz is 8, and calcite is only 9. So even if you weren't sure that diamonds were the hardest substance on the planet, it's surely the hardest of your answer choices.

9. **D.** The endocrine system involves all the organs and glands that regulate hormones, which, in turn, affect growth and metabolism. The musculoskeletal system deals with muscles and bones. The nervous system involves nerves and the process of sensing electrical messages throughout the body. The digestive system turns food into energy and takes the nutrients needed to sustain the body.

10. **A.** The moon shines by reflecting sunlight. Like Earth, half of the moon is always lit by the sun's direct rays, and the other half is in shadow.

11. **D.** By definition, an element is a chemical substance made up of a single type of atom. A nucleus is part of an atom. Microscopic refers to the size of something—namely, that it's so small that it can be viewed only with a microscope. A compound is a combination of two or more elements.

12. **B.** Choice A is wrong because the sense of sight is vision. Choice C is wrong because the sense of hearing is audition. Choice D is wrong because the sense of touch is somatic sensation.

13. **A.** Choice B is wrong because iron is needed to make hemoglobin, the protein used to carry oxygen throughout the body. Choice C is wrong because iodide is a component of radioactive waste. Choice D is wrong because fluoride helps prevent tooth decay.

14. **D.** Rain is water condensation that accumulates in clouds. All the other choices refer to different forms of condensation near the ground: dew is liquid, frost is frozen, and fog is vapor.

15. **A.** Even if you didn't know that cartilage acts as a cushion in joints, you could get this right through process of elimination. Choice B is wrong because muscles are tissues that cause motion and are used to move joints. Choice C is wrong because tendons connect muscles to bones. Choice D is wrong because ligaments connect bones to other bones at joints.

16. **A.** You can eliminate answers B and D right away because they are not metals: oxygen is a gas and calcium is a mineral. Aluminum is the most abundant metal in Earth's crust, with iron coming in second.

17. **B.** The stomach helps break down food so that it can be absorbed into the system. The large intestine deals with the waste products of food after all the nutrition is taken out by the small intestine (which is the most complex part of the digestion process). The pancreas produces secretions and hormones to aid in digestion.

18. **A.** Stratus clouds are the ones that look like there's a blanket in the sky. Cirrus clouds are thin and whispy, and found high in the sky. Cumulus clouds look billowy, like cotton balls. Cirrocumulus clouds are high in the sky but are patchy, like a blending of the thinness of cirrus clouds and puffiness of cumulus.

19. **D.** Newtons measure force. Both Centigrade and Celsius measure temperature. Kilograms measure mass.

20. **C.** A cyclone is characterized by a swirling or rotating motion in the same direction the Earth is turning. Orographic lifting refers to movement of masses of air as it travels over terrain. A thunderstorm is a storm in which the air and clouds become electrically charged. A front is the line of demarcation between two air masses.

21. **C.** As the name suggests, unreactive gases do not react to other elements or nearly anything. This includes combining and exploding.

22. **C.** Carbohydrates are quickly and easily converted into sugar, the body's main source of energy. Insulin and enzymes are created by the body to aid in digestion and the absorption and metabolism of food. Cholesterol is a fat-like substance the body produces to help with the production of cells and hormones.

23. **A.** Glaciers are made of ice, not rock. Coral reefs are produced by living creatures, not the weathering of rock. Fossils are remains of a living organism preserved in rock. Sediment is what's left of rock after it has been worn down by time and erosion and transported by wind or water.

24. **B.** The 365-day calendar year marks one entire revolution of Earth around the sun.

25. **B.** A tornado may be accompanied by lightning or electrical activity in the atmosphere, but it is not defined by these characteristics. Snowstorms deliver frozen crystals of water, not electricity. Tsunamis are not even storms, but tidal waves. This leaves thunderstorms, which are defined by the electrical activity they create.

# Arithmetic Reasoning

1. **B.** First calculate how much 6% of $2.2 million is: $2,200,000 × .06 = $132,000. Next, figure out what 40% of $132,000 is: $132,000 × .40 = $52,800. Finally, subtract the second total from the first: $132,000 – $52,800 = $79,200.

2. **C.** First figure out the difference between the election totals: 5,500 – 3,080 = 2,402. Then calculate what percentage 2,402 votes is of the 5,500 total: 2,402 ÷ 5,500 = .44 or 44%. Next, subtract 100 – 44 to find out the percentage of votes the winning candidate got: 56. Last, find the difference between the percentages: 56% – 44% = 12%. Candidate B lost by 12%.

3. **C.** This is a factorial. Calculate: 5! = 5 × 4 × 3 × 2 × 1 = 120.

4. **D.** The number of men = 29. The number of women = 116. Make these the numerator and denominator of a fraction, and then reduce: $\frac{29}{116} = \frac{1}{4}$

5. **B.** This is a rate question. Your job is to figure out the time based on the distance and rate. Plug your values into this equation and solve:

$$\text{Time} = \frac{\text{Distance}}{\text{Rate}}$$
$$\text{Time} = \frac{120}{60} = 2$$

6. **A.** Calculate how much 15% of $23,462 is ($3,519.30). Then subtract that number from $23,462. The answer is $19,942.70.

7. **C.** This is straight-up adding decimals: $\begin{array}{r} 3.45 \\ +7.32 \\ \hline 10.77 \end{array}$

8. **B.** This is a multistep process using simple math. First add each of the values of hay and multiply the sum by 25: (22 + 30 + 35 + 32) × 25 = 119 × 25 = $2,975. Now divide this amount by 4, the number of years in the question, to find the average: $743.75.

9. **D.** Multiply .25 × 52 to find out how much the value of a bond increases in a year: $13. Now multiply 13 × 7 to calculate how much the bond's value will increase in 7 years: $91. Now add that to the base amount of the bond: 25 + 91 = $116.

10. **A.** $9 \times 9 = 81$

11. **B.** Start by adding the cost of each of the types of supplies you need to buy:

    Pencils: $1.25

    Markers: $1.75

    Erasers: $.50

    Paper: $2.50

    $1.25 + 1.75 + .50 + 2.50 = 6$

    Now multiply that amount by the number of children who need supplies to get the total cost: $\$6 \times 3 = \$18$.

12. **B.** Figure out how many students make up 75% of the class by multiplying $28 \times .75 = 21$. This means that 21 students are going to camp and 7 are not. Since the question asks for the ratio of students who are going to camp versus those going on vacation, your ratio should read 21:7. Now reduce to 3:1.

13. **D.** Add the scores and divide by 6: $89 + 63 + 75 + 80 + 85 + 92 = 484$; $\dfrac{484}{6} = 80.6$.

14. **C.** Calculate how many women make up ¾ of respondents: $.75 \times 36 = 27$. Now calculate how many men make up $\dfrac{5}{6}$ of the respondents: $.83 \times 90 = 74.7$. You can round this up to 75. Since you know that 102 (27 + 75) people are pursuing college, subtract this amount from the total number of respondents: $126 - 102 = 24$.

15. **A.** Your total number of cookies is 14. If you were looking to find your chances of picking an oatmeal cookie at random, the probability would be $\dfrac{2}{14}$, or $\dfrac{1}{7}$ when you reduce, since there are only three oatmeal cookies in the jar. However, the question asks about your chances of picking any of the *other* cookies. Since there are 12 cookies that are not oatmeal your probability is $\dfrac{12}{14}$, which reduces to $\dfrac{6}{7}$.

16. **C.** Use what you know about Blake to figure out Draydon's age (she is $\dfrac{1}{3}$ of Blake's age): $\dfrac{1}{3} \times \dfrac{18}{1} = \dfrac{18}{3} = 6$. Now add 3 to that (the number of years Sabrina is older than Draydon), and you have 9 as Sabrina's age.

17. **B.** We can use the Distance = Rate × time formula here. We know that the distance is 426 miles and the time is 6 hours. Plug these numbers into the formula and solve:

    $$426 = r \times 6$$
    $$\dfrac{426}{6} = r$$
    $$71 = r$$

18. **A.** Divide the amount of the commission by the amount of the sale to find the rate of commission: $3425\overline{)670.00000}^{\,.19562}$ . Round up to get the answer that fits best: 19.6%.

19. **D.** First, figure out the area of the floor by multiplying length times width: $6.5 \times 12.5 = 81.25$. Now calculate the area of each tile: $2 \times 2 = 4$. Last, divide 81.25 by 4: 20.31. Since we're talking about whole tiles in this question and your decimal shows that more than 20 tiles will be needed, you have to round to the nearest full tile. Your answer is 21.

20. **C.** $\dfrac{3}{5} \times 185 = \dfrac{3}{5} \times \dfrac{185}{1} = \dfrac{555}{5} = 111$

21. **B.** First figure out how many widgets are produced in an hour: $\dfrac{45}{2} = 22.5$. Now figure out how many hours it would run during half of a seven-day workweek. Since the factory works only six hours per day, multiply that by 7: $6 \times 7 = 42$. Now divide that amount by 2, since you want to find out how many hours the factory produces widgets in half of a workweek: $\dfrac{42}{2} = 21$. Now multiply that amount by 22.5: $21 \times 22.5 = 472.5$.

22. **A.** Calculate the amount of money you made for the down payment: $3,985 ÷ 3 = $1,328.33. This is the value of one third of the car's price, or what is owed after your down payment.

23. **D.** Calculate how long it would take Jim to walk 7 miles. You can use a proportion for this: $\frac{45}{2.5} = \frac{t}{7}$. Cross multiply to figure out the missing value:

$45 \times 7 = t \times 2.5$

$315 = t \times 2.5$

$\frac{315}{2.5} = t$

$126 = t$

It will take Jim 126 minutes to walk to the park. Subtract this from 12:30, and you'll find he has to leave his house at 10:24 A.M.

24. **B.** Though this may look like a complicated question, it's really simple subtraction. Since those whom you gave the bracelets to got only one each, subtract 24 from 30 to get your answer of 6.

25. **C.** Division will do the trick here. Divide 3,689 by 8.49 $\left( 849\overline{)368900.00}^{\,434.51} \right)$ to find that you need to work 434.51 hours to earn the money for the trip.

26. **A.** The value of a radius is half the diameter: $\frac{22}{2} = 11$

27. **A.** There are 15 beads total. Three are blue. Write out a ratio of $\frac{3}{15}$ and reduce to $\frac{1}{5}$.

28. **D.** Figure out how many members of the faculty do not have doctorates: 132 − 17 = 115. From this number, you can eliminate answers A and B, since you can estimate that 115 is well over 56% of 132. Now divide that number by the number of total faculty to get the percentage: $\frac{115}{132}$ = .87.

29. **C.** Multiply the number of total seats by the percentage sold already: .38 × 1,500 = 570. Now subtract this total from 1,500: 1,500 − 570 = 930.

30. **D.** Calculate the cost for each person by multiplying the cost of a game by the number of times per week they go:

Nora: 5 × 3.75 = 18.75

Jan: 2 × 3.75 = 7.50

Blaine: 3 × 3.75 = 11.25

Now add the sums to get $37.50.

# Word Knowledge

1. **B.** If you do a quick swap of the underlined word for the answer choices, you can eliminate answers C and D right away; they just don't make sense. If you had *inconsistent* evidence, the police would likely not be able to make an arrest, since such evidence would be unreliable. The best choice here is answer B, which means something that can be touched or is actual.

2. **A.** Break this word down into its base word: *expect*. When you expect something, you anticipate it. Answer A has the base word of "anticipate." All the other answer choices don't fit.

3. **C.** The sentence tells us that the woman's ideas were creative, so the correct answer will have something to do with creativity. *Frigid* is cold, *optimal* is favorable, and *dispassionate* is without passion or enthusiasm. This leaves *clever*, which involves showing mental skill and creativity.

4. **D.** *Opulent* means "luxurious" or "finely appointed." Answers A and C are the opposite of this meaning, and answer B has nothing to do with luxury. Answer D is most likely, especially since *luxury* is the base word in this choice.

5. **B.** This is a good word to break down by roots. *Omni* means "all-encompassing" and *potent* means "power." The correct answer will mean "all-powerful." Answers A and C have that encompassing aspect of the prefix but say nothing about power. Answer D just doesn't fit with what we're looking for, whereas answer B is a decent fit, since *supremacy* implies encompassing power.

6. **A.** *Germane* means "appropriate" and has a neutral connotation. Answers C and D have negative and positive connotations, respectively, and answer B is the opposite of "appropriate." If something is suited to something else, it is appropriate, making A the best choice.

7. **C.** When you think of *meander*, think of a winding river that snakes its way down a mountain making lots of twists and turns. Many water parks also have a "meandering river" ride where you float lazily on an inner tube around a long, twisty circle. A river can't *navigate, attack,* or *forgive,* but it sure can *zig-zag,* which makes C your best choice.

8. **A.** A great way to remember the definition of *atrocious* is to remember your Mary Poppins: "Supercalifragilisticexpialidocious. Even though the sound of it is something quite atrocious!" A very long word like that certainly does sound "awful," which is what it means.

9. **C.** One of the most revered aircraft carriers in the United States is the *Intrepid*, which is now a museum in New York City. The military would never name an enormous ship in its fleet designed to be used in times of war with a word that means *meek* (shy) or *arrogant* (full of oneself). Such a vessel needs to project strength and valor—guts, if you will.

10. **D.** *Succinct* describes something that's short, sweet, and to the point. *Amuse, math,* and *heavy* don't make sense. However, when you're *blunt*, you get to the point fast and with few words.

11. **A.** The root *voc* tells you that this word has something to do with speaking, and the suffix *ous* tells you that this word is an adjective. Even if you know nothing else about this word, you can get this answer correct. *Decision* is a noun, so it's out. A voice might be singular, but it can't be selective. Given the choice between *singular* and *loud*, the latter is the best choice, since volume is a more logical attribute for a voice than how many there are. By the way, *vociferous* means "crying out loudly."

12. **B.** *Frugal* means "to be cautious with money." Maybe you remember The Frugal Gourmet, a chef who made a career out of teaching people how to make first-class meals on a budget. Any way you slice it, "cheap" is the best answer.

13. **D.** *Judicious* refers to someone who is practical and expedient in their decisions. *Intuitive* (using one's feelings) and *instructive* (giving direction) just don't fit. Someone who is *judicious* may be judgmental, but that is not a characteristic needed to define the word. *Prudent* is the best choice.

14. **C.** To be *astute* is to be very aware or intuitive. Answers A and D are the opposite of this. Answer B has nothing to do with this definition.

15. **B.** Something that is *abrasive* is harsh or causes friction. Within the context of the sentence, *abrasive* refers to harsh speech. Answers A, C, and D have nothing to do with being harsh, as *incredulous* means "unbelievable," *available* means "open," and *instinctive* means "going with a feeling." Answer B is correct because *tactless* means "speaking without concern for others' feelings or reactions," which is usually harsh.

16. **D.** A good little mnemonic for *incorrigible* is "You don't want to encourage incorrigible behavior," which gives you a clue that such behavior is negative. Answers A, B, and C describe behavior that is not generally negative, making answer D your best choice.

17. **B.** You can make an association here, as *stringent* means the same as "strict," "severe," and "stern." Answer A has nothing to do with these things. While you may be tempted to go with either answers C or D, remember that you're looking for a word that defines the underlined word. Someone can sometimes be offensive or wicked while being stringent, but they are always severe, which is why answer B is the best answer.

18. **D.** A search that encompasses hundreds of miles is very large. This means the answer you want has something to do with size. Answer D is the only one that addresses size, as *heroic* describes bravery, *fortuitous* describes a chance happening, and *intimate* describes a degree of personal interaction.

19. **B.** As we said earlier, the root in *potent* means "power." Your correct answer here will have some connection to this idea. The only one that fits the bill is answer B.

20. **C.** Even if you didn't know the exact definition of *bigotry*, you've likely heard the word used in conjunction with negative sentiments, which gives it a negative meaning. Answer B is positive and answer D is neutral, as *transcendence* means "to go beyond." Both answers A and C are negatives, but *antagonism* means "aggression," while *chauvinism* means "prejudice," which is what bigotry is.

21. **A.** To *belittle* is to reduce the importance of something. Answer A is the only answer choice that reflects this meaning. Answer B is the opposite, and the other answers have nothing to do with this definition.

22. **D.** The base word here is *oppose*, which means "to go against." The first three answers run counter to this definition, as they all indicate relationships that go with or help. Even if you didn't know the meaning of *antagonist*, the prefix *ant* in answer D is a good sign that this word goes against something.

23. **B.** *Eloquent* is an adjective that describes beautiful or well-spoken speech. Such speech may be elegant or relatable, but it does not need to be in order to be considered eloquent. If speech is mumbled, it is the opposite of elegant. This leaves answer B, *articulate*, as the best choice.

24. **B.** *Florid* describes something that is greatly embellished. Answers A and C do not match this definition. Answer D applies to growth, not embellishment, whereas answer B refers specifically to decorating or embellishing a great deal.

25. **C.** The prefix *di* means "two" and the root *logue* means "speak." This word refers to two speakers engaging in communication. Though each answer choice involves some kind of communication, only answer C, *chat*, involves two participants, by definition.

26. **A.** When you go to a bookstore, chances are, you're going to look at books. You can't *interact* with them, since they are not alive. You likely wouldn't *eliminate* them, especially if going to a bookstore is a favorite activity. *Sanctify* means "to make something holy," which doesn't really make sense, either. Answer A, *examine*, is the logical choice.

27. **C.** A tap on the bumper of a car isn't likely to cause much damage to either vehicle. Therefore, you can eliminate answers A and D. Likewise, such an accident probably would not damage the inside of the car, which eliminates answer B from the running as well.

28. **A.** *Mischief* is the base word here and implies causing trouble without intent to harm. *Obedient* refers to doing what you're told. *Forgiven* means "to be pardoned." *Uninitiated* means "lacking experience." Answer A, *playful*, is the best choice, since it's the only one even remotely related to the underlined word.

29. **D.** Physical therapy for broken bones usually results in some kind of recovery. Swap out answer choices here to find that D is the only one that makes sense in the sentence.

30. **D.** *Reticence* means "quiet" or "reserved in nature." Answer A is the opposite. Answer B has nothing to do with this meaning. Answer C, in addition to having no connection with *reticence*, is also the wrong part of speech.

31. **B.** Someone who has been through a bad divorce is likely to be wary of getting married again. Answer A runs opposite to this idea. Answer C refers to confusion, which doesn't fit, either. Answer D has nothing to do with being wary.

32. **C.** A *predecessor* is someone who comes before another. An *instigator* causes something to happen. An *infiltrator* is a spy. A *substitute* stands in for someone. An *ancestor* is someone who lives before another in a family line, making it the best choice.

33. **A.** When you *procrastinate*, you push off what you can do today until tomorrow. In other words, you delay having to do something. Answer B means "to go through with strength." Answer C means "to get revenge." Answer D means "to go after."

34. **D.** Students in an early morning class are likely to still be feeling the effects of sleep. The teacher in the sentence is using inspirational material to bring their spirits up (*uplift*). Clearly, D is your best bet.

35. **B.** To be *militant* is to be extremely aggressive, which means answers C and D are not a good fit. Though militants can run on instinct (answer A), they are not defined by it. Answer B, *revolutionary*, suggests aggression to an extreme.

# Paragraph Comprehension

1. **A.** The main idea of this passage is stated in the first sentence.

2. **A.** Use process of elimination here. No mention of strategy on Spain's part was made in the passage, nor did the passage mention Canada or European wars. The best choice is answer A because by making the purchase "Jefferson was able to secure trade access to the port of New Orleans and greatly increase the United States' standing as a formidable country."

3. **D.** The passage does not support any answer choice other than D.

4. **B.** The speaker is clearly arguing for people to become involved in the fight against deforestation. Every choice other than answer B goes against that stance.

5. **C.** If you swap out *myriad* for the answer choices, you'll find that answer C makes the most sense. There's no indication of a specific amount, its proportions, or level of interest.

6. **B.** As we said before, the speaker is clearly urging action against deforestation. She's not thinking it over or lacking in enthusiasm, which eliminates the other answers as possibilities.

7. **B.** This is a specific detail question, and the answer is found in the last sentence: "The internal temperature must be raised to at least 205° Celsius to produce caffeol oil." Caffeine and coloring aren't mentioned in the passage. Flavor is, but it says that caffeol oil produces the flavor we associate with coffee. It does not mention extra flavor anywhere.

8. **D.** This is an inference question. You need to use information in the passage to prove each answer true or false. The passage says that green coffee beans must be roasted before they can be consumed. This eliminates answer A. The passage says that coffee beans come from berries, but it says nothing about them tasting like berries. It also says that coffee beans must be fermented before they're cleaned. These two details eliminate answers B and C. The first sentence clearly states that coffee beans are "roasted seeds of coffee berries," which makes answer D the best choice.

9. **C.** *Mandate* means "to require." If you use the swapping technique with this question, you'll see that answer C is the only choice that fits the sentence.

10. **A.** The passage talks about the census, why it's conducted, and how it's used. No opinion or conclusion is stated, so *persuade* and *evaluate* aren't possible answers. The information is very neutral and does not ask the reader to take any action, which eliminates *incite* as an answer. More than anything, the passage informs the reader about the census, making answer A the best answer.

11. **C.** This is another inference question. There's no information in the passage about vitamin C being helpful for test preparation, running speed, or better sleep. It does say that it can help wounds heal faster. Because a paper cut is a wound, it's logical to think that adding vitamin C to your diet can be beneficial.

12. **D.** This is a main idea question. In the passage, the main idea is the first sentence: "Vitamin C is an essential nutrient for maintaining good health." The best choice is answer D because it includes these key ideas.

13. **A.** This is an inference question. The information in the passage contradicts answer B, and there is no information to support answers C and D. Answer A is directly supported by the second sentence in the passage.

14. **C.** "Monitor the actions of our elected officials" tells us that the speaker is urging people to keep an eye on politicians. This sets up the rest of the sentence, which talks about holding them responsible for their actions. The only choice that fits this idea is answer C.

15. **B.** This is another inference question. The best approach is to go to each answer choice and ask why the author would agree with it:

(A) "Too many people come to council meetings": The author wouldn't agree because the passage says, "Not enough people attend their local town council meetings."

(B) "Elected officials must answer to the public": This is a good choice because the author says, "It's our responsibility as American citizens to monitor the actions of our elected officials and hold them accountable."

(C) "Council meetings are the best place to air a grievance about the community": There's no mention of grievances or public speaking in the passage.

(D) "Town councils should recognize citizens more often": There's no reference to citizens being recognized in the passage.

# Mathematics Knowledge

1. **B.** Use FOIL for this:

   First: $a \times a = a^2$

   Outer: $8 \times a = 8a$

   Inner: $5 \times a = 5a$

   Last: $5 \times 8 = 40$

   Your new expression is: $a^2 + 8a + 5a + 40$

   Combine like terms: $a^2 + 13a + 40$

2. **A.** Plug in 4 wherever you see $b$:

   $5 \times b^3 + \dfrac{3b}{2}$

   $5 \times 4 \times 4 \times 4 + \dfrac{3 \times 4}{2}$

   Now solve according to order of operations:

   Multiply: $(5 \times 4 \times 4 \times 4 = 320) + \left( \dfrac{3 \times 4}{2} = \dfrac{12}{2} \right)$

   Divide: $320 + \left( \dfrac{12}{2} = 6 \right)$

   Add: $320 + 6 = 326$

3. **C.** When multiplying two like variables with exponents, keep the variable the same and add the exponents: $y^2 \times y^3 \times y^4 \times y^5 = y^{2+3+4+5} = y^{14}$.

4. **D.** A vertex is the point where the two lines that make up an angle intersect. Area is the space an object occupies. An operation is an action you need to take with a value. A term is a single number or variable, or combinations of them.

5. **A.** Solve this like any other equation:

   $4x - 3 < 5 + 2y$

   $4x = \cancel{-3 + 3} < 5 + 3 + 2y$

   $4x < 8 + 2y$

   $x < \dfrac{8 + 2y}{4}$

   $x < 2 + 2y$

6. **B.** Move your decimal points in this equation and add zeroes after the 4 in the dividend to find your answer. Take the division as far as you have to in order to get to one of the answer choices: $32.6 \div 4 = .1226$.

   Remember to round if you have the option. In this case, since you came up with .1226, you would round up to .123.

7. **A.** Start by combining like terms:

$x + 2y - 4x + 6 = 2$

$2y (x + -4x) + 6 = 2$

$2y - 3x + 6 = 2$

Now subtract 6 from both sides:

$2y - 3x + 6 - 6 = 2 - 6$

$2y - 3x = -4$

Next, add $-3x$ to both sides:

$2y - 3x + 3x = -4 + 3x$

$2y = -4 + 3x$

Finally, divide both sides by 2:

$$\frac{2y}{2} = \frac{-4 + 3x}{2}$$

$$y = -2 + \frac{3x}{2}$$

8. **D.** Use the total surface area formula for rectangular solids here: $2lw + 2wh + 2lh$. The question has $l = 3$, $w = 10$, and $h = 5$:

$(2 \times 3 \times 10) + (2 \times 10 \times 5) + (2 \times 3 \times 5)$

$60 + 100 + 30 = 190$ m²

9. **A.** Take out the decimal points and multiply these two numbers as usual:

```
   12475
 ×   202
   24950
  000000
+2495000
 2519950
```

Now count the number of decimal places in the original question. 12.475 has three places, while 20.2 has two. The decimal point in your final answer will be five places from the right: 25.19950.

10. **C.** Turn your mixed number into an improper fraction by multiplying 6 × 4 and then adding 1 (from the numerator): $6\frac{1}{4} = \frac{25}{4}$. Now multiply the mixed fraction by the reciprocal of $\frac{5}{8}$: $\frac{25}{4} \times \frac{8}{5} = \frac{200}{20} = 10$.

11. **B.** Attack this like any other equation and solve for $x$:

$3x + 5 \times 5 \neq 7 - 12$

$3x + 25 \neq -5$

$3x + 25 - 25 \neq -5 - 25$

$3x \neq -30$

$x \neq \frac{30}{3} = 10$

12. **D.** This is a quadratic expression. You can either FOIL the answer choices or factor the expression: $b^2 + 14b - 24$.

Set up your binomials: $(b\ )(b\ )$

Now list factors of 24:

$1 \times 24$

$2 \times 12$

$3 \times 8$

$4 \times 6$

If you add 2 and 12, you get 14, which is the middle term; if you multiply them, you get the final term, which is 24. Add these terms to your binomial shells. Now we figure out the signs. Since one of our original terms is negative, both signs in the final binomials will be negative. The final answer is $(b - 2)(b + 12)$.

13. **A.** A parallelogram is a quadrilateral with opposite sides that are parallel and equal in length. Trapezoids and rhombi are types of parallelograms with their own distinct properties that distinguish them from simply having the definition of a parallelogram. A polygon is an enclosed figure with three or more sides.

14. **C.** Use the Pythagorean Theorem here to solve for the missing value: $a^2 + b^2 = c^2$.

$(6 \times 6) + b^2 = (7.8 \times 7.8)$

$36 + b^2 = 60.84$

$b^2 = 60.84 - 36 = 24.84$

$b = \sqrt{24.84}$

Since your answer choices don't ask for an exact answer, $\sqrt{24.84}$ is enough to get you through this question.

15. **C.** This one is all about order of operations. Start with the brackets, since they tell you that what's inside must be solved before moving on to anything else:

Parentheses: $(6 + 4 = 10)$; $(14 - 8 = 6)$

New expression: $[(10)^2 + (6)]$

Exponents: $(10 \times 10 = 100)$

New expression: $[100 + (6)]$

Addition: $100 + (6) = 106$

Now that the expressions in the brackets have been solved, take a look at the new expression: $106 - \frac{2}{3} \times \frac{9}{2}$. Go back to the beginning of order of operations and start again. Since there are no parentheses or exponents, start with multiplication:

Multiply: $\frac{2}{3} \times \frac{9}{2} = \frac{18}{6} = 3$

New expression: $106 - 3$

Subtraction: $106 - 3 = 103$

16. **A.** This is another proportion. Cross multiply and solve for the missing value:

$\frac{3}{6} = \frac{a}{12}$

$3 \times 12 = 6a$

$36 = 6a$

$\frac{36}{6} = a$

$6 = a$

17. **C.** These are similar triangles, since they have internal angles that are equal to each other and, therefore, proportional sides. The degrees of angles $g$, $d$, and $f$ are the same in each triangle. This means that side $a$ is proportional to side $x$, side $c$ is proportional to side $y$, and side $b$ is proportional to side $z$ (with the same proportion).

18. **B.** With scientific notation, you move the decimal point to the right of the leftmost digit. With 16597000000, you'd move the decimal 10 places to the left to get 1.6597000000. Now drop all of the 0s after the 7 to get 1.6597. Finally, multiply this number by 10 to the 10th power (the number of decimal spaces you moved): $1.6597 \times 10^{10}$.

19. **D.** Turn the mixed number into an improper fraction and set up a new expression:

$2\frac{4}{5} - \frac{7}{8} = \frac{14}{5} - \frac{7}{8}$.

Now make the denominators the same by multiplying each fraction by its opposite denominator:

$\frac{14}{5} \times \frac{8}{8} = \frac{112}{40}$

$\frac{7}{8} \times \frac{5}{5} = \frac{35}{40}$

Finally, subtract the two new fractions and reduce: $\frac{112}{40} - \frac{35}{40} = \frac{77}{40} = 1\frac{37}{40}$

20. **B.** Isosceles right triangles have two equal sides.

21. **C.** This is a trapezoid because it's a quadrilateral with at least two sides that run parallel to each other. A rhombus has two sets of sides that run parallel. A hexagon is a six-sided polygon. A chord is a segment in a circle that touches any two points of the edge.

22. **D.** This is factorial, so calculate: $8 \times 7 \times 6 \times 5 \times 4 \times 3 \times 2 \times 1 = 40,320$.

23. **A.** Both terms here are perfect squares. Calculate the square roots of both terms and place in a set of binomial expressions: $\sqrt{c^2} = c$; $\sqrt{121} = 11$: $(c\ 11)\ (c\ 11)$. We need a positive and negative sign here to make these work when FOIL is applied, so our answer is $(c + 11)\ (c - 11)$.

24. **A.** Adjacent angles share a common side. *Congruent* and *similar* are terms used to describe triangles. A straight angle is one that's 180°.

25. **D.** All sides of a square are equal. Multiply 15.2 × 15.2 = 231.04 to find the area.

# Electronics Information

1. **A.** Choices B and D are wrong because there are no neutral charges in current flow. Choice C is wrong because it describes the flow of electrons instead of current.

2. **C.** Choices A and D are wrong because they describe conductor material rather than insulator. Choice B is wrong because it is not a material typically associated with wiring.

3. **D.** The diode looks like an arrow pointing in the direction that current flows.

4. **B.** The formula for this problem is Watts = Volts × amps. Insert the values you have and solve for the missing amount.

5. **D.** Choice A is wrong because a gas-powered generator uses a different symbol. Choices B and C are wrong because they are not power sources.

6. **B.** Choice A is wrong because protons aren't involved in electric current. Choice C is wrong because ohms measure the resistance in a current. Choice D is wrong because amps measure current; they don't push it along.

7. **C.** Choice A is wrong because conductors are the materials through which electricity can pass. Choice B is wrong because a switch is an electrical control signal. Choice D is wrong because a circuit is a system of connected conductors that direct the path of electricity.

8. **D.** To calculate frequency, divide wave speed by wavelength.

9. **B.** The resistor diagram looks like a never-ending letter *W*.

10. **A.** To determine amps, you must divide volts by resistance.

11. **A.** The other choices are all incorrect because they have nothing to do with resistance.

12. **A.** Low-range frequencies have the longest wavelengths, making them easier to hear.

13. **D.** To answer this question, use the following equation: $\Omega = \dfrac{\text{volts}}{\text{amps}}$.

14. **C.** Choice A is wrong because an ohmmeter is used to measure resistance. Choice B is wrong because a voltmeter is used to measure the difference in voltage. Choice D is wrong because it is used to measure current.

15. **A.** Choices B, C, and D are wrong because they are all types of current, and therefore cannot measure another type of current.

16. **B.** The diagram illustrates a DC voltage capacitor. Choice A is wrong because it describes a bridge rectifier. Choice C is wrong because it describes cells, batteries, and regulated power supplies. Choice D is wrong because it describes a transformer.

17. **B.** Choice A is wrong because scattered wavelengths occur during dispersion. Choice C is wrong because rectilinear propagation is the movement of waves in a straight line. Choice D is wrong because the bending of waves occurs during diffraction.

18. **C.** To solve for the missing value, you use the following formula: $\text{amps} = \dfrac{\text{volts}}{\text{resistance}}$.

19. **C.** Wave speed is calculated by multiplying wavelength and frequency.

20. **D.** Good conductors of electricity offer low resistance, such as copper. Choice A is wrong because it is the opposite of the right answer. Choice B is wrong because there is no exact resistance number used to determine "a good conductor." Choice C is wrong because gauge refers to wire thickness, not resistance.

# Automotive and Shop Information

1. **A.** Refer back to the seven steps we listed in the beginning of the chapter that are involved in starting a car. After turning the key, the next set of activities are as follows: power transfers from the battery (power source) through the ignition switch to the ignition coil, which sends power to the distributor (if present) and spark plugs.

2. **B.** The solenoid is also called a relay because it receives current from the battery and passes it on to the starter. This function is similar to that of a relay runner in a race.

3. **C.** When switches are in the open position, power cannot be passed through the circuit. When the circuit is closed, it is complete.

4. **B.** A disc brake is distinguishable by brake pads, calipers, and rotors. Choice D is wrong because a secondary brake is another way of referring to an emergency brake.

5. **D.** Choice A is wrong because the slide pin is used to hold the calipers together. Choice B is wrong because the wheel hub holds the rotors and allows the car to turn. Choice C is wrong because the rotors don't house the brake pads, but they provide a rubbing surface for friction material and help disperse heat during braking.

6. **C.** Choice A is wrong because the brake lines hold brake fluid and sometimes get air bubbles in them. The bleed valve is opened to empty the brake lines of fluid and air. Choice B is wrong because the brake pad is designed to apply friction to both sides of the disc brake. Choice D is wrong because the dust cap is used to keep contaminants, such as dust and dirt, out of the hub bearing.

7. **A.** Resonators are used as a silencing mechanism to help mufflers reduce exhaust gas noise. They are used when standard-size mufflers are too large to fit under the car, and smaller mufflers cannot silence the exhaust noise sufficiently.

8. **B.** Catalytic converters were designed in the 1970s to control harmful exhaust pollutants like nitrogen gas, carbon dioxide, and water vapor.

9. **D.** Choice A is wrong because the exhaust pipe is the first step in the process of transporting gases and vapors through the exhaust system. Choice B is wrong because catalytic converters control harmful emissions. Choice C is wrong because the hanger holds the tailpipe onto the undercarriage of the vehicle.

10. **C.** The four-stroke process is as follows: intake, compression, combustion, exhaust.

11. **A.** The piston starts the Otto Cycle, or four-stroke process, in the up position. During the compression stroke, the piston moves down and then starts back up. When it reaches the top of the stroke, it becomes the combustion step. Finally, the exhaust stroke finds the piston in the down position again.

12. **D.** Choice A is wrong because it describes the brake system. Choice B is wrong because the electrical system is responsible for providing the initial source of power to the ignition system. Choice C is incorrect because it describes the cooling system.

13. **A.** Choice B is wrong because the fuel filter keeps rust and dirt particles out of the fuel before they reach the engine. Choice C is wrong because the fuel pump feeds fuel to the engine from the fuel tank. Choice D is wrong because the alternator is not even part of the fuel system.

14. **D.** Hot fluid flows through a series of radiator tubes to be cooled by a fan system and air coming through the front grille.

15. **B.** Choice A is wrong because it is the inverse of the correct choice. Choice C is wrong because brake fluid is located in the brake lines, not the cylinder. Choice D is wrong because calipers are not part of a drum brake system; brake drums are attached to the wheel.

16. **B.** The pein of the hammer is depicted by the ball-shaped sphere of steel directly across from the hammer head.

17. **D.** The hammer best suited for driving rivets into sheet metal is a tinner's hammer.

18. **A.** Hand drills are characterized by a cranking handle, a chuck, and a drill bit, as depicted in the diagram.

19. **D.** The other three choices are all reasons to use a power drill, not a hand drill.

20. **C.** None of the other choices resemble this type of tool.

21. **A.** Choice B is wrong because it describes the role of a block plane. Choice C is wrong because it describes the role of a hand screw. Choice D is wrong because it describes the role of a pipe clamp.

22. **B.** A jack plane is a type of plane tool, which falls under the category of shaping.

23. **C.** A chisel is a type of shaping tool, not a saw.

24. **C.** Choices A and B are wrong because a pistol grip drill is handheld, as is a hammer drill. Choice D is wrong because a jigsaw is a type of saw, not drill.

25. **A.** Choice B is wrong because rasps are used for wood surfaces only. Choices C and D are wrong because they don't have tiny ridgelike grooves used for smoothing surfaces.

# Mechanical Comprehension

1. **B.** The ball cannot do work on the bat if the bat struck it; however, the bat can do work on the ball in this situation.

2. **B.** A 2nd-class lever positions the load between the fulcrum and the effort.

3. **A.** To calculate this equation, you should per-form the following procedure:

   Multiply the larger weight by *x*. That is the left side of the equation.

   Multiple the smaller weight by (the distance between the two weights minus *x*). That is the right side of the equation.

   Solve for *x*.

   $50x = 25(15 - x)$

   $50x = 350 - 25x$

   $75x = 350$

   $x = 5$

   You now know that the larger weight should be 5 feet from the fulcrum. Since the two weights were 15 feet apart to begin with, you can deduce that the second weight must be 10 feet from the fulcrum.

4. **A.** Choice B is wrong because a 3rd-class lever is exemplified by tongs, tweezers, and staplers. Choice C is wrong because a 1st-class lever is exemplified by a seesaw, scissors, or a hammer claw. Choice D is wrong because a 4th-class lever doesn't exist.

5. **D.** Each time a pulley is introduced to a pulley system, the mechanical advantage increases.

6. **D.** Balancing the weight on a 1st-class lever requires that both ends of the rod have equal weights; in addition, the weights must be posi-tioned equidistant from the fulcrum.

7. **A.** The easiest way to calculate mechanical advantage (without regard to friction and other unknown factors) is to count the number of rope lengths you have in the pulley system. In this case, there is one pulley with one rope section. Therefore, you have a mechanical advantage of 1.

8. **B.** Gear ratio is used to determine the rate at which two gears turn.

9. **C.** To determine gear ratio by number of teeth, divide the larger number of teeth by the smaller number. In this case, $\frac{200}{40} = 5$. Therefore, you have a 5:1 ratio.

10. **B.** Gears perform each of the other tasks listed. Although gears may cause an object to *feel* lighter, they don't actually change the weight of the object.

11. **D.** Choice A is wrong because friction occurs when two objects rub against one another. Choice B is wrong because acceleration occurs when there is a rate of increase of velocity. Choice C is wrong because speed is defined as distance traveled over a unit of time.

12. **A.** Negative acceleration is calculated in the same manner as acceleration. The change in velocity per hour is divided by the time interval.

13. **B.** When speed and direction are unchanging, velocity is said to be constant.

14. **C.** The law of reciprocal action is considered Newton's third law.

15. **A.** A 1st-class lever is characterized by a fulcrum located in between the load and the effort.

16. **A.** Newton's second law states that the accel-eration of an object is directly proportional to the net force acting on the object; further-more, the object accelerates in the direction of the net force acting on it.

17. **B.** None of the other formulas represent force.

18. **B.** Newton's second law applies to this question.

19. **D.** Most countries use mass to measure an object, which is why you may be more familiar with the term *kilogram* than *Newton*. However, a Newton is the metric expression of weight.

20. **A.** None of the other choices offers the appro-priate formula for mass.

21. **D.** Choice A is wrong because mass is defined by the volume and density of an object. Choice B is wrong because speed is distance traveled per unit of time. Choice C is wrong because acceleration is the rate of increase of velocity.

22. **C.** Work is calculated by multiplying force times distance.

23. **A.** Kinetic energy is calculated using the following formula: $KE = \frac{1}{2}mv^2$.

24. **B.** Work is calculated by multiplying force times distance.

25. **A.** Plug the numbers into the formula as follows:
$$18\,(10) = x(30 - 10)$$
$$180 = 30x - 10x$$
$$180 = 20x$$
$$9 = x$$

# Assembling Objects

1. **B.** This is a pretty simple one. Answer A has the B connection in the wrong place on the *g*. Answer C has a *p* instead of a *g*, and answer D is mirrored.

2. **A.** The shapes in answer B are changed from the sample and one is mirrored, which eliminates it as a possibility. Choices C and D both have shapes different from the sample. Answer A is your best bet.

3. **C.** Both shapes in answer C have been rotated so that points A and B are connected in the right place. The A connection in answer A is wrong. There's a star shape instead of an *X* shape in answer B, and the triangle in answer D has been changed.

4. **C.** The shapes in answers A and D are not the same shape or size as those of the sample. Answer B contains mirrored images, which means it can't be correct.

5. **A.** Notice the little flag on the dot indicating point B in the sample. This tells you the angle the connecting line has to come in at. The line in answer B comes into point B at a different angle than that in the sample. The A connection in answer C is in the wrong place, and the B connection in answer D is also wrong.

6. **D.** Some of the shapes in answers A and B do not match those in the sample. Answer C is all mirrored pieces. Everything in answer D is the same as the sample.

7. **C.** The five-sided figure in answer A is mirrored. The flower shape in answer B has five petals instead of six, and the five-sided figure in answer D has been replaced by a rectangle.

8. **B.** All the answer choices except answer B contain at least one shape that doesn't match the sample.

9. **D.** The star in answer A is different from the sample. The triangle in answer B is smaller and a different shape. There's an extra piece in answer C. This makes answer D the best choice.

10. **D.** Choices A and C have one connector placed on the wrong section of one of the objects. The top object in choice B is rotated too much and at an angle to make the connection to point A exactly the same as it is in the example.

11. **D.** The A connection in answer A and the B connection in answer C are in the wrong place. The top shape in answer B is not the same as in the example.

12. **C.** There are extra pieces and changed shapes in answer A. The cross in answer B is markedly different from the sample, and the second triangle is missing. In answer D, at least one of the triangles is the wrong shape. Even though the circle is behind the cross in answer C, it's still your best choice.

13. **D.** The top shape in answer A and the bottom shape in answer B are different from the sample. Both the A and B connections in answer C are in the wrong place.

14. **B.** There are no quadrilaterals in answer A, which eliminates it as a possibility. One of the quadrilaterals in answer C is not the same as the sample, and the triangle in D doesn't have a flat bottom like the one in the sample.

15. **C.** The B connection in answer A is in the wrong place and the rounded object doesn't match the sample. Answers B and D have incorrect shapes included in the connection. This leaves only C as a possible choice.

16. **A.** There's a rectangle in answer B that should not be there. The hexagon in answer C was changed to an octagon and there is a piece missing. Answer D has five pieces instead of four.

17. **A.** Answer B has the B connection in the wrong place. Instead of a number symbol in answer C, there is an *S*, and the B connection is in the wrong place. Finally, the figures are mirrored in answer D.

18. **C.** The rounded rectangle from the sample now has squared edges in answer A. In answer B, the star was replaced by a triangle. The rectangle in answer D has been replaced with another trapezoid.

19. **C.** The bottom shape is mirrored in answer A. The bottom shapes in answers B and D do not match the sample.

20. **A.** The diamond in answer B has been split into two shapes. The seven-sided figure in answer C was replaced with a pentagon. There are five shapes in answer D, and the smaller rectangle is now the same size as the larger one.

21. **D.** The rounded rectangle in answer A has been replaced by a regular one. The A connection and the B connection in answer B is in the wrong place. The angle the B connection comes in on answer C doesn't match the sample.

22. **B.** The angles in two of the shapes are skewed in answer A. Two pieces in both answers C and D have also been changed in shape and size.

23. **C.** The B connection in answer A is in the wrong place. The ampersand in answer B is mirrored. Both the A and B connections are in the wrong place in answer D.

24. **A.** The proportions of all the shapes in answer B are off. There are two rectangles in answer C instead of just one. In answer D, the shield has been replaced with an oval.

25. **B.** The A and B connections in answers A and C are in the wrong place. There's a *p* in answer D instead of an *h*.

# General Science

**Time:** 11 Minutes

**Questions:** 25

**Directions:** This section tests your general knowledge in the area of science. Carefully read each question below and choose the answer choice that best answers the question.

1. The study of plants is called
    - (A) botany.
    - (B) ecology.
    - (C) zoology.
    - (D) chemistry.

2. If a species' body composition changes in response to survival needs, the theory of _____ applies.
    - (A) cell regeneration
    - (B) gene therapy
    - (C) evolution
    - (D) homeostasis

3. All of the following are aspects of thermodynamics theory except:
    - (A) Energy never disappears.
    - (B) Energy transfer cannot be completed in single-cell organisms.
    - (C) Energy gets converted to other forms.
    - (D) Energy transfer is not completely efficient.

4. Theoretically, archaea falls under the taxonomic classification of
    - (A) kingdom.
    - (B) phylum.
    - (C) class.
    - (D) order.

5. Plants appear green because

    (A) photosynthesis produces green energy.

    (B) chlorophyll absorbs all red and blue light, causing plants to appear green.

    (C) the chloroplasts absorb green light.

    (D) they grow from seeds.

6. Which chemical reaction represents the process of photosynthesis?

    (A) $6CO_2 + 6H_2O$ (+ light energy) $C_6H_{12}O_6 + 6O_2$

    (B) $8CO + 6H_2O$ (+ light energy) $C_6H_{12}O_6 + 8O_2$

    (C) $6CO_4 + 12H_2O$ (+ light energy) $C_6H_{12}O_6 + 6O_4$

    (D) $6CO + 6H_2O$ (+ light energy) $C_6H_{12}O_2 + O_2$

7. An important element essential to human life that plants produce is

    (A) light.

    (B) carbon dioxide.

    (C) oxygen.

    (D) water.

8. A habitat that is characterized by small land masses that are wet, cloudy, and windswept is called a(n)

    (A) tropical forest.

    (B) oceanic island.

    (C) freshwater wetland.

    (D) ocean.

9. How many cells are in the adult human body?

    (A) hundreds

    (B) thousands

    (C) millions

    (D) billions

10. Which cell organelle contains digestive enzymes?

    (A) ribosome

    (B) golgi

    (C) mitochondria

    (D) lysosome

11. The two main types of cell division are

    (A) DNA and RNA.

    (B) mitosis and meiosis.

    (C) endoplasmic and cell plasma.

    (D) nucleus and nucleotide

12. Weightlifters' muscles get larger due to

    (A) protein growth.

    (B) chromosome change.

    (C) mitosis cell division.

    (D) metabolism conversion.

13. Which biological term is used to describe the basic unit of heredity?

    (A) nucleotide

    (B) gene

    (C) metabolism

    (D) amino acid

14. Which of the following is most commonly found in meats and eggs?

    (A) amino acids

    (B) proteins

    (C) carbohydrates

    (D) vitamin C

15. Muscles, veins, arteries, and capillaries are all part of the

    (A) respiratory system.

    (B) digestive system.

    (C) circulatory system.

    (D) excretory system.

16. The kidneys

    (A) pass solid waste out of the body.

    (B) pull oxygen all the way through the lungs.

    (C) allow blood to deposit carbon dioxide and pick up oxygen.

    (D) filter waste from the blood.

17. The body's main source of energy comes from

    (A) fats.

    (B) carbohydrates.

    (C) minerals.

    (D) vitamins.

18. Which of the following serves as a vehicle for carrying nutrients needed by the body?

    (A) proteins

    (B) fats

    (C) roughage

    (D) water

19. Which portion of our diet includes fibrous, indigestible foods?

    (A) fats

    (B) vitamins

    (C) roughage

    (D) proteins

20. From surface to center, the layers of Earth are

    (A) crust, mantle, outer core, inner core.

    (B) mantle, inner core, outer core, crust.

    (C) crust, inner core, outer core, mantle.

    (D) mantle, crust, inner core, outer core.

21. When liquid molten rock flows beneath Earth's surface, it is called

    (A) magma.

    (B) lava.

    (C) volcano.

    (D) nickel.

22. The outer core of Earth is made up primarily of

    (A) iron and copper.

    (B) iron and nickel.

    (C) nickel and magnesium.

    (D) nickel and copper.

23. The air pressing down on Earth is measured in terms of

    (A) warm front.

    (B) barometric pressure.

    (C) temperature.

    (D) cumulonimbus.

24. A rock or minor planet orbiting the sun is known as a(n)

    (A) comet.

    (B) meteor.

    (C) asteroid.

    (D) astronomical unit.

25. Which planet is the brightest?

    (A) Mercury

    (B) Pluto

    (C) Jupiter

    (D) Venus

# Arithmetic Reasoning

**Time:** 36 Minutes

**Questions:** 30

**Directions:** This section tests your ability to reason through mathematical problems using basic arithmetic. Carefully read each question and choose the answer choice that best answers the question.

1. John wants to give his two employees a raise. Employee 1 earns $245 per week, and Employee 2 earns $396 per week. If he increased their weekly pay by 6%, how much more would he have to allocate to pay his employees per 4-week month?

    (A) $34.76
    (B) $38.46
    (C) $134.23
    (D) $153.84

2. Mr. X has four dates per week. At this rate, how many dates will he have over the course of a year?

    (A) 208
    (B) 215
    (C) 287
    (D) 306

3. Jon makes $32,890 per year. Amy makes $545.50 per week. How much more per week does Jon make?

    (A) $32.50
    (B) $56.20
    (C) $87.00
    (D) $632.50

4. Out of the 750 books in the local library, 150 are romance novels, 200 are mysteries, and the rest are nonfiction books. What percentage of the total collection are romance novels?

    (A) 20%
    (B) 25%
    (C) 50%
    (D) 55%

5. If you made $15,625.35 during the first half of the year and 7% more for the second half of the year, what's the total amount of money you made over the entire year?

    (A) $30,050.67
    (B) $32,344.47
    (C) $42,433.74
    (D) $82,779.23

6. The produce section of a grocery store held a sale on peaches. Over the course of the sale, 125 peaches were sold. During the same time, 85 regular-priced apples were also sold. What is the ratio of peaches to apples sold during this sale period?

    (A) 85:210
    (B) 125:210
    (C) 17:25
    (D) 25:17

7. Thirty-two is what percentage of 128?

    (A) 15%

    (B) 20%

    (C) 25%

    (D) 55%

8. Bailey brings three kids to the movies with her. The price for adults is $5.25 and for children is $3.75. In the lobby, she meets her friend and invites her to come see the movie with her and the kids. Assuming that Bailey and her friend are adults, how much will it cost for all five people to see the movie?

    (A) $9.52

    (B) $10.50

    (C) $11.25

    (D) $21.75

9. If you travel at a consistent rate of 13 miles per hour, about how long will it take you to travel 87 miles?

    (A) $6\frac{9}{13}$ hours

    (B) $6\frac{2}{13}$ hours

    (C) $7\frac{2}{4}$ hours

    (D) $9\frac{3}{6}$ hours

10. If you add –12 to –13, you get

    (A) 25

    (B) –25

    (C) –1

    (D) 1

11. April's mother is 67 and is 32% older than April. About how old is April?

    (A) $40\frac{1}{2}$

    (B) $45\frac{1}{2}$

    (C) $46\frac{3}{4}$

    (D) $48\frac{1}{2}$

12. $5 \times 4 \times 3 \times 2 \times 1$ is also known as a(n)

    (A) constant.

    (B) inequality.

    (C) factorial.

    (D) variable.

13. Jack makes $0.35 on every copy of his new CD that is sold. If each costs $14.95, what portion of sales goes to Jack?

    (A) 2.34%

    (B) 6.23%

    (C) 6.75%

    (D) 7.54%

14. Your garden is 4 feet wide by 6 feet long. You want to build another garden for your friend that is bigger but still proportionate. If you make your friend's garden to be 9 feet wide, how long would it have to be to still be in proportion to yours?

    (A) 8 feet

    (B) 9 feet

    (C) 10.8 feet

    (D) 13.5 feet

15. For every $2 that you spend at a particular restaurant, 75¢ is given to charity. If you spend $138 there over the course of the month, how much of your money will have been donated?

    (A) $28.55

    (B) $51.75

    (C) $103.50

    (D) $151.75

16. What part of the following expression would you evaluate first according to order of operations: $[2 \times 4 + (3^2 - 3)^4] + (-6) - 9$.

    (A) $(3^2 - 3)$

    (B) $2 \times 4$

    (C) $(3^2 - 3)^4$

    (D) $[2 \times 4 + (3^2 - 3)^4]$

17. Jordan makes $622 per week as a waitress. If she has to pay 12% of that to her landlord for rent, how much does she have left over for other expenses each month?

    (A) $298.56

    (B) $345.65

    (C) $2,189.44

    (D) $2,488

18. Emma and Tim both collect baseball cards. If Emma has 32 cards and hers outnumber Tim's cards by a ratio of 4:1, how many cards does Tim have?

    (A) 6

    (B) 8

    (C) 24

    (D) 32

19. If you could wash four loads of laundry at the Laundromat for $10.75, how many full loads could you wash for $23.63?

    (A) 6

    (B) 7

    (C) 8

    (D) 9

20. Your latest scores on a particular video game are 10,965; 15,637; and 16,222. What is your average score based on these numbers?

    (A) 14,274.67

    (B) 15,274.67

    (C) 23,724.67

    (D) 42,824

21. Four-sixths plus ⅞ equals:

    (A) $\dfrac{12}{11}$

    (B) $\dfrac{11}{12}$

    (C) $1\dfrac{2}{5}$

    (D) $1\dfrac{5}{8}$

22. Barry is organizing a trip to the botanical gardens for himself and 14 friends. Among them, they have five cars. Two hold four passengers, two hold five passengers, and one holds only three passengers. How many more people would they have to invite to fill up all the cars?

    (A) 3

    (B) 4

    (C) 5

    (D) 6

23. You have to move 27 one-pound bags of sand from the garage to your car. You can carry two bags at a time. How many trips will you have to make to move all the bags?

    (A) 11
    (B) 13
    (C) 14
    (D) 16

24. Private Snuffy can complete 50 push-ups in three minutes, which is 15 more than his closest competitor in his training class. What percentage would his competitor need to increase his numbers to reach Snuffy's performance?

    (A) 28%
    (B) 30%
    (C) 38%
    (D) 43%

25. At what percentage would a savings account have to accrue annual interest to increase a deposit of $235 to about $263 in a year?

    (A) 2%
    (B) 6%
    (C) 12%
    (D) 21%

26. $2 \times 2 \times 2 \times 2 \times 2$ is another way of writing

    (A) $2^2$
    (B) $2^3$
    (C) $2^4$
    (D) $2^5$

27. The square root of 169 is:

    (A) 11
    (B) 12
    (C) 13
    (D) 14

28. The odds on a horse in a race are paid 9:1. If you placed a $75 bet on the horse and it won, how much money would you win?

    (A) $525
    (B) $675
    (C) $775
    (D) $955

29. One lap on a track is equal to one quarter of a mile. If you ran 29 laps, about how many miles have you traveled?

    (A) 6
    (B) 7
    (C) 8
    (D) 9

30. In the following expression, which number is a base?

    $$7^6 + 14 - 12 + (-3)$$

    (A) 7
    (B) 14
    (C) –12
    (D) –3

# Word Knowledge

**Time:** 11 Minutes

**Questions:** 35

**Directions:** This section tests your knowledge of and ability to use vocabulary. Read each question and choose the answer choice that most nearly means the same as the underlined word.

1. Conceited most nearly means

    (A) humble.
    (B) noble.
    (C) proud.
    (D) loud.

2. Insurmountable most nearly means

    (A) conquered.
    (B) undefeatable.
    (C) friendly.
    (D) surrounded.

3. Extraordinary most nearly means

    (A) unexpected.
    (B) reliable.
    (C) morose.
    (D) melancholy.

4. Open most nearly means

    (A) simple.
    (B) advanced.
    (C) meager.
    (D) accepting.

5. Intricate most nearly means

    (A) frigid.
    (B) optimal.
    (C) complex.
    (D) dispassionate.

6. Antediluvian most nearly means

    (A) outdated.
    (B) incorrect.
    (C) beloved.
    (D) normal.

7. Profuse most nearly means

    (A) hard.
    (B) generous.
    (C) merited.
    (D) difficult.

8. After my mother's funeral, I thanked her friends for being so solicitous in their kind offer to help with the preparations.

    (A) grateful
    (B) false
    (C) active
    (D) concerned

9. The calm attorney was known for her forbearance when facing particularly aggressive opponents in court.

    (A) temper
    (B) vitality
    (C) patience
    (D) abrasiveness

10. Regal most nearly means

    (A) majestic.
    (B) ruddy.
    (C) uninterested.
    (D) ruined.

11. <u>Insipid</u> most nearly means

    (A) brave.

    (B) darkened.

    (C) angered.

    (D) trite.

12. <u>Foresight</u> most nearly means

    (A) affluence.

    (B) intuition.

    (C) contagion.

    (D) influence.

13. <u>Frequent</u> most nearly means

    (A) obstructive.

    (B) censorious.

    (C) recurrent.

    (D) blatant.

14. Even though the newspapers were all predicting a landslide win for the other candidate, the mayor was <u>resolute</u> in his belief that he would win the election.

    (A) steadfast

    (B) depressed

    (C) anxious

    (D) appreciative

15. The increasing length of the war quickly <u>depleted</u> the country's finances and manpower.

    (A) infused

    (B) drained

    (C) sustained

    (D) marginalized

16. <u>Ubiquitous</u> most nearly means

    (A) somniferous.

    (B) omnipotent.

    (C) omniscient.

    (D) omnipresent.

17. The <u>duplicitous</u> thief betrayed his comrade by giving him less than an equal cut of their latest heist.

    (A) demented

    (B) honorable

    (C) dishonest

    (D) disavowed

18. <u>Capitulate</u> most nearly means

    (A) surrender.

    (B) delay.

    (C) waver.

    (D) intrude.

19. It took a while for the exchange student to <u>assimilate</u> into her new family's culture, but soon she was speaking French and darting about the village like a native.

    (A) construct

    (B) reject

    (C) blend

    (D) grieve

20. <u>Benevolent</u> most nearly means

    (A) inferior.

    (B) egotistic.

    (C) blinded.

    (D) giving.

21. <u>Lanky</u> most nearly means

    (A) stout.

    (B) gangly.

    (C) broad.

    (D) small.

22. <u>Metamorphosis</u> most nearly means

    (A) transformation.

    (B) incantation.

    (C) inclination.

    (D) excitation.

23. <u>Obligate</u> most nearly means

    (A) exist.

    (B) deceive.

    (C) appreciate.

    (D) compel.

24. <u>Enrich</u> most nearly means

    (A) treat.

    (B) stir.

    (C) augment.

    (D) react.

25. <u>Indoctrinate</u> most nearly means

    (A) force.

    (B) train.

    (C) incite.

    (D) believe.

26. Her <u>sanguine</u> smile and optimistic words of encouragement in even the toughest circumstances helped make Jane the ideal candidate for team leader.

    (A) darkening

    (B) threatening

    (C) confident

    (D) unconscious

27. <u>Mystify</u> most nearly means

    (A) perplex.

    (B) clarify.

    (C) deify.

    (D) stupefy.

28. Because of my dyslexia, I often <u>transpose</u> *p* and *b* when I write the word *plumber*; it ends up looking like *blumper*.

    (A) impress

    (B) switch

    (C) ruin

    (D) berate

29. <u>Bait</u> most nearly means

    (A) mislead.

    (B) carry on.

    (C) bleed.

    (D) harass.

30. The anesthetic from my dental work earlier in the day was still in effect, thus making me <u>garble</u> my words in the meeting.

    (A) jumble

    (B) squeak

    (C) plait

    (D) berate

31. <u>Belie</u> most nearly means

    (A) predict.

    (B) confirm.

    (C) contradict.

    (D) forage.

32. <u>Heady</u> most nearly means

    (A) upset.

    (B) thrilling.

    (C) delusory.

    (D) exhausting.

33. Knowing that everyone else in the house was sick, I thought I'd take some extra vitamin C to try to <u>fortify</u> my immune system so I would not get sick, too.

    (A) strengthen

    (B) enlighten

    (C) enliven

    (D) invigorate

34. <u>Dictate</u> most nearly means

    (A) passive.

    (B) aggressive.

    (C) utter.

    (D) behave.

35. <u>Gracious</u> most nearly means

      (A) tangible.

      (B) raucous.

      (C) tactless.

      (D) congenial.

# Paragraph Comprehension

**Time:** 13 Minutes

**Questions:** 15

**Directions:** This section tests your ability to read and understand written information, as well as come to logical conclusions based on a text. Read each passage and answer the questions that follow. Choose the answer choice that best answers the question.

*Use the following passage to answer questions 1–2:*

(1) The Nile River is an important source of water in Africa. (2) Authorities have argued over the years about its exact length, as no definite consensus on its source has been reached. (3) As of 2006, it is estimated to be about 4,175 miles long, flowing south to north through Burundi, Egypt, Ethiopia, Kenya, Rwanda, Sudan, Tanzania, Uganda, and Zaire.

(4) Settlements and farms tend to center around the river. (5) Its use as a source of water for agricultural purposes has resulted in the production of many different types of foods upon which these countries rely for sustenance and income. (6) The Nile also serves as a source of hydroelectric power that helps support many communities in the countries through which it flows.

1. How many countries does the Nile run through?

      (A) 6

      (B) 7

      (C) 8

      (D) 9

2. Which sentence best conveys the main point of the passage?

      (A) 1

      (B) 2

      (C) 3

      (D) 4

*Use the following passage to answer questions 3–5:*

(1) Antarctica is the only continent that acts as a living laboratory for scientific research. (2) Though the benefits of having such a vast land that has not had much interference from human inhabitants are great, the extreme climate makes long-term study a challenge. (3) Maintaining temporary settlements that can support the manpower and equipment necessary to conduct experiments in temperatures that average –56° throughout the year and can drop below –150° in the winter is a constant issue.

(4) Furthermore, because of Antarctica's position over the southern pole of the Earth, it is lit by the sun for only six months throughout the year. (5) This presents issues for generating and maintaining sources of power during the months when the sun does not shine on the continent, especially since there are no sources of energy that can be drawn from towns or villages.

3. A research team planning to conduct a study in Antarctica might face issues with

   (A) providing heat that would protect their team members and equipment.
   (B) providing food and shelter for their team members and equipment.
   (C) providing light and electricity to conduct experiments and use computer equipment.
   (D) all of the above.

4. Which sentence best conveys the main point of the passage?

   (A) 1
   (B) 2
   (C) 4
   (D) 5

5. The tone of this passage can be described as

   (A) impassioned.
   (B) accusatory.
   (C) matter-of-fact.
   (D) sour.

*Use the following passage to answer questions 6–7:*

Animals are often classified by the type of food they eat. Most people are familiar with the two main types of this classification system: carnivores and herbivores. Carnivores are animals that eat only the flesh of other animals. Herbivores are plant eaters or vegetarians. They do not consume meat at all. What many people are not aware of is the third class, named omnivores. The name comes from the roots *omni*, which means "all" or "all-encompassing," and *vore*, which means "to devour." In short, omnivores eat both meat and plants to provide for their bodies.

6. According to the passage, humans can generally be classified as

   (A) carnivores.
   (B) herbivores.
   (C) omnivores.
   (D) semivores.

7. The root *herb* most likely means

   (A) having to do with plants.
   (B) having to do with meat.
   (C) having to do with men.
   (D) having to do with speaking.

*Use the following passage to answer questions 8–10:*

My class is so excited to be going to their first Broadway show. Even though we all live within comfortable proximity to New York City, many of us are too encumbered by our daily responsibilities to take the time to add cultural enrichment into our lives. It's easier and less of a drain on your time and money to consume television and Internet media versus having to purchase tickets to art exhibits, concerts, or plays. Also, the amount of time you have to schedule is considerable when you take into account covering the distance between your house and the venue, any transportation delays that may happen along the way, and the time you will actually spend enjoying the experience once you get to your destination. Even though these obstacles may prevent some from taking advantage of the wealth of cultural experience New York City has to offer, making the time to do so is always rewarding.

8. According to the passage, one of the reasons more people in the New York City area don't seek out cultural enrichment more is

   (A) lack of transportation.

   (B) demands on time and money.

   (C) lack of interest in the arts.

   (D) increases in interesting television programming.

9. The author would most likely agree with

   (A) a union strike that causes plays in New York City to have to be cancelled.

   (B) increases in ticket prices to Broadway shows.

   (C) a board of education proposal to set aside funding for an annual trip to the Museum of Modern Art for high school juniors.

   (D) a class about how to read and navigate a trip using maps.

10. The author's purpose is to

   (A) examine obstacles people experience in accessing cultural experience and encourage them to overcome those obstacles.

   (B) dissuade moviegoers from seeing the latest action film.

   (C) encourage students to conduct research about cultural activities.

   (D) admonish those who do not include cultural experiences in their lives.

*Use the following passage to answer questions 11–13:*

We decided to take our trip to Florida rather suddenly. The opportunity to take the family to visit the theme parks in the Orlando area for so little money was one we could not pass up. We have only a week to make all of our preparations. This includes: notifying our jobs that we needed a few days off; telling the girls' schools that they would not be in class and arranging for their assignments in advance; hiring a house sitter that could make sure the mail was taken in and the cats had food and water; and arranging for transportation to and from the airport. We also need to get identification for the girls, as they are too young to have driver's licenses and we didn't have enough time to apply for passports. Their birth certificates will have to do, though I'm not sure where they are right now.

11. The trip the author is talking about is

    (A) unexpected.
    (B) unwelcome.
    (C) inconvenient.
    (D) unfavorable.

12. What type of identification will the author use for her children?

    (A) student IDs
    (B) driver's licenses
    (C) passports
    (D) birth certificates

13. The author's tone is

    (A) upset.
    (B) relaxed.
    (C) hurried.
    (D) defiant.

*Use the following passage to answer questions 14–15:*

Listening is a skill that needs to be developed and is not simply innate to human beings. There is a big difference between physically hearing what is going on around you and understanding and processing that information. Internal and external forces, such as preoccupied thoughts and background noise, can command more of our attention than we realize. The result is that we do not actively listen to the messages around us, and much of the information presented to us does not add to our consciousness or intellect.

14. Based on information from the passage, one way to listen better would be to

    (A) conduct conversations in loud areas.
    (B) decrease the amount of background noise when conversing with someone.
    (C) concentrate on past experiences instead of on what's being said.
    (D) think about upcoming events.

15. In the passage, the word <u>innate</u> most nearly means

    (A) inborn

    (B) acquired

    (C) blessed

    (D) opportune

# Mathematics Knowledge

**Time:** 24 Minutes

**Questions:** 25

**Directions:** This section tests your knowledge of basic mathematics, algebra, and geometry. Carefully read each question and choose the answer choice that reflects the best answer.

1. If $x = 8$ and $y = 2$, then $y^3 + 2x - (x^2 + 11) =$

    (A) 60

    (B) 23

    (C) –51

    (D) 51

2. $\sqrt{144} =$

    (A) 11

    (B) 12

    (C) 14

    (D) 20

3. $(6x + 2)(2x - 4) =$

    (A) $12x^2 + (-20x) + (-8)$

    (B) $12x^2 + (-28x) + (-8)$

    (C) $12x^2 + (-28x) + 8$

    (D) $12x^2 + (-28x) + (-8)$

4. If angle $a = 102°$, then angle $d =$

    (A) 32°

    (B) 65°

    (C) 78°

    (D) 102°

5. If $7x - 12 \geq 3x + 8$, then $x$

    (A) $\geq 5$.

    (B) $\geq 5$.

    (C) $\geq 20$.

    (D) $\geq 20$.

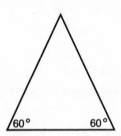

6. The area of this rhombus is:

 (A) 36

 (B) 72

 (C) 144

 (D) 150

7. On line segment AC, point B is located 4 away from points A and C. Point B is the

 (A) midpoint.

 (B) vertex.

 (C) radius.

 (D) ray.

8. What is the value of the third angle in this triangle?

 (A) 36°

 (B) 45°

 (C) 60°

 (D) 90°

9. Factor: $y^2 - 13y + 30$

 (A) $(y - 3)(y - 10)$

 (B) $(y - 6)(y - 12)$

 (C) $(y + 3)(y + 10)$

 (D) $(y + 3)(y - 10)$

10. You're laying carpet in a room that is 12 feet long by 30 feet wide. You have only half the amount of carpet needed to complete the job. How many more square feet of carpet do you need to get?

 (A) 50 ft²

 (B) 80 ft²

 (C) 95 ft²

 (D) 180 ft²

11. If in a right triangle, $a = 5$ and $b = 7$; $c$ equals about

 (A) 8.60.

 (B) 12.

 (C) 17.2.

 (D) 74.

12. 22% =

 (A) $\dfrac{1}{22}$

 (B) $\dfrac{1}{4}$

 (C) .22

 (D) 2.2

13. A number that stands by itself in an expression or equation is called a(n)

 (A) operation.

 (B) variable.

 (C) coefficient.

 (D) constant.

14. $\dfrac{9}{11} \div \dfrac{3}{7} =$

 (A) $\dfrac{27}{77}$

 (B) $1\dfrac{10}{11}$

 (C) $\dfrac{77}{27}$

 (D) $2\dfrac{23}{27}$

15. In scientific notation, 6,538,900,000 is:

(A) $6.5389 \times 10^9$

(B) $65.389 \times 10^8$

(C) $653.89 \times 10^7$

(D) $6538.9 \times 10^6$

16. $\dfrac{7}{10}$ is the same as:

(A) $7 \times 10$

(B) $7 \div 10$

(C) $7 - 10$

(D) $7 + 10$

17. Your office is holding a pool to predict when your boss's baby will be born. There are 20 spots total, and employees can pick only 1 spot. If there are only five spots left and you choose one of them, what is the probability of you winning the pool?

(A) $\dfrac{1}{2}$

(B) $\dfrac{1}{5}$

(C) $\dfrac{1}{20}$

(D) $\dfrac{2}{20}$

18. 16% of 642 =

(A) 10.272

(B) 102.72

(C) 1027.2

(D) 10,272

19. $\dfrac{8}{9} + \dfrac{4}{7} =$

(A) $\dfrac{2}{3}$

(B) $\dfrac{3}{8}$

(C) $\dfrac{12}{16}$

(D) $1\dfrac{29}{63}$

20. Factor: $y^2 - 9$

(A) $(y - 3)(y - 3)$

(B) $(y + 3)(y + 3)$

(C) $(y - 3)(y + 3)$

(D) $(y - 6)(y + 3)$

21. When multiplying or dividing positive and negative numbers, an even number of negatives will result in

(A) a negative answer.

(B) a positive answer.

(C) a neutral answer.

(D) an unequal answer.

22. Adding the values of all three sides of a triangle will give you its

(A) perimeter.

(B) area.

(C) absolute value.

(D) hypotenuse.

23. A proportion

(A) compares products.

(B) compares two values.

(C) compares sums.

(D) compares ratios.

24. What is the greatest common factor of 42 and 68?

(A) 2

(B) 4

(C) 8

(D) 12

25. If $p = 4$, solve for $x$: $2x + p^2 - 14 = 0$.

(A) 0

(B) 1

(C) −1

(D) 2

# Electronics Information

**Time:** 9 Minutes

**Questions:** 20

**Directions:** This section tests your knowledge of basic electronics principles and applications. Carefully read each question and choose the answer choice that reflects the best answer.

1. What does the letter $I$ represent in terms of electricity?

   (A) power
   (B) current
   (C) ampere
   (D) resistance

2. What type of particle is required in the production of electricity?

   (A) proton
   (B) neutron
   (C) electron
   (D) diode

3. Electricity always takes the _____ path to the ground.

   (A) least resistant
   (B) longest
   (C) lowest
   (D) most circuitous

4. Why do household wires require insulators?

   (A) because cold electrons move too slowly
   (B) because exposed wires release dangerous gases into the air
   (C) because insulators allow people to handle wires without getting shocked
   (D) all of the above

5. Which of the following appliances would require the most current?

   (A) nightlight
   (B) 100-wattt lightbulb
   (C) hair dryer
   (D) none of the above—current is the same for every appliance

*Use this diagram for questions 6–8.*

6. What does the previous symbol represent?

   (A) diode
   (B) capacitor
   (C) transformer
   (D) a sequence of resistors in a circuit

7. More specifically, the diagram depicts what?

   (A) parallel series of resistors in a circuit
   (B) parallel series of diodes
   (C) perpendicular series of transformers
   (D) parallel series of capacitors

8. This electronic device is used to prevent a circuit from suffering damage due to too much current:

   (A) resistor
   (B) transformer
   (C) switch
   (D) fuse

9. This symbol can be compared to a "One Way" road sign that is used to direct traffic down one-way streets?

(A)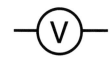

(B) ———

(C) ———▷|———

(D) ——o⁄o——

——(V)——

*Use the diagram to answer questions 10–11.*

10. What does the previous diagram illustrate?

(A) voltage

(B) voltmeter

(C) amperes

(D) vertical current

11. What is the purpose of the diagram?

(A) to demonstrate the amount of force an electrical source applies

(B) to measure voltage

(C) to determine how much current is flowing through the circuit

(D) to determine the direction of current flow

12. The acronym "LED" stands for

(A) lamp ending diagram.

(B) light energy direction.

(C) light emitting diode.

(D) load electricity diagram.

13. What material typically is used to make a diode?

(A) silicon

(B) copper

(C) rubber

(D) machined steel

14. Which of the following symbols represents a component that turns electrical energy into kinetic energy?

(A) —(M)—

(B) —⊗—

(C) ▽

(D) ⌇

15. Which of the following is an example of a load?

(A) electrons

(B) copper

(C) lightbulb

(D) current

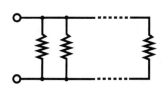

16. The previous diagram illustrates which of the following?

(A) resistors in a parallel circuit

(B) series circuit

(C) diode

(D) transformer

17. Ohm's law states that electric current is directly proportional to _____.

(A) resistance

(B) voltage

(C) amperes

(D) watts

18. Which of the following is NOT a factor pertaining to the amount of resistance in a wire?

    (A) gauge

    (B) length

    (C) composition

    (D) color

19. If you have 20 volts and 5 amps, how much resistance do you have?

    (A) 100 ohms

    (B) 4 ohms

    (C) 25 ohms

    (D) not enough information

20. If you have 10 ohms of resistance and 2 amps of current, how much voltage do you have?

    (A) 5 volts

    (B) 8 volts

    (C) 6 volts

    (D) 20 volts

# Automotive and Shop Information

**Time:** 11 Minutes

**Questions:** 25

**Directions:** This section tests your knowledge of automotive components and principles, as well as general shop tools and applications. Carefully read each question and choose the answer choice that reflects the best answer.

1. Which system makes the light and power systems work?

    (A) exhaust system

    (B) electrical system

    (C) fuel system

    (D) suspension system

2. Which system deals with the movement of the wheels and the manner in which cars react to terrain?

    (A) exhaust system

    (B) electrical system

    (C) fuel system

    (D) suspension system

3. When the engine receives a full cylinder of gas and air, this is known as which stroke in the Otto Cycle?

    (A) intake

    (B) compression

    (C) combustion

    (D) exhaust

4. Brake pistons move under what type of pressure?

    (A) air

    (B) fluid

    (C) heat

    (D) mechanical

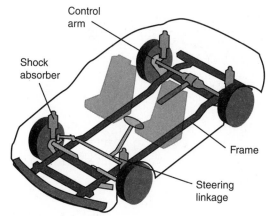

Control arm

Shock absorber

Frame

Steering linkage

*Use this diagram to answer questions 5–7.*

5. Which part of the diagram helps smooth the jolting of a bumpy road?

    (A) control arm
    (B) frame
    (C) shock absorber
    (D) steering linkage

6. Which part shown in the diagram can pivot in two places to handle wheel activity?

    (A) control arm
    (B) frame
    (C) shock absorber
    (D) steering linkage

7. Which part shown in the diagram has a series of arms, rods, and ball sockets that allow the wheels to swivel as needed?

    (A) control arm
    (B) frame
    (C) shock absorber
    (D) steering linkage

8. Approximately how many spark plug explosions does it take per minute for a four-cylinder engine to drive 50 miles per hour?

    (A) 40
    (B) 400
    (C) 4,000
    (D) 2,000

9. How many coils are found in a typical coil pack for a six-cylinder engine?

    (A) 3
    (B) 4
    (C) 5
    (D) 6

10. Once your car is running, how does the battery get recharged?

    (A) Energy from the spark plugs is transferred to the battery.
    (B) The solenoid sends electric current to the battery.
    (C) The alternator recharges it.
    (D) The voltage regulator monitors and recharges the battery.

11. Which part of the car's battery stores energy?

    (A) positive post
    (B) negative post
    (C) lead plates
    (D) battery cables

12. Where are fuse boxes generally located in a car?

    (A) near the bottom of the dashboard or under the hood
    (B) near the top of the dashboard or under the driver's seat
    (C) in the trunk or in the driver's door panel
    (D) none of the above

13. Which of the following is NOT true of diesel fuel?

    (A) It vaporizes at a higher temperature than gasoline.
    (B) It gets better gas mileage than gasoline.
    (C) It is more dense than gasoline.
    (D) It burns less efficiently than gasoline.

14. In newer cars, fuel pumps tend to be mounted where?

    (A) alongside the fuel filter

    (B) on top of the fuel injector

    (C) inside the fuel tank

    (D) wherever there is space

15. Which of the following is NOT a key function of the exhaust system?

    (A) reduce engine noise

    (B) maintain performance

    (C) reduce or eliminate harmful emissions

    (D) absorb road bumps

16. Which tool is often used in creating pockets for door hinges?

    (A) cold chisel

    (B) file

    (C) wood chisel

    (D) rasp

17. Which type of saw generally has 8–15 teeth per inch, with alternating cutting edges on the blade, and cuts wood against the grain?

    (A) hack saw

    (B) crosscut saw

    (C) miter saw

    (D) circular saw

18. Which type of hammer is best used when a steel-headed tool could damage the material being hammered into?

    (A) curved claw

    (B) rubber mallet

    (C) ball pein

    (D) engineer's

19. Which part of a hand drill turns the main shaft?

    (A) cranking handle

    (B) cranking chuck

    (C) cranking bit

    (D) cranking miter

20. If you want a screw to lie flush with a piece of wood, which type of drill bit should you use for your project?

    (A) carbide-tipped masonry bit

    (B) spade bit

    (C) countersink

    (D) auger

21. A pipe wrench is actually a form of what other kind of wrench?

    (A) open end

    (B) combination end

    (C) adjustable end

    (D) all of the above

22. An Allen wrench is

    (A) V-shaped.

    (B) L-shaped.

    (C) T-shaped.

    (D) I-shaped.

23. This tool is also known as a ratchet and is used to tighten different-sized nuts and bolts:

    (A) hand screw

    (B) Phillips head screwdriver

    (C) monkey wrench

    (D) socket wrench

24. Which tool is used to stop leaks and features a metallic strap or band?

    (A) bar clamp

    (B) pipe clamp

    (C) vise grip

    (D) band clamp

25. A jackhammer can be categorized as what type of drill?

   (A) drill press
   (B) hammer drill
   (C) claw drill
   (D) circular drill

# Mechanical Comprehension

**Time:** 19 Minutes

**Questions:** 25

**Directions:** This section tests your knowledge and application of basic mechanical principles. Carefully read each question and choose the answer choice that reflects the best answer.

1. Which of the following types of energy is NOT found in a rubber band?

   (A) potential energy
   (B) kinetic energy
   (C) elastic energy
   (D) electromagnetic energy

2. Suppose you have an object whose mass is 20 kilograms and is located 2 meters above Earth. What is the object's gravitational potential energy?

   (A) 40 joules
   (B) 98 joules
   (C) 200 joules
   (D) 392 joules

3. Matter is

   (A) energy of motion.
   (B) how fast an object is moving.
   (C) speed, plus the direction of motion.
   (D) anything that occupies space and has mass.

4. You have an object whose gravitational potential energy equals 6,272 joules, and the mass equals 64 kilograms. What is the height above Earth's surface?

   (A) 9.8 meters
   (B) 10 meters
   (C) 98 meters
   (D) 1,000 meters

5. How can you determine the ratio of the gears?

   (A) measure the width of each gear
   (B) measure the circumference of each gear
   (C) count the teeth and multiply them together
   (D) count the teeth and divide the larger number by the smaller number

6. When Sergeant Bob does push-ups, the force of his hands against the ground results in equal pressure from the ground against his hands. This is known as what law?

    (A) the law of reciprocal action

    (B) the law of reaction

    (C) the law of reverse inertia

    (D) the law of resistance

7. Suppose it takes you 800 joules of work to move a distance of 50 meters against a force. If you cut your distance in half, what happens to your workload?

    (A) It stays the same.

    (B) It doubles.

    (C) It gets halved.

    (D) No way to tell.

8. If instead you double the force you are acting against, what happens to your workload?

    (A) It stays the same.

    (B) It doubles.

    (C) It gets halved.

    (D) No way to tell.

9. If instead you double the force you are carrying *and* cut the distance in half, what happens to your workload?

    (A) It stays the same.

    (B) It doubles.

    (C) It gets halved.

    (D) No way to tell.

10. When you lean against the countertop in your kitchen, the countertop also pushes against you. Which one of Newton's laws does this concept apply to?

    (A) first

    (B) second

    (C) third

    (D) all three

11. If the gear in the middle of the previous diagram causes the other gears to turn in opposite directions, it is a

    (A) compound gear.

    (B) fixed gear.

    (C) moveable gear.

    (D) driving gear.

12. An object is in mechanical equilibrium

    (A) when it simplifies the workload.

    (B) when it undergoes Newton's third law.

    (C) when its acceleration and velocity are equal.

    (D) when there is no acceleration.

13. Suppose you have a 70-kilogram object that needs to be lifted 15 meters. In a basic two-wheeled pulley system, how much weight does it feel like you're lifting?

    (A) 35 kilograms

    (B) 55 kilograms

    (C) 70 kilograms

    (D) 140 kilograms

14. Suppose you have a 20-kilogram object that needs to be lifted 40 meters. In a basic four-wheeled pulley system, how far do you have to pull the rope?

    (A) 20 meters

    (B) 60 meters

    (C) 80 meters

    (D) 160 meters

15. What is a force-distance trade-off?

    (A) the definition of simple machines

    (B) the concept behind building simple machines

    (C) when an object feels lighter, but you are forced to pull the rope farther to raise it the original distance

    (D) when an object becomes lighter through the addition of pulleys, but the pulleys are placed farther away from the object

16. The type of gear that is more versatile and quieter than a spur gear, and is commonly found in car transmissions is called a

    (A) helical gear.

    (B) bevel gear.

    (C) worm gear.

    (D) compound gear.

17. When gears reduce the speed of machinery, this is known as

    (A) simple mechanics.

    (B) gear reduction.

    (C) gear advantage.

    (D) speed reduction.

18. When two objects with different masses free-fall, why might they theoretically fall at the same speed?

    (A) The object with the smaller mass also has proportionately more force acting on it.

    (B) Gravitational pull causes everything to fall at the same speed when there is no air resistance.

    (C) The law of acceleration causes all objects to accelerate at the same rate.

    (D) Wind resistance and air friction would have an equalizing effect on the two objects.

19. Suppose you are in a cycling race. When the race begins, you increase your speed from 0 kilometers per hour to 40 kilometers per hour over the course of 10 seconds. What is your rate of acceleration?

    (A) 30 kilometers per second$^2$

    (B) 4 kilometers per second$^2$

    (C) 50 kilometers per second$^2$

    (D) 40 kilometers per second$^2$

20. If you are traveling at a speed of 30 miles per hour, what is the distance you cover in one minute?

    (A) 2 miles

    (B) 30 miles

    (C) $\frac{1}{2}$ mile

    (D) 1 mile

21. Consider the following figures. An object has a mass of 50 kilograms, acceleration of 8 kilometers per second$^2$, and a speed of 20 kilometers per hour. Using the relevant figures, calculate the amount of force needed to set this object in motion.

    (A) 400

    (B) 160

    (C) 800

    (D) 20

22. What does mass measure?

    (A) the gravitational force exerted on an object

    (B) the amount of material in an object

    (C) the density of cells in an object

    (D) the volume of an object

23. What kind of movement constitutes motion?

    (A) movement of mass
    (B) movement measured by Newtons
    (C) kinetic energy
    (D) any kind

24. Kinetic energy is energy that has been converted from another kind of energy. Which of the following does NOT convert to kinetic energy?

    (A) chemical
    (B) potential
    (C) negative acceleration
    (D) all of the above

25. Potential energy exists in

    (A) any object that exists in a force field.
    (B) any object that has kinetic energy.
    (C) any object that can retain its original shape, even after being rearranged.
    (D) any object.

# Assembling Objects

**Time:** 15 Minutes

**Questions:** 25

**Directions:** This section tests your ability to visualize how objects fit together. Carefully read each question and choose the answer choice that reflects the best answer.

1. In the following diagram, which figure best shows how the objects in the first box would touch if points A and B were connected?

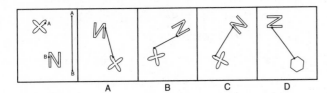

2. Which answer choice best shows how the objects in the first box would appear if they were fitted together?

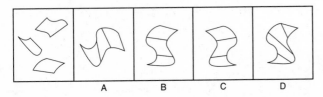

3. In the following diagram, which figure best shows how the objects in the first box would touch if points A and B were connected?

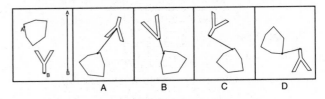

4. Which answer choice best shows how the objects in the first box would appear if they were fitted together?

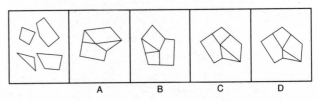

5. In the following diagram, which figure best shows how the objects in the first box would touch if points A and B were connected?

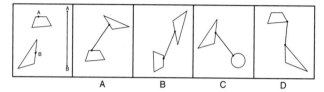

6. Which answer choice best shows how the objects in the first box would appear if they were fitted together?

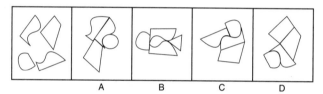

7. In the following diagram, which figure best shows how the objects in the first box would touch if points A and B were connected?

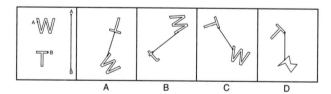

8. Which answer choice best shows how the objects in the first box would appear if they were fitted together?

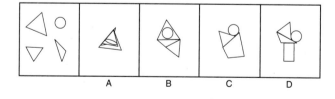

9. In the following diagram, which figure best shows how the objects in the first box would touch if points A and B were connected?

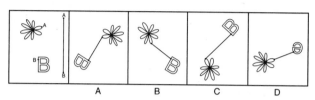

10. Which answer choice best shows how the objects in the first box would appear if they were fitted together?

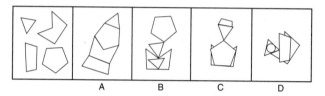

11. In the following diagram, which figure best shows how the objects in the first box would touch if points A and B were connected?

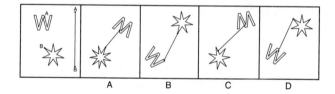

12. Which answer choice best shows how the objects in the first box would appear if they were fitted together?

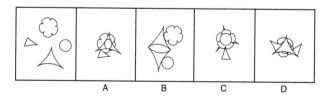

13. In the following diagram, which figure best shows how the objects in the first box would touch if points A and B were connected?

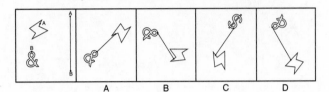

14. Which answer choice best shows how the objects in the first box would appear if they were fitted together?

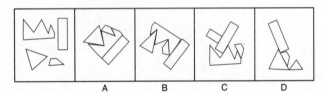

15. In the following diagram, which figure best shows how the objects in the first box would touch if points A and B were connected?

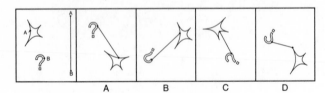

16. Which answer choice best shows how the objects in the first box would appear if they were fitted together?

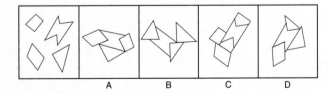

17. In the following diagram, which figure best shows how the objects in the first box would touch if points A and B were connected?

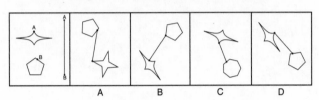

18. Which answer choice best shows how the objects in the first box would appear if they were fitted together?

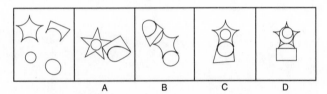

19. In the following diagram, which figure best shows how the objects in the first box would touch if points A and B were connected?

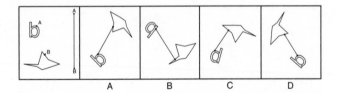

20. Which answer choice best shows how the objects in the first box would appear if they were fitted together?

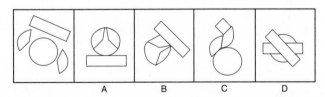

21. In the following diagram, which figure best shows how the objects in the first box would touch if points A and B were connected?

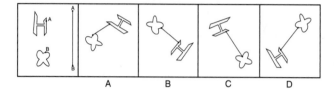

22. Which answer choice best shows how the objects in the first box would appear if they were fitted together?

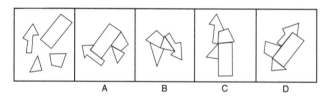

23. In the following diagram, which figure best shows how the objects in the first box would touch if points A and B were connected?

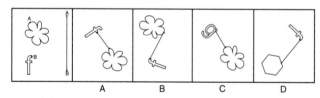

24. Which answer choice best shows how the objects in the first box would appear if they were fitted together?

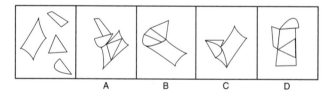

25. In the following diagram, which figure best shows how the objects in the first box would touch if points A and B were connected?

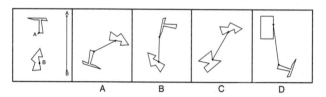

# Answers and Explanations

## General Science

1. **A.** Choice B is wrong because ecology is the study of the environment. Choice C is wrong because zoology is the study of animals. Choice D is wrong because chemistry is the study of matter.

2. **C.** Choice A is wrong because cell theory states that all living organisms are made up of cells. Choice B is wrong because gene theory states that traits get passed on from generation to generation through genes. Choice D is wrong because homeostasis theory addresses an animal's ability to maintain a constant internal temperature.

3. **B.** All the other choices are correct statements regarding thermodynamics theory.

4. **A.** The archaea kingdom, in particular, has been a source of great debate among scientists.

5. **B.** All the other choices were false statements.

6. **A.** None of the other choices have the correct photosynthesis formula.

7. **C.** During photosynthesis, plants convert carbon dioxide, water, and sunlight to sugar and oxygen.

8. **B.** Choice A is wrong because tropical forests are characterized by enormous trees and lush plants. Choice C is wrong because freshwater wetlands are characterized by shallow waters, such as marshes and ponds. Choice D is wrong because oceans are characterized by water that covers nearly 75 percent of Earth.

9. **D.** Some human bodies even have trillions of cells, depending on how large they are.

10. **D.** Choice A is wrong because ribosomes contain RNA units to build proteins. Choice B is wrong because golgi allow newly made proteins to mature and become functional. Choice C is wrong because mitochondria convert nutrients into energy.

11. **B.** Mitosis is the process of cell division in which each cell completely divides and has its own nucleus. Meiosis is the process of cell division used in sexual reproduction.

12. **C.** All cells undergo mitosis except those involved with sexual reproduction. Hair, muscle, nail, and skin cells all undergo mitosis as they grow and replace old cells.

13. **B.** Choice A is wrong because nucleotides play an important role in metabolism. Choice C is wrong because metabolism is a set of chemical reactions that allows organisms to grow, reproduce, maintain structure, and respond to the environment. Choice D is wrong because amino acids also play a role in metabolism.

14. **B.** Proteins are most commonly found in meats, eggs, dairy, seeds, and nuts.

15. **C.** Choice A is wrong because the respiratory system includes the mouth, nose, trachea, lungs, and diaphragm. Choice B is wrong because the digestive system includes the mouth, throat, esophagus, stomach, liver, gall bladder, and the like. Choice D is wrong because the excretory system includes the kidneys, liver, lungs, and skin.

16. **D.** Choice A is wrong because it describes the large intestine. Choice B is wrong because it describes the diaphragm. Choice C is wrong because it describes the lungs.

17. **B.** Choice A is wrong because while fats do provide us with energy, most dietary energy comes from carbohydrates. Choice C is wrong because the main job of minerals is to assist in normal body functions. Choice D is wrong because vitamins play a key role in many chemical processes.

18. **D.** Choice A is wrong because the main function of protein is to assist in growth and muscle repair. Choice B is also wrong—see the explanation about fats in the preceding answer. Choice C is wrong because roughage is designed to ensure a healthy digestive system.

19. **C.** See previous answer explanations for additional information on choices A, B, and D.

20. **A.** The crust is closest to the surface of Earth, running about 10 miles deep. The mantle comes next and extends inward approximately 1,800 miles toward the center of Earth. Following the mantle is the outer core, which is nearly 3,000 miles deep. Lastly, the inner core is thought to be approximately 900 miles deep.

21. **A.** Choice B describes liquid molten rock that flows above Earth's surface. Choices C and D do not describe any form of liquid rock.

22. **B.** None of the other choices depict the main elements found in Earth's outer core.

23. **B.** Choice A is wrong because a warm front occurs when an advancing mass of warm air rises over a mass of cold air. Choice C is wrong because temperature is a degree of hotness or coldness in the environment. Choice D is wrong because cumulonimbus is a type of cloud.

24. **C.** Choice A is wrong because a comet is a small, frozen mass of dust and gas revolving around the sun. Choice B is wrong because a meteor is also known as a shooting star. Choice D is wrong because an astronomical unit is the distance from Earth to the sun.

25. **D.** Choice A is wrong because Mercury is the hottest planet. Choice B is wrong because Pluto is the coldest planet. Choice C is wrong because Jupiter is the largest planet.

# Arithmetic Reasoning

1. **D.** John currently pays $245 + $396 = $641 to his employees each week. If he increases this by 6% (641 × .06 = 38.46), he will have to allocate $38.46 more per week to pay his employees. Multiply this by 4 and you will find how much more he has to pay per month: $38.46 × 4 = $153.84.

2. **A.** Since there are 52 weeks in a year, multiply 52 × 4 to find that Mr. X will have been on 208 dates over the course of a year.

3. **C.** Divide 32,890 by 52 to figure out Jon's weekly salary: $632.50. Now subtract:

    632.50
    -545.50
    ‾‾‾‾‾‾‾
    87.00

4. **A.** According to the question, 150 out of 750 books are romances. This is a ratio of $\frac{150}{750}$, which reduces to $\frac{1}{5}$, which is also the fraction form of 20%.

5. **B.** Multiply 15,625.35 by .07 to figure out how much more you made the second half of the year: 15,625.35 × .07 = 1,093.77. Now multiply 15,625.35 × 2 to find your regular annual earnings: $31,250.7. Finally, add 1,093.77 to this amount to find you've made $32,344.47 for the year.

6. **D.** Your ratio of peaches to apples is 125:85, which reduces to 25:17.

7. **C.** Divide 32 by 128. The answer is 25%.

8. **D.** Figure out how much Bailey will have to pay for both the children and the adults:

    Adults: 5.25 × 2 = 10.50

    Children: 3.75 × 3 = 11.25

    Now add the products. Admission for all five people will cost $21.75.

9. **A.** Use the Distance = Rate × time formula here:

    $$87 = 13 \times t$$
    $$\frac{87}{13} = t$$
    $$6\frac{9}{13} = t$$

10. **B.** Translate this into an expression: −12 + −13. When you add two negatives, you go down the number line, so add the two numbers and place a negative in front of your answer: 12 + 13 = −25.

11. **B.** Calculate 32% of 67: .32 × 67 = 21.44. Now subtract this amount from 67:

    67.00
    −21.46
    ‾‾‾‾‾‾
    45.56

    April is about $45\frac{1}{2}$ years old.

12. **C.** When you have a list of numbers multiplied in order from greatest to least, you have a factorial.

13. **A.** Divide .35 by 14.95 and then multiply by 100 to get 2.34%.

14. **D.** Set up a proportion here based on your garden's dimensions and those of your neighbor's. Use a variable to stand in for the unknown quantity: $\frac{4}{6} = \frac{9}{x}$. Now cross multiply to solve for $x$:

    $$6 \times 9 = 4x$$
    $$54 = 4x$$
    $$\frac{54}{4} = x$$
    $$13.5 = x$$

15. **B.** Calculate the percentage of every dollar that goes to charity by dividing $0.75 by 2. This leaves you with $0.375. Now multiply that amount by $138: $138 × .375 = $51.75.

16. **A.** Since parentheses come first in order of operations, you should look for those. The only expression in parentheses is inside the brackets. Brackets are a step up from parentheses, so you would look there first anyway. So it's logical that among the expressions within the brackets, you would solve $(3^2 - 3)$ first. Exponents are second, so $(3^2 - 3)^4$ is not correct. Answer D, $[2 \times 4 + (3^2 - 3)^4]$, is also not correct because you would not solve the whole expression first, but one smaller part.

17. **C.** Multiply $622 \times 4$ to find out how much she makes per month ($2,488). Next, multiply this amount by .12: $2,488 \times .12 = $298.56. Now subtract this amount from $2,488: $2,488 - $298.56 = $2,189.44. This is how much Jordan has to spend on other expenses.

18. **B.** Start your calculation with a proportion: $\frac{4}{1} = \frac{32}{x}$. Now cross multiply and solve for $x$:

    $32 \times 1 = 4x$

    $\frac{32}{4} = x$

    $8 = x$

    This tells us that Tim has eight cards.

19. **C.** Divide 10.75 by 4 to find out that one load costs $2.6875.

    Now divide $23.63 by this amount to get 8.79. Since this number is not nine full loads, you have to round down to eight, because you need to find the number of entire loads the amount will pay for. You'll have change left over, but eight loads in the wash.

20. **A.** Add all the numbers to get 42,824.

    Now divide that number by 3 to get this: $42,824 \div 3 = 14,274.67$

21. **B.** Translate this into two fractions: $\frac{4}{6} + \frac{2}{8}$. Multiply each fraction by the opposite denominator to get a common denominator:

    $\frac{4}{6} \times \frac{8}{8} = \frac{32}{48}$

    $\frac{2}{8} \times \frac{6}{6} = \frac{12}{48}$. Finally, add these two new fractions together and reduce: $\frac{32}{48} + \frac{12}{48} = \frac{44}{48} = \frac{11}{12}$.

22. **D.** Including Barry, 15 people are scheduled to go on the trip. The total number of seats available are $4 + 4 + 5 + 5 + 3 = 21$. Subtract $21 - 15 = 6$. He needs six more people to fill all the cars.

23. **C.** If you take two bags at a time, you can move 26 bags in 13 trips. You will have to make one more to get the remaining bag, so your total is 14 trips.

24. **D.** Divide 15 by 35 (the number of push-ups the competitor can complete) to find that Snuffy's competitor would need to increase his numbers by 42.8% to catch up to Snuffy. Round this up to 43 and you have your answer.

25. **C.** Subtract $263 - 235 = 28$. Now multiply each of the answer choices by 235. The one that equals 28 is the correct answer:

    $235 \times .02 = 4.7$

    $235 \times .06 = 14.1$

    $235 \times .12 = 28.2$

    $235 \times .21 = 49.35$

    Answer C is the best choice.

26. **D.** This is an extended way of writing $2^5$.

27. **C.** $13 \times 13 = 169$

28. **B.** Start with a proportion to show the ratio of the odds and how much money is bet: $\frac{9}{1} = \frac{x}{75}$. Now cross multiply and solve for $x$:

    $9 \times 75 = x$

    $675 = x$

29. **B.** Divide 29 by 4 to get 7.25. Round this down, since it's below half. The best answer is B.

# Word Knowledge

1. **C.** *Conceited* means "to be full of oneself." Answer A is the opposite of this. Answer B describes honorable moral character. Answer D describes something that makes a lot of sound.

2. **B.** *Surmount* means "to overcome." Add the prefix *in*, and the meaning changes to "unable to overcome." Answer A is the opposite of this meaning. The other two answer choices don't make sense.

3. **A.** *Extraordinary* is something that's special or unexpected. Answer B is the opposite of this meaning. *Morose* and *melancholy* are similar in that they both refer to something that's gloomy, sad, or depressing.

4. **D.** *Open* has several definitions. From the answer choices, it's clear that you're looking for the adjective form, which means "accepting."

5. **C.** Something that is *intricate* artfully combines many things to make a whole. *Frigid* means "cold." *Optimal* means "the best." *Dispassionate* means "without strong emotion." *Complex* is the best choice.

6. **A.** The prefix *ante*, which means "before," tells you that there is some kind of time connection. The only answer choice that has any connection to time is A, which is the main definition of the word.

7. **B.** *Profuse* means "generous" or "widespread." None of the other answers make sense with this definition.

30. **A.** The main number or variable in a term is called the base, while the raised number is the exponent. In this question, the only place this is applicable is with the term $7^6$. Clearly, 7 is the base and 6 is the exponent.

8. **D.** You can infer from the sentence that the "kind offer" was most likely out of concern for the aggrieved daughter. The other answer choices don't make sense in this context.

9. **C.** *Forbearance* describes restraint or grace under pressure, which the lawyer in the sentence is known for having, according to the context clues. Even if you didn't know this, if you swapped out the underlined word with any of the other answer choices, they wouldn't have made sense in this context.

10. **A.** A good association here is "His regal, royal majesty." Each of these words means the same thing: noble, ceremonial, imperial, and so on.

11. **C.** *Insipid* means "dull" or "uninteresting." *Trite* means "overused" or "clichéd." The other answer choices have nothing to do with either, which makes answer C the best choice.

12. **B.** Break down this word into smaller parts. *Sight* obviously means "to see." The prefix *for* means "coming before." With this as a working definition, answer B makes the most sense, since it talks about instinct and knowledge. *Affluence* is a state of wealth and power. A *contagion* is something that spreads disease (think *contagious*). *Influence* is having the ability to affect something.

13. **C.** How is *frequent* being used here? Is it an adjective or a verb? The fact that the answer choices are all adjectives tells us we're dealing with the definition of *frequent* that means doing something "often." *Obstructive* is "getting in the way." *Censorious* is "critical." *Blatant* is "obvious."

14. **A.** The sentence talks about someone who believes against the odds. The mayor is determined to keep hope alive. *Steadfast* means to stay firm in a belief. Answer B and D don't make sense with the context clues in the sentence, which tell us the underlined word would mean the opposite of what the beginning of the sentence implies. Answer D just doesn't make sense.

15. **B.** Logic (and history) tells us that a lengthy war drains resources. It would not infuse (increase), sustain (keep steady), or marginalize (keep out of the center of attention) money or manpower.

16. **D.** *Ubiquitous* means "all around." *Somniferous* is something that causes sleep (the root *som* means "sleep"). *Omnipotent* means "all powerful." *Omniscient* means "all knowing." *Omnipresent* means "all encompassing."

17. **C.** The context clues tell us the thief is being deceitful or dishonest. *Demented* means "irrational," which could apply in this context. However, there is no indication about the thief's intent other than to cheat his partner. *Disavowed* is to deny association or knowledge of something, which clearly doesn't fit in this case.

18. **A.** *Capitulate* means "to agree" or "to surrender." To "waver" is to go back and forth, and to "intrude" is to interrupt, neither of which makes sense.

19. **C.** The context clue, "like a native," tells us that the student's situation has changed and that though she felt foreign at the beginning of the sentence, by the end she fits in much better. *Blend* is the only answer choice that works with this meaning.

20. **D.** The root *bene* means "good," so the correct answer will have something to do with being good or having attributes considered to be good. *Inferior* means "less than." *Egotistic* means "concerned with the self." *Blinded* means "unable to see." *Giving* is the best choice, since this is generally considered a "good" attribute.

21. **B.** *Long, lanky,* and *gangly* are often used interchangeably when describing someone who is very tall and thin. They all have negative connotations to them. All of the other words describe sizes that oppose long and thin.

22. **A.** If you read Franz Kafka's *Metamorphosis* (about a man who turns into a bug) or remember grade school science class lessons about caterpillars turning into butterflies, you know answer A is the best choice. *Incantation* is a spell. *Inclination* is a desire. *Excitation* is something that creates excitement.

23. **D.** When you're *obligated* to do something, you're responsible for seeing it done. This *compels* (drives) you to do it. *Exists* means "to be." *Deceive* means "to trick." *Appreciate* means "to value."

24. **C.** *Enrich* means "to enhance." Even if you didn't know that *augment* means "to change or enhance," you could eliminate every other answer choice.

25. **B.** To *indoctrinate* is to teach someone about a belief or ideology. *Force* and *believe* don't fit here. To *incite* means to start something. Any way you look at it, answer B is the only choice that has anything to do with teaching, and it is your best choice.

26. **C.** Leaders need to be strong, and the sentence describes Jane as being inspirational and optimistic. The correct answer will have something to do with this. The only answer that comes close is C. (*Sanguine* has several definitions, and "confident" is one of them.)

27. **A.** Mysteries are mystifying because they cause confusion and puzzle people's minds. *Perplex* means "to confuse." *Clarify* means "to make clear." To *deify* is to make something a god or godlike. To *stupefy* is to astonish or amaze, not necessarily to confuse.

28. **B.** In the sentence, we see that the *p* and *b* in the sentence have been switched, or transposed.

29. **D.** *Bait* has many definitions. In this case, *bait* means "to tease or harass," since none of the other words are related to any other definition of bait (a lure, to lure, an attack by a dog, and so on).

30. **A.** Anyone who has had their mouth numbed in the dentist's chair knows that the anesthetic impairs one's ability to speak. Using context clues, you can figure out that to *garble* is to make something unintelligible or all messed up. *Jumble* means "to mix up." *Plait* means "to braid." *Berate* means "to scold."

# Paragraph Comprehension

1. **D.** Sentence 2 lists Burundi, Egypt, Ethiopia, Kenya, Rwanda, Sudan, Tanzania, Uganda, and Zaire as the countries the Nile runs through.

2. **A.** The main point of the passage is best described in sentence 1: "The Nile River is an important source of water in Africa." The rest of the passage backs up this statement with specific examples and details.

31. **C.** To *belie* is to give a false impression or contradict the truth.

32. **B.** A good mnemonic to make here is "Intoxication goes right to your head." *Heady* means "intoxicating" or "exhilarating." The only word you might have trouble with in this question is *delusory*, which means "deceptive." It's a form of *delusion* and does not fit.

33. **A.** The sentence is clearly telling us that *fortify* means "to strengthen," since the speaker's goal is not to get sick. The other choices don't make sense in the sentence.

34. **C.** The root *dict* means "to speak," so the correct answer will have to do with speaking. *Utter* is another word for "speak." Answers A and B are adjectives, which means they can't be right, since *dictate* is a verb. Answer D has nothing to do with speaking.

35. **D.** The base word here is *grace*, which means the correct answer will have something to do with elegance or politeness. *Tangible* means "able to be touched." *Raucous* means "loud." To be *tactless* is to be unconcerned with how one's actions impacts others. *Congenial* means "friendly" or "pleasant." Out of all of these choices, D is your best bet.

3. **D.** From the information in the passage about the inhospitable living conditions, lack of power, and lack of sunlight, all the answer choices would be issues a research team planning to study in Antarctica would face.

4. **B.** Sentence 2 says, "Though the benefits of having such a vast land that has not had much interference from human inhabitants are great, the extreme climate makes long-term study a challenge." The majority of the passage supports this statement, making it the main idea.

5. **C.** The speaker's tone really doesn't convey any emotion, which makes C the best choice.

6. **C.** Even if they choose to be vegetarians or vegans, humans are omnivores, since, categorically, we eat both meat and plants in our diets.

7. **A.** You can infer from the passage that *herb* has to do with plants, since it's part of the word defined as "plant-eater."

8. **B.** The passage states that "many of us are too encumbered by our daily responsibilities to take the time to add cultural enrichment into our lives." Specifically, it discusses demands on time and money as barriers to cultural enrichment. The other answer choices aren't supported by information from the passage.

9. **C.** From the author's tone, you can infer that he or she would support any effort that would enable people to enjoy culture more easily or frequently. Answer C is the only one that would accomplish this.

10. **A.** Answer A is directly supported by the final sentence in the passage: "Even though these obstacles may prevent some from taking advantage of the wealth of cultural experience New York City has to offer, making the time to do so is always rewarding."

11. **A.** The only indication we get from the passage that applies to the answer choices is that the trip was last-minute and unexpected.

12. **D.** The last sentence says she will use birth certificates. The passage says she doesn't have passports and the kids are too young for driver's licenses. Student IDs are never mentioned.

13. **C.** Since time is the main issue throughout this paragraph, the author's tone is most likely hurried rather than upset. She is definitely neither relaxed or defiant.

14. **B.** The passage states, "Internal and external forces, such as preoccupied thoughts and background noise, can command more of our attention than we realize." Based on this information, it stands to reason that if you decrease the amount of background noise, you will be able to listen better. All the other answer choices are contradicted by information from the passage.

15. **A.** *Innate* means "at birth." Answer B is contradicted by the context of the sentence in which *innate* is used. Answers C and D just don't make sense.

# Mathematics Knowledge

1. **C.** When you plug in the numbers given in the question, you have $2^3 + 2 \times 8 - (8^2 + 11)$. Follow order of operations to solve.

2. **B.** The square root of 144 is 12 because $12 \times 12 = 144$.

3. **A.** Use FOIL here.
   $(6x + 2)(2x - 4) = 12x^2 + (-24x) + 4x + (-8)$
   Now combine like terms.
   $(6x + 2)(2x - 4) = 12x^2 + (-20x) + (-8)$

4. **C.** Looking at the diagram, you can see that the angle is acute, so any answers over 90° are out. This eliminates answer D. Angles *a* and *d* are supplementary, which means that the total of their degrees is 180. To solve, subtract 102 from 180, and you'll see that the value of angle *d* is 78.

5. **A.** Solve this inequality like an equation. Start by moving $3x$ to the left of the $\geq$ symbol, and $-12$ to the right. Don't forget to change them to the opposite sign, so $3x$ becomes $-3x$ and $-12$ becomes 12.

   $7x - 3x \geq 8 + 12$

   Combine like terms:

   $4x \geq 20$

   Now divide both sides by 4: $\dfrac{4x}{4} \geq \dfrac{20}{4}$.

   Because we did not multiply or divide the inequality by a negative number, the symbol stays the same. The final answer is $x \geq 5$.

6. **C.** To calculate the area of a rhombus, we multiply the base times the height. Here it's $24 \times 6$, which equals 144.

7. **A.** Because point B is equidistant from the two endpoints, it marks the midpoint.

8. **C.** The two sides on the bottom are 60°, which means the other angle has to be 60° as well. This makes the triangle equilateral.

9. **A.** This is a quadratic expression. You can either FOIL the answer choices or factor the expression: $y^2 - 13y + 30$.

   $(y\ )(y\ )$

   List factors of 30:

   $1 \times 30$

   $2 \times 15$

   $3 \times 10$

   If you add $-3$ and $-10$, you get $-13$, which is the middle term. Multiply them to get the positive 30 term. The final answer is $(y - 3)$ $(y - 10)$.

10. **D.** Calculate the area of the room. Since we know it's a rectangle, multiply the length times the width to get 360 ft². Then divide by half to find the missing amount: 180 ft².

11. **A.** Use the Pythagorean Theorem here to solve for the missing value: $a^2 + b^2 = c^2$.

    $(5 \times 5) + (7 \times 7) = c^2$

    $25 + 49 = c^2$

    $74 = c^2$

    $\sqrt{74} = c$

    $8.6 = c$

12. **C.** Another way of writing 22% is .22.

13. **D.** A constant is a number that stands by itself in an expression or equation.

14. **B.** Remember, when you divide fractions, you're really multiplying them. The first fraction stays the same, but you flip the numbers of the second fraction (which is called a reciprocal), multiply across, and reduce:

    $\dfrac{9}{11} \div \dfrac{3}{7} = \dfrac{9}{11} \times \dfrac{7}{3} = \dfrac{63}{33} = 1\dfrac{10}{11}$

15. **A.** With scientific notation, you move the decimal point to the right of the leftmost digit. With 6538900000, you'd move the decimal 9 places to the left to get 6.538900000. Now drop all the 0s after the 9 to get 6.5389. Finally, multiply this number by 10 to the ninth power (the number of decimal spaces you moved): you then get $6.5389 \times 10^9$.

16. **B.** Using a fraction bar to separate terms means division.

17. **C.** This is less complicated than it looks. You are choosing 1 spot out of 20, which makes your chances of winning $\dfrac{1}{20}$. Whoever else has chosen does not make a difference in your calculations.

18. **B.** Multiply the two terms without regard to the decimal points:

$$
\begin{array}{r}
642 \\
\times 16 \\
\hline
3852 \\
+6420 \\
\hline
10272
\end{array}
$$

In the product, add the two decimal places back in to get 102.72.

19. **D.** Make the denominators the same by multiplying each fraction by its opposite denominator:

$$\frac{8}{9} \times \frac{7}{7} = \frac{56}{63}$$

$$\frac{4}{7} \times \frac{9}{9} = \frac{36}{63}$$

Now add the two new fractions and reduce:

$$\frac{56}{63} + \frac{36}{63} = \frac{92}{63} = 1\frac{29}{63}$$

20. **C.** Both terms here are perfect squares. Calculate the square roots of both terms and place in a set of binomial expressions: $\sqrt{y^2} = y$ ; $\sqrt{9} = 3$ :(y 3) (y 3). Since the sign in the original expression is negative, one sign in your binomials will be negative and the other positive: (y − 3) (y + 3).

21. **B.** An even number of negatives results in a positive answer: $\frac{-27}{-3} = 9$ (two negatives); (−4) (−6)(−8)(−10) = 1,920 (four negatives).

22. **A.** Perimeter is the distance around an object, no matter what type of object it is.

23. **D.** The definition of a proportion is a comparison of ratios.

24. **A.** Let's start with prime factorization of both 42 and 68:

$$
\begin{array}{ll}
2\underline{|42} & 2\underline{|68} \\
3\underline{|21} & 2\underline{|34} \\
7\underline{|7} & 17\underline{|17} \\
1 & 1
\end{array}
$$

Now multiply common factors:

42 = 2×3×7

68 = 2×2×17

The only shared factor here is 2, which makes it your highest common factor.

25. **C.** Plug in your value for p and solve using order of operations.

# Electronics Information

1. **B.** Choice A is wrong because power is represented by the letter *P*. Choice C is wrong because amperes are represented by the letter *A*. Choice D is wrong because resistance is measured by the Ohm symbol, Ω.

2. **C.** Electricity is comprised of electrons, all of which carry a negative charge. Choice A is wrong because protons have a positive charge. Choice B is wrong because neutrons do not carry any charge. Choice D is wrong because a diode is not a type of atom.

3. **A.** Because electricity always takes the least resistant path to the ground, people have to be very careful what they touch; a fallen tree on a power line could give someone a very serious shock.

4. **C.** None of the other choices offer truthful statements.

5. **C.** While voltage seldom varies, current frequently varies based on the needs of each object using it.

6. **D.** The other choices are incorrect.

7. **A.** Choices B, C, and D are all wrong because *series* and *parallel* refer to circuits, not the other terms listed.

8. **D.** Choice A is wrong because a resistor is used to provide resistance to the current flowing through a circuit. Choice B is wrong because a transformer is used to transfer electricity from one source to another. Choice C is wrong because a switch is used to open or close a circuit.

9. **C.** Choice A is wrong because it represents a capacitor. Choice B is wrong because it represents a wire. Choice D is wrong because it represents a switch. Choice C represents a diode, which allows current to flow in only one direction.

10. **B.** None of the other terms apply to this diagram.

11. **B.** Choice A is wrong because it describes voltage. Choice C is wrong because it describes amperes. Choice D is wrong because it touches on principles of magnetism, polarity, and so forth.

12. **C.** None of the other choices correctly describe the acronym.

13. **A.** Choice B is wrong because copper is used in conductors. Choice C is wrong because rubber is used for insulators. Choice D is wrong because it is not a material commonly used for diodes.

14. **A.** Choices B, C, and D are wrong because they represent lamps, aerials, and fuses, respectively.

15. **C.** Choice A is wrong because electrons create electricity when they are grouped together and traveling in the same direction. Choice B is wrong because copper is an example of a conductor. Choice D is wrong because current is the flow of electricity.

16. **A.** The other choices are incorrect.

17. **B.** Choice A is wrong because current is *inversely* proportional to resistance. Choice C is wrong because ampere is current. Choice D is wrong because watts measure power.

18. **D.** All other choices reflect factors pertaining to resistance in a wire.

19. **B.** To calculate this question, use the following formula and plug in the numbers you have: $amps = \dfrac{volts}{resistance}$.

20. **D.** To calculate this question, use the following formula and plug in the numbers you have: volts = amps × ohms.

# Automotive and Shop Information

1. **B.** Choice A is wrong because the exhaust system converts excess gases from the engine and releases them to the air. Choice C is wrong because the fuel system stores and supplies fuel to the combustion chamber of the engine, where it combines with air, vaporizes, and burns to give the engine energy. Choice D is wrong because the suspension system deals with the movement of the wheels and the manner in which the car reacts to terrain.

2. **D.** Choice B is wrong because the electrical system makes the lights and power systems work. See additional explanations in the previous answer.

3. **A.** Choice B is wrong because, during the compression stroke, the piston is moving upward, compressing the fuel–air mixture. Choice C is wrong because the combustion stroke occurs when the spark plug emits a spark to ignite the gasoline mixture. Choice D is wrong because the exhaust stroke causes the exhaust valve to open, and exhaust exits via the tailpipe.

4. **B.** Brake pistons move under hydraulic pressure, also known as fluid pressure.

5. **C.** Choice A is wrong because the control arm manages the motion of the wheels. Choice B is wrong because the frame supports the car's engine and body. Choice D is wrong because the steering linkage allows the wheels to turn as a result of the motion of the steering wheel.

6. **A.** See explanations in the previous answer for additional guidance.

7. **D.** See explanations in the previous answer for additional guidance.

8. **C.** It takes more than 4,000 explosions per minute inside for the car we described to travel down the road.

9. **A.** Each coil has a spark plug wire coming out either side of the coil; as a result, each side of the coil can serve one spark plug.

10. **C.** Each of the other choices contain false statements and parts that have nothing to do with battery recharge.

11. **C.** A car battery has six cells that are stacked with positive and negative lead plates, which store energy.

12. **A.** Fuse panels, or fuse boxes, help control the function of many things, such as the headlights, dashboard lights, radios, and clocks.

13. **D.** Diesel burns more efficiently than gasoline.

14. **C.** In older cars, fuel pumps either didn't exist or were mounted outside the fuel tank.

15. **D.** Absorbing road bumps is a function of the suspension system.

16. **C.** Choice A is wrong because a cold chisel is used when cutting cold metals to remove waste metal. Choices B and D are wrong because files and rasps are used to smooth rough edges.

17. **B.** Choice A is wrong because a hack saw does not have alternating cutting edges. Choice C is wrong because a miter saw cuts using both sides of the blade. Choice D is wrong because a circular saw can cut with *or* against the grain, not necessarily just one way.

18. **B.** Choices A, C, and D are all wrong because they all have steel heads.

19. **A.** Choices B and C both list other hand drill parts, although they are not supposed to be prefaced with the word *cranking*. In addition, their job is not to turn the main shaft of the drill. Choice D is not a component of a hand drill.

20. **C.** A countersink is used to create a hole in which the top part of the hole is enlarged. That way, the screw head will go all the way down into the wood so that the surface of the wood is smooth.

21. **C.** A pipe wrench is a more specific version of an adjustable-end wrench. The adjustable clamps on one end are designed especially to grip a variety of objects used by mechanics, plumbers, and handymen.

22. **B.** None of the other choices offer the right answer.

23. **D.** Socket wrenches are frequently used for automotive repairs and other household projects. They come equipped with removable and varying-sized sockets.

24. **B.** A pipe clamp is used to hold a pipe in place so that it can be cut, threaded, lifted, or suspended. It is designed as described in the question.

25. **B.** Choice A is wrong because a drill press is usually bolted to the floor or to a workbench; as a result, it cannot possibly perform the kind of demolition work that a jackhammer does. Choices C and D are the names of a hammer and a saw, respectively.

# Mechanical Comprehension

1. **D.** When you stretch a rubber band, it has potential energy—the possibility of doing work. When you release it, it has kinetic energy—motion energy. The fact that the rubber band can be stretched and retain its original shape suggests that it has elastic energy.

2. **D.** The formula for gravitational potential energy is $PE = mgh$, or mass × gravity × height above Earth:

    $PE = 2 \times 9.8 \times 20$

    $PE = 392$ joules

3. **D.** Choice A is the definition of kinetic energy. Choice B is the definition of speed. Choice C is the definition of velocity.

4. **B.** Use the same formula from question 2 and solve for the missing value.

5. **D.** Gear ratio can be calculated by counting the number of rotations each gear makes. The other option is to count the teeth on each gear. Divide the number of teeth on the larger gear by the number of teeth on the smaller gear.

6. **A.** Newton's third law is known as the law of reciprocal action, which states that, for every action, there is an equal and opposite reaction.

7. **C.** Work is directly proportionate to distance traveled.

8. **B.** Work is directly proportionate to force.

9. **A.** See the explanations for the previous two answers.

10. **C.** Newton's third law of reciprocal action states that, for every action, there is an equal and opposite reaction.

11. **D.** Choices A, B, and C all describe types of pulleys instead of gears.

12. **D.** None of the other choices offer accurate statements.

13. **A.** A two-wheeled pulley system offers mechanical advantage that causes an object to feel half as heavy.

14. **D.** In a four-wheeled pulley system, the object gains enough mechanical advantage to make it feel four times easier to lift. However, it also forces you to pull the rope four times farther to raise the object to the intended height.

15. **C.** None of the other choices offer factual statements.

16. **A.** Choice B is wrong because bevel gears are often used in car differentials, not transmissions. Choice C is wrong because worm gears are also sometimes found in certain high-performance car differentials. Choice D is wrong because it is not a type of gear, but rather a combination of gears.

17. **B.** Choices A, C, and D are not the correct terms for the description that was given.

18. **A.** None of the other choices offer factual statements.

19. **B.** Acceleration is calculated using the following formula: (Final rate of velocity – initial rate of velocity) ÷ Time. In this case, you would subtract 0 from 40 and divide by 10. This gives you 4 km per second$^2$.

20. **C.** Speed is calculated by dividing distance by time.

21. **A.** Force = Mass × acceleration.

22. **B.** Choice A is wrong because it defines weight. Choices C and D don't describe mass or weight.

23. **D.** Any kind of movement is considered motion.

24. **C.** Choices A and B both convert to kinetic energy. Choice C, however, is not a form of energy.

25. **A.** Choice B is wrong because objects have potential energy before they ever get kinetic energy. Choice C is wrong because it describes elastic energy. Choice D is wrong because not every object has potential energy (although, most do).

# Assembling Objects

1. **C.** The N in answer A is mirrored. The connection points are in the wrong place on both shapes in answer B. Answer D replaces the X shape with a hexagon.

2. **B.** The center shape in answer A is different from the sample. Answer C is mirrored. The shapes in answer D are different from the sample and an extra shape has been added.

3. **C.** The connection points in answers A and D are in the wrong places. Answer B replaces the Y shape with a V shape.

4. **C.** Answers A and D have different shapes than those in the sample. The triangle in answer B is not the same as the one in the sample.

5. **B.** The triangle in answer A is not the same as in the sample. The circle in answer C replaces the trapezoid shape from the sample. The connection points in answer D are in the wrong places.

6. **C.** The rounded shape from the sample has been turned into a complete circle in answer A, and the quadrilateral from the sample is a triangle in answer B. One of the curved shapes from the sample is a quadrilateral in answer D.

7. **C.** One of the shapes in answers B and D have been changed. The connection point on the T is in the wrong place.

8. **B.** The circle from the sample is replaced with an oval in answer A. Two of the triangles from the sample have been replaced with one quadrilateral in answer C, and now there are three pieces to this puzzle instead of four. The third triangle from the sample has been replaced by a rectangle in answer D.

9. **A.** The flower in answer B is shaped differently than the one in the sample. The B in answer C is mirrored and the one in answer D has been replaced by an e.

10. **A.** There are two triangles instead of one in answer B. The quadrilateral in answer C is smaller than the one in the sample. The pentagon is missing in answer D.

11. **D.** The star in answer A has nine points, not seven, as in the sample. The connection point on the W in answer B and on the star in answer C is in the wrong place.

12. **C.** In answer A, the circle is now an oval. The small triangle in answer B has been replaced with a large, curvy one. In answer D, there are five shapes instead of the four shown in the sample.

13. **B.** The angled shape in answer A has been mirrored. The ampersand in answer C has been replaced with a dollar sign. In answer D, the connection on the angled shape is in the wrong place.

14. **A.** The triangle in answer B doesn't match the one from the sample. There is an extra rectangle in answer C and no triangle. The large jagged piece is missing in answer D.

15. **A.** The connection point on the question mark in answer A is in the wrong place. The connection point on the starlike shape in answer C is in the wrong place. The question mark in answer D is mirrored.

16. **A.** In answers B and D, one of the four-sided shapes now has three sides. Answer C has five pieces instead of the four shown in the sample.

17. **D.** The star shape in answer A is not the same as in the sample. In answer B, both connection points are off. In answer C, the five-sided shape now has seven sides.

18. **C.** The star in answer A is different from the one in the sample. Answer B has two ovals instead of an oval and a circle. The shape with the flat bottom and curved top has been replaced with a rectangle in answer D.

19. **D.** The connection to the angled shape in answer A comes in at the wrong angle. Both connection points in answer B are in the wrong places. The *b* in answer C has been mirrored.

20. **A.** Three of the shapes in answer B don't match the sample. The rectangle in answer C is now a square. In answer D, the shapes have changed and there are now only three instead of four.

21. **D.** The connection point to the *H* shape in answer A is wrong. The *H* shape in answer B has been mirrored. The *X*-like shape in answer C has been rounded out.

22. **D.** The shape of the arrow is changed in answer A. There is no large rectangle in answer B. Two shapes in answer C are mirrored.

23. **B.** Both connection points in answer A are in the wrong places. The *f* in answer C has been changed into a *g*. The flower shape in answer D has been replaced with a hexagram.

24. **B.** The shape of the triangle is changed in answer A. Only two of the shapes in answer C match the sample. The largest shape from the sample is missing from answer D.

25. **A.** The connection point to the *T* shape in answer B is wrong. Both shapes in answer C are different from those in the sample, while only one is different in answer D.

# General Science

**Time:** 11 Minutes

**Questions:** 25

**Directions:** This section tests your general knowledge in the area of science. Carefully read each question and choose the answer choice that best answers the question.

1. When force is applied to an object and results in the movement of that object to a higher energy state, this is called:

   (A) friction.
   (B) momentum.
   (C) force.
   (D) work.

2. Mass multiplied by velocity is the formula for

   (A) gravity.
   (B) momentum.
   (C) work.
   (D) speed.

3. The ratio of distance traveled in a given time period to the time it took is

   (A) velocity.
   (B) speed.
   (C) acceleration.
   (D) force.

4. The rate of change of velocity of an object is

   (A) speed.
   (B) physics.
   (C) acceleration.
   (D) friction.

5. If a car increases its speed by 10 miles per hour every second, this is known as

   (A) constant acceleration.
   (B) constant velocity.
   (C) negative velocity.
   (D) nonconstant acceleration.

6. In which state of matter are atoms extremely cold and unexcited?

   (A) solid
   (B) liquid
   (C) plasma
   (D) Bose–Einstein Condensate

7. Hard, closely packed molecules that can hold their own shape fall under which state of matter?

   (A) liquid

   (B) plasma

   (C) solid

   (D) gas

8. When you combine 1 atom of carbon with 2 atoms of oxygen, what type of chemical structure do you have?

   (A) compound

   (B) electron

   (C) atom

   (D) element

9. The subscript number of a compound symbol represents the number of

   (A) chemical bonds.

   (B) atoms.

   (C) neutrons and electrons.

   (D) negative elements.

10. Neutrons affect the _____ and _____ of an atom.

    (A) mass, charge

    (B) charge, magnetism

    (C) bond strength, density

    (D) mass, radioactivity

11. Which type of eclipse is dangerous to look at?

    (A) lunar

    (B) planetary

    (C) solar

    (D) binary

12. Which of the following is NOT one of Kepler's laws of planetary motion?

    (A) The planets move in elliptical orbits.

    (B) An imaginary line joins the center of a planet to the center of the sun and sweeps the same amount of space all the time.

    (C) The time it takes a planet to orbit the sun is based on how far away from the sun it is.

    (D) The distance from Earth to the sun is measured in astronomical units.

13. Twice a year, day and night are the same length all over the world. This is known as what?

    (A) Lunar New Year

    (B) solstice

    (C) equinox

    (D) astronomical equivalency

14. A celestial body larger than an asteroid that moves around and receives light from a star is known as a(n)

    (A) galaxy.

    (B) asteroid.

    (C) meteorite.

    (D) planet.

15. The prefix *cirro* describes clouds that are

    (A) high in the sky.

    (B) midlevel in the sky.

    (C) low in the sky.

    (D) transparent.

16. When two different types of air masses meet, this is known as what?

    (A) clouds
    (B) barometric pressure
    (C) front
    (D) tornado

17. Clouds form in the

    (A) troposphere.
    (B) stratosphere.
    (C) mesosphere.
    (D) thermosphere.

18. Because the atomic molecules are so spread out in the thermosphere, this causes it to be very

    (A) hot.
    (B) cold.
    (C) wet.
    (D) thick.

19. Which gas is NOT commonly found in the atmosphere?

    (A) oxygen
    (B) argon
    (C) nitrogen
    (D) hydrogen

20. Which of the following is the scale used to determine rock hardness?

    (A) Ohm's
    (B) Kepler's
    (C) Hertz's
    (D) Mohs

21. Skeletons of living organisms found in rock are called

    (A) shale.
    (B) fossils.
    (C) graphite.
    (D) archeology.

22. Igneous rock that was formed and remains underground is known as

    (A) lava.
    (B) intrusive rock.
    (C) extrusive rock.
    (D) sediment.

23. Another word for *polypeptide* is

    (A) amino acid.
    (B) nucleotide.
    (C) riboflavin.
    (D) protein.

24. Which of the following is an example of tissue?

    (A) circulatory system
    (B) femur
    (C) muscle
    (D) cell

25. Which of the following habitats are formed by movements in Earth's crust?

    (A) deserts
    (B) grasslands
    (C) mountains
    (D) tropical forests

# Arithmetic Reasoning

**Time:** 36 Minutes

**Questions:** 30

**Directions:** This section tests your ability to reason through mathematical problems using basic arithmetic. Carefully read each question and choose the answer choice that best answers the question.

1. Amy bought three pairs of shoes at $17.95, $22.95, and $26.95 each. She added a pair of socks for $5.65 and a necklace for $18.50 to her purchase. Assuming there is no sales tax, what was her total at the register?

   (A) $68
   (B) $75
   (C) $92
   (D) $560

2. If you have three quarters, two pennies, six dimes, and a nickel in your pocket, what's the probability you'll pull out a penny the next time you pick out a coin?

   (A) $\frac{1}{4}$

   (B) $\frac{1}{6}$

   (C) $\frac{1}{2}$

   (D) $\frac{1}{12}$

3. Miriam is three times as old as Kenny. If Kenny is half of Adriana's age, and she is 42, how old is Miriam?

   (A) 18
   (B) 21
   (C) 45
   (D) 63

4. Barry needs to make 15% more money this year than his annual salary pays. Instead of getting a raise, Barry is offered extra hours at work at a rate of $11.50 per hour. If his annual salary is $32,425, about how many extra hours would he have to work to make the money that he needs?

   (A) 423
   (B) 444
   (C) 482
   (D) 499

5. You read six books in a month. At this rate, how many do you read in a week?

   (A) 1.5
   (B) 2.2
   (C) 2.8
   (D) 2.9

6. Your college tuition is $326 per credit. An increase of 7% is announced for the following semester. What will the new cost of tuition per three-credit class be?

   (A) $22.82
   (B) $348.82
   (C) $1,046.46
   (D) $3,046.46

7. In a group discussion, $\frac{3}{5}$ of the participants favor the proposed change to the rules. If there are 30 people in the group, how many will likely vote to approve the measure?

    (A) 6
    (B) 18
    (C) 29
    (D) 30

8. A sandbox is 3 feet wide, 3 feet long, and 3 feet tall. How much sand can it hold?

    (A) 9 ft$^2$
    (B) 9 ft$^3$
    (C) 27 ft$^2$
    (D) 27 ft$^3$

9. A man visits his wife's grave six times per year since her passing. If he has been there 27 times, how long has it been since he lost his wife?

    (A) 4.5 years
    (B) 5 years
    (C) 5.5 years
    (D) 6 years

10. Recording studio time costs $235 per hour. If it takes four sessions of eight hours at a time to record a whole CD, how much would it cost to record CDs for five new artists?

    (A) $1,175
    (B) $37,600
    (C) $67,300
    (D) $73,600

11. A salesperson makes a 16% commission on everything she sells. If she sold $6,283 worth of merchandise this month and put 12% of her earnings into a savings account, how much did she add to the account this month?

    (A) $10.28
    (B) $95.65
    (C) $120.63
    (D) $1,005.28

12. Which of the following numbers is not an integer:

    (A) 1
    (B) –1
    (C) 2
    (D) 2.3

13. A dance club starts letting people in at 10:00 P.M. In the first hour, 10 men and 15 women are admitted, and none leave. In the second hour, 25 men and 20 women are admitted. Again, none leave. In the third hour, 11 women and 7 men leave and no more people are admitted into the club. What is the ratio of men to women in the club by 1 A.M.?

    (A) 7:6
    (B) 5:8
    (C) 8:3
    (D) 11:1

14. Your lunches at the local diner this week cost you $4.65, $5.32, and $7.27. Assuming you left a 15% tip for each meal, what's the average amount of money you spent on lunch?

    (A) $2.58
    (B) $6.61
    (C) $9.35
    (D) $17.24

15. If you can type 36 words per minute, about how long would it take you to type a 453-word essay?

    (A) 4

    (B) 6

    (C) 13

    (D) 25

16. Which of the following is a prime number?

    (A) 1

    (B) 4

    (C) 9

    (D) 11

17. Marc bought three times as many carrots as Dave. Dave bought half as many as Jen. If Jen bought 10 carrots, how many did Marc buy?

    (A) 10

    (B) 15

    (C) 25

    (D) 40

18. Using order of operations, which term would you address first in the following expression? $-6 + -3 - 4^3 + 6$

    (A) $-6 + -3$

    (B) $(-3) - 4^3$

    (C) $4^3 + 6$

    (D) $4^3$

19. In a gymnastics competition, Mary received a 5.4, 3.9, 4.8, 4.9, and 5.1 for her floor routine. What is her average score?

    (A) 4.28

    (B) 4.82

    (C) 15.7

    (D) 24.5

20. Negative six minus negative six equals:

    (A) 0

    (B) 6

    (C) –12

    (D) 18

21. A room measures 16.2 feet long by 8.5 feet wide. What is its area?

    (A) 24.7 ft²

    (B) 137.7 ft²

    (C) 321.84 ft²

    (D) 898.23 ft²

22. Erin needs to buy six apples to make her famous pie. She needs three golden delicious, one granny smith, and one red delicious. At the store, she finds golden delicious apples marked down 10% from their usual price of 89¢ apiece. The granny smith and red delicious apples are marked at 75¢ and 65¢ apiece, respectively. If she doesn't have to pay tax on her purchase, how much money will she need to buy all the apples she needs?

    (A) 80¢

    (B) $1.80

    (C) $2.80

    (D) $3.80

23. The answer to an addition problem is a

    (A) product.

    (B) quotient.

    (C) sum.

    (D) difference.

24. When the numerator is less than the denominator, you have a(n)

    (A) proper fraction.

    (B) improper fraction.

    (C) mixed number.

    (D) simplified fraction.

25. In three years, Jed will be four times as old as Terry. If Terry will be 12 next year, how old is Jed now?

    (A) 14
    (B) 23
    (C) 53
    (D) 85

26. A MEPS site has 68 potential recruits come in on Saturday to take the ASVAB. Of those who come in, 72% will pass the AFQT. About how many recruits will have to retake the ASVAB to get into the military?

    (A) 10
    (B) 19
    (C) 49
    (D) 80

27. On opening day at the amusement park, there were 26 ice cream vendors and 42 hot dog vendors providing food for the park's patrons. What's the ratio of ice cream vendors to hot dog vendors?

    (A) 6:7
    (B) 13:21
    (C) 14:23
    (D) 9:26

28. What is 345.876 divided by 23.1?

    (A) 8.64
    (B) 11.78
    (C) 12.85
    (D) 14.97

29. A CD collection has 25 titles. Of these, 10 are classic rock, 3 are hard rock, and the rest are adult contemporary. What is the probability that you could choose a classic rock CD the first time you reached for a random title and a hard rock CD the second time (assuming you kept the first CD with you and did not return it to the collection)?

    (A) $\dfrac{1}{20}$

    (B) $\dfrac{3}{40}$

    (C) $\dfrac{5}{20}$

    (D) $\dfrac{5}{40}$

30. How many minutes are in a day?

    (A) 60
    (B) 240
    (C) 1,440
    (D) 86,400

# Word Knowledge

**Time:** 11 Minutes

**Questions:** 35

**Directions:** This section tests your knowledge of and ability to use vocabulary. Read each question and choose the answer choice that most nearly means the same as the underlined word.

1. Nuisance most nearly means

    (A) annoyance.
    (B) forbearance.
    (C) clarity.
    (D) argument.

2. Authoritative most nearly means

    (A) loud.
    (B) irritating.
    (C) commanding.
    (D) conceited.

3. <u>Perverse</u> most nearly means

(A) able.

(B) wicked.

(C) appreciative.

(D) wired.

4. <u>Sonorous</u> most nearly means

(A) religious.

(B) grave.

(C) jubilant.

(D) echoing.

5. I went back to the classroom so I could <u>retrieve</u> the pencil case I left in my desk.

(A) recover

(B) collect

(C) embrace

(D) forget

6. Believing everything everyone tells you is not an <u>astute</u> way to collect information.

(A) forgivable

(B) efficient

(C) discerning

(D) pardonable

7. <u>Efface</u> most nearly means

(A) implement.

(B) thicken.

(C) break.

(D) erode.

8. <u>Palatable</u> most nearly means

(A) edible.

(B) cross.

(C) insipid.

(D) brave.

9. When her money ran out for the third time that month, the girl <u>entreated</u> her parents to send some more for her basic expenses.

(A) annoyed

(B) begged

(C) smiled

(D) soothed

10. <u>Variance</u> most nearly means

(A) quickness.

(B) ability.

(C) likeability.

(D) difference.

11. Jade's friends loved how friendly and <u>gregarious</u> she got when they went out on Friday nights.

(A) reticent

(B) reserved

(C) sociable

(D) suspicious

12. The <u>spare</u> room had only a cot and a pillow in it.

(A) small

(B) unadorned

(C) ornate

(D) spacious

13. <u>Superfluous</u> most nearly means

(A) unnecessary.

(B) essential.

(C) immortal.

(D) gracious.

14. <u>Affix</u> most nearly means

(A) argue.

(B) berate.

(C) stick.

(D) savor.

15. <u>Hasten</u> most nearly means

    (A) accelerate.

    (B) pause.

    (C) cry.

    (D) drop.

16. Seattle's <u>temperate</u> climate makes it ideal for those who are not overly fond of extreme cold or hot weather.

    (A) lacking

    (B) excessive

    (C) seasonal

    (D) moderate

17. <u>Viral</u> most nearly means

    (A) spreadable.

    (B) secret.

    (C) submissive.

    (D) surreptitious.

18. The heartfelt tribute video <u>evoked</u> tears from the late musician's most devoted fans.

    (A) extinguished

    (B) stirred

    (C) belied

    (D) criticized

19. <u>Increment</u> most nearly means

    (A) blaze.

    (B) gel.

    (C) increase.

    (D) concern.

20. <u>Raze</u> most nearly means

    (A) demolish.

    (B) uplift.

    (C) create.

    (D) fasten.

21. <u>Vituperative</u> most nearly means

    (A) creative.

    (B) impassioned.

    (C) blasé.

    (D) offensive.

22. With the help of the increased winds and dry weather, the smoking leaves where the cigarette had been dropped had quickly turned into a <u>conflagration</u> that endangered whole neighborhoods.

    (A) inference

    (B) blaze

    (C) creation

    (D) beast

23. <u>Auspicious</u> most nearly means

    (A) egotistic.

    (B) unfortunate.

    (C) favorable.

    (D) interrogative.

24. <u>Baleful</u> most nearly means

    (A) sinister.

    (B) loose.

    (C) flammable.

    (D) sticky.

25. Blake did not want to serve on a jury, so he did not register to vote in hopes that he could <u>circumvent</u> being added to the list of county residents that makes up the jury pool.

    (A) volunteer

    (B) facilitate

    (C) celebrate

    (D) avoid

26. <u>Lather</u> most nearly means

   (A) censure.
   (B) foam.
   (C) rubber.
   (D) hide.

27. <u>Vapid</u> most nearly means

   (A) clever.
   (B) uninspiring.
   (C) mean-spirited.
   (D) energizing.

28. <u>Clarity</u> most nearly means

   (A) transparency.
   (B) reason.
   (C) tranquility.
   (D) abrasiveness.

29. <u>Invigorate</u> most nearly means

   (A) appreciate.
   (B) value.
   (C) refresh.
   (D) concentrate.

30. Though she smiled when she said she was delighted to be part of the committee, her resentful tone proved her words to be <u>spurious.</u>

   (A) serious
   (B) believable
   (C) angry
   (D) disingenuous

31. <u>Blockade</u> most nearly means

   (A) brink.
   (B) passage.
   (C) cordon.
   (D) crater.

32. <u>Vocation</u> most nearly means

   (A) occupation.
   (B) interest.
   (C) belief.
   (D) relief.

33. <u>Grill</u> most nearly means

   (A) undermine.
   (B) interrogate.
   (C) appreciate.
   (D) blast.

34. <u>Malady</u> most nearly means

   (A) prize.
   (B) windfall.
   (C) function.
   (D) woe.

35. <u>Emblazon</u> most nearly means

   (A) display.
   (B) forget.
   (C) explode.
   (D) speak.

# Paragraph Comprehension

**Time:** 13 Minutes

**Questions:** 15

**Directions:** This section tests your ability to read and understand written information, as well as come to logical conclusions based on a text. Read each passage and answer the questions that follow. Choose the answer choice that best answers the question.

*Use the following passage to answer questions 1–3:*

> Vinegar is an extremely <u>versatile</u> substance that can be used all around the house. First, its highly acidic properties make it an excellent natural food preservative. Mixing vinegar with garlic, dill, and other spices produces a brine that can be used to pickle vegetables or marinate meats.
>
> Vinegar is also an effective nonchemical cleaner that can be used on all sorts of surfaces, including metal, wood, glass, fabrics, and linoleum. Though its odor is very pungent and distinct in itself, vinegar solutions can be used to clean and deodorize coffeemakers, microwaves, sinks, and bathrooms. It can also be used to treat areas of the house that have been soiled by pets. It even works as a natural way to prevent infestations of fleas and ticks on animals.

1. In the passage, the word <u>versatile</u> most nearly means

    (A) having many uses.
    (B) malodorous.
    (C) gentle.
    (D) pleasing.

2. Vinegar might be a good substance to help treat a(n)

    (A) fever.
    (B) coffee stain on the rug.
    (C) heartburn.
    (D) abrasion.

3. One reason you might choose to bathe your pet in a vinegar solution is that

    (A) you want to make their coat shine.
    (B) you want them to stop wetting the rug.
    (C) you want to clean paint off of their fur.
    (D) you want to get rid of fleas.

*Use the following passage to answer questions 4–5:*

Most people think of communication in terms of a one-way process where a sender encodes a message that is transmitted to a receiver. However, advancing research in communication studies indicates that most communication is systemic, meaning that conception and transmission of a message is only one part of the equation. Listener-centric models of communication are taking center stage today. These assert that communication takes place simultaneously through verbal and nonverbal signals from sender to receiver and back. Furthermore, internal communication, such as thoughts and perception of external stimuli, are also taking place and influencing how both the sender and receiver interpret messages and form their responses.

4. A good title for this passage might be:

    (A) Listen Up: Things Are Not What They Seem

    (B) Sender-Focused Communication Is the Future

    (C) Communication as an Interactive Process

    (D) Listener-Centric Communication Models Gain Acceptance

5. According to the passage, thoughts and evaluating perceptions are forms of

    (A) external communication.

    (B) internal communication.

    (C) external stimuli.

    (D) external foci.

*Use the following passage to answer questions 6–7:*

Pablo Neruda was a Chilean poet best known for his contributions to the surrealist movement in the 1970s. He was born Neftalí Ricardo Reyes Basoalto, but he wrote under the pseudonym Pablo Neruda as a teenager because his father did not approve of his taking an interest in writing. Neruda's work features a variety of voices that swing from highly romantic and excited to deeply troubled and depressed. This is of little surprise, since surrealism is characterized by building dreamlike situations through which the unreal becomes real and is examined through artistic interpretation. The spectrum of emotions and thoughts brought to life through surrealistic writing and art stands out among other styles and genres for its tendency to flaunt unreality while exploring very real ideas.

6. Surrealism is

    (A) a type of poem.

    (B) no longer seen in the artistic community.

    (C) a genre of artistic expression.

    (D) grounded in reality.

7. In the passage, the word pseudonym most nearly means

    (A) false name.

    (B) deception.

    (C) recitation.

    (D) belief.

*Use the following passage to answer questions 8–10:*

(1) Competition for consumer attention has gotten drastically out of hand over the past few decades. (2) When media first started to become an established part of our lives, we were restricted to advertisements that could be printed in magazines or newspapers, or broadcast on television or the radio. (3) With the increasing pervasiveness of the Internet; the advent of cell phones and video messaging; and the appearance of programmed media in venues like hotel lobbies, elevators, and even bathrooms and the DMV, consumers are inundated with communication of all sorts.

(4) It's getting to the point where you can't go anywhere without being constantly pressed for your attention to some product, service, or other item essential to your existence. (5) Is there nothing we can do to lessen the amount of communicational baggage we are forced to carry around with us all the time?

8. The speaker comes across as

    (A) calm.

    (B) understanding.

    (C) complacent.

    (D) frustrated.

9. The speaker would most likely NOT support

    (A) the removal of news tickers from the bottoms of television screens.

    (B) digital billboards attached to sides of buses.

    (C) reduced dependence on cell phones.

    (D) more time playing board games with her family.

10. Which sentence best expresses the main idea of the passage?

    (A) 1

    (B) 2

    (C) 4

    (D) 5

*Use the following passage to answer questions 11–13:*

Is capital punishment a just punishment for murder? This is one of the most debated topics in American society, and exemplifies the type of argument that asks one of the essential questions of our existence: what is justice? Because laws are created by people, one could say that justice is what is deemed to be moral and right by the majority of people. But what of those who do not agree with these ideas? Are their impressions of justice any more or less valid within the scope of the universe?

Is there any such thing as a universal right or wrong? Certainly, most cultures find killing to be wrong, yet every culture kills, whether it is deemed to be right or wrong. Does this mean that killing is a universal right, even though large numbers of people believe it to be wrong? Questions such as these will likely never be answered, because for every definitive opinion given, there will also be a counter-opinion that is just as persuasive. Therefore, arguing for or against capital punishment is a futile task.

11. The speaker in this passage is

   (A) addressing a text.
   (B) arguing with someone else.
   (C) debating with himself.
   (D) responding to a comment.

12. This passage consists of

   (A) a series of questions, answers, and speculation.
   (B) incontrovertible facts.
   (C) academic research.
   (D) biased opinion.

13. In the end, the speaker decides that

   (A) debating the topic is essential.
   (B) every academic should debate this topic.
   (C) there will be only one answer to this debate.
   (D) debating the topic is useless.

*Use the following passage to answer questions 14–15:*

Guido " Guy" Fawkes is remembered as a key player in the failed attempt to assassinate England's King James I in 1605. As a member of a secret group of dissenters who wanted to overthrow the Protestant government that persecuted Puritans and Catholics, Fawkes was charged with making sure the Gunpowder Plot of 1605 went off without a hitch.

The plan was to ignite a cache of explosives underneath Parliament while King James and most of the aristocracy were present. One of the members of Fawkes's group, however, betrayed the plan to a member of Parliament. Authorities were sent to intercept Fawkes as he was about to light the explosives, and instead of dying in the fire as he intended to, Fawkes was arrested for treason.

Though the plot did not come to fruition, Fawkes is remembered throughout Great Britain today through an annual Bonfire Night commemorating the event that was supposed to take place, as well as references in literature, movies, television, and more.

14.  It can be inferred that Guy Fawkes was

    (A) politically disinterested.

    (B) a revolutionary.

    (C) loyal to King James I.

    (D) looking forward to traveling to Spain.

15.  In the passage, the phrase <u>come to fruition</u> most nearly means

    (A) have much impact.

    (B) last very long.

    (C) come to happen.

    (D) mean anything in the scope of history.

# Mathematics Knowledge

**Time:** 24 Minutes

**Questions:** 25

**Directions:** This section tests your knowledge of basic mathematics, algebra, and geometry. Carefully read each question and choose the answer choice that reflects the best answer.

1.  If $b = 6$, $b + 12 - 3b \times 2b =$

    (A) 12

    (B) –12

    (C) 198

    (D) –198

2.  $\dfrac{5}{9} \div \dfrac{3}{9} =$

    (A) $\dfrac{5}{27}$

    (B) $1\dfrac{2}{3}$

    (C) $\dfrac{3}{5}$

    (D) $2\dfrac{3}{5}$

3. $3^{-4} =$

    (A) $\dfrac{12}{1}$

    (B) $\dfrac{1}{12}$

    (C) $\dfrac{1}{81}$

    (D) $\dfrac{81}{1}$

4. You have a cylindrical barrel that is 5 feet tall and 6 feet wide. What is its volume?

    (A) 30 ft³

    (B) 47.1 ft³

    (C) 52.3 ft³

    (D) 141.3 ft³

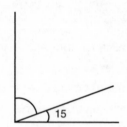

5. If the previous angles are complementary, the value of the missing angle is:

    (A) 75

    (B) 90

    (C) 130

    (D) 180

6. In $c^2 + 3x + 12$, $c^2$ is a

    (A) coefficient.

    (B) constant.

    (C) equation.

    (D) term.

7. Factor $a^2 - 13a + 22$

    (A) $(a - 12)(a - 1)$

    (B) $(a - 2)(a - 11)$

    (C) $(a + 2)(a - 11)$

    (D) $(a + 1)(a - 12)$

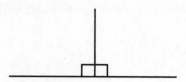

8. These angles are

    (A) supplementary.

    (B) complementary.

    (C) adjacent.

    (D) parallel.

9. If $12x + 6 > 6x - 4$, then $x >$

    (A) −2

    (B) 2

    (C) −5

    (D) 5

10. $b^5 \div b^4 =$

    (A) $b^{-1}$

    (B) $b$

    (C) $b^2$

    (D) $b^3$

11. All four sides are congruent and angles are right angles in a

    (A) pentagon.

    (B) hexagon.

    (C) triangle.

    (D) square.

12. When you know the value of any two sides of a right triangle, you use _____ to calculate the other side.

    (A) $A = \dfrac{1}{2}bh$

    (B) the Pythagorean Theorem

    (C) $A = \dfrac{1}{2} \times h\left(b_1 + b_2\right)$

    (D) $A = \pi r^2$

13. If in a right triangle $a = 6$ and $b = 9$, $c =$

    (A) 10.816

    (B) 11.618

    (C) 12.562

    (D) 17.853

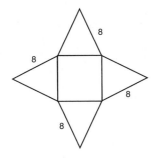

14. If the triangles in the figure are equilateral, the area of the square is:

    (A) 10

    (B) 16

    (C) 24

    (D) 64

15. The greatest common factor of 24 and 36 is:

    (A) 8

    (B) 9

    (C) 12

    (D) 16

16. The area of a circle with a diameter of 11 inches is:

    (A) 52.425 in²

    (B) 94.985 in²

    (C) 268.598 in²

    (D) 379.94 in²

17. What action breaks down a number into the product of its prime factors?

    (A) simplification

    (B) factorial

    (C) scientific notation

    (D) prime factorization

18. Solve for $a$: $\dfrac{9}{13.5} = \dfrac{a}{6}$

    (A) 4

    (B) 8

    (C) 12

    (D) 16

19. The total surface area of a cylindrical solid that has a radius of 5 feet and a height of 12 feet is:

    (A) 60 ft²

    (B) 112 ft²

    (C) 533.8 ft²

    (D) 635.6 ft²

20. The least common multiple of 12 and 8 is:

    (A) 16

    (B) 24

    (C) 32

    (D) 36

21. The value of the external angle is:

    (A) 38°

    (B) 46°

    (C) 86°

    (D) 125°

22. The area of a trapezoid with a height of 9, a top base value of 6, and a bottom base value of 14 is:

    (A) 20

    (B) 50

    (C) 80

    (D) 10

23. All of the following are tests to determine whether two triangles are congruent EXCEPT:

    (A) Are all three corresponding side values equal?

    (B) Are two corresponding angles and the side they share equal?

    (C) Are two sides perpendicular?

    (D) Are two corresponding angles and a side they don't share equal?

24. Factor: $42x^2 + 28x$.

    (A) $2x(21x + 14)$

    (B) $14x(3x + 2)$

    (C) $14x(3x - 2)$

    (D) $21x(2x + 7)$

25. Simplify $\dfrac{18y + 27}{9}$.

    (A) $\dfrac{9}{18y + 27}$

    (B) $\dfrac{6y + 9}{3}$

    (C) $2y - 3$

    (D) $2y + 3$

# Electronics Information

**Time:** 9 Minutes

**Questions:** 20

**Directions:** This section tests your knowledge of basic electronics principles and applications. Carefully read each question and choose the answer choice that reflects the best answer.

1. The previous symbol represents

    (A) fuse.

    (B) capacitor.

    (C) diode.

    (D) DC voltage capacitor.

2. As you drive down the road unbuckled, your car gives you a gentle reminder in the form of a bell sound. The sound occurs every three seconds. You choose to ignore it for five minutes. What is the frequency of the seatbelt alarm?

    (A) 20 times per minute

    (B) 60 times per minute

    (C) 3 times per minute

    (D) 5 times per minute

3. What is the formula to calculate resistance?

    (A) Ohms = Amps × watts

    (B) Ohms = Watts ÷ amps

    (C) Ohms = Volts × amps

    (D) Ohms = Volts ÷ amps

4. The previous symbol represents

(A) fuse.

(B) motor.

(C) voltmeter.

(D) amplifier.

5. If you have 10 amps and 100 watts, how many volts do you have?

(A) 10

(B) 1,000

(C) 90

(D) 100

6. The formula for amperes is:

(A) Amps = Volts ÷ resistance

(B) Amps = Volts ÷ watts

(C) Amps = Volts × resistance

(D) Amps = Volts × watts

7. The idea that waves generally move in a straight line is called what?

(A) interference

(B) refraction

(C) rectilinear propagation

(D) longitudinal

8. The previous symbol represents

(A) aerial.

(B) resistor.

(C) transformer.

(D) lamp.

9. What do electrons flow through?

(A) insulators

(B) conductors

(C) loads

(D) ammeters

10. How much electrical force is required for most household appliances?

(A) 100 watts

(B) 100 volts

(C) 120 watts

(D) 120 volts

11. The previous symbol represents

(A) AC voltage capacitor.

(B) wire.

(C) battery.

(D) switch.

12. What does a basic circuit start with?

(A) resistor

(B) load

(C) power source

(D) diode

13. What is the formula for voltage?

(A) Volts = Amps × watts

(B) Volts = Watts ÷ amps

(C) Volts = Ohms × amps

(D) Volts = Amps ÷ ohms

14. Which type of current is commonly used by the power company for industrial and residential customers alike?

(A) alternating

(B) direct

(C) amplified

(D) frequency modulated

15. Computer clock speed is measured using which type of unit?

   (A) Newton
   (B) Hertz
   (C) joule
   (D) kilogram

16. If you have a wave that measures 6 meters between peaks, an amplitude of 8 meters, and a frequency of 24 Hertz, what is the wave speed?

   (A) 48
   (B) 4
   (C) 3
   (D) 144

17. Which of the following is true of high frequencies?

   (A) They have low pitches and long wavelengths.
   (B) They have low pitches and short wavelengths.
   (C) They have high pitches and short wavelengths.
   (D) They have high pitches and long wavelengths.

18. The previous symbol represents

   (A) battery.
   (B) capacitor.
   (C) diode.
   (D) DC voltage capacitor.

19. When sound waves bend around an object, this is known as what?

   (A) dispersion
   (B) diffraction
   (C) deflection
   (D) distancing

20. What is the formula for wattage?

   (A) Watts = Amps × ohms
   (B) Watts = Volts ÷ amps
   (C) Watts = Volts × amps
   (D) Watts = Volts ÷ ohms

# Automotive and Shop Information

**Time:** 11 Minutes

**Questions:** 25

**Directions:** This section tests your knowledge of automotive components and principles, as well as general shop tools and applications. Carefully read each question and choose the answer choice that reflects the best answer.

1.  What drives the piston downward into the exhaust stroke of the Otto Cycle?

    (A) ignition of gasoline
    (B) hydraulics
    (C) compression
    (D) the weight of the cylinder

2.  About how many times per minute (on average) do the spark plugs have to ignite the fuel–air mixture for a car engine to run properly?

    (A) dozens
    (B) hundreds
    (C) thousands
    (D) millions

3.  When you turn the key to start the car, what device are you engaging?

    (A) alternator
    (B) spark plug
    (C) distributor cap
    (D) solenoid

4.  Which of the following is NOT a type of ignition system in use by cars today:

    (A) mechanical ignition
    (B) hydraulic ignition
    (C) electronic ignition
    (D) distributorless ignition

5.  Of the systems listed in question 4, which one is the most modern?

    (A) mechanical ignition
    (B) hydraulic ignition
    (C) electronic ignition
    (D) distributorless ignition

6.  When battery power is converted to ignite the fuel–air mixture, how many volts (on average) do the spark plugs receive in newer cars?

    (A) more than 50
    (B) more than 500
    (C) more than 50,000
    (D) more than 100,000

7.  Why is it better to get as many volts as possible from the battery to the spark plugs?

    (A) More volts create cooler sparks.
    (B) More volts create hotter sparks.
    (C) More volts spark faster.
    (D) More volts spark slower.

8.  The ignition switch holds battery power back until what?

    (A) the spark plugs ignite
    (B) you activate the ignition with your key
    (C) the solenoid relays the current
    (D) the alternator stops working

9.  Everything in your car that uses electricity is connected to what?

    (A) brake lines
    (B) coil pack
    (C) voltage regulator
    (D) ignition switch

10. What can happen to a parking brake that goes unused for lengthy periods of time?

    (A) It can get corroded.
    (B) The brake cable can snap.
    (C) The brake cable can become loose.
    (D) The hydraulics stop functioning.

11. What device is used to alert drivers that brake pads are worn and should be replaced?

    (A) small metal clip
    (B) slide pin
    (C) ceramic blocks
    (D) steel drums

12. Another term for *backing plate* is:

    (A) wheel
    (B) hub plate
    (C) mounting plate
    (D) wheel well

13. What causes brake pads to press against the rotors?

    (A) calipers
    (B) hydraulic pressure
    (C) friction
    (D) brake shoes

14. On which system do emergency brakes operate?

    (A) electronic system
    (B) mechanical system
    (C) hydraulic system
    (D) none of the above

15. Which element of the suspension system helps prevent the car from rolling during a sharp turn?

    (A) steering linkage
    (B) stabilizer bars
    (C) control arm
    (D) damper

16. During which phase of a woodworking project should a rasp be used?

    (A) before sawing
    (B) after sanding
    (C) after sawing, before sanding
    (D) before and after sawing

17. Which type of saw should you use to cut the corners of a picture frame?

    (A) hack
    (B) jigsaw
    (C) miter
    (D) table

18. How much does an engineer hammer typically weigh?

    (A) between 1 and 5 pounds
    (B) between 5 and 10 pounds
    (C) between 10 and 15 ounces
    (D) between 50 and 20 ounces

19. Which hammer features a flat, octagonal-shaped head with a sharp, beveled pein?

    (A) curved claw
    (B) ball pein
    (C) tinner's
    (D) engineer

20. Which type of screwdriver provides more stability for the connection of the screw and screwdriver?

    (A) flathead
    (B) cabinet
    (C) torx
    (D) Phillips

21. What is the purpose of an auger drill bit?

    (A) to bore a larger hole than a twist bit will allow
    (B) to drill into tile
    (C) to create a hole in which the top of the hole is enlarged
    (D) to drill deep, large holes in wood

22. Twist bits are most commonly made of

   (A) high-speed steel or carbon steel.
   (B) nickel.
   (C) titanium.
   (D) machined steel or metal.

23. The combination-end wrench has an open end at one end and a _____ design at the other end.

   (A) clamp
   (B) socket
   (C) box
   (D) screw

24. Which tool is often used when assembling ready-to-finish furniture?

   (A) Allen wrench
   (B) hand screw
   (C) bar clamp
   (D) socket wrench

25. A jigsaw has what type of blade?

   (A) circular, jagged
   (B) narrow, reciprocating
   (C) wide, reciprocating
   (D) circular, short teeth

# Mechanical Comprehension

**Time:** 19 Minutes

**Questions:** 25

**Directions:** This section tests your knowledge and application of basic mechanical principles. Carefully read each question and choose the answer choice that reflects the best answer.

1. Suppose you have an object whose mass is 50 kilograms, and it is located 4 meters above Earth. What is the object's gravitational potential energy?

   (A) 200 joules
   (B) 490 joules
   (C) 540 joules
   (D) 1,960 joules

2. What is the definition of negative acceleration?

   (A) slowing down
   (B) Acceleration – $x$
   (C) Acceleration ÷ Speed
   (D) 0 – Acceleration

3. Work is

   (A) something that changes an object at rest into an object in motion.
   (B) transferring energy through force over a distance.
   (C) any object that changes distance over a period of time.
   (D) energy of motion.

4. When potential energy is released, it is converted to what type of energy?

   (A) work
   (B) chemical
   (C) motion
   (D) gravitational

5. A spring has three main types of energy. What are they?

    (A) potential, light, and sound

    (B) kinetic, potential, and thermal

    (C) elastic, kinetic, and potential

    (D) electromagnetic, potential, and elastic

6. 9.8 m/sec/sec is the calculation for

    (A) energy.

    (B) force.

    (C) gravity.

    (D) velocity.

7. What is the kinetic energy of a tricycle moving at 2 kilometers per hour if it weighs 10 kilograms?

    (A) 20 joules

    (B) 10 joules

    (C) 40 joules

    (D) 12 joules

8. Which of the following objects has greater kinetic energy? Object 1 is a paper airplane with a mass of 2 kilograms and a velocity of 15 kilometers per hour; object 2 is a rolling ball with a mass of 4 kilograms and a velocity of 10 kilometers per hour.

    (A) Object 1 has greater kinetic energy.

    (B) Object 2 has greater kinetic energy.

    (C) Object 1 has the same kinetic energy as object 2.

    (D) Not enough information.

9. If you have two variables, force times distance, what are you trying to calculate?

    (A) mass

    (B) matter

    (C) work

    (D) motion

10. According to Newton's first law, an object tends to resist changes in motion unless

    (A) it undergoes negative acceleration.

    (B) it has an equal and opposite reaction to the motion.

    (C) a force is exerted upon it.

    (D) gravitational pull forces the change.

11. This is an example of a

    (A) 1st-class pulley.

    (B) fixed pulley.

    (C) moveable pulley.

    (D) compound pulley.

12. Velocity is a measure of both the _____ and _____ in which an object moves.

    (A) speed, acceleration

    (B) speed, distance

    (C) speed, direction

    (D) speed, force

13. During freefall, how quickly do objects accelerate downward?

    (A) $9.8 \text{ m/s}^2$

    (B) $8.9 \text{ m/s}^2$

    (C) $3.14 \text{ m/s}^2$

    (D) $6.2 \text{ m/s}^2$

14. What is an inward force that causes an object to turn?

    (A) gravitational pull
    (B) centrifugal force
    (C) centripetal force
    (D) metric force

15. When a gear causes a motor or mechanism to slow down, what is the result?

    (A) increased speed
    (B) increased motion
    (C) more forceful output
    (D) more forceful input

16. This type of gear is designed such that the teeth are angled inward. The result is that contact spreads slowly across each tooth. What type of gear is this?

    (A) helical
    (B) spur
    (C) bevel
    (D) worm

17. Suppose you have a bicycle wheel that turns one time for every six full pedal rotations. What is the gear ratio?

    (A) 1:6
    (B) 6:1
    (C) 2:1
    (D) 1:2

18. If you are a cyclist going uphill, which gear ratio would offer easier pedaling for you?

    (A) 1:4
    (B) 2:1
    (C) 9:3
    (D) 4:1

19. When an axel is connected to a stationary object, such as a hook or a wall, this is known as what type of pulley?

    (A) fixed
    (B) stationary
    (C) immobile
    (D) compound

20. The definition of *fulcrum* is

    (A) the weight of a lever.
    (B) the load that is placed on either side of a lever.
    (C) the mechanical advantage associated with a lever.
    (D) the object on which a lever pivots.

21. Which of the following is NOT an example of a 2nd-class lever?

    (A) wheelbarrow
    (B) nutcracker
    (C) scissors
    (D) wrench

22. If you place two weights on a 1st-class lever and one weight is heavier than the other, which one should sit closer to the fulcrum for the lever to balance?

    (A) the lighter weight
    (B) the heavier weight
    (C) neither; they should sit equidistant
    (D) not enough information to tell

23. When weight and distance are balanced on either side of the fulcrum, a lever is considered

    (A) complete.
    (B) 1st class.
    (C) balanced.
    (D) 2nd class.

24. Suppose you have a 20-kilogram weight on one side of a 1st-class lever, and it is placed 6 meters from the fulcrum. Suppose you have another 12-kilogram weight to place on the other side. How far apart should the objects be from one another to achieve balance?

    (A) 16 meters

    (B) 6 meters

    (C) 12 meters

    (D) 20 meters

25. Which type of lever is pictured?

    (A) 1st class

    (B) 2nd class

    (C) 3rd class

    (D) 4th class

# Assembling Objects

**Time:** 15 Minutes

**Questions:** 25

**Directions:** This section tests your ability to visualize how objects fit together. Carefully read each question and choose the answer choice that reflects the best answer.

1. In the following diagram, which figure best shows how the objects in the first box would touch if points A and B were connected?

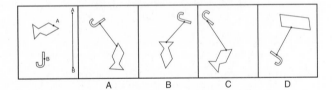

2. Which answer choice best shows how the objects in the first box would appear if they were fitted together?

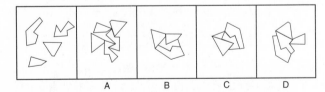

3. In the following diagram, which figure best shows how the objects in the first box would touch if points A and B were connected?

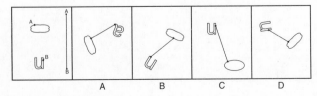

4. Which answer choice best shows how the objects in the first box would appear if they were fitted together?

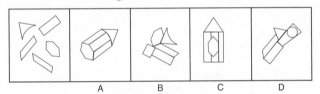

5. In the following diagram, which figure best shows how the objects in the first box would touch if points A and B were connected?

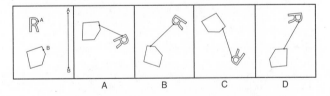

6. Which answer choice best shows how the objects in the first box would appear if they were fitted together?

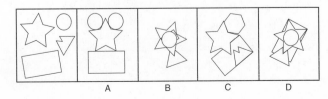

7. In the following diagram, which figure best shows how the objects in the first box would touch if points A and B were connected?

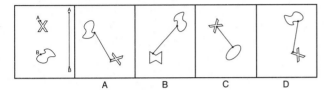

8. Which answer choice best shows how the objects in the first box would appear if they were fitted together?

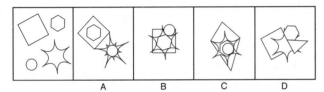

9. Which answer choice best shows how the objects in the first box would appear if they were fitted together?

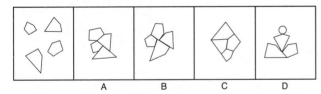

10. In the following diagram, which figure best shows how the objects in the first box would touch if points A and B were connected?

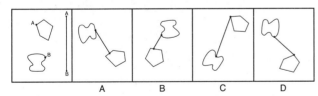

11. In the following diagram, which figure best shows how the objects in the first box would touch if points A and B were connected?

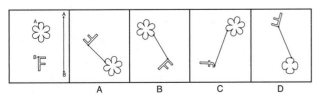

12. Which answer choice best shows how the objects in the first box would appear if they were fitted together?

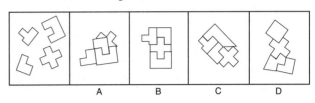

13. In the following diagram, which figure best shows how the objects in the first box would touch if points A and B were connected?

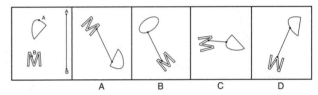

14. Which answer choice best shows how the objects in the first box would appear if they were fitted together?

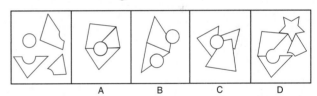

15. In the following diagram, which figure best shows how the objects in the first box would touch if points A and B were connected?

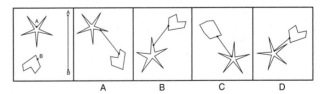

16. Which answer choice best shows how the objects in the first box would appear if they were fitted together?

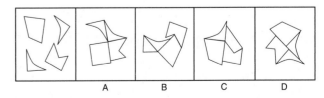

17. In the following diagram, which figure best shows how the objects in the first box would touch if points A and B were connected?

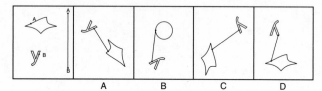

18. Which answer choice best shows how the objects in the first box would appear if they were fitted together?

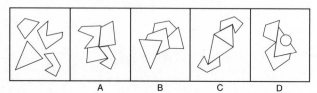

19. In the following diagram, which figure best shows how the objects in the first box would touch if points A and B were connected?

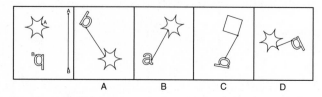

20. Which answer choice best shows how the objects in the first box would appear if they were fitted together?

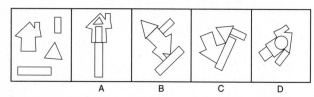

21. In the following diagram, which figure best shows how the objects in the first box would touch if points A and B were connected?

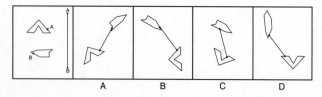

22. Which answer choice best shows how the objects in the first box would appear if they were fitted together?

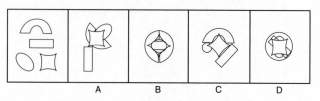

23. In the following diagram, which figure best shows how the objects in the first box would touch if points A and B were connected?

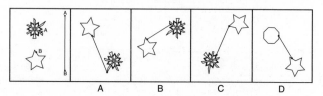

24. Which answer choice best shows how the objects in the first box would appear if they were fitted together?

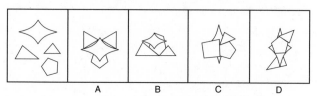

25. In the following diagram, which figure best shows how the objects in the first box would touch if points A and B were connected?

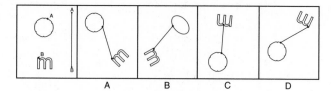

# Answers and Explanations

## General Science

1. **D.** Choice A is wrong because friction is defined as two objects rubbing against one another. Choice B is wrong because momentum is defined as an impelling force or strength. Choice C is wrong because force is defined as any influence that can cause a change in the velocity of an object.

2. **B.** Choice A is wrong because gravity is a force of attraction between mass and Earth. Choice C is wrong because the definition of work is a force that is applied to one object and results in the movement of that object. Choice D is wrong because speed is defined as distance traveled in a given time period.

3. **B.** Choice A is wrong because velocity is defined as the rate of motion in a specific direction. Choice C is wrong because acceleration is defined as the rate of change of velocity of an object. Choice D is wrong because force is defined as any influence that can cause a change in the velocity of an object.

4. **C.** See previous explanations for the definitions of choices A, B, and D.

5. **A.** Constant acceleration means an object increases speed by the same amount every second.

6. **D.** Bose–Einstein Condensates are so cold that all molecular activity comes to a halt.

7. **C.** Choice A is wrong because liquids cannot hold their own shape. Choices B and D are wrong because plasmas and gases have atoms that are quite spread out.

8. **A.** A compound is created when two or more elements are combined or bonded.

9. **B.** Choices A, C, and D are false statements.

10. **D.** Although neutrons have no charge, they are still a very important part of an atom.

11. **C.** Choice A is wrong because, in a lunar eclipse, the moon passes behind Earth, blocking sunlight from the moon. Since the moon doesn't create its own light, it is safe to view. Choices B and D are not types of eclipses.

12. **D.** All the other choices are Kepler's laws; choice D is a true statement but is not one of Kepler's laws.

13. **C.** Choice A is wrong because Lunar New Year is a holiday that occurs in January every year and is celebrated in Asian countries; it is also called Chinese New Year. Choice B is wrong because solstice occurs twice each year when the days begin getting either longer or shorter, depending on whether it is summer or winter solstice. Choice D has nothing to do with the length of days and nights.

14. **D.** Choice A is wrong because a galaxy is a group of stars, gas, and dust held together by gravity. Choice B is wrong because an asteroid is a rock or minor planet orbiting the sun. Choice C is wrong because a meteorite is an object from outer space, such as a rock that falls into Earth.

15. **A.** Choice B is wrong because midlevel clouds are identified with the prefix *alto*. Choice C is wrong because low-level clouds do not have a prefix. Choice D is wrong because it has nothing to do with cloud prefix identification.

16. **C.** Choice A is wrong because clouds are formations of gaseous water. Choice B is wrong because barometric pressure is the weight of air as it pushes down on a portion of Earth. Choice D is wrong because a tornado results from barometric pressure that has plummeted.

17. **A.** Choice B is wrong because this is where the ozone exists. Choice C is wrong because the mesosphere is the coldest region in the atmosphere. Choice D is wrong because this is the atmospheric layer closest to space.

18. **B.** Even though the atoms in the thermosphere have very high energy, there is very little heat. Heat is felt when energy is transferred from one atom to another. When atoms are very spread out, they cannot easily transfer energy.

19. **D.** The atmosphere generally has the other gases listed in choices A, B, and C. In addition, you may find ozone and carbon dioxide in the atmosphere.

20. **D.** Choice A is wrong because ohms are used to measure resistance in electric circuits. Choice B is wrong because Kepler is famous for his planetary laws. Choice C is wrong because Hertz is the name of the scientist who first proved the existence of electromagnetic waves.

21. **B.** Choice A is wrong because shale is a soft, sedimentary rock that often houses fossils. Choice C is wrong because graphite is a type of rock. Choice D is wrong because archaeology is the study of past human life.

22. **B.** Choice A is wrong because lava is liquid molten rock that flows above Earth's surface. Choice C is wrong because extrusive rock is igneous rock that has cooled on the surface of Earth. Choice D is wrong because sediment is worn-down particles of igneous rock that settles in the beds of lakes, streams, and oceans.

23. **D.** Choice A is wrong because amino acids form chains of polypeptides, or proteins. Choice B is wrong because nucleotides are joined molecules that comprise the structural units of DNA and RNA. Choice C is wrong because riboflavin is a vitamin.

24. **C.** Choice A is wrong because it describes a system. Choice B is wrong because it describes a bone. Choice D is wrong because a bunch of cells together comprise tissue, but a single cell does not.

25. **C.** Mountains cover 20 percent of Earth's surface and can be found on every continent. They are most frequently formed by the collision of tectonic plates.

# Arithmetic Reasoning

1. **C.** Use simple addition.

2. **B.** This is a probability question, so start by counting the total number of coins in your pocket: 3 + 2 + 6 + 1 = 12. Since the question asks about the chances you'll pull out a penny, use this value as the top number of your fraction to figure out the probability. The total number of coins will be the bottom number. Finally, reduce: $\frac{2}{12} = \frac{1}{6}$.

3. **D.** Start by calculating Kenny's age: .5 × 42 = 21. Now multiply that value by 3 to get Miriam's age, which is 63.

4. **A.** Calculate 15% of 32,425: 32,425 × .15 = 4,863.75. Now divide this amount by 11.50 to get 422.934. Round this up and you'll have 423 as your answer.

5. **A.** Divide 6 by 4 (number of weeks in a month) to get the answer: 1.5.

6. **C.** First calculate how much a 7% increase in your per-credit tuition will be: .07 × $326 = $22.82. Now add this amount to the current per-credit price: $326 + $22.82 = $348.82. Finally, multiply this total by 3: $348.82 × 3 = $1,046.46.

7. **B.** Calculate $\frac{3}{5} \times \frac{30}{1} = \frac{90}{5} = 18$.

8. **D.** This is a volume question. Since we're dealing with a rectangular solid, plug in the numbers from the question into the following formula:

   $V = l \times w \times h$

9. **A.** Divide 27 by 6 to get 4.5.

10. **B.** Start by multiplying the number of hours by sessions for one CD: 4 × 8 = 32. Now multiply this number by the number of artists to see how many total hours will be needed to record all the music: 32 × 5 = 160. Finally, multiply this amount by $235 to get the total cost: 160 × $235 = $37,600.

11. **C.** First figure out how much the salesperson made by multiplying .16 × $6,283 = $1,005.28. Now figure out how much she puts in her savings account: .12 × $1,005.28 = $120.63.

12. **D.** An integer is any whole number and its opposite. Answer D is a decimal, not a whole number.

13. **A.** Start by figuring out how many men and women come and go by 1 A.M.:

    Men: 10 + 25 + (–7) = 28

    Women: 15 + 20 (–11) = 24

    Now set up your ratio like it's said in the question (men to women) and reduce: 28:24 = 7:6.

14. **B.** Add the cost of all your lunches, and then multiply that sum by .15 to calculate that you've paid $2.586 in tips. Now add $17.24 + $2.586 = $19.826 to get the total amount spent throughout the month. Finally, divide this total by 3 to get an average of $6.6086, which rounds up to $6.61.

15. **C.** Divide 453 by 36 to find it would take 12.58 minutes to type the essay. Round this up to 13 to get your answer.

16. **D.** A prime number is an integer that can be divided only by 1 and itself. One is not a prime number because 1 is its only factor.

17. **B.** Jen buys 10 carrots. This means Dave bought 5 carrots. Since Marc bought three times the number of carrots as Dave, he bought 15 carrots.

18. **D.** Since there are no parentheses, you address the exponent first, which is answer D.

19. **B.** This is a simple average question. Add up all of the scores and divide by 5: 5.4 + 3.9 + 4.8 + 4.9 + 5.1 = 24.1 ÷ 5 = 4.82.

20. **A.** This translates to –6 – –6. The two negative signs cancel each other out and make a positive. Therefore, you are really dealing with –6 + 6, which equals 0.

21. **B.** Multiply length times width to get the area of a rectangle: 16.2 × 8.5 = 137.7 ft².

22. **D.** Calculate the cost of each apple:

Golden delicious: $.89 – (.89 × .10) = .89 – .089 = $.80

Granny smith: $.75

Red delicious: $.65

Now multiply by the number you need of each and add the products:

Golden delicious: $.80 × 3 = $2.40

Granny smith: $.75 × 1 = $.75

Red delicious: $.65 × 1 = $.65

$2.40 + $.75 + $.65 = $3.80

23. **C.** A product is the answer to a multiplication problem. A quotient is the answer to a division problem. A difference is the answer to a subtraction problem.

24. **A.** When the numerator is either equal to or greater than the denominator, you have an improper fraction. When you simplify an improper fraction, you break it down into a mixed fraction (a whole number and a fraction together in one term). A simplified fraction is one that is in its smallest form.

25. **C.** According to the question, Terry is 11 right now. That means in 3 years, he'll be 14. In 3 years, Jed will be four times this number: 4 × 14 = 56. So today Jed is 53, since 56 – 3 = 53.

26. **B.** Since you have to retake the ASVAB if you don't pass it, you need to figure out how many recruits passed the test and subtract that from the total number who took the test:

Pass: .72 × 68 = 48.96 (round up to 49)

Fail: 68 – 49 = 19

27. **B.** Set up the ratio just like it's said in the question, and reduce: 26:42 = 13:21.

28. **D.** Move your decimal points and divide to get 14.97.

29. **A.** Find the probability of both of these events and then multiply to get your answer:

Classic rock: $\dfrac{10}{25}$

Hard rock: $\dfrac{3}{24}$

Notice that the denominator in the hard rock fraction is 24, not 25. This is because, according to the question, you did not return the classic rock CD, so you thus reduced the total number of CDs you could have chosen from.

Now multiply the fractions and reduce:

$\dfrac{10}{25} \times \dfrac{3}{24} = \dfrac{30}{600} = \dfrac{3}{60} = \dfrac{1}{20}$

30. **C.** There are 60 minutes in an hour and 24 hours in a day: 60 × 24 = 1,440.

# Word Knowledge

1. **A.** Something that is a *nuisance* is annoying. *Forbearance* means "calm" or "patience." *Clarity* means "clearness." *Argument* means "a position" or "a disagreement."

2. **C.** Though those who are authoritative may be loud, irritating, or conceited, what defines them is their power to command.

3. **B.** *Perverse* can mean "stubborn" or "wicked." None of the other answer choices make sense with this definition.

4. **D.** The root *son* means "sound," so your answer will have something to do with sound. That eliminates choices A and B. You may like option C as an answer, but you can be jubilant (excited, happy) without emitting sound. You cannot echo without sound, though.

5. **A.** The sentence tells us that the pencil case belongs to the speaker and implies that she was previously in the classroom. This means she needs to get it again. If she were to collect it, this would imply it's the first time she's getting the pencil case in her possession, which goes against the context clues in the sentence.

6. **C.** When you take all information to be fact, you're simply collecting it, not evaluating it at all. The context clues tell us that the underlined word is the opposite of what the sentence is talking about (see the *not* before *astute*). Therefore, *discerning* (evaluative) is the correct answer.

7. **D.** *Efface* means "to rub or wear away," so this answer makes the most sense.

8. **A.** Connect the base word in *palatable* to your mouth, and you'll get a good clue to the meaning of the word. Something that's palatable tastes good and can be eaten. *Cross* means "angry." *Insipid* means "uninteresting." *Brave* talks about nerve.

9. **B.** Swap out your answer choices here, and *begged* will be the only one that makes sense.

10. **D.** An association you can make here is in the base word, *vary*, which means "to change." *Variance*, therefore will have something to do with change. Answer D is the only choice that implies this.

11. **C.** Using the context clues, you can tell Jade is friendly and active with her friends. Answers A and B mean "quiet" and "keeping to oneself." Answer D means "doubtful." Answer C makes the most sense.

12. **B.** Don't be fooled here into thinking "spare room" means "extra room." If you look at the context clues in the sentence, you'll see that it's talking about how it's decorated. There is very little in the room and no indication of its size. Answer B is the best choice.

13. **A.** *Superfluous* means "extra," and answer A is the only one that makes sense with this definition.

14. **C.** *Affix* means "to fasten" something. A good mnemonic: "affix a sticker." *Berate* means "to scold." *Savor* means "to enjoy."

15. **A.** The base word here is *haste*, which means "speed" or "hurry." The correct answer will have to do with hurrying, which is what you do when you accelerate.

16. **D.** The context clues of "ideal for those who are not overly fond of extreme cold or hot weather" tell us that *temperate* relates to conditions somewhere in the middle.

17. **A.** Think about how viruses spread—really easily—and you'll be able to remember the definition of *viral*. *Submissive* means "passive." *Surreptitious* means "secretive."

18. **B.** *Evoke* means "to cause." You can infer from the sentence that the fans were emotionally moved by the tribute, which makes all the other answer choices not fit.

19. **C.** *Increment* is an increase in something. None of the other answer choices make sense.

20. **A.** A good connection to make is "raze one building to make room for another," as this is often the context in which you hear *raze* being used. However, it does not mean to build them; it means to destroy or demolish them.

21. **D.** *Vituperative* describes speech that intends to harm and offend. It may be impassioned or creative, but it is not defined by this. *Blasé* means uncaring, so that doesn't fit.

22. **B.** The sentence talks about a small flame that grows large. The only answer that makes sense is answer B.

23. **C.** *Auspicious* means "positive" or "lucky." To be *egotistic* is to be concerned with one-self. *Unfortunate* is the opposite of *auspicious*. *Interrogative* refers to questioning.

24. **A.** *Baleful* is a negative word that means "menacing" or "threatening." Answer A is the only one that makes sense.

25. **D.** It's obvious from the context of the sentence that Blake is trying to avoid jury duty.

26. **B.** Think of when you shampoo your hair. The foam that forms is called lather.

27. **B.** *Vapid* means "dull" or "uncreative." Answers A and D don't fit with this, nor does answer C.

28. **A.** We talked earlier about *clarity*, meaning "being clear" or "transparent." *Tranquility* refers to peace, and *abrasiveness* means "grainy."

29. **C.** *Invigorate* means "to add life to" or "to refresh." None of the other answer choices come anywhere close to this definition.

30. **D.** The sentence tells us that the woman is being false with her words. *Disingenuous* means "insincere."

31. **C.** Look to the base word here, which is *block*. A blockade prevents transportation. *Brink* means "edge." *Passage* is the opposite. A *crater* is a sunken hole. A *cordon* is a barrier.

32. **A.** *Vocation* is another word for a job.

33. **B.** *Grill* is being used as a verb here. When you grill someone, you question them thoroughly.

34. **D.** The prefix *mal* tells you the word is a neg-ative. Answers A through C are either positive or neutral.

35. **A.** To *emblazon* is to splash or make something very noticeable. Answer A makes the most sense.

# Paragraph Comprehension

1. **A.** In the sentence, *versatile* describes many uses.

2. **B.** The passage says vinegar is a good cleaner and deodorizer for coffee and fabric.

3. **D.** The passage states that a vinegar solution is good for treating a flea infestation. None of the other choices is supported.

4. **D.** This is the best choice because it talks about listener-centric communication and its increased recognition, which is the main idea of the passage.

5. **B.** The passage talks about thoughts and evalu-ating perceptions as internal communication.

6. **C.** The final sentence in the passage directly supports answer C.

7. **A.** The sentence this word is used in talks about how Neruda used a different name.

8. **D.** Throughout the passage, the speaker uses language that indicates she is upset with the situation, an emotion that runs counter to answers A through C.

9. **B.** All the other answer choices advocate activities that take you away from media interaction.

10. **A.** The passages focuses on the information presented in the first sentence: "Competition for consumer attention has become drastically out of hand over the past few decades."

11. **C.** Since no other source of information is being presented to us, it can be assumed that all the debate is coming from the speaker.

12. **A.** Answer B is too extreme and inaccurate. Answer C is unfounded by the information in the passage. There is no indication of bias one way or another in the speaker's words, which eliminates answer D.

13. **D.** The final sentence reads, "Therefore, arguing for or against capital punishment is a futile task."

14. **B.** The passage talks about Fawkes being part of a plan to overthrow the government, which defines being a revolutionary. This goes against answers A and C. Answer D has no relevance to the passage.

15. **C.** If you swap out the answer choices with the word in the passage, this answer makes the most sense.

# Mathematics Knowledge

1. **D.** Substitute 6 for $b$ and solve:

   $b + 12 - 3b \times 2b =$

   $6 + 12 - (3 \times 6) \times (2 \times 6)$

   $6 + 12 - 18 \times 12$

   $6 + 12 - 216$

   $18 - 216$

   $-198$

2. **B.** Since we're dividing fractions, flip the second fraction and multiply across to get your answer. Then reduce:

   $$\frac{5}{9} \div \frac{3}{9} = \frac{5}{9} \div \frac{9}{3} = \frac{45}{27} = 1\frac{18}{27} = 1\frac{2}{3}$$

3. **C.** A negative exponent, such as $3^{-4}$ doesn't tell you the number of times to multiply the base by itself. Instead it tells you how many times to divide the number itself from 1. Start by calculating the value of $3^4$: $3 \times 3 \times 3 \times 3 = 81$. Now write the answer as a fraction and flip it:

   $$\frac{81}{1} \rightarrow \frac{1}{81}.$$

4. **D.** Volume for a cylindrical solid uses the formula $V = \pi r^2 h$. If you plug in your values from the question, you get the following:

   $V = 3.14 \times 3^2 \times 5$

   $V = 3.14 \times 9 \times 5$

   $V = 141.3 \text{ ft}^3$

   Note that 3 stands in for the value of the radius. That's because this value is half the diameter, which is represented by the width value in the question.

5. **A.** Complimentary angles are two angles that share a common side and whose combined value equals 90°.

6. **D.** A term is a single number, variable, or combinations thereof. A coefficient is a number that multiplies a variable. A constant is a number that stands by itself in an expression or equation. An equation is a mathematical statement that shows two equal expressions.

7. **B.** This is a quadratic expression. You can either FOIL the answer choices or factor the expression: $a^2 + 13a - 22$.

$(a\ )(a\ )$

List factors of 22:

$1 \times 22$

$2 \times 11$

If you add 2 and 11, you get 13, which is the middle term. Since one of our original terms is negative, both signs in the final binomials will be negative. The final answer is $(a - 2)(a - 11)$.

8. **A.** Supplementary angles together make a straight line. The sum of the angles equals 180°.

9. **C.** Solve like any other equation, keeping track of the direction of the inequality.

$12x + 6 > 6x - 4$

$12x + 6 - 6 > 6x - 4 + (-6)$

$12x > 6x - 10$

$\dfrac{12x}{6x} > \dfrac{6x - 10}{6x}$

$2x > -10$

$x > \dfrac{-10}{2}$

$x > -5$

10. **B.** When you divide powers, treat it like a fraction and reduce. Write out the base the number of times indicated in the exponent and cancel out like terms:

$$b^5 \div b^4 = \dfrac{b^5}{b^4} = \dfrac{b \times b \times b \times b \times b}{b \times b \times b \times b} = \dfrac{\cancel{b} \times \cancel{b} \times \cancel{b} \times \cancel{b} \times b}{\cancel{b} \times \cancel{b} \times \cancel{b} \times \cancel{b}} = \dfrac{b}{1} = b$$

11. **D.** Pentagons have five sides. Hexagons have six sides. Triangles have three sides.

12. **B.** Answer A is the formula for finding the area of a triangle, not a right triangle. Answer C is used to find the area of a trapezoid. Answer D is used to find the area of a circle.

13. **A.** Use the Pythagorean Theorem here to solve for the missing value: $a^2 + b^2 = c^2$.

$(6 \times 6) + (9 \times 9) = c^2$

$36 + 81 = c^2$

$117 = c^2$

$\sqrt{117} = c$

$10.816 = c$

14. **D.** All sides of an equilateral triangle are equal. Therefore, each of the sides of the square equals 8. To calculate the area of a square, you multiply the value of 2 sides: $8 \times 8 = 64$.

15. **C.** Calculate prime factorization on both 24 and 36:

$2\underline{|24}\quad 2\underline{|36}$
$2\underline{|12}\quad 2\underline{|18}$
$2\underline{|6}\quad\ \ 3\underline{|9}$
$3\underline{|3}\quad\ \ 3\underline{|3}$
$1\qquad\ \ 1$

Now multiply common factors:

$24 = 2 \times [2 \times 2 \times 3]$

$36 = [2 \times 2 \times 3] \times 3$

The shared factors here are $2 \times 2 \times 3$, which, when multiplied, gives you a highest common factor of 12.

16. **B.** To calculate the area of a circle, use the following formula: $A = \pi r^2$. Since you know the diameter is 11, divide that by 2 and use that value for the radius. Your math should look like this:

A = 3.14 × 5.5 × 5.5

A = 94.985 in²

17. **D.** This is the definition of prime factorization.

18. **A.** To solve for the missing value, cross multiply and complete the equation:

$13.5a = 9 \times 6$

$13.5a = 54$

$a = \dfrac{54}{13.5}$

$a = 4$

19. **C.** To calculate total surface area, use the formula $TSA = 2\pi r(r + h)$. Plug in your values and solve.

20. **B.** To find the LCM of two numbers, calculate prime factorization on both 8 and 12:

    2|8    2|12
    2|4    2|6
    2|2    3|3
    1      1

    Our common factors are 2 and 3. Next, multiply each factor by the greatest number of times it appears in any one factorization. Since 2 appears three times and 3 appears once, your expression will be 2 × 2 × 2 × 3 = 24.

21. **A.** You can calculate the value of this external angle because you know the value of the adjacent internal angle and, together, the angles equal 180°. Subtract the value of the internal angle from 180 to get 38 as your answer.

22. **D.** Use the following formula to calculate the area of a trapezoid: $A = \dfrac{1}{2} \times h\left(b_1 + b_2\right)$.

$$A = \frac{1}{2} \times h\left(b_1 + b_2\right)$$

$$A = \frac{1}{2} \times 9\left(6 + 14\right)$$

$$A = \frac{1}{2} \times 20$$

$$A = 10$$

23. **C.** The four tests to determine if two triangles are congruent are:

    ♦ Are all three corresponding side values equal?

    ♦ Are two corresponding sides and the angle they make equal?

    ♦ Are two corresponding angles and the side they share equal?

    ♦ Are two corresponding angles and a side they don't share equal?

24. **B.** Start by breaking down each term into prime factors:

    $42x^2 = 2 \times 3 \times 7 \times x \times x$

    $28x = 2 \times 2 \times 7 \times x$

    What do both of these have in common? $2 \times 7 \times x$ (which equals $14x$). Next, simplify each of these by crossing out one 2, 7, and $x$ in each expression:

    $42x^2 = \cancel{2} \times 3 \times \cancel{7} \times x \times \cancel{x}$

    $28x = 2 \times \cancel{2} \times \cancel{7} \times \cancel{x}$

    Now combine like terms and place the new expression in parentheses with $14x$ outside: $42x^2 + 28x = 14x\,(3x + 2)$.

25. **D.** Simply divide the upper part of the fraction by 9 to get $2y + 3$.

# Electronics Information

1. **A.** See the symbol chart in Chapter 12, page 129, for additional guidance.

2. **A.** Over the course of 60 seconds, your seatbelt alarm will sound 20 times. You allow this to continue for 5 minutes, resulting in a total of 100 alarms. To calculate frequency, you divide the total number of times an event takes place by the total length of time that has elapsed. In this case, 100 ÷ 5 = 20.

3. **D.** None of the other choices offer the correct formula.

4. **D.** See the symbol chart in Chapter 12, page 129, for additional guidance.

5. **A.** To calculate volts, use the following formula: Watts = Volts × amps.

6. **A.** None of the other choices offer the correct formula.

7. **C.** Choice A is wrong because interference occurs when two waves come into contact with one another. Choice B is wrong because refraction occurs when a wave changes direction after striking a reflective surface. Choice D is wrong because longitudinal is a type of wave, not a principle of wave movement.

8. **C.** See the symbol chart in Chapter 12, page 129, for additional guidance.

9. **B.** Choice A is wrong because insulators surround the conductors through which electrons flow. Choice C is wrong because loads are circuit parts that convert one type of energy to another. Choice D is wrong because ammeters are used to measure current.

10. **D.** Electrical force refers to voltage, so choices A and C are wrong. Choice B is also wrong because most household appliances in the United States either run on 120 volts, or occasionally 240 volts. In other countries, most appliances run on 220 volts.

11. **B.** See the symbol chart in Chapter 12, page 129, for additional guidance.

12. **C.** A power source is required to get electrons moving along their path. This is why a hair dryer cord that isn't plugged in is basically useless.

13. **C.** None of the other choices offer the correct formula.

14. **A.** Choice B is wrong because it is commonly used by batteries. Choices C and D are wrong because they are actually radio waves.

15. **B.** CPU clock speed, AC power, and waves are all measured in Hertz (Hz).

16. **D.** Wave speed is calculated by multiplying wavelength and frequency.

17. **C.** Low frequencies have long wavelengths and low pitches, and B and D were simply incorrect statements.

18. **A.** See the symbol chart in Chapter 12, page 129, for additional guidance.

19. **B.** Choice A is wrong because dispersion occurs when a wave is split up by frequency. Choices C and D are wrong because they are not terms commonly associated with waves bending around obstacles.

20. **C.** None of the other choices offer the correct formula.

# Automotive and Shop Information

1. **A.** The Otto Cycle is a four-stroke process that ignites the engine as follows. The pistons start in the up position. When the intake valve opens, the crankshaft drives the pistons down to receive a full cylinder of fuel and air. This is known as the intake step. As the pistons slide back up, they compress the mixture, which is why the next step is called compression. When the pistons reach the top position once again, the spark plugs emit a spark to ignite the mixture. This is known as the combustion step.

The ignition of gasoline drives the pistons back down so that they can release exhaust gases through the exhaust system.

2. **C.** A smoothly running engine is like a finely tuned orchestra. Everything has to be timed just right, and the spark plugs have to work around the clock to get the job done for the engine. The number of times they have to fire varies with the number of rotations per minute the engine makes, but generally fire at least 1,000 times per minute.

3. **D.** The solenoid acts as a relay runner would in a race. When the solenoid receives battery power combined with electric current from the ignition switch, it becomes engaged. It passes the battery power on to the starter.

4. **B.** Although hydraulics are used in cars today, they are not considered a type of ignition system.

5. **D.** Ignition systems made prior to 1975 were called mechanical ignitions. During the 1970s and 1980s, the electronic ignition system became popular. In the mid-1980s, the distributorless system was invented, and it is still in use today.

6. **C.** In older cars, the batteries could convert to only about 20,000 volts; however, newer cars can get two and a half times that number.

7. **B.** When a car can transform a higher number of volts, a hotter spark results.

8. **B.** Choices A, C, and D are all fictitious statements.

9. **D.** The ignition switch acts as an intermediary between the battery and the rest of the car's electronic components.

10. **A.** When parking brakes go unused, they can become corroded and eventually inoperable.

11. **A.** As brake pads get worn, a small metal clip scrapes against the rotor. The sound of scraping metal alerts the driver that the pads need to be replaced.

12. **C.** The other terms are not interchangeable with *backing plate*.

13. **B.** Choice A is wrong because calipers are designed to house the brake pads. Choice C is wrong because friction is the result of the pads squeezing either side of a disc brake. Choice D is wrong because brake shoes are a component of drum brakes, whereas brake pads are part of the disc brake system.

14. **B.** Emergency brakes are considered secondary braking devices because they operate using a mechanical system. They are designed this way so that if the hydraulic system used by the primary disc or drum brakes fails, the emergency brake can still slow the car.

15. **B.** Choice A is wrong because the steering linkage is designed to allow cars to swivel and turn. Choice C is wrong because the control arm is designed to manage the motion of the wheels. Choice D is wrong because *damper* is another term for the shock absorber. The shock absorber is built to smooth the jolt of a bump in the road.

16. **C.** The sharp teeth of a rasp help smooth rough edges from a saw. However, the teeth are too rough to smooth the wood as well as sandpaper.

17. **C.** Miter saws come in both the hand tool and the powered tool variety. Either one is ideal for making picture frames because of the angle on which the saw cuts.

18. **A.** Another word for an engineer hammer is *baby sledge* because of the size, weight, and shape of an engineer hammer.

19. **C.** Choice A is wrong because a curved claw has a claw instead of a pein. Choice B is wrong because a ball pein has a ball-shaped pein instead of a sharp, beveled pein. Choice D is wrong because an engineer's hammer resembles a baby sledge.

20. **D.** Because of the *X* shape on the end of a Phillips head screwdriver and the matching shape on the screw, the tool fits snugly inside the head of the screw. This causes less slippage than a flathead.

21. **D.** Choice A is wrong because it describes a spade bit. Choice B is wrong because it describes a carbide-tipped masonry bit. Choice C is wrong because it describes a countersink.

22. **A.** Twist bits can also be found in titanium nitrade, but it is much less common to use this material.

23. **C.** Combination-end wrenches use a box design to slip vertically over fasteners, which means you can't accidentally use the wrong size; it just won't fit.

24. **A.** None of the other tools are commonly used on this type of project.

25. **B.** A jigsaw's blade is designed to allow it to make intricate cuts and curves in a variety of different directions.

# Mechanical Comprehension

1. **D.** The formula for gravitational potential energy is $PE = mgh$, or mass × gravity × height above Earth:

   $PE = 4 \times 9.8 \times 50$

   $PE = 1,960$ joules

2. **A.** None of the other answers represent negative acceleration.

3. **B.** Choice A is the definition of force. Choice C is the definition of motion. Choice D is the definition of kinetic energy.

4. **C.** Motion energy is another term for kinetic energy, which is what potential energy is converted to.

5. **C.** When a spring is tightly coiled, it has potential energy. When it is released, the ensuing movement demonstrates kinetic energy. The ability to restore its original structure demonstrates elastic energy.

6. **C.** On Earth, acceleration due to gravity is approximately 9.8 meters per second per second.

7. **A.** Kinetic energy is determined by taking half the value of (mass times velocity squared).

8. **A.** Object 1 has a kinetic energy of 225 joules. Object 2 has a kinetic energy of 200 joules. These calculations were computed using the formula for kinetic energy, which is described in the previous answer.

9. **C.** Work = Force × distance

10. **C.** Choices A and D are wrong because they are not involved with any of Newton's laws of motion. Choice B is wrong because it refers to Newton's third law.

11. **D.** This pulley system blends several fixed or movable pulleys to maximize mechanical advantage.

12. **C.** None of the other choices offer the combination of factors that defines velocity.

13. **A.** Objects that are free falling are under the influence of gravity only, which means that they accelerate at a rate of 9.8 m/s$^2$.

14. **C.** Choice A is wrong because gravitational pull is the force that causes an object to fall toward Earth. Choice B is wrong because centrifugal force is an outward force that causes an object to turn. Choice D is wrong because it is not specifically related to circular motion.

15. **C.** Gears offer the mechanical advantage of slowing the work process but increasing the force of output.

16. **A.** Choice B is wrong because a spur gear does not have teeth that are angled inward. Choice C is wrong because bevel gears are mounted on perpendicular shafts with a variety of teeth styles. Choice D is wrong because a worm gear has teeth that mesh with a partially threaded shaft instead of another gear.

17. **B.** Ratios are determined by counting the number of rotations for each gear and dividing the larger number by the smaller number.

18. **D.** With a 4:1 ratio, the force is easier, even if the process takes longer. This is called gear reduction.

19. **A.** A fixed pulley is mounted to a stationary object. Although there is only a mechanical advantage of 1 with this type of pulley, it still has the advantage of making the work *seem* easier.

20. **D.** Choice A is wrong because the weight of the lever actually has nothing to do with a fulcrum. Choice B is wrong because the load on either side of the lever is completely separate from the pivot point. Choice C is wrong because the mechanical advantage of a lever has nothing to do with a fulcrum.

21. **C.** A pair of scissors operates under the principle of a 1st-class lever.

22. **B.** This answer can be determined using the following formula: Heavy weight × $X$ = Lower weight (distance between the two objects − $X$). Although we didn't use any numbers in this question, if you plugged in a set of numbers, you would be able to see the answer.

23. **C.** A 1st- and 3rd-class lever are depicted as such due to the placement of force, fulcrum, and effort, not because of balancing purposes.

24. **A.** This answer was derived from the formula described previously in the answer to question 22:

$$20(6) = 12(x - 6)$$
$$120 = 12x - 72$$
$$192 = 12x$$
$$16 = x$$

In this case, $x$ is the distance between the two weights on the lever.

25. **C.** A 3rd-class lever positions the effort between the fulcrum and the load.

# Assembling Objects

1. **C.** The larger shape in answer A is mirrored and the A connection is too far toward the top. Answer B has the A connection in the wrong place. Answer D has the sharp-angled object changed.

2. **B.** There are five shapes instead of four in answer A. Several shapes were changed in answers C and D.

3. **D.** The *u* in answer A has been changed to an *a*. Connection point A in answer B is in the wrong spot. The connector line reaching point B in answer C comes in at the wrong angle.

4. **A.** One of the four-sided figures in answer B is smaller than in the sample. The rectangular shapes in answer C have been changed. Only the slanted rectangular shape and the full rectangle are the same as in the sample in answer D.

5. **C.** The A connection point in answer A is in the wrong place. The *R* in answer B is mirrored. The D connection point in answer D is in the wrong place.

6. **D.** The mountain shape has been replaced with two circles in answer A. The rectangle in answer B is much smaller than it should be. The circle is now a hexagon in answer C.

7. **D.** The B connection is in the wrong place in answer A. One of the objects in both answers B and C has been completely replaced.

8. **B.** The star shape in answer A is different from the sample. The large square has been replaced with a diamond in answer C. The circle has been replaced with a triangle in answer D.

9. **C.** The four-sided shape is three-sided in answer A. The irregular five-sided figure is a proportional pentagon in answer B. One of the angular shapes has been replaced with a circle in answer D.

10. **D.** The connection points in answers A and C are in the wrong places. The five-sided figure in answer B is now a perfect pentagon.

11. **D.** Answer B has the A connection at the top middle of the flower petal, whereas the sample has it on the side of the petal. Answers C and D have shapes that don't match the sample.

12. **B.** The *L* shape is duplicated in answer A, and one of the other shapes is missing. The largest shape has been changed from the sample in answer C. There are two new shapes in answer D.

13. **C.** The B connection in answer A is in the wrong place. The rounded object in answer B has been replaced with an oval. Both connection points in answer D are wrong.

14. **A.** There is an extra circle in answer B. The largest piece in answer C is longer than in the sample. In answer D, the circle has been replaced with a star.

15. **D.** Both connection points in answer A are wrong. The star is misshapen in answer B. The A connection point in answer C is wrong and the angular shape has been changed.

16. **D.** The disproportional four-sided figure has been replaced with a rectangle in answer A. The curved triangle has been replaced with a flat one in answer B and a four-sided shape in answer C.

17. **C.** The A connection point in answer A is in the wrong place. The angled shape in answer B has been replaced with a circle. The B connection point in answer D is in the wrong place.

18. **B.** The triangle is now a four-sided figure in answer A. One of the pieces of the sample has been duplicated and replaces another piece in answer C. There is also an extra triangle. One of the original shapes has been replaced with a circle in answer D.

19. **A.** The *q* in answer B has been changed to *a*. The star in answer C is now a square. The B connection point in answer D is in the wrong place.

20. **B.** The triangle in answer A is much smaller than it should be and also has different angles. The house has been replaced with an arrow shape in answer C. The triangle is now a circle in answer D.

21. **B.** The B connection point in answer A is in the wrong place. Both connection points in answer C are in the wrong place. The angled shape in answer D has been replaced.

22. **A.** There are two rainbow shapes in answer B now instead of one. The oval in answer C has been turned into a circle. The rainbow in answer D is now a circle.

23. **B.** The A connection point in answer A is in the wrong place. Both connection points in answer C are in the wrong place. The snowflake shape in answer D has been replaced with an octagon.

24. **D.** One of the triangles has been changed to match the other in answer A. The pentagon in answer D has changed, as has the size of the star shape. The larger triangle in answer C has been replaced with a four-sided figure.

25. **D.** The A connection point in answer A is in the wrong place. The circular shape in answer B has been replaced with an oval. The B connection point in answer C is in the wrong place.

# AFQT Practice Test

## Arithmetic Reasoning

**Time:** 36 Minutes

**Questions:** 30

**Directions:** This section tests your ability to reason through mathematical problems using basic arithmetic. Carefully read each question and choose the answer choice that best answers the question.

1. If you made $726.35 per week for the first half of the month and 10% more per week for the second half of the month, what's the average amount of money you made over the entire month?

    (A) $1,452.70
    (B) $1,597.97
    (C) $2,905.40
    (D) $3,050.67

2. The average time a song on a particular CD plays is 2 minutes and 35 seconds. Assuming all of the songs on the CD are about the average length, how many complete songs could you play during a 10-minute car ride to the store?

    (A) 3
    (B) 4
    (C) 5
    (D) 6

3. A cylindrical pool is 6 feet tall and 10 feet wide at its diameter. How much water can it hold?

    (A) 147 ft²
    (B) 471 ft²
    (C) 147 ft³
    (D) 471 ft³

4. Aaron wants to dedicate at least 20% of his free time after work three days per week to working out in the gym. If he has 7 hours of free time after work on an average day, how many hours will he have to spend at the gym in a week to meet this goal?

(A) 1.4
(B) 4.2
(C) 4.3
(D) 5.2

5. Two runners leave the same starting point at the same time. Runner A moves at a pace of 4.2 miles per hour. Runner B moves at a pace of 3.6 miles per hour. After 2.25 hours, how much farther has Runner A gone?

(A) 1.35 miles
(B) 1.82 miles
(C) 2.45 miles
(D) 8.12 miles

6. You want to cash in part of your 401(k) early to put a down payment on a house. Currently, you have $15,689 in your account. You're allowed to take up to 50% of this amount to put toward the purchase of a new home and will have to pay a 12% penalty. How much money will you have after the penalty is paid, if you take the full amount allowed?

(A) $6,903.16
(B) $7,844.50
(C) $8,362.78
(D) $9,956.22

7. Sarah will be 6 on her birthday next week. If Max takes her out for ice cream today and he is 6 times her age, how old is he?

(A) 15
(B) 25
(C) 30
(D) 36

8. Emily has to write a 12-page paper for her history class. After working all night, she has completed 7 pages. What percent of the total paper does she have left to complete?

(A) 35%
(B) 42%
(C) 58%
(D) 100%

9. A child's toy wish list has a train, airplane, doll, video game, and soccer ball on it. What's the probability she will get a toy that's a vehicle?

(A) $\frac{1}{5}$

(B) $\frac{2}{5}$

(C) $\frac{3}{5}$

(D) $\frac{4}{5}$

10. Fourteen is what fraction of twenty-one?

(A) $\frac{2}{3}$

(B) $\frac{7}{8}$

(C) $\frac{2}{21}$

(D) $\frac{14}{3}$

11. The members of your team are 25, 18, 21, 23, 28, and 26. What's the average age?

(A) 20.5
(B) 23.5
(C) 26.3
(D) 141

12. Murray decided to buy a sofa for $1,937. When he had the sales clerk ring up his purchase, he found that he had to pay 7% sales tax and that

the sofa was 15% off. How much did Murray end up paying for the sofa in all?

    (A) $1,478.04

    (B) $1,528.40

    (C) $1,646.48

    (D) $1,761.73

13. Your friend is an avid collector of sci-fi memorabilia and acquires 6 new pieces per quarter year to add to her collection. If she's been collecting at this rate for 15 years, how many pieces of memorabilia does your friend's collection contain?

    (A) 24

    (B) 180

    (C) 275

    (D) 360

14. Ray mowed three lawns, cleaned two gutters, and raked three yards. If he charges $22 for each job he performs on the ground and $28 for any job he needs to climb a ladder for, how much money did he make doing these jobs?

    (A) $56

    (B) $132

    (C) $188

    (D) $210

15. If it takes 4 cups of sugar to make one batch of brownies that yields 24 pieces, how many cups of sugar would you need to make 132 brownies?

    (A) 22

    (B) 23

    (C) 25

    (D) 28

16. It has been 16 years since Jane has seen a Broadway play. For Max, it has been only $\frac{1}{3}$ as long. How many years has it been since he's seen a Broadway play?

    (A) $4\frac{1}{3}$ years

    (B) $5\frac{1}{3}$ years

    (C) $5\frac{2}{3}$ years

    (D) $5\frac{7}{25}$ years

17. Your son leaves for sleep-away camp on Monday, June 26. He promises to write you every day until he gets home on August 4, and twice every Sunday. If he does not write home on the day he arrives, how many letters can you expect to get by the time he comes home?

    (A) 23

    (B) 39

    (C) 44

    (D) 48

18. Private Joe can bench press 125 pounds on a 15-pound bar. Private Jane can bench press 135 pounds on a 10-pound bar. How much more weight can Private Jane press?

    (A) 5 pounds

    (B) 8 pounds

    (C) 10 pounds

    (D) 12 pounds

19. You're used to getting up at 8 A.M. In boot camp, you have to get up at 4:30 A.M. Assuming you go to bed at the same time every night, how much less sleep will you get over the course of one full week?

    (A) About $\frac{1}{4}$ of a day

    (B) About $\frac{1}{2}$ of a day

    (C) About $\frac{2}{4}$ of a day

    (D) About 1 day

20. You buy a new phone for $185 and receive a 35% rebate check in the mail. How much is the check for?

    (A) $46.75

    (B) $64.75

    (C) $67.54

    (D) $76.45

21. A lecture hall has 266 people attending a speech about biology. Of these people, 60 are history majors, 144 are biology majors, and the rest are undeclared. What is the ratio of history majors to biology majors?

    (A) 5:12

    (B) 30:31

    (C) 12:5

    (D) 31:30

22. Of your neighbors, $\frac{5}{8}$ are in favor of a block party and $\frac{1}{6}$ are in favor of a block-long garage sale. None are in favor of any other kind of activity. How many are in favor of having some kind of neighborhood activity?

    (A) $\frac{6}{8}$

    (B) $\frac{3}{8}$

    (C) $\frac{19}{24}$

    (D) $\frac{21}{19}$

23. What is negative four plus positive eight?

    (A) –4

    (B) 4

    (C) –12

    (D) 12

24. If for every time a bicycle wheel turns once, you have to pedal three times, what's the ratio of wheel turns to times you have to pedal?

    (A) 3:1

    (B) 1:3

    (C) 2:3

    (D) 2:4

25. Your monthly rent is $875. If it increases by $200 for the last three months of the year, how much will you pay in rent over the course of the entire year?

    (A) $1,075

    (B) $3,225

    (C) $7,875

    (D) $11,100

26. In 724.9654, the 6 is in the

    (A) ones place

    (B) tens place

    (C) tenths place

    (D) hundredths place

27. A dance club has 125 women whose hair is either blond, brunette, red, or black. Twenty percent are blond, 20% are brunette, and 20% are redheaded. What is the ratio of women with black hair to those who are brunette?

    (A) $\frac{2}{1}$

    (B) $\frac{1}{2}$

    (C) $\frac{50}{2}$

    (D) $\frac{25}{4}$

28. On Tuesday, Bill bought $89.75 worth of items from the grocery store. On Wednesday, he returned the $1.29 spaghetti, the $2.47 box of dog treats, and the $5.63 value package of floor cleaner to the store. After having returned the items, how much money did he end up spending at the store between the two days?

    (A) $9.40
    (B) $18.80
    (C) $80.36
    (D) $99.20

29. If Assembly Line A can produce 14 boxes of chocolate per half hour and Assembly Line B can produce twice as much as that, how many boxes can they produce together over 12 hours?

    (A) 168
    (B) 336
    (C) 672
    (D) 1,008

30. If you rounded $25.36 to the nearest dime, you would have

    (A) $25.30
    (B) $25.37
    (C) $25.40
    (D) $30.00

# Word Knowledge

**Time:** 11 Minutes

**Questions:** 35

**Directions:** This section tests your knowledge of and ability to use vocabulary. Read each question and choose the answer choice that most nearly means the same as the underlined word.

1. Desecrate most nearly means

    (A) cater.
    (B) violate.
    (C) package.
    (D) surround.

2. Grueling most nearly means

    (A) difficult.
    (B) empty.
    (C) nourishing.
    (D) arresting.

3. Listless most nearly means

    (A) disorganized.
    (B) bored.
    (C) confused.
    (D) impotent.

4. Excel most nearly means

    (A) master.
    (B) recognize.
    (C) interest.
    (D) complete.

5. Stride most nearly means

    (A) progress.

    (B) originate.

    (C) break.

    (D) listen.

6. Provoke most nearly means

    (A) speak.

    (B) release.

    (C) call.

    (D) incite.

7. Vogue most nearly means

    (A) search.

    (B) fad.

    (C) model.

    (D) belief.

8. Haughty most nearly means

    (A) tight.

    (B) severe.

    (C) smug.

    (D) giving.

9. Liberal most nearly means

    (A) progressive.

    (B) conservative.

    (C) fastidious.

    (D) outspoken.

10. Garner most nearly means

    (A) placate.

    (B) generate.

    (C) invest.

    (D) blanket.

11. Conviction most nearly means

    (A) mask.

    (B) felony.

    (C) certainty.

    (D) bluster.

12. Accomplice most nearly means

    (A) bereavement.

    (B) relation.

    (C) cohort.

    (D) caregiver.

13. Optimistic most nearly means

    (A) oppressive.

    (B) secretive.

    (C) positive.

    (D) owed.

14. Although the teacher had told her student that if he did not improve his homework grades he would not pass the course, he still took a blasé attitude to her comments and completing his assignments.

    (A) studious

    (B) unconcerned

    (C) slight

    (D) average

15. Translucent most nearly means

    (A) crystalline.

    (B) motionless.

    (C) vague.

    (D) beautiful.

16. Lackluster most nearly means

    (A) muddy.

    (B) vengeful.

    (C) optimistic.

    (D) shiny.

17. Compensate most nearly means

    (A) annihilate.

    (B) move.

    (C) provide.

    (D) repay.

18. Our <u>ruse</u> would have worked if our little brother hadn't told mother that we were only pretending to be sick.

    (A) regret.
    (B) trick.
    (C) incite.
    (D) flower.

19. <u>Languid</u> most nearly means

    (A) belonging.
    (B) fortunate.
    (C) drooping.
    (D) trusted.

20. The damage the illness did to my immune system leaves me <u>vulnerable</u> to all sorts of common infections.

    (A) exposed
    (B) over-the-top
    (C) brilliant
    (D) aged

21. <u>Prosaic</u> most nearly means

    (A) appreciative.
    (B) supporting.
    (C) dull.
    (D) artistic.

22. When Paige received an expensive new sports car for her 16th birthday, her brother was <u>indignant</u>, because he'd only gotten a new game system for his.

    (A) angry
    (B) healthy
    (C) average
    (D) pacified

23. <u>Calling</u> most nearly means

    (A) arrangement.
    (B) fortune.
    (C) officiant.
    (D) vocation.

24. <u>Misrepresent</u> most nearly means

    (A) stutter.
    (B) deceive.
    (C) orate.
    (D) gripe.

25. <u>Astronomical</u> most nearly means

    (A) valid.
    (B) stellar.
    (C) negligent.
    (D) huge.

26. <u>Infer</u> most nearly means

    (A) ramble.
    (B) diverge.
    (C) conclude.
    (D) reluctant.

27. <u>Fastidious</u> most nearly means

    (A) painstaking.
    (B) generous.
    (C) arousing.
    (D) eager.

28. Although Jimmy was <u>apprehensive</u> about being away from home for the first time, it helped that he had his best friend with him as he took the bus to camp.

    (A) anxious
    (B) fantastical
    (C) courteous
    (D) reluctant

29. When the man thought about the negative consequences, he knew he would <u>rue</u> lying to get more money from his insurance company.

    (A) listen
    (B) anticipate
    (C) regret
    (D) welcome

30. <u>Perimeter</u> most nearly means

    (A) measurement.
    (B) boundary.
    (C) charity.
    (D) consent.

31. <u>Conservative</u> most nearly means

    (A) calculating.
    (B) accepting.
    (C) innovative.
    (D) traditionalist.

32. <u>Frantic</u> most nearly means

    (A) beleaguered.
    (B) overworked.
    (C) wild.
    (D) produced.

33. <u>Sacred</u> most nearly means

    (A) revered.
    (B) exceptional.
    (C) belated.
    (D) perfect.

34. <u>Gravity</u> most nearly means

    (A) ineptitude.
    (B) mirth.
    (C) seriousness.
    (D) pull.

35. <u>Malicious</u> most nearly means

    (A) official.
    (B) inappropriate.
    (C) designed.
    (D) harmful.

# Paragraph Comprehension

**Time:** 13 Minutes

**Questions:** 15

**Directions:** This section tests your ability to read and understand written information, as well as come to logical conclusions based on a text. Read each passage and answer the questions that follow. Choose the answer choice that best answers the question.

Websites are a series of single pages that are interconnected through hyperlinks. The structure of a website consists of a central page, called a home page, which contains the main information a visitor needs to know about the site. There is also a navigation bar that gives a listing of the other main information sections. After clicking the mouse on a specific link on the navigation bar, the corresponding page will come up on the screen.

1. According to the passage, what would you use to click on a specific link when visiting a website?

    (A) navigation bar
    (B) hyperlink
    (C) mouse
    (D) Weblog

*Use the following passage to answer questions 2–3:*

Drinking coffee can help treat a headache. Caffeine works to block certain chemicals in the brain that make you sleepy and, in the process, causes blood vessels to tighten up. Closing off or restricting the flow of blood vessels that are feeding a headache can help bring relief.

2. Caffeine affects the

    (A) brain.
    (B) cardiovascular system.
    (C) only A.
    (D) both A and B.

3. The author would most likely support

    (A) drinking coffee as a sleep aid.
    (B) drinking coffee as a natural headache remedy.
    (C) using coffee as a treatment for areas of the brain that need more blood.
    (D) all of the above.

*Use the following passage to answer questions 4–6:*

Colombia is the northwestern-most country in South America. Its northern border with Panama is the only direct land connection between Central and South America. Grassy plains, expansive mountain ranges, marshland, and coastal lowlands dominate the country's topography. Colombia's main products include coffee, cattle, sugar cane, chemicals, coal, and petroleum.

4. In this paragraph, the word <u>topography</u> most nearly means

    (A) exports.
    (B) landforms.
    (C) imports.
    (D) elevation of mountains.

5. The tone of this passage is

    (A) positive.
    (B) urgent.
    (C) negative.
    (D) neutral.

6. What country separates Central and South America?

    (A) Panama
    (B) Guatemala
    (C) Colombia
    (D) Uruguay

*Use the following passage to answer questions 7–8:*

We have to get the new deck built before the end of the month. I've called three contractors already and can't find one that can complete the task for the right price. I'm thinking of asking a co-worker about the contractor he hired to build the new addition onto his house. He seemed to be happy with the man's work.

7. The next step the speaker will likely take is to

(A) do the work himself.

(B) hire one of the contractors that did not come in at price.

(C) contact his co-worker about his contractor.

(D) look for other contractors in the phone book.

8. According to the paragraph, the speaker is concerned about

(A) time.

(B) cost.

(C) reliability.

(D) all of the above.

*Use the following passage to answer questions 9–11:*

Wind farms are one of the leading sources of sustainable energy in the United States. Such farms contain one or more turbines with giant blades that are turned by the wind. This action converts the kinetic energy of the wind into mechanical energy through the rotation of the blades. The mechanical energy is then routed to a generator within the turbine, which converts that energy into yet another form, electricity.

9. A good title for this passage would be

(A) Wind Farms Produce the Most Electricity in the Nation

(B) Sustainable Energy Now!

(C) Wind Farms: A Sustainable Energy Source Based on Science

(D) The U.S. Switches its Power Supply to Wind Energy

10. According to the passage, wind has

(A) kinetic energy.

(B) potential energy.

(C) mechanical energy.

(D) rotational energy.

11. The purpose of this passage is to

(A) incite action.

(B) inform.

(C) publicize.

(D) editorialize.

*Use the following passage to answer questions 12–15:*

The introduction of electronic devices that keep us constantly connected to work, friends, and family, coupled with the increasingly long workweek, is resulting in chronic exhaustion among U.S. adults. This increases levels of stress the body experiences and thus leads to increased levels of adrenaline. This means that, chemically, our bodies are constantly on edge, which costs a lot of physical and mental energy.

Most adults aren't even aware of the amount of stress they are under during a normal workday because they have become desensitized to the effects in order to get through the tasks they have on their plate. The physical costs of this desensitization, however, are greater than one might imagine.

12. In this passage, the word <u>desensitized</u> most nearly means

   (A) more able to physically handle something.

   (B) becoming more aware of one's surroundings.

   (C) losing the ability to feel or notice something.

   (D) more able to remember.

13. According to the passage, a cause of exhaustion is

   (A) lack of time away from work.

   (B) constant interaction with electronic communication devices.

   (C) chemical imbalances caused by external stressors.

   (D) all of the above.

14. The tone of this passage is

   (A) flippant.

   (B) concerned.

   (C) glib.

   (D) bored.

15. The speaker would most likely support

   (A) a stress-awareness campaign being distributed to employees at Fortune 500 companies.

   (B) an increase in the number of hours in the standard workweek.

   (C) the introduction of computer software that would forward calls to a built-in hands-free phone in your car.

   (D) a political candidate whose agenda includes increasing the country's gross national product.

# Mathematics Knowledge

**Time:** 24 Minutes

**Questions:** 25

**Directions:** This section tests your knowledge of basic mathematics, algebra, and geometry. Carefully read each question and choose the answer choice that reflects the best answer.

1. Reduce the following to lowest terms:
   $$\frac{6x+9}{2x+6} =$$
   (A) $1\frac{1}{2}$

   (B) $\frac{3(x+3)}{2(x+3)}$

   (C) $\frac{3}{2}$

   (D) $\frac{2(2x+3)}{2(x+3)}$

2. The following diagram is an example of a

   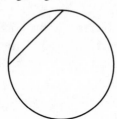

   (A) circumference.
   (B) chord.
   (C) radius.
   (D) diameter.

3. $k^2 - 2k + 6$ is a
   (A) coefficient.
   (B) constant.
   (C) quadratic expression.
   (D) variable.

4. $(b - 7)(b + 4) =$
   (A) $b^2 - 3b + 28$
   (B) $b^2 - 3b - 28$
   (C) $b^2 - 11b - 28$
   (D) $b^2 - 11b + 28$

5. $2\frac{5}{6} \div \frac{2}{7} =$
   (A) $9\frac{11}{12}$

   (B) $12\frac{9}{11}$

   (C) $\frac{12}{119}$

   (D) $6\frac{11}{12}$

6. $4 + a^2 < 2a - 3$ means
   (A) $4 + a^2$ is less than $2a - 3$
   (B) $4 + a^2$ is greater than $2a - 3$
   (C) $4 + a^2$ is equal to $2a - 3$
   (D) $4 + a^2$ is greater than or equal to $2a - 3$

7. A mathematical constant that appears in many formulas involving circles is
   (A) $\neq$
   (B) $\Omega$
   (C) $\leq$
   (D) $\pi$

8. Factor: $b^2 - 10b - 24$

 (A) $(b + 3)(b - 8)$
 (B) $(b + 3)(b + 8)$
 (C) $(b + 2)(b - 12)$
 (D) $(b - 4)(b + 12)$

9. $7! =$

 (A) $-14$
 (B) $28$
 (C) $4,005$
 (D) $5,040$

10. $\dfrac{a^2 d}{cd} \times \dfrac{4y}{2ay}$

 (A) $\dfrac{2c}{a}$

 (B) $\dfrac{2a}{c}$

 (C) $\dfrac{4a}{c}$

 (D) $\dfrac{4c}{a}$

11. $x^0 =$

 (A) $0$
 (B) $1$
 (C) $2$
 (D) $3$

12. The square root of 196 is

 (A) $14$
 (B) $15$
 (C) $16$
 (D) $17$

13. $3 + 2[1 + 2(1 + 2)]^2$

 (A) $36$
 (B) $49$
 (C) $98$
 (D) $101$

14. In the following diagram, what is the value of angle 3?

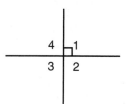

 (A) $30°$
 (B) $45°$
 (C) $90°$
 (D) $180°$

15. $(x^3)^3$

 (A) $x^{-4}$
 (B) $x^6$
 (C) $x^9$
 (D) $x^{-9}$

16. The three internal angles of a triangle always add up to

 (A) $90°$
 (B) $90 \text{ ft}^2$
 (C) $180°$
 (D) $180 \text{ ft}^2$

17. Factor: $a^2 - 49$

 (A) $(a - 7)(a - 7)$
 (B) $(a + 7)(a + 7)$
 (C) $(a + 7)(a - 7)$
 (D) none of the above

18. Solve for $a$: $\dfrac{3}{a} = \dfrac{9}{12}$

 (A) $4$
 (B) $5$
 (C) $6$
 (D) $7$

19. If $a = 2$, $a - 6 + 3a - 4a =$

    (A) 3

    (B) –3

    (C) 6

    (D) –6

20. $\dfrac{4}{8} \times \dfrac{10}{5} =$

    (A) $\dfrac{1}{4}$

    (B) $\dfrac{1}{2}$

    (C) 1

    (D) 2

21. Simplify: $(2x^2)(14x) + x - xy =$

    (A) $28x^3 + x - xy$

    (B) $x(28x^2 + 1 - y)$

    (C) $28x^3 + x^2y$

    (D) $28x^5y$

22. Factor: $10y + 15xy + 50y^2$

    (A) $y(10 + 15x + 50y)$

    (B) $5(2y + 3xy + 10y)$

    (C) $5x(2 + 3y + 10y^2)$

    (D) $5y(2 + 3x + 10y)$

23. What is the area of a pool table that is 8.2 feet long by 5.6 feet wide?

    (A) 45.9 ft$^2$

    (B) 45.9 ft$^3$

    (C) 52.9 ft$^2$

    (D) 54.9 ft$^3$

24. You have a box that is 4 feet tall, 4 feet wide, and 3 feet long. What is its volume?

    (A) 48 ft$^2$

    (B) 48 ft$^3$

    (C) 88 ft$^2$

    (D) 88 ft$^3$

25. A monomial is

    (A) any expression that has more than three terms.

    (B) expressions with three terms joined by operations.

    (C) a polynomial that has just one term.

    (D) an expression with two terms joined by operations.

# AFQT Practice Test Answers and Explanations

## Arithmetic Reasoning

1. **D.** Multiply your weekly pay by .10 (10%) to find out how much more you made in the last two weeks of the month: 72.64. Now add this to your weekly rate: 798.99. Multiply the original rate of pay by 2 and your new rate by 2, then add the products: (726.35 × 2) + (798.99 × 2) = 1452.7 + 1597.97 = $3,050.67.

2. **A.** Convert your time into seconds. Ten minutes equals 600 seconds; 2 minutes and 35 seconds equals 155 seconds. Now divide 600 by 155 to get 3.87. Since the question asks how many *complete* songs you could play during the ride, you have to round down to 3 instead of rounding up to 4, since you know three can definitely play in this time.

3. **D.** This is a volume question. Think back to geometry for this one and calculate the volume of a cylinder using the following formula: $V = \pi r^2 h$. Plug in the numbers from the question to get the following (remember, radius is half the value of diameter, and pi is about 3.14):

   $V = 3.14 \times 5^2 \times 6$

   $V = 3.14 \times 25 \times 6$

   $V = 78.5 \times 6$

   $V = 471$

   Volume is always expressed in cubes, so your answer is 471 ft³.

4. **B.** Calculate 20% of 7 to get the amount of time he wants to spend at the gym per day: 1.4 hours. Now multiply by the number of days he will go, and you have 4.2 hours in the gym per week total.

5. **A.** Calculate the distance per rate each runner goes using the Distance = Rate × time formula:

   Runner A: $D = 4.2 \times 2.25 = 9.45$

   Runner B: $D = 3.6 \times 2.25 = 8.1$

   Now subtract Runner A's distance from Runner B's to get 1.35 miles.

6. **A.** Fifty percent of 15,689 is 7,844.5. Multiply this amount by the penalty percentage: $7,844.5 \times .12 = 941.34$. Subtract this amount from 7,844.5 to find you'll have $6,903.16 to put toward your house.

7. **C.** Max is 30 because Sarah is 5 today and he is 6 times older.

8. **B.** A simple equation will help you with this one: $7 = y \times 12$. Isolate the $y$ by dividing both sides by 12:

   $$\frac{7}{12} = \frac{y \times \cancel{12}}{\cancel{12}}$$

   $$\frac{7}{12} = y$$

   $$.583 = y$$

   This shows that she has completed about 58% of her paper. Now subtract this amount from the total (100%), and you'll find she has 42% left to complete.

9. **B.** Two out of the total items on the list are vehicles. Since there are five items total, the probability is $\frac{2}{5}$.

10. **A.** Use the same equation here that we did in question 8. But instead of calculating the percentage, we're looking for the fraction:

    $$14 = y \times 21$$

    $$\frac{14}{21} = \frac{y \times \cancel{21}}{\cancel{21}}$$

    $$\frac{14}{21} = y$$

    $$\frac{2}{3} = y$$

11. **B.** Add all the numbers together to get 141. Divide this sum by the number of terms you added to get it—in this case, 6.

12. **D.** Start by figuring out what the discounted price of the sofa is: $1,937 \times .15 = 290.55$; $1,937 - 290.55 = 1,646.48$. Now multiply that amount by the sales tax: $1,646.48 \times .07 = 115.2515$. Finally, add that amount to 1,646.48 to get your final answer of $1,761.73.

13. **D.** First, find out how many new pieces your friend acquires per year by multiplying 6 × 4. This gives you 24 pieces. Now multiply that by 15 to find that she has 360 pieces of sci-fi memorabilia.

14. **C.** Ray does six ground jobs and two ladder jobs. He earns $132 and $56, respectively. Add them together to find that he earned $188 that day.

15. **A.** A quick way to solve this is to turn it into a proportion: $\frac{4 \text{ cups}}{24 \text{ brownies}} = \frac{x \text{ cups}}{132 \text{ brownies}}$. To solve for $x$, multiply 4 × 132 to get 528. Now divide 528 by 24 to get the value of $x$: $\frac{132}{24} = 22$.

16. **B.** Multiply your two amounts to find the answer: $\frac{16}{1} \times \frac{1}{3} = \frac{16}{3} = 5\frac{1}{3}$.

17. **C.** First count the number of days between June 26 and August 4 (remember he did not write on the day he arrived at camp):

    June = 4 days

    July = 31 days

    August = 4 days

    Add them together: 4 + 31 + 4 = 39. Now calculate how many Sundays occur during this time. If June 26 is a Monday, then July 2, 9, 16, 23, and 30 are Sundays your son will be at camp. Add 5 to 39 to find that you'll expect 44 letters.

18. **A.** Add the total weight each can lift and subtract Private Joe's number from Private Jane's:

    Private Joe: 125 + 15 = 140

    Private Jane: 135 + 10 = 145

    The difference is 5 pounds.

19. **D.** You lose 3.5 hours of sleep per day. Multiply this over a seven-day week, and you end up losing 24.5 hours total. This equals about a whole day.

20. **B.** Multiply 185 by .35 to get $64.75.

21. **A.** The ratio is 60:144. Both of these numbers have 12 as a common factor. If you divide both by 12, you have 5:12, which is your final answer.

22. **C.** Add your fractions here.

23. **B.** Write this as an expression: –4 + 8. You start on the negative side of the number line and move eight steps to the right. When you stop, you're at +4.

24. **B.** Write this like you would say it: 1 wheel turn equals 3 times you have to pedal, or 1:3.

25. **D.** Out of 12 months, you pay $875 for nine months ($875 × 9 = $7,875). For three months, you pay $1,075 ($1,075 × 3 = $3,225). For the whole year, you pay $11,100 (that is, $7,875 + $3,225 = $11,100).

26. **D.** The second place to the right of the decimal point is the hundredths place. The first place to the right is the tenths. The other two places in the answers are to the left of the decimal.

27. **A.** Twenty-five women in the club are brunette, since 20% of 125 is 25. Those with hair colors other than brunette, blond, and red make up 40% of the women, which equals about 50. Written the way the question reads, the ratio of women with other colors of hair to those who are brunette is $\frac{50}{25} = \frac{2}{1}$.

28. **C.** Add up the total of the items Bill returned: 1.29 + 2.47 + 5.63 = 9.39. Now subtract this amount from the total of his bill on Tuesday: 89.75 – 9.39 = $80.36.

29. **D.** First calculate how much Assembly Line A can produce in an hour: 14 × 2 = 28. Now multiply that number by 12 to see how much it can produce in 12 hours: 28 × 12 = 336. Now multiply that number by 2 to determine how much Assembly Line B can produce in that amount of time: 336 × 2 = 672. Add 336 + 672 to get the total they both make in 12 hours.

30. **C.** The nearest dime in this case would be $.40, since 36 would round up to 40, not down to 30.

# Word Knowledge

1. **B.** Chances are, you've heard the word *desecrate* used in negative ways, such as to desecrate a grave or something holy. The word means "to soil or violate." All the other answer choices are neutral, but answer B is definitely negative.

2. **A.** If something is *grueling*, it is difficult or challenging. Answers B and C don't fit this description. Answer D, *arresting*, means "visually stunning," which also doesn't fit. An interesting association you might make with the word *grueling* is "Gruel is difficult to swallow."

3. **B.** *Listless* means "without energy or interest." Answers A and C don't fit with this definition. Answer D, *impotent*, means "powerless."

4. **A.** To excel means to do something extremely well. Answers B through D don't agree with this definition, but you may feel reluctant to choose A as your answer. Remember that *master* can be used as both a noun and a verb, and its verb form means "to become very skilled."

5. **A.** If you're familiar with the Stride Rite brand of shoes, making the connection between *stride* and its definition of "moving forward," "walking," or "progressing" will be a natural one.

6. **D.** Don't confuse *insight*, which means "perceptiveness," with *incite*, which means "to provoke" or "to start something." Although calling and speaking (answers C and A, respectively) may be involved with inciting, they are not necessary to define the word. The same is true of answer B, *release*. This makes D the best choice.

7. **B.** An easy association with the word *vogue* is to think about the fashion magazine with the same name. Fashion is all about what's the best now, and those perceptions are fleeting, just like fads are. Answers A and D have

nothing to do with this, and though you might be tempted to choose answer C because of the link between *fashion* and *model*, *fad* is the choice that most nearly means "vogue."

8. **C.** *Haughty* means someone is arrogant or smug. The word speaks directly to someone's high opinion of himself. None of the other answer choices do this.

9. **A.** Liberal politicians are most associated with progressive beliefs. Answer B is the opposite of this, as "conservative" means to act with restraint or to be traditional. Answer C means "to pay close attention to detail." And though if you are liberal you may be outspoken (answer D), *liberal* is not defined by such a quality.

10. **B.** *Garner* means the same as "generate." A cool association for *garner*: Jennifer Garner generates interest wherever she goes. *Placate* means "to soothe," *invest* means "to have a stake in something," and *blanket* means "to cover."

11. **C.** *Conviction* can have many meanings. The one we're most familiar with is likely being found guilty of a crime. However, none of the answer choices reflect this definition (answer B, *felony*, describes the crime itself, not being found guilty). Another definition of *conviction* is a strong belief. Answer A means "to cover or conceal," and answer D means "to speak without real belief," which is the opposite of what we're looking for. Answer C is your best bet.

12. **C.** A good way to remember what *accomplice* means is to associate it with the word *accompany*, which means to "go with." An accomplice is someone who aids in a crime. Answer A means "mourning," answer B means "to have a connection to," and answer D means "someone who aids someone else in their care." Though

answers B and D may seem like possible choices, if you carefully consider their meanings, you'll see that they don't connect like answer C does. A *cohort* is a "partner in crime."

13. **C.** *Optimistic* refers to being positive or having a positive outlook. Answers A and B have negative connotations/meanings to them. *Oppressive* refers to something that holds something else back, and to be *secretive* is to hold information back. Answer D really has nothing to do with what we're looking for.

14. **B.** Context clues in the sentence indicate that the answer we're looking for shows that the student did not change his attitude and/or did not think the teacher's advice was important. The only answer choice that reflects this is B. *Studious* means "interested in or engaging in study." The other answer choices don't really make any sense.

15. **A.** Two roots that can help you in this question. *Trans* means "through," and *luc* means "light." From this, you can deduce that *translucent* has to do with light being able to pass through something. The only answer that fits is *crystalline*, which describes something very clear.

16. **A.** Break this word into smaller words, and you'll get a good clue to its definition. To *lack* is to not have, and *luster* means "shine." Answer D is the opposite of this. Answers B and C don't really have anything to do with lacking shine. However, if something is *muddy* (answer A), it will definitely not shine.

17. **D.** *Compensate* means to pay someone for something, so the answer you're looking for has something to do with payment. Answer A means "to destroy." Answer B means "to change something's position." Answer C means "to give." While you may be thinking C is a good choice, when you see that answer D

means "to pay someone back," you'll find that it's the stronger choice.

18. **B.** The sentence tells us that the children were pretending to be sick, which means *ruse* has something to do with pretending or tricking. Answers A and D don't make sense with what we're looking for. Answer C not only doesn't make sense, but it's also the wrong part of speech (a verb when we need a noun).

19. **C.** The Latin root *lang* means "to be weakened." The correct answer choice will have something to do with inability to support something. The only one that makes sense is answer C, *drooping*, which implies a lack of strength to hold oneself upright.

20. **A.** If you use Swap It Out for this question, you'll find that answers B and C don't fit. This leaves A and D for you to consider. The sentence talks about how an illness damaged the immune system, which implies that some harm has made it exposed. Age is not necessary to define this, so answer A is the best choice.

21. **C.** *Prosaic* means something is straightforward or lacking in imagination. This eliminates answer D. Answers A and B don't really fit the meaning we're working with, whereas answer C fits it exactly.

22. **A.** The sentence implies that the brother is upset at the unfairness of the situation. *Healthy* and *average* are simply not strong enough to match a starved appetite. *Pacified* has to do with calming, which is the opposite of what we need. Your answer is *angry*. It's not an exact match, but remember, you're looking for the best choice out of the four you're given.

23. **D.** *Calling* can be either a noun or a verb. A quick look at the answer choices tells you that you're dealing with the noun form of the word (all the answers are nouns). In this case, *calling* means some kind of job or profession. Answers A and B don't fit. Answer C means someone who acts in an official capacity of some kind. While this can be a job, it doesn't have to be and doesn't define job or profession. Answer D, "vocation," does.

24. **B.** The answer we're looking for has something to do with standing in for someone in a bad way. Answer A means "to not be able to speak fluidly." Answer C means "to speak publicly." Answer D means "to complain." None of these are a great fit. Answer B, *deceive*, means "to knowingly present an impression that is not the truth." While this isn't the best match in definition, the idea is the same: representing an image with bad or ill intent.

25. **D.** A good association to make with *astronomical* is to think of it in terms of space. Space, the universe, and everything associated with them are so large that you can't even conceive of it all. Answer A means "correct." Answer B refers to the average or everyday. Answer C means "careless." This makes answer D the best choice.

26. **C.** When you infer, you use all the information you are given to come to your own conclusion about what's going on. Answer A means "to talk on and on." Answer B means "to split apart from something." Answer D means that you don't really want to do something. Answer C is the best choice, as it means "to come to a conclusion."

27. **A.** As we said earlier, *fastidious* means "to pay close attention to detail." The only answer choice that makes sense here is A, *painstaking*, which means "to pay very close attention to detail."

28. **A.** If you swap out the answer choices with the underlined word, you'll find that *anxious* is the only one that makes sense in this context.

29. **C.** In the sentence, the man is considering negative consequences for actions he has already committed. When this happens, he likely regrets those actions. Our answer has to do with regret. Answers B and D run counter to this, and answer A has nothing to do with it.

30. **B.** If you think back to our discussions on geometry, you'll remember that a *perimeter* is the distance around something, or its boundary. You can make the same connection here. You can cross off answers C and D right away. Answer A has a vague connection to the math side of this word, but we're looking for answer B, which speaks to its actual meaning.

31. **D.** We had *liberal* earlier, and now we have *conservative*, its opposite. So we're looking for an answer that's the opposite of *progressive* (looking to change). That eliminates answers B and C right away. Answer A means "to scheme," which doesn't define the opposite of *progressive*. Answer D, *traditionalist*, does represent ideas that support how things have always been.

32. **C.** One of Harrison Ford's famous movies is entitled *Frantic*. Why? The character he plays has his wife mysteriously disappear while the couple is in Paris. He has to find her against huge odds before anything bad happens to her, which makes him frantic to save her. Answers B and D don't make sense with this association. Answer A, *beleaguered*, means "to be annoyed or harassed," which isn't the case here. Answer C is the best choice.

33. **A.** Something that is revered is holy or sacred. *Exceptional* means "special," but not necessarily "holy." *Belated* means "late," which doesn't make sense. *Perfect* means "without flaws," which also doesn't necessarily mean "holy."

34. **C.** *Gravity* is another one of those words that has multiple definitions. If you look at the answer choices, you'll see that there really isn't any one that describes a pull toward Earth. This means you have to think of another definition. Your original thought can help you here. The pull of gravity helps you experience weight, so you can associate it with being heavy. *Gravity*, when used in respect to a situation, refers to being very serious—or heavy, as opposed to light. *Ineptitude* is not being skilled at something. *Mirth* is amusement, and *surface* is simply the outer portion of an object.

35. **D.** If you remember back to Chapter 5, we discussed *malice* as an intent to harm. *Malicious* is the adjective form of this word, which makes D the only choice that fits.

# Paragraph Comprehension

1. **C.** The last sentence talks about using a mouse to click on links.

2. **D.** The passage talks about caffeine affecting both the brain and blood vessels. Since blood vessels are part of the cardiovascular system, both A and B are correct.

3. **B.** The passage contradicts answers A and C, which makes answer D wrong as well.

4. **B.** The sentence uses the word *topography* to describe a variety of geographic landforms.

5. **D.** This is an informative passage that has no sense of emotion coming from the speaker. This makes "neutral" the most logical choice.

6. **A.** The second sentence in the passage says that Panama "is the only direct land connection between Central and South America."

7. **C.** The passage doesn't give us any indication that the speaker wants to or even can perform the work himself. Because he's posing the possibility of seeking a recommendation from his co-worker, it's unlikely that his next step will be to hire someone he's gotten a quote from already or to look for someone he knows nothing about. Contacting his co-worker is the next logical step, based on the information in the passage.

8. **D.** The speaker says, "We have to get the new deck built before the end of the month," "I've called three contractors already and can't find one that can complete the task for the right price," and "I'm thinking of asking a co-worker about the contractor he hired … he seemed to be happy with the man's work." All this implies that he is concerned about time, cost, and reliability.

9. **C.** This makes the most sense, since the passage describes the scientific process of how wind turbines make electricity. There is no emotion present, which rules out answer B. And although the passage says that wind farms are a "leading" source of sustainable energy, there's no indication that all of the U.S. power supply comes from this energy source or that this source produces the most energy in the country.

10. **A.** The sentence "This action converts the kinetic energy of the wind into mechanical energy through the rotation of the blades" tells us that the wind has kinetic energy.

11. **B.** Since this passage describes a process without emotion or any call to action, it is clearly intended to inform.

12. **C.** The sentence talks about being unaware of physical effects. It doesn't talk about any increased physical ability or memory, which eliminates answers A and D. Answer B runs contrary to how the word is used in the sentence.

13. **D.** Each of the answer choices is mentioned in the passage. This makes D the best choice.

14. **B.** *Flippant* and *glib* imply speaking in an uncaring way. The speaker obviously cares about this subject; she appears to be concerned with the negative consequences of this lifestyle. This makes B the best choice.

15. **A.** The author states that "most adults aren't even aware of the amount of stress they are under during a normal workday because they have become desensitized to the effects in order to get through the tasks they have on their plate." This supports answer A.

# Mathematics Knowledge

1. **A.** Factor out what you can from each side of the division bar. Then get rid of terms that cancel each other out:
$$\frac{3x+9}{2x+6}=\frac{3(x+3)}{2(x+3)}=\frac{3}{2}=1\frac{1}{2}$$

2. **B.** A chord is a segment in a circle that touches any two points of the edge. A diameter is a type of chord, but its endpoints have to go directly through the center of the circle. The line in this diagram does not.

3. **C.** This is an example of a quadratic expression: quadratic expression: $ax^2 + bx + c$.

4. **B.** Use FOIL here: $(b - 7)(b + 4)$

    First: $b \times b = b^2$

    Outer: $b \times 4 = 4b$

    Inner: $-7 \times b = -7b$

    Last: $-7 \times 4 = -28$

    Your new expression is: $b^2 + 4b - 7b - 28$

    Combine like terms: $b^2 - 3b - 28$

5. **B.** Turn $2\frac{5}{6}$ into an improper fraction: $2 \times 6 + 5 = 17$. So your new fraction is $\frac{17}{6}$. Since you're dividing fractions, multiply $\frac{17}{6}$ by the reciprocal of $\frac{2}{7}$: $\frac{17}{6} \times \frac{7}{2} = \frac{119}{12}$. Now turn your product back into a mixed number by dividing 12 into 119. You get $9\frac{11}{12}$.

6. **A.** The < symbol shows that the value to the left is less than the value to the right.

7. **D.** A mathematical constant that appears in many formulas involving circles is known as pi ($\pi$).

8. **C.** FOIL the answer choices to find that only C produces the original expression.

9. **D.** This is a factorial, so you need to calculate $7 \times 6 \times 5 \times 4 \times 3 \times 1 = 5,040$.

10. **B.** Multiply straight across and then take out lowest terms:
$$\frac{a^2d}{cd} \times \frac{4y}{2ay} = \frac{4a^2dy}{2acdy} = \frac{2a}{c}$$

11. **B.** Any base to the 0 power equals 1.

12. **A.** $14 \times 14 = 196$

13. **D.** Start with the inner expression in parentheses (not the brackets, which indicate that all processes within must be addressed first), and find 3 to be the answer. The parentheses around the 3 indicate that we must multiply. Within the brackets, we multiply 2 × 3 first, then add 1 + 6. Next, apply the exponent to the 7 to get 49. Next, multiply 2 × 49 to get 98; finally, add the 3.

14. **C.** These angles are perpendicular, which makes them all 90°.

15. **C.** When you apply an exponent to terms in parentheses that have powers, you multiply exponents to simplify the expression: $(x^3)^3 = x^{3\times3} = x^9$.

16. **C.** The three internal angles of a triangle always add up to 180°.

17. **C.** This involves simple factoring, since you have a binomial made up of squares. Break it into two binomial expressions that have the roots of the squares. In this case, $\sqrt{a^2} = a$ and $\sqrt{49} = 7$. Since our original expression has a negative, at least one of our signs is going to be a negative as well. If we FOIL the binomials, the two middle terms will have to cancel each other out in order to give us our original expression. This means one sign will be negative and the other positive. In this case, it doesn't matter which. The correct answer is $(a + 7)(a - 7)$.

18. **A.** Cross multiply to solve for the missing value. If 3 × 12 = 36, then $a$ × 9 = 36. Divide both sides by 9 and find that $a$ = 4.

19. **D.** Plug in the value of $a$ into the expression, and then follow order of operations:

    a − 6 + 3a − 4a

    2 − 6 + (3)(2) − (4)(2)

    Multiply first: 2 − 6 + 6 − 8

    Solve left to right: 2 − 6 = −4; −4 + 6 = 2; 2 − 8 = −6

20. **C.** Multiply straight across and simplify:
    $\frac{4}{8} \times \frac{10}{5} = \frac{40}{40} = 1$.

21. **B.** Combine as many like terms as possible here, and then see what you can factor out:

    $(2x^2)(14x) + x - xy$

    $28x^3 + x - xy$

    $x(28x^2 + 1 - y)$

22. **D.** Common factors are 5 and $y$, which, when multiplied, equal 5$y$. Now break down each term into prime factors:

    $10y = 2 \times 5 \times y$

    $15xy = 5 \times 3 \times x \times y$

    $50y^2 = 5 \times 5 \times 2 \times y \times y$

    Simplify each of these by crossing out one $5 \times y$ in each expression:

    $10y = 2 \times \cancel{5 \times y}$

    $15xy = 3 \times \cancel{5 \times} x \times y$

    $50y^2 = 2 \times y \times \cancel{5 \times} 5 \times y$

    Simplify each term and place the new expression in parentheses with 5$y$ outside: $10y + 15xy + 50y^2 = 5y(2 + 3x + 10y)$.

23. **A.** This is a simple area problem. Multiply length times width and express in square feet: 8.2 × 5.6 = 45.9 ft².

24. **B.** This is a volume problem. Multiply your height by width by depth, and express in cubic feet: 4 × 4 × 3 = 48 ft³.

25. **C.** Know about the root *mon*, which means "one," to help you remember that a monomial is a polynomial that has just one term.

# ASVAB Scores by Military Job

Now that you have a good understanding of how the ASVAB is structured, the types of questions you'll see, and the manner in which your scores will be computed, you'd probably like to know how those scores translate to jobs in the military. Combinations of scores from the ten ASVAB subtests, called composite scores or line scores, determine qualification for a military job. Each branch of service has different formulas for each job category, which we outline below. Note that these computations are subject to change, so it's best to check with a recruiter or www.official-asvab.com/military_app.htm for the most up-to-date information.

## Army

We begin the list of composite scores with the Army, the oldest and largest branch of service. The Army determines job qualification from 10 separate composite scores from various subtests of the ASVAB. If you're not sure what the acronyms stand for, check the list on the inside front cover of the book for explanations.

- ◆ Clerical (CL)—Noninteger weighted linear combination of all subtests.
- ◆ Combat (CO)—Noninteger weighted linear combination of all subtests.
- ◆ Electronics (EL)—Noninteger weighted linear combination of all subtests.
- ◆ Field Artillery (FA)—Noninteger weighted linear combination of all subtests.
- ◆ General Maintenance (GM)—Noninteger weighted linear combination of all subtests.
- ◆ General Technical (GT)—VE + AR
- ◆ Mechanical Maintenance (MM)—Noninteger weighted linear combination of all subtests.
- ◆ Operators and Food (OF)—Noninteger weighted linear combination of all subtests.

◆ Surveillance and Communications (SC)—Noninteger weighted linear combination of all subtests.

◆ Skilled Technical (ST)—Noninteger weighted linear combination of all subtests.

The Army calls all of its enlisted jobs a Military Occupational Specialty, or MOS. The Army has grouped these occupations according to industry, or job field (in Army language). For an updated list of Army MOSs with their corresponding composite scores, check out www.army.com/enlist/line_score.html. This website categorizes each MOS in accordance with the job field to which it belongs. For example, you can find a Field Artillery Surveyor (MOS 13S) under the Field Artillery category. Likewise, you can find an Air and Missile Defense Crewmember (MOS 14S) under the category of Air Defense.

# Navy

The next-oldest branch of service is the Navy. It uses 11 composite scores to determine job qualifications:

◆ General Technical (GT)—AR + VE

◆ Electronics (EL)—AR + EI + GS + MK

◆ Basic Electricity and Electronics (BEE)—AR + GS + 2MK

◆ Engineering (ENG)—AS + MK

◆ Mechanical Maintenance (MEC)—AR + AS + MC

◆ Mechanical Maintenance 2 (MEC2)—AO + AR + AS

◆ Nuclear Field (NUC)—AR + MC + MK + VE

◆ Operations Specialist (OPS)—VE + AR + MK + AO

◆ Hospitalman (HM)—GS + MK + VE

◆ Administrative (ADM)—MK + VE

Unlike the Army, the Navy refers to its jobs as Ratings instead of MOSs. The Navy has fewer jobs than the Army, so they are listed individually instead of by field. To view the full inventory of Navy enlisted jobs, go to www.navycs.com/asvab-test.html. The Coast Guard has only a few enlisted positions. The following website breaks down the youngest service's ASVAB score requirements by military job: www.uscg.mil/HQ/CapeMay/Education/cgmilcareerdev.asp#aschools.

# Marine Corps

The Marine Corps uses four composite scores to determine job qualification:

◆ Clerical (CL)—VE + MK

◆ Electronical (EL)—AR + MK + EI + GS

◆ Mechanical (MM)—AR + MC + AS + EI

◆ General Technical (GT)—VE + AR + MC

As in the Army, the Marines call their jobs Military Occupational Specialties (MOSs). Each MOS is further categorized according to occupational fields. Check out www.military.com/ASVAB/0,,ASVAB_MOS_USMC.html for up-to-date ASVAB scores needed for each MOS.

# Air Force

Just like the last three branches of service that we've discussed, the Air Force has its own listing of composite scores. Listed here are the combination of subtests per composite:

◆ Mechanical (M)—AR + VE + MC + AS

◆ Administrative (A)—VE + MK

◆ General (G)—VE + AR

◆ Electronic (E)—AR + MK + EI + GS

The Air Force calls its enlisted jobs Air Force Specialty Codes, or AFSCs. The Air Force divides its AFSCs into main groups, including Operations, Maintenance & Logistics, Support, Medical & Dental, Legal & Chaplain, Finance & Contracting, and Special Investigations. Each of these categories includes one or more career fields, similar to those of the Army and Marine Corps. Similar AFSCs are listed together under a career field. For example, under the heading of "Operations," you can find a career field called "Aircrew Operations." In this career field, you might find an In-Flight Refueling Specialist, a Flight Engineer, an Aircraft Loadmaster, and the like. For a complete list of Air Force Career Fields and their corresponding jobs, check out www.military.com/ASVAB/0,,ASVAB_MOS_USAF.html.

# Appendix B

# MEPS Locations

As you go through the enlistment process, you will make at least one trip to the nearest Military Entrance Processing Station (MEPS). This is a major part of the enlistment procedure, as MEPS is the place where you will complete your military physical exam and all of the final contractual paperwork. Furthermore, you will be sworn in at MEPS, and you will very likely take your ASVAB exam there as well.

In this appendix we've provided a comprehensive listing of MEPS locations nationwide. Not every state has a MEPS station, but for those that do, we list each location with the appropriate mailing address and the nearest major city.

## Alabama

Montgomery
Maxwell Air Force Base—Gunter Annex
705 McDonald Street
Building 1512
Montgomery, AL 36114-3110
Phone: 334-416-7863
Fax: 334-416-5034
E-mail: mntg-sec@mepcom.army.mil

## Alaska

Anchorage
1717 C Street
Anchorage, AK 99501
Phone: 907-274-9142
Fax: 907-274-7268
E-mail: anch-sec@mepcom.army.mil

## Arizona

Phoenix
1 North 1st Street
Suite 613
Phoenix, AZ 85004-2357
Phone: 602-258-1703
Fax: 602-258-8206
E-mail: phoe-sec@mepcom.army.mil

## Arkansas

Little Rock
1520 Riverfront Drive
Little Rock, AR 72202-1724
Phone: 501-666-6377
Fax: 501-663-5863
E-mail: nlrk-sec@mepcom.army.mil

# California

Los Angeles
5051 Rodeo Road
Los Angeles, CA 90016
Phone: 323-292-2202, ext. 221
Fax: 323-292-0004
E-mail: losa-sec@mepcom.army.mil

Sacramento
3870 Rosin Court
Suite 105
Sacramento, CA 95834-1648
Phone: 916-564-0253
Fax: 916-564-0268
E-mail: sato-sec@mepcom.army.mil

San Diego
4181 Ruffin Road
Suite B
San Diego, CA 92123
Phone: 858-874-2400, ext. 261
Fax: 858-874-0415
E-mail: sndi-sec@mepcom.army.mil

San Jose
546 Vernon Avenue
Mountain View, CA 94043
Phone: 650-603-8201
Fax: 650-603-8225
E-mail: snjo-sec@mepcom.army.mil

# Colorado

Denver
275 New Custom House
19th and Stout Street
Denver, CO 80202
Phone: 303-623-1020, ext. 223
Fax: 303-623-5506
E-mail: denv-sec@mepcom.army.mil

# Florida

Jacksonville
4051 Philips Highway
Jacksonville, FL 32207-7299
Phone: 904-737-6861
Fax: 904-448-6794
E-mail: jacv-sec@mepcom.army.mil

Miami
7789 NW 48th Street
Suite 150
Miami, FL 33166
Phone: 305-463-0891, ext. 248
Fax: 305-629-8923
E-mail: miam-sec@mepcom.army.mil

Tampa
3520 West Waters Avenue
Tampa, FL 33614-2716
Phone: 813-932-0079, ext. 1105
Fax: 813-932-8763
E-mail: tamp-sec@mepcom.army.mil

# Georgia

Atlanta
1500 Hood Avenue
Building 720
Fort Gillem, GA 30297-5000
Phone: 404-469-3090
Fax: 404-469-5367
E-mail: atla-sec@mepcom.army.mil

# Hawaii

Honolulu
490 Central Avenue
Pearl Harbor, HI 96860
Phone: 808-471-8725
Fax: 808-471-2888
E-mail: hono-sec@mepcom.army.mil

## Idaho

Boise
550 West Fort Street
MSC 044
Boise, ID 83724-0101
Phone: 208-334-1450, ext. 202
Fax: 208-334-1580
E-mail: bois-sec@mepcom.army.mil

## Illinois

Chicago
2834 Green Bay Road
North Chicago, IL 60064-3094
Phone: 847-688-4874
General Information: HQ-MPA-INFO@mepcom.
army.mil

## Indiana

Indianapolis
5541 Herbert Lord Drive
Indianapolis, IN 46216
Phone: 317-554-0531, ext. 201
Fax: 317-554-0541
E-mail: indi-sec@mepcom.army.mil

## Iowa

Des Moines
7105 NW 70th Avenue
Building S-71
Johnston, IA 50131
Phone: 515-224-0125, ext. 312
Fax: 515-224-4906
E-mail: desm-sec@mepcom.army.mil

## Kentucky

Louisville
600 Dr. Martin Luther King, Jr., Place
Room 477
Louisville, KY 40202
Phone: 502-582-5921, ext. 2222
Fax: 502-582-6566
E-mail: lvil-sec@mepcom.army.mil

## Louisiana

New Orleans
4400 Dauphine Street
Building 603-1C
New Orleans, LA 70146-5900
Phone: 504-943-0470, ext. 225
Fax: 504-943-5670
E-mail: newo-sec@mepcom.army.mil

Shreveport
2715 Alkay Drive
Shreveport, LA 71118-2509
Phone: 318-671-6080, ext. 203
Fax: 318-671-6097
E-mail: shrv-sec@mepcom.army.mil

## Maine

Portland
510 Congress Street
3rd Floor
Portland, ME 04101-3403
Phone: 207-775-0910
Fax: 207-775-2947
E-mail: porm-sec@mepcom.army.mil

## Maryland

Baltimore
850 Chisholm Avenue
Fort Meade, MD 20755
Phone: 301-677-0422
Fax: 301-677-0440
E-mail: balt-sec@mepcom.army.mil

## Massachusetts

Boston
Barnes Building
495 Summer Street
4th Floor
Boston, MA 02210
Phone: 617-753-3100
Fax: 617-426-7486
E-mail: bost-sec@mepcom.army.mil

Springfield
551 Airlift Drive
Westover JARB
Springfield, MA 01022-1519
Phone: 413-593-9543, ext. 200
Fax: 413-593-9485
E-mail: spri-sec@mepcom.army.mil

## Michigan

Detroit
1172 Kirts Boulevard
Troy, MI 48084-4846
Phone: 248-244-8534
Fax: 248-244-9352
E-mail: detr-sec@mepcom.army.mil

Lansing
120 East Jolly Road
Lansing, MI 48910
Phone: 517-887-1714
Fax: 517-877-9160
E-mail: lans-sec@mepcom.army.mil

## Minnesota

Minneapolis
Bishop Henry Whipple Federal Building
1 Federal Drive
Suite 3300
Fort Snelling, MN 55111-4080
Phone: 612-725-1772
Fax: 612-725-1749
E-mail: minn-sec@mepcom.army.mil

## Mississippi

Jackson
664 South State Street
Jackson, MS 39201
Phone: 601-355-3835, ext. 203
Fax: 601-352-5708
E-mail: json-sec@mepcom.army.mil

## Missouri

Kansas City
10316 NW Prairie View Road
Kansas City, MO 64153-1350
Phone: 816-891-9490
Fax: 816-891-8258
E-mail: kans-sec@mepcom.army.mil

St. Louis
Robert A. Young Federal Building
1222 Spruce Street
St. Louis, MO 63103-2816
Phone: 314-331-4040
Fax: 314-331-5699
E-mail: stlu-sec@mepcom.army.mil

## Montana

Butte
22 W. Park Street
Butte, MT 59701
Phone: 406-723-8883, ext. 222
Fax: 406-782-7797
E-mail: butt-sec@mepcom.army.mil

## Nebraska

Omaha
5303 F Street
Omaha, NE 68117-2805
Phone: 402-733-7474, ext. 4
Fax: 402-733-7660
E-mail: omah-sec@mepcom.army.mil

## New Jersey

Fort Dix
Building 5645 Texas Avenue
Fort Dix, NJ 08640
Phone: 609-562-6050, ext. 2306
Fax: 609-562-5207
E-mail: dixx-sec@mepcom.army.mil

## New Mexico

Albuquerque
505 Central Avenue NW
Suite A
Albuquerque, NM 87102-2113
Phone: 505-246-8020
Fax: 505-246-8861
E-mail: albq-sec@mepcom.army.mil

## New York

Albany
Leo W. O'Brien Federal Building
North Pearl Street & Clinton Avenue
Albany, NY 12207
Phone: 518-320-9860
Fax: 518-320-9869
E-mail: alba-sec@mepcom.army.mil

Buffalo
2024 Ent Avenue
Building 799
Niagara Falls ARS, NY 14304-5000
Phone: 716-501-9012
Fax: 716-501-9027
E-mail: buff-sec@mepcom.army.mil

New York City
Fort Hamilton Military Community
116 White Avenue
Brooklyn, NY 11252-4705
Phone: 718-630-4646
Fax: 718-765-7338
E-mail: newy-sec@mepcom.army.mil

Syracuse
6001 East Molloy Road
Building 710
Syracuse, NY 13211-2100
Phone: 315-455-3012
Fax: 315-455-7807
E-mail: syra-sec@mepcom.army.mil

## North Carolina

Charlotte
6125 Tyvola Centre
Charlotte, NC 28217-6447
Phone: 704-665-6620
Fax: 704-665-6678
E-mail: char-sec@mepcom.army.mil

Raleigh
2625 Appliance Court
Raleigh, NC 27604
Phone: 919-834-7787
Fax: 919-755-1303
E-mail: rale-sec@mepcom.army.mil

## North Dakota

Fargo
225 Fourth Avenue North
Fargo, ND 58102
Phone: 701-234-0473
Fax: 701-234-0597
E-mail: farg-sec@mepcom.army.mil

## Ohio

Cleveland
20637 Emerald Parkway Drive
Cleveland, OH 44135-6023
Phone: 216-267-1286, ext. 201
Fax: 216-522-9860
E-mail: clev-sec@mepcom.army.mil

Columbus
775 Taylor Road
Gahanna, OH 43230
Phone: 614-868-8430, ext. 220
Fax: 614-856-9065
E-mail: cooh-sec@mepcom.army.mil

## Oklahoma

Oklahoma City
301 Northwest 6th Street
Suite 150
Oklahoma City, OK 73102
Phone: 405-609-8700
Fax: 405-609-8639
E-mail: okcy-sec@mepcom.army.mil

## Oregon

Portland
7545 NE Ambassador Place
Portland, OR 97220-1367
Phone: 503-528-1630
Fax: 503-528-1640
E-mail: poro-sec@mepcom.army.mil

## Pennsylvania

Harrisburg
4641 Westport Drive
Mechanicsburg, PA 17055
Phone: 717-691-6180
Fax: 717-691-8039
E-mail: hari-sec@mepcom.army.mil

Pittsburgh
William S. Moorhead Federal Building
1000 Liberty Avenue
Suite 1917
Pittsburgh, PA 15222-4101
Phone: 412-395-5873
Fax: 412-395-5454
E-mail: pitt-sec@mepcom.army.mil

## Puerto Rico

San Juan
Highway 28
GSA Building 651
Guaynabo, PR 00968
Phone: 787-277-7500
Fax: 787-277-7507
E-mail: snju-sec@mepcom.army.mil

## South Carolina

Fort Jackson
2435 Marion Avenue
Fort Jackson, SC 29207
Phone: 803-751-5141
Fax: 803-751-5744
E-mail: jack-sec@mepcom.army.mil

## South Dakota

Sioux Falls
2801 South Kiwanis Avenue
Suite 200
Sioux Falls, SD 57105
Phone: 605-334-0280
Fax: 605-332-8412
E-mail: siou-sec@mepcom.army.mil

## Tennessee

Knoxville
9745 Parkside Drive
Knoxville, TN 37922
Phone: 865-531-8221, ext. 221
Fax: 865-531-8741
E-mail: kxvi-sec@mepcom.army.mil

Memphis
480 Beale Street
Memphis, TN 38103-3232
Phone: 901-526-2100
Fax: 901-527-7832
E-mail: memp-sec@mepcom.army.mil

Nashville
20 Bridgestone Park
Nashville, TN 37214-2428
Phone: 615-833-1347, ext. 112
Fax: 615-833-2570
E-mail: nash-sec@mepcom.army.mil

## Texas

Amarillo
1100 South Fillmore
Suite 100
Amarillo, TX 79101
Phone: 806-379-9037
Fax: 806-374-9332
E-mail: amar-sec@mepcom.army.mil

Dallas
Federal Building
207 South Houston Street
Suite 400
Dallas, TX 75202
Phone: 214-655-3200
Fax: 214-655-3213
E-mail: dall-sec@mepcom.army.mil

El Paso
6380 Morgan Avenue
Suite E
El Paso, TX 79906-4611
Phone: 915-568-3505
Fax: 915-568-4477
E-mail: elpa-sec@mepcom.army.mil

Houston
701 San Jacinto Street
P.O. Box #52309
Houston, TX 77052-2309
Phone: 713-718-4220
Fax: 713-718-4228
E-mail: hous-sec@mepcom.army.mil

San Antonio
1950 Stanley Road
Suite 103
San Antonio, TX 78234-5102
Phone: 210-295-9031
Fax: 210-295-9151
E-mail: snan-sec@mepcom.army.mil

## Utah

Salt Lake City
2830 South Redwood Road
Salt Lake City, UT 84119-2375
Phone: 801-975-3701
Fax: 801-975-3715
E-mail: salt-sec@mepcom.army.mil

## Virginia

Fort Lee
2011 Mahone Avenue
Fort Lee, VA 23801-1707
Phone: 804-765-4180
Fax: 804-765-4190
E-mail: leee-sec@mepcom.army.mil

## Washington

Seattle
4735 East Marginal Way South
Seattle, WA 98134-2385
Phone: 206-766-6400, ext. 7525
Fax: 206-766-6430
E-mail: seat-sec@mepcom.army.mil

Spokane
Federal Building
920 W. Riverside Avenue
2nd Floor
Spokane, WA 99201
Phone: 509-353-3105
Fax: 509-353-3104
E-mail: spok-sec@mepcom.army.mil

## West Virginia

Beckley
409 Wood Mountain Road
Glen Jean, WV 25846
Phone: 304-465-0208
Fax: 304-465-3194
E-mail: beck-sec@mepcom.army.mil

## Wisconsin

Milwaukee
11050 West Liberty Drive
Milwaukee, WI 53224
Phone: 414-359-1315
Fax: 414-359-1390
E-mail: milw-sec@mepcom.army.mil

# Appendix C

# Resources

You can find tons of great resources out there to help you prepare for the ASVAB overall, bone up on specific subject areas, and gain extra practice. You can also find out a lot about your career options, enlistment requirements, and other information to help you make the best decision possible for your future. We recommend checking out the following books and websites.

## Books

Dennis, Johnnie T., and Gary F. Moring. *The Complete Idiot's Guide to Physics*. Alpha Books, 2006.

DePree, Christopher. *The Complete Idiot's Guide to Astronomy*. Alpha Books, 2001.

Guch, Ian. *The Complete Idiot's Guide to Chemistry*. Alpha Books, 2006.

Handwerker, Mark J. Science Essentials, High School Level: Lessons and Activities for Test Preparation. Jossey-Bass, 2004.

Hewitt, Paul G., John A. Suchocki, and Leslie A. Hewitt. *Conceptual Physical Science, 4th Edition*. Addison Wesley, 2007.

Kelley, W. Michael. *The Complete Idiot's Guide to Algebra*. Alpha Books, 2007.

Lynn, Vyvyan, and Tony Molla. *The Complete Idiot's Guide to Auto Repair*. Alpha Books, 2007.

Miller, Mark Richard, and Rex Miller. *Audel Machine Shop Tools and Operations, 5th Edition*. Audel, 2004.

Moulton, Glen E. *The Complete Idiot's Guide to Biology*. Alpha Books, 2004.

Seifert, Mark F. *The Complete Idiot's Guide to Anatomy, Illustrated*. Alpha Books, 2008.

Staub, Catherine. *Wiring 1-2-3*. The Home Depot, 2001.

Stradley, Laura, and Robin Kavanagh. *The Pocket Idiot's Guide to the ASVAB*. Alpha Books, 2009.

Szecsei, Denise. *The Complete Idiot's Guide to Geometry*. Alpha Books, 2007.

Thompson, Frances McBroom. *Math Essentials, High School Level: Lessons and Activities for Test Preparation*. Jossey-Bass, 2005.

# Websites

Algebra Help.com: www.algebrahelp.com/

Armed Forces Careers.com: www.armedforcescareers.com

Army.com ASVAB prep: www.army.com/enlist/asvab.html

ASVAB Career Exploration Program (for high school students): www.asvabprogram.com

Careers in the Military.com: www.careersinthemilitary.com/

How Stuff Works.com: www.howstuffworks.com/

March 2 Success.com: www.march2success.com/

Merriam-Webster's Word of the Day: www.merriam-webster.com/cgi-bin/mwwod.pl

Military.com website: www.military.com/

Military Entrance Processing Command website: www.mepcom.army.mil/

Navy Armed Forces Qualification Test Requirements: www.navycs.com/asvab-test.html

Official Air Force website: www.airforce.com

Official Army website: www.goarmy.com

Official Coast Guard website: www.gocoastguard.com/

Official Marine Corps website: www.marines.com

Official Navy website: www.navy.com

Official Site of the ASVAB Testing Program: www.official-asvab.com/

Prefixsuffix.com: www.prefixsuffix.com

Purplemath.com: www.purplemath.com/index.htm

Today's Military.com: www.todaysmilitary.com/

# Index

# E

# O

obtuse angles, 88
occupational specialties
Air Force, 4-5
Army, 5-6
Coast Guard, 7
Marines, 8
Navy, 9
oceanic islands, 110
oceans, 110
ohmmeters, 130
ohms, 125
Ohm's law, 129-130
one-wheeled pulley systems, 168
open-end wrenches, 155
operational organizations, Army, 5
operations (arithmetic)
definition, 83
order of, 73
opportunities, branch selection, 3
Air Force, 4-5
Army, 5-6
Coast Guard, 6-7
Marines, 8
Navy, 9
order classification (taxonomy), 108
order of operations (arithmetic), 73
ordinance occupations, Coast Guard, 7
organisms, taxonomy, 107
organs, 110
Otto Cycle, 137
outer core (Earth), 115

# P

PAP (Paper and Pencil Test), 19-21, 30
Paper and Pencil Test (PAP), 19-21, 30
paragraph breakdown (PC subtest), 54-55

Paragraph Comprehension subtest. *See* PC subtest
parallel circuits, 129
parallel lines, 88
parallelograms, 91
parentheses (order of operations), 73
parts of speech, 42
passages (engines), 143
PC (Paragraph Comprehension) subtest, 16
expectations, 50
inference questions, 53-54
main idea questions, 50-51
paragraph breakdown, 54-55
practice, 61-66
purpose questions, 51
reasons for taking, 49-50
specific detail questions, 52-53
tone questions, 51-52
vocabulary-in-context questions, 53
percents, 79
perimeter
definition, 87
determination, 90
Periodic Table of Elements, 120
perpendicular lines, 88
phases (astronomical), 118
Phillips head screwdrivers, 154
photosynthesis, 108
phylum classification (taxonomy), 108
physical examinations, 10
physical science review
chemistry, 120-121
physics, 121-122
physics, 121-122
pi, 92
pipe clamps, 156
pipe wrenches, 156
pipes (exhaust systems), 142
pistol grips, 157
pistons, 138
plane tools, 152
planets, 118-119
planning strategies, 31-32

accessing recruiters, 32
breaking down material, 33-34
concentrate on career goal, 32
relaxation prior to test, 34-35
scheduling study time, 34
timing self on practice tests, 33
plasma, 121
plasma cell membrane (cells), 111
*The Pocket Idiot's Guide to the ASVAB*, 136
polar regions, 109
polygons
definition, 87
quadrilaterals, 91
polynomials, 85-86
positive connotation, simple definition questions, 41-42
positive numbers (arithmetic), 73-74
potential energy, 160-161
power, 125
power tools, 156-157
practice
AI (Auto Information) subtest, 183-186
AO (Assembling Objects) subtest, 192-195
AR (Arithmetic Reasoning) subtest, 71, 93-98
ES (Electronic Skills) subtest, 180-183
GS (General Science) subtest, 177-180
MC (Mechanical Comprehension) subtest, 189-192
MK (Mathematics Knowledge) subtest, 98-102
PC (Paragraph Comprehension) subtest, 61-66
SI (Shop Information) subtest, 186-189
test-taking strategies, 27-28
timing tests, 33
WK (Word Knowledge) subtest, 57-61